Congressional
Procedures
and the
Policy Process

WALTER J. OLESZEK

Congressional Procedures and the Policy Process

FIFTH EDITION

A DIVISION OF CONGRESSIONAL QUARTERLY INC.
WASHINGTON, D.C.

CQ Press
A Division of Congressional Quarterly Inc.
1414 22nd Street, N.W.
Washington, D.C. 20037
(202) 822-1475; (800) 638-1710

www.cqpress.com

Cover Design: Dennis Anderson

Printed and bound in Canada

05 04 03 02 01   5 4 3 2 1

♾ The paper used in this publication meets the minimum requirements of the American National Standard for Information Sciences--Permanence of Paper for Printed Library Materials, ANSI Z39.48-1992.

Library of Congress Cataloging-in-Publication Data

In process

ISBN: 1-56802-492-4
        1-56802-448-7 (pbk)

For Janet, Mark, and Eric

Contents

Tables, Figures, and Boxes   xi

Preface   xv

1 Congress and Lawmaking   1

    The Constitutional Context 2
    Functions of Rules and Procedures 5
    Rules and Policy Making in Congress 10
    Congressional Decision Making 17
    The House and Senate Compared 23
    Pressures on Members 30

2 The Congressional Budget Process   41

    Overview 41
    Authorization-Appropriations Process 43
    Prelude to Budget Reform 56
    The 1974 Budget Act 56
    Evolution of the Budget Process 66
    The Surplus Era 69

3 Preliminary Legislative Action   75

    Categories of Legislation 77
    Bill Referral Procedure 79
    Consideration in Committee 86
    The Committee Chairman's Role 89
    Hearings 91
    The Markup 95
    The Report 101
    Bypassing Committees 103

4 Scheduling Legislation in the House   109

    The House Legislative Calendars 110
    Minor and Noncontroversial Bills 110

Privileged Legislation   117
Major Legislation   118
Legislation Blocked in Committee   138
Final Scheduling Steps   142

5   **House Floor Procedure**   148

Adoption of the Rule   150
Committee of the Whole   151
General Debate   153
The Amending Process   158
Voting   169
Final Procedural Steps   173

6   **Scheduling Legislation in the Senate**   181

Flexible Scheduling System   181
Noncontroversial Bills   187
Major Legislation   191
Unanimous Consent Agreements   194
The Track System   202
Scheduling Procedures Compared   203

7   **Senate Floor Procedure**   207

Legislative and Calendar Days   209
Daily Order of Business   210
Debate in the Modern Senate   211
Bills Considered by Unanimous Consent   215
The Amending Process   217
Bills Without Unanimous Consent   227
Procedures to Circumvent Committees   236

8   **Resolving House-Senate Differences**   245

Obscurity of the Process   245
Agreement Without a Conference   247
Preconference Considerations   248
Conference Committee Process   250
Presidential Approval or Veto   268

9 **Legislative Oversight**   274

Techniques of Oversight   278
Oversight Trends   289
Lack of Consensus on Oversight   291

10 **A Dynamic Process**   298

Glossary of Congressional Terms   309

Selected Bibliography   323

Selected Internet Sources   327

Index   329

Tables, Figures, and Boxes

TABLES

1-1 Contract with America Scorecard at One Hundred Days   21
1-2 Major Differences between the House and Senate   24

2-1 Authorization-Appropriations Rules Compared   51

3-1 From Bill to Law, 1979–1999   76
3-2 Jurisdiction of House Committee on Education and
       the Workforce   81
3-3 Procedural Differences at Preliminary Stages of the
       Legislative Process   101

4-1 The Corrections Calendar and Suspension of the Rules   113
4-2 Motions to Suspend the Rules in the House, by Party
       of Sponsor, 100th to 105th Congresses   115
4-3 Committees with Direct Access to the Floor
       for Selected Legislation   117
4-4 Open versus Restrictive Rules, 95th to 105th Congresses   126

5-1 Major Characteristics, House and Committee of the Whole   153

6-1 House and Senate Scheduling Compared   184
6-2 Purposes and Features of a Complex
       Unanimous Consent Agreement   197
6-3 Comparison of House Special Rule and Senate
       Unanimous Consent Agreement   204

7-1 Selected Bicameral Differences in the Amendment Process   219
7-2 Attempted and Successful Cloture Votes, 1919–1999   235

8-1 Bicameral Reconciliation of Legislation, 99th (1985–1987),
       103d (1993–1995), and 105th (1997–1999) Congresses   248

FIGURES

1-1 How a Bill Becomes Law   14
1-2 A Daily Message for House Republicans   33

2-1 The Graying of the Budget   68

3-1 House Committee Report   104

4-1 Calendars of the United States House of Representatives
      and History of Legislation   111
4-2 House Whip Notice   143

5-1 Floor Plan of the House of Representatives   149
5-2 The Basic Amendment Tree   166

6-1 Distribution of Senate and House Votes, 102d Congress,
      by Day of Week   185
6-2 Senate *Calendar of Business*   188
6-3 Senate Whip Notice   189

7-1 Senate Floor Plan and Seating Chart   208
7-2 Amendment to Insert   221

8-1 Conference Report   263
8-2 Public Law   270

BOXES

1-1 Major Sources of House and Senate Rules   6
1-2 Leadership Structure of Congress   18

2-1 Basic Purposes of Authorizations Acts   44
2-2 Structure of a Regular Appropriations Act   46
2-3 Congressional Budget Process Timetable   59
2-4 Senate Reconciliation Directives   63

3-1 For the Record   80
3-2 Standing Committees, 106th Congress   82
3-3 A Jurisdictional Accommodation   87
3-4 Selected Formal Rules Governing Hearings Procedures   93
3-5 Judicial Bypass   105

4-1 Reading a Special Rule   124
4-2 Tax-Hike Rule Waiver   128
4-3 Open Debate and Political Maneuvering   135

5-1 Some Tests of Germaneness   164
5-2 Methods of Voting in the House   170

5-3   Rules Changes Open the Process but Strengthen
      the Reins of Power   174

6-1   Schedule of Sen. Mike DeWine, R-Ohio   182
6-2   Wrapping Up the Senate's Day   190

7-1   A Unanimous Consent Agreement   216
7-2   A Cloture Motion   232
7-3   Ending a Senate Filibuster   233
7-4   Placing a Measure on the Calendar   240

8-1   Instruction of Conferees   256
8-2   Senate Procedure Change on Appropriations Bills   261
8-3   Picking Procedural Locks   266
8-4   Calling Up a Conference Report:
      Unanimous Consent Agreement   267
8-5   Calling Up a Conference Report: House Rule   268

9-1   A Committee Veto   281

Preface

Congress is constantly adapting to change. New procedures, processes, and practices come about in response to developing conditions and circumstances. Some procedural innovations are incorporated formally into the rules of the House or Senate; others evolve informally. For all their variability over time, the rules of the House and Senate are constant in this sense: they establish the procedural context within which individual members and the two chambers raise issues and make (or avoid making) decisions. Members of Congress must rely upon rules and procedures to expedite or delay legislation, to secure enactment, or to bring about the defeat of bills.

Congressional Procedures and the Policy Process was first published in 1978, in the aftermath of major changes that affected legislative decision making and the political system. The result of many of these developments on Capitol Hill was to diffuse policy-making influence widely throughout Congress. Six years later, when the second edition appeared, the House and Senate had undergone further procedural transformations. The House, for instance, began gavel-to-gavel television coverage of its floor proceedings. The third edition was published in the late 1980s. By then, the Senate also had begun gavel-to-gavel television coverage of its floor proceedings. Furthermore, Congress had revamped its budgetary practices with the enactment of Gramm-Rudman-Hollings I and II; the House Rules Committee had crafted unique new rules for regulating floor decision making; and greater use had been made of comprehensive bills, or packages, to process much of Congress's annual workload. One effect of these and other changes was to recentralize authority in fewer legislative hands.

The fourth edition was updated during another time of momentous change on Capitol Hill. After forty years as the "permanent minority," Republicans captured control of the House in the November 1994 elections and reclaimed control of the Senate as well.

Significant procedural and political developments have occurred on Capitol Hill since the mid-1990s. Partisanship is sharper in both the House and the Senate; both chambers have introduced procedural innovations; and Congress now operates in a fiscal environment shaped by surpluses, not deficits. Accordingly, I have incorporated in this fifth edition discussion of new rules and practices and new examples and materials that highlight the elements of stability and change in Congress's decision-making procedures.

The fundamental objective of *Congressional Procedures and the Policy Process* is to discuss how Congress makes laws and how its rules and procedures shape domestic and foreign policy. The theme of the book is that the interplay of rules, procedures, precedents, and strategies is vital to understanding how Congress works. I emphasize the rules and procedures most significant to congressional lawmaking; I do not attempt to survey all the rules and procedures used by Congress.

Every chapter of the fifth edition has been revised to incorporate new developments and insights. Chapter 1 presents an overall view of the congressional process. Chapter 2 examines Congress's budget process, which shapes much of the legislative decision making.

Chapter 3 turns to the initial steps of the legislative process—the introduction of legislation, referral of bills to House and Senate committees, and committee action on measures. Chapter 4 explains how legislation that has emerged from committee is scheduled for floor consideration in the House. Chapter 5 then examines the main features of floor decision making in the House. In Chapter 6 the spotlight is put on the Senate, with discussion of how legislation is scheduled in that chamber. Senate floor action is the subject of Chapter 7.

Chapter 8 describes how House-Senate differences are reconciled when each chamber passes a different version of the same bill and then discusses the president's veto power. Chapter 9 deals with how Congress monitors the implementation of the laws it has passed. Finally, Chapter 10 reexamines the legislative process, pulling together the major themes of the book.

Anyone who writes five editions of a book is intellectually indebted to numerous scholars and colleagues, and I welcome the opportunity to acknowledge their generous advice and assistance. Let me start with the talented people associated with CQ Press. Colleen McGuiness, the editor of this edition, did a careful and thorough job of reviewing the manuscript and contributed greatly to the book's readability. She made the final product much better than it would have been without her skillful assistance. My sincere thanks also extend to Gwenda Larsen, who coordinated the numerous phases of the book's development; Ann O'Malley, who steered the book through the production process; and Ann Davies, the managing editor of textbooks and reference, who was in overall charge of ensuring that deadlines were met. Finally, my sincere appreciation goes to Brenda Carter, director of the college division, who encouraged and helped me with this book over the years.

Much credit for whatever understanding I have of the congressional process goes in large measure to my colleagues at the Congressional Research Service (CRS). Over the years I have learned the intricacies of the House and Senate from scores of CRS associates. Their research endeavors have expanded understanding of Congress's role and responsibilities. I especially want to acknowledge Mildred Amer, Stanley Bach, Richard Beth, Faye Bullock, Paul Dwyer, Louis Fisher, Roger Garcia, Frederick Kaiser, Robert Keith, Michael Koempel, Ronald Moe, John Pontius, Morton Rosenberg, Paul Rundquist, Richard Sachs, James Saturno, Judy Schneider, Stephen Stathis, Sylvia Streeter, and Lorraine Tong. CRS, I should note, bears no responsibility whatsoever for the views or interpretations expressed within these pages. I must also emphasize that whatever errors remain in this book are mine alone.

I am indebted also to scores of past and present House and Senate members and professional congressional aides who have shared ideas and observations and deepened my understanding of the legislative process. My deep gratitude goes to all the parliamentarians of the House and Senate for trying to improve my understanding of Congress's procedural intricacies. I also want to thank Matt Pinkus, a long-time House staff aide, who read several chapters of this edition and offered helpful suggestions.

In addition, I am grateful to numerous colleagues in academia who have created, with their research studies, a reservoir of knowledge about congressional activities and operations. Here I would like especially to acknowledge my longtime collaborators in various projects—Roger H. Davidson, C. Lawrence Evans, and James Thurber—who are always generous with their time and who provide excellent suggestions. My intellectual debt also extends to Donald R. Wolfensberger, director of The Congress Project at the Woodrow Wilson International Center for Scholars and former staff director of the House Rules Committee, and University of Alabama professor Stephen A. Borrelli for their thoughtful reviews and useful suggestions for improving this edition of the book.

Finally, I dedicate this fifth edition to family members—Janet, Mark, and Eric. They provided a loving and encouraging home environment, good humor, and support throughout.

Walter J. Oleszek

CHAPTER 1

Congress and Lawmaking

O N JANUARY 20, 1999, Sen. Orrin G. Hatch, R-Utah, chairman of the Judiciary Committee, introduced a bill to reduce violent juvenile crime and to rehabilitate juvenile criminals. Hatch used a little-known procedure (Senate Rule XIV) to place the bill directly on the Senate's legislative calendar, bypassing the committee referral stage and allowing the bill to be called up for floor action at any time. There the bill languished until a tragic event riveted the attention of the nation.

On April 20, 1999, a shooting occurred at Columbine High School in Littleton, Colorado. Fourteen students and a teacher were killed by two Columbine teenagers before they took their own lives. A month later, on May 20, the Senate passed the juvenile justice bill, but it had been transformed through the floor amendment process into a gun control measure. Vice President Al Gore, in his role as president of the Senate, cast the tie-breaking vote (51-50) on a controversial amendment requiring background checks before guns could be purchased at gun shows.

Scores of parliamentary procedures were employed during Senate consideration of this legislation: filibusters, filling the amendment tree, unanimous consent agreements, and more. When the bill was transmitted to the House, it also encountered a variety of procedural maneuvers. In a surprise move, the GOP leadership through its control of the House Rules Committee split the Senate's bill into two separate measures—one dealing with crime and culture and the other addressing gun controls. This procedural tactic, in the judgment of some analysts, was "aimed at giving wavering lawmakers political cover in the aftermath of the Littleton shootings: They could oppose gun control, while at the same time supporting an array of measures to curb juvenile crime and regulate violence in the media." [1] On largely partisan votes, the House on June 17, 1999, passed the juvenile justice bill; the next day, it defeated the bill stipulating gun curbs. The House-approved legislation did not contain the Senate provisions regarding background checks at gun shows, child-safety locks, or a ban on violent juveniles owning guns.

The Senate subsequently passed an amended version of the House bill. The conference committee—made up of members from each chamber known as conferees, who were appointed to work out bicameral disagreements—convened once in August 1999. Legislative gridlock ensued for more than a year after Columbine, despite repeated adoption of motions to instruct the gun control conferees to meet. Compromises were hard to come by between the parties and chambers as proponents argued for stronger gun control measures and opponents urged tougher enforcement of existing gun laws. Democratic president Bill Clinton also weighed in with criticism of GOP-proposed changes to the legislation. Further polarizing the debate were the lobbying efforts of the National Rifle Association, the U.S. Chamber of Commerce, civil liberties organizations, and the entertainment industry, among others.

Conflicts and disputes are commonplace when Congress debates controversial issues, such as gun control. These matters arouse the partisan or ideological zeal of lawmakers on each side of the issue and make compromises hard to come by. As Rep. John D. Dingell, D-Mich., said, "Legislation is hard, pick-and-shovel work," and it often "takes a long time to do it."[2] Whether Congress can overcome the procedural and substantive wrangling regularly associated with many bills is subject to many factors. What remains constant, however, is Congress's ability to initiate ideas on its own and to refine and crystallize public debate.

Congress is an independent policy maker as well as the nation's premier forum for addressing the economic, social, and political issues of the day—from agriculture to housing, environment to national defense, health to taxes. However, it is not impermeable to pressures from other governmental and nongovernmental forces (including the executive branch, the media, members' constituents, and lobbying groups), from being a bicameral legislature, and from sweeping procedural changes implemented in the past few decades. The lawmaking process, which can be complicated and variable, is governed by rules, procedures, precedents, and customs and is open to the use of some generally predictable strategies and tactics.

This book examines the most significant House and Senate rules and practices that influence the lawmaking process. Usually, no idea on Capitol Hill can avoid a range of parliamentary processes if it expects to become law. Thus, a number of questions arise: Why does Congress have rules? How do House and Senate rules differ and what impact do those differences have on policy making? How are rules applied strategically to accomplish partisan goals? What procedures frame budgetary debates on Capitol Hill? Can House and Senate rules be set aside to expedite consideration of legislation?

THE CONSTITUTIONAL CONTEXT

Congress's central role in policy making can be traced to the writers of the Constitution. James Madison, Alexander Hamilton, and the others developed a political system that established Congress as the lawmaking body and set out its relationship with the other branches of government and with the people. Several familiar basic principles underlie the specific provisions of the Constitution: limited government, separation of powers, checks and balances, and federalism. Each principle continues to shape lawmaking today despite the enormous changes that have transformed and enlarged the role of government in American society.

Limited Government

The framers of the Constitution wanted a strong and effective national government, but at the same time they wanted to avoid concentrating too much power in the central government lest it threaten personal and property rights. The Constitution is filled with implicit and explicit "auxiliary precautions" (Madison's phrase), such as checks and balances and a bill of rights. Limitation of government, the framers believed, could be achieved by dividing power among three branches of national government and between the nation and the states. The division of power ensured both policy conflicts and cooperation because it made officials in the several branches responsive to different constituencies, responsibilities, and perceptions of the public welfare. The framers believed that the "accumulation of all powers, legislative, executive, and judiciary, in the same hands . . . may justly be pronounced the very definition of tyranny."[3] As men of practical experience, they had witnessed firsthand the abuses of King George III and his royal governors. They also wanted to avoid the possible "elective despotism" of their own state legislatures.[4] Wary of excessive authority in either an executive or a legislative body, the framers also were familiar with the works of influential political theorists, particularly Locke and Montesquieu, who stressed concepts such as the separation of powers, checks and balances, and popular control of government.

Separation of Powers

The framers combined their practical experience with a theoretical outlook and established three independent branches of national government, none having a monopoly of governing power. Their objective was twofold. First, the separation of powers was designed to restrain the power of any one branch. Second, it was meant to ensure that cooperation would be necessary for effective government. As Justice Robert Jackson wrote in a 1952 Supreme Court case (*Youngstown Co. v. Sawyer*, 343 U.S. 579, 635): "While the Constitution diffuses power the better to secure liberty, it also contemplates that the practice will integrate the dispersed powers into a workable government." The framers held a strong bias in favor of lawmaking by representative assemblies, and so they viewed Congress as the prime national policy maker. The Constitution names Congress the first branch of government, assigns it "all legislative power," and grants it explicit and implied responsibilities through the so-called elastic clause (Section 8 of Article I). This clause empowers Congress to make "all Laws which shall be necessary and proper for carrying into Execution" its enumerated or specific powers.

In sharp contrast, Articles II and III, creating the executive and judicial branches, respectively, describe only briefly the framework and duties of these governmental units. Although separation of powers implies that Congress "enacts" the laws, the president "executes" them, and the Supreme Court "interprets" them, the framers did not intend such a rigid division of labor. The Constitution creates a system not of separate institutions performing separate functions but of separate institutions sharing functions (and even competing for predominate influence in exercising them). The overlap of powers is fundamental to national decision making. The founders did grant certain unique responsibilities to each branch and ensured their separateness by, for example, prohibiting any officer from serving in more than one branch simultaneously. They linked the branches through a system of checks and balances.

Checks and Balances

An essential corollary of separation of powers is checks and balances. The framers realized that individuals in each branch might seek to aggrandize power at the expense of the other branches. Inevitably, conflicts would develop. In particular, the Constitution provides an open invitation to struggles for power by Congress and the president.

To restrain each branch, the framers devised a system of checks and balances. Congress's own legislative power was effectively "checked" by the establishment of a bicameral body consisting of the House of Representatives and the Senate. The laws Congress passes may be vetoed by the president. Treaties and high-level presidential appointments require the approval of the Senate. Many decisions and actions of Congress and the president are subject to review by the federal judiciary.

Checks and balances have a dual effect; they encourage cooperation and accommodation among the branches—particularly between the popularly elected Congress and the president—and they introduce the potential for conflict. Since 1789 Congress and the president have cooperated with each other and protected their own powers. Each branch depends in various ways on the other. When conflicts occur, they are resolved most frequently by negotiation, bargaining, and compromise.

Federalism

Just as the three branches check each other, the state and federal governments also are countervailing forces. This division of power is another way to curb and control governing power. While the term *federalism* (like *separation of powers* or *checks and balances*) is not mentioned in the Constitution, the framers understood that federalism was a plan of government acceptable to the thirteen original states. The Constitution's "supremacy clause" makes national laws and treaties the "supreme Law of the Land"; however, powers not granted to the national government remain with the states and the people. The inevitable clashes that occur between levels of government are often arbitrated by the Supreme Court or worked out through practical accommodations or laws.

Federalism has infused "localism" into congressional proceedings. As a representative institution, Congress and its members respond to the needs and interests of states and congressional districts. The nation's diversity is given ample expression in Congress by legislators whose tenure rests on the continued support of their constituents. Federalism is an especially prominent theme at the start of the twenty-first century as many lawmakers seek to return federal functions to state and local governments.

Thus, the Constitution outlines a complicated system. Power is divided among the branches and between levels of government, and popular opinion is reflected differently in each. Both Congress and the president, each with different constituencies, terms of office, and times of election, can claim to represent majority sentiment on national issues. Given each branch's independence, formidable powers, different perspectives on many issues, and intricate mix of formal and informal relationships, important national policies reflect the judgment of both the legislative and the executive branches and the views of pressure groups and influential persons.

FUNCTIONS OF RULES AND PROCEDURES

Any decision-making body needs a set of rules, procedures, and conventions—formal and informal—to function. These rules and conventions establish the procedural context for both collective and individual policy-making action and behavior (see Box 1-1).

In the case of Congress, the Constitution authorizes the House and Senate to formulate their own rules of procedure and also prescribes some basic procedures for both houses, such as overrides of presidential vetoes. Thomas Jefferson, who as vice president compiled the first parliamentary manual for the U.S. Senate, emphasized the importance of rules to any legislative body.

> It is much more material that there be a rule to go by, than what that rule is; that there may be a uniformity of proceeding in business not subject to the caprice of the Speaker or captiousness of the members. It is very material that order, decency, and regularity be preserved in a dignified public body.[5]

Rules and procedures in an organization serve many functions. Among them are to provide stability, legitimize decisions, divide responsibilities, protect minority rights, reduce conflict, and distribute power.

Stability

Rules provide stability and predictability in personal and organizational affairs. Individuals and institutions can conduct their day-to-day business without having to debate procedure. Universities, for example, have specific requirements for bachelor's, master's, and doctorate degrees. Students know that if they are to progress from one degree to the next they must comply with rules and requirements. Daily or weekly changes in those requirements would cause chaos on any campus. Similarly, legislators need not decide each day who can speak on the floor, offer amendments, or close debate. Such matters are governed by regularized procedures that continue from one Congress to the next and afford similar rights and privileges to every member.

BOX 1-1 Major Sources of House and Senate Rules

U.S. Constitution. Article I, Section 5, states: "Each House may determine the Rules of Its Proceedings." In addition, other procedures of Congress are addressed, such as quorums, adjournments, and roll calls.

Standing Rules. The formal rules of the House are contained in the *Constitution, Jefferson's Manual, and Rules of the House of Representatives,* commonly called the House Manual. The Senate's rules are in the *Senate Manual Containing the Standing Rules, Orders, Laws, and Resolutions Affecting the Business of the United States Senate.* Each chamber prints its rule book biennially as a separate document.

Precedents. Each chamber, particularly the larger House, has scores of precedents, or unwritten law, based upon past rulings of the chair. The modern precedents of the Senate are compiled in one volume prepared by the Senate parliamentarian. It is revised and updated periodically, printed as a Senate document, and entitled *Senate Procedure: Precedents and Practices.* House precedents are contained in several sources. Precedents from 1789 to 1936 are found in eleven volumes: *Hinds' Precedents of the House of Representatives* (from 1789 through 1907) and *Cannon's Precedents of the House of Representatives* (from 1908 through 1936). Precedents from 1936 through 1999 can be found in the multivolume series entitled *Deschler's Precedents of the United States House of Representatives,* volumes one to nine, and *Deschler-Brown Precedents of the United States House of Representatives,* volumes ten to fifteen. Asher C. Hinds, Clarence Cannon, Lewis Deschler, and William Holmes Brown were parliamentarians of the House. A summary of important precedents through 1984 is found in *Procedure*

To be sure, House and Senate rules change in response to new circumstances, needs, and demands. The history of Congress is reflected in the evolution of the House and Senate rules. Increases in the size of the House in the nineteenth century, for instance, produced limitations on debate for individual representatives. As veteran Democratic senator Robert C. Byrd, W. Va., said about Senate proceedings:

> The day-to-day functioning of the Senate has given rise to a set of traditions, rules, and practices with a life and history all its own. The body of principles and procedures governing many senatorial obligations and routines ... is not so much the result of reasoned deliberations as the fruit of jousting and adjusting to circumstances in which the Senate found itself from time to time.[6]

Procedural evolution is a hallmark of Congress. The modern House and Senate differ in important ways from how they operated only a few decades ago. For example, the House today operates with more procedural and political powers centralized in the Speaker than it did in the past. In the *in the U.S. House of Representatives.* In addition, *House Practice: A Guide to the Rules, Precedents, and Procedures of the House* (1996) examines selected contemporary precedents as of the 104th Congress.

Statutory Rules.   Provisions of many public laws have the force of congressional rules. These rulemaking statutes include, for example, the Legislative Reorganization Act of 1946 (PL 79-601), the Legislative Reorganization Act of 1970 (PL 91-510), and the Congressional Budget and Impoundment Control Act of 1974 (PL 93-344).

Jefferson's Manual.   When Thomas Jefferson was vice president (1797–1801), he prepared a manual of parliamentary procedure for the Senate. Ironically, the House in 1837 made it a formal part of its rules, but the Senate did not grant it such status. The provisions of his manual, according to the House Manual, "govern the House in all cases to which they are applicable and in which they are not inconsistent with the standing rules and orders of the House."

Party Rules.   Each of the two major political parties in each chamber has its own set of party rules. Some of these party regulations directly affect legislative procedure. The House Republican Conference, for example, has a provision that affects the Speaker's use of the suspension of the rules procedure.

Informal Practices and Customs.   Each chamber develops its own informal traditions and customs. They can be uncovered by examining sources such as the *Congressional Record* (the substantially verbatim account of House and Senate floor debate), scholarly accounts, and other studies of Congress. Committees and party groups may also prepare manuals of legislative procedure and practice.

contemporary Senate the filibuster (extended debate) is a growth industry. Infrequently employed a few decades ago, use or threatened use of the filibuster is today almost a daily occurrence.

Legitimacy

Students typically receive final course grades that are based on their classroom performance, examinations, and term papers. They accept the professors' evaluations if they believe in their fairness and legitimacy. If professors suddenly decided to use students' political opinions as the basis for final grades, a storm of protest would arise against such an arbitrary procedure. In a similar fashion, members of Congress and citizens generally accept legislative decisions when they believe the decisions have been approved according to orderly and fair procedures.

From 1993 to 1995 Congress grappled with the issue of applying to itself the laws it passes for the private sector and executive branch. Issues of legitimacy abound in this area. As Rep. Earl Pomeroy, D-N.D., highlighted in a story he told the House Rules Committee:

> Mr. Chairman, at one town meeting recently a constituent stood up and said, "Congressman, how are we supposed to believe the laws you guys pass are good for America, when you're telling us they're not good for Congress?" He was right. To ensure confidence in our laws we need to apply them to ourselves as well.[7]

Hence, Congress devised a process consistent with constitutional principles to bring itself into compliance with appropriate laws (employment, civil rights, and health and safety laws, for example). The landmark bill, titled the Congressional Accountability Act of 1995, was signed into law by the president.

Division of Labor

Any university requires a division of labor if it is to carry out its tasks effectively and responsibly, and rules establish the various jurisdictions. Hence there are history, chemistry, and art departments; admissions officers and bursars; and food service and physical plant managers, all with specialized assignments. For Congress, committees are the heart of the legislative process. They provide the division of labor and specialization that Congress needs to handle about ten thousand measures that are introduced biennially and to review the administration of scores of federal programs. Like specialized bodies in many organizations, committees do not make final policy decisions but initiate recommendations that are forwarded to their respective chambers.

The jurisdiction, or policy mandate, of Congress's standing (permanent) committees is outlined in the House and Senate rules. Legislation generally is referred to the committee (or committees) having authority over the subject matter. As a result, the rules generally determine which committee, and thus which members and their staffs, will exercise significant influence over a particular issue such as defense, taxes, health, or education.

Rules also prescribe the standards that committees are expected to observe during their policy deliberations. These include quorum requirements, public notice of committee meetings and hearings, and the right to counsel for witnesses. These rules also allocate staff resources to committees and subcommittees.

Protect Minority Rights

Colleges and universities have procedures and practices to make certain that minority ideas and beliefs are protected from suppression. Tenure for faculty members ensures that professors are free to expound unconventional views without fear of reprisal from academic administrators. Student handbooks are replete with policies and guidelines to ensure fairness and due process in the adjudication of academic grievances or violations. A fundamental purpose of the collegiate experience presumably is to encourage students to explore new areas, to examine diverse ideas, and to engage persons who think and believe differently than they do.

Congress provides procedural protections for individual lawmakers regardless of their party affiliation and for the minority party. However, the House and Senate differ in the extent to which they emphasize majority rule versus minority rights. The principle of majority rule is embedded in the rules, precedents, and practices of the House. Still, numerous procedural protections exist for minority members and viewpoints. For example, the minority party is always represented on every standing committee; any lawmaker with contrary views can claim one-third of the debate time on conference reports if the Republican and Democratic floor managers both support it; and any committee member is entitled to have supplemental, additional, or minority views printed in committee reports on legislation. As House Democratic Whip David Bonior, Mich., declared: "This body, unlike the other, operates under the principle that a determined majority should be allowed to work its will while protecting the rights of the minority to be heard."[8]

The Senate, by contrast, operates with rules and procedures that advantage minority rights. Prime examples include the right of every senator to speak at great length (the filibuster) and to offer amendments, including nongermane amendments. If the House errs on the side of majority rule (decision over deliberation), the Senate tilts toward minority rights. As Professor Richard F. Fenno Jr. said about the awesome procedural prerogatives afforded each senator: "Every member of the Senate has an atomic bomb and can blow up the place. That leads to accommodation."[9]

Conflict Resolution

Rules reduce conflicts among members and units of organizations by distinguishing appropriate actions and behavior from the inappropriate. For example, universities have procedures by which students may drop or add classes. There are discussions with faculty advisers, completion of appropriate paperwork, and the approval of a dean. Students who informally try to drop or add classes may encounter conflicts with their professors as well as sanctions from the dean's office. Most of the conflicts can be avoided by observance of established procedures. Similarly, congressional rules reduce conflict by, for example, establishing procedures to fill vacancies on committees when several members are competing for the same position or to settle bicameral disputes on legislation. As Rep. Clarence A. Cannon, D-Mo. (1923–1964), a former House parliamentarian and subsequently the chairman of the Appropriations Committee, explained:

> The time of the House is too valuable, the scope of its enactments too far-reaching, and the constantly increasing pressure of its business too great to justify lengthy and perhaps acrimonious discussion of questions of procedure which have been authoritatively decided in former sessions.[10]

Distribution of Power

A major consequence of rules is that they generally distribute power in any organization. Rules, therefore, often are a source of conflict themselves. During the 1960s many campuses witnessed struggles among students, faculty, and administrators involving the curriculum. The charge of irrelevance in course work was a frequent criticism of many students. As a result, the rules of the game for curriculum development were changed on many campuses. Students, junior faculty, and even community groups became involved in reshaping the structure and content of the educational program. Recent years have witnessed comparable concerns as groups on various campuses persuaded university officials to adopt rules, guidelines, or codes regarding speech that is perceived as offensive, for example, to minority groups or women (the so-called political correctness movement).

Like universities, Congress distributes power according to its rules and customs. Informal party rules establish a hierarchy of leadership positions in both chambers. House and Senate rules accord prerogatives to congressional committee chairmen that are unavailable to others.

Rules are not neutral devices. They help to shore up the more powerful members and influence the attainment of member goals such as winning reelection, gaining internal influence, or winning congressional passage of legislation. As former Speaker Newt Gingrich, R-Ga., once said: "The rules of the House are designed for a Speaker with a strong personality and an agenda."[11] Thus, attempts to change the rules almost invariably are efforts to redistribute power.

RULES AND POLICY MAKING IN CONGRESS

Rules play similar roles in most complex organizations. Congress has its own characteristics that affect the functions of the rules. First, members owe their positions to the electorate, not to their congressional peers or to influential congressional leaders. No one in Congress has authority over the other members comparable to that of university presidents and tenured faculty over junior faculty or to that of a corporation president over lower-level executives. Members cannot be fired except by their constituency. (Under the Constitution either chamber may expel a member by a two-thirds vote, but the authority is rarely used.) And each member has equal voting power in committees and on the floor of the House or Senate.

The rules of Congress, unlike those of many organizations, are especially sensitive to the rights of minorities, including the minority party, ideological minorities, and individual members. Skillful use of the rules enables the minority to check majority action by delaying, defeating, or reshaping legislation. Intensity often counts as much as numbers—an apathetic majority may find it difficult to prevail over a well-organized minority. Except in the few instances when extraordinary majorities are needed, such as overriding presidential vetoes (a two-thirds vote), Senate ratification of treaties (two-thirds), and ending extended debate (a filibuster) in the Senate (three-fifths), the rules of the House and Senate require a simple majority to decide public policies.

Congress also is different from other organizations in its degree of responsiveness to external groups and pressures. The legislative branch is not so self-contained an institution as a university or a corporation. Congress is involved with every significant national and international issue. Its agenda compels members to respond to changing constituent interests and needs. Congress also is subject to numerous other influences, particularly the president, pressure groups, political parties, and state and local officials.

Finally, Congress is a collegial, not hierarchical, body. Power flows not from the top down, as in a corporation, but in practically every direction. While presidents can say, as did Harry S. Truman, "The buck stops here," responsibility in Congress is circular, with everybody and nobody appearing responsible for action or inaction. "The congressional system is not set up to have the buck stop somewhere," observed Charles E. Schumer, D-N.Y. (House 1981–1999; Senate-1999).[12] There is often little centralized authority at the top; congressional policies are not announced but made by shifting coalitions that vary from issue to issue. Congress's deliberations are more accessible to the public than those of perhaps any other kind of organization. These are some of the characteristics that set Congress apart from other bodies. Inevitably these differences affect the decision-making process.

Procedure and Policy

Legislative procedures and policy making are inextricably linked in at least four ways. First, procedures affect policy outcomes. Congress processes legislation by complex rules and procedures that permeate the institution. Some matters are only gently brushed by the rules, while others become locked in their grip. Major civil rights legislation, for example, failed for decades to win congressional approval because southern senators used their chamber's rules and procedures to kill or modify such measures.

Congressional procedures are employed to define, restrict, or expand the policy options available to members during floor debate. They may prevent consideration of certain issues or presage policy outcomes. Such structured procedures enhance the policy influence of certain members, committees, or party leaders; facilitate expeditious treatment of issues; grant priority to some policy alternatives but not others; and determine, in general, the overall character of policy decisions.

Second, policy decisions often are expressed as procedural moves. As Robert H. Michel, R-Ill., who served as House minority leader from 1981 to 1995, said about the procedure-substance linkage:

> Procedure hasn't simply become more important than substance—it has, through a strange alchemy, become the substance of our deliberations. Who rules House procedures rules the House—and to a great degree, rules the kind and scope of political debate in this country.[13]

Or as Representative Dingell phrased it, "If you let me write the procedure, and I let you write the substance, I'll [beat] you every time."[14]

Representatives and senators, on various occasions, prefer not to make clear-cut decisions on certain complex and far-reaching public issues. Should a major weapons system be continued or curtailed? Should the nation's energy production needs take precedence over environmental concerns? Should financial assistance for the elderly be reduced and priority given to aiding disadvantaged children? On questions such as these, members may be cross-pressured—the president may exert influence one way while constituent interests dictate another approach. Legislators sometimes lack adequate information or time to make informed judgments. They may be reluctant to oppose powerful pressure groups. Or they may feel that an issue does not lend itself to a simple "yes" or "no" vote.

As a result, legislators employ various procedural devices to handle knotty problems. A matter may be postponed on the ground of insufficient study in committee. Congress may direct an agency to prepare a detailed report before an issue is considered. An outside commission may be established to study a problem. Or a measure may be tabled by the House or Senate, a procedural vote that effectively defeats a proposal without rendering a clear judgment on its substance.

Third, the nature of the policy can determine the use of certain procedures. The House and Senate generally consider noncontroversial measures under expeditious procedures; controversial proposals normally involve lengthy deliberation. Extraordinary circumstances sometimes prompt Congress to use expedited procedures to pass legislation, such as suspension of the rules, which limits debate to forty minutes and prohibits floor amendments. Emergency bills or legislation with overwhelming bipartisan support can be passed quickly by way of the suspension route.

Fourth, policy outcomes are more likely to be influenced by members with procedural expertise. Members who are skilled parliamentarians are better prepared to gain approval of their proposals than those who are only vaguely familiar with the rules. Just as carpenters and lawyers must learn their trade, members of Congress need to understand the rules if they expect to perform effectively. Congressional procedures are confusing to members. "To table, to refer to committee, to amend—so many things come up," declared a junior senator. "You don't know whether you are coming or going."[15] John W. McCormack, D-Mass., who served as House Speaker from 1962 to 1971, once advised House newcomers:

> Learn the rules and understand the precedents and procedures of the House. The congressman who knows how the House operates will soon be recognized for his parliamentary skills—and his prestige will rise among his colleagues, no matter what his party.[16]

Members who know the rules will always have the potential to shape legislation to their ends and to become key figures in coalitions trying to pass or defeat legislation. Those who do not understand the rules reduce their proficiency and influence as legislators. Some members even become parliamentary watchdogs or use guerrilla warfare tactics to harass the opposition or to stymie majority steamrollers.

Conventional versus Unconventional Lawmaking

A fundamental strength of Congress's lawmaking process is its capacity to adjust and adapt to new circumstances. This has been a principal characteristic of the legislative process from Congress's very beginning. The House and Senate, not surprisingly, regularly make formal or informal modifications to their procedures and practices. Thus, the procedures associated with lawmaking are often a moving target. What is conventional or orthodox in one era or for specific types of bills may seem unconventional or unorthodox when different patterns of congressional decision making emerge.

Recently, a number of commentators and scholars have discussed what to them are procedural deviations from a textbook Congress or the regular order. The regular order refers to what the House or Senate rulebook prescribes for the consideration of legislation. Most of the time in each chamber many of these rules are not observed because they are too cumbersome to apply in practice. Instead, each chamber creates special orders, such as rules in the House or unanimous consent agreements in the Senate. Thus, the regular order can be conceived as the default procedures in the standing rules that will be observed absent their being set aside, the customary practice of each chamber.

Speaking of the regular order as a specifically prescribed way by which ideas become laws is somewhat misleading. Instead, this term generally refers to procedural expectations or norms that have come into being regarding how legislation should normally be considered in the House or Senate. During the 1950s, 1960s, and early 1970s, for instance, the regular order, or textbook version of lawmaking, meant introduction and referral of bills to committees; committee hearings, markups, and reports; wide amendment opportunities on the House or Senate floor; the bicameral resolution of chamber differences on legislation; and presidential consideration. This pattern still holds true for most public laws enacted by Congress (see Figure 1-1).

However, the fundamental point is that variations have always existed from the procedural expectations prevalent in certain eras. During the 1990s and early 2000s, those variations have increased in significant measure because Congress is less insular and more permeable to outside forces than ever before. Understandably, changes in the broader political environment—the election of activist lawmakers who do not want to defer to committee chairmen, the proliferation of interest groups, the rise in issue complexity, partisan polarization, breakthroughs in communications technology, clashes with presidents, crises, and more—are reflected in the procedural practices and politics of the House and Senate.

Contemporary lawmaking is a more fluid and less predictable process. Party leaders and individual members simply have more procedural room for

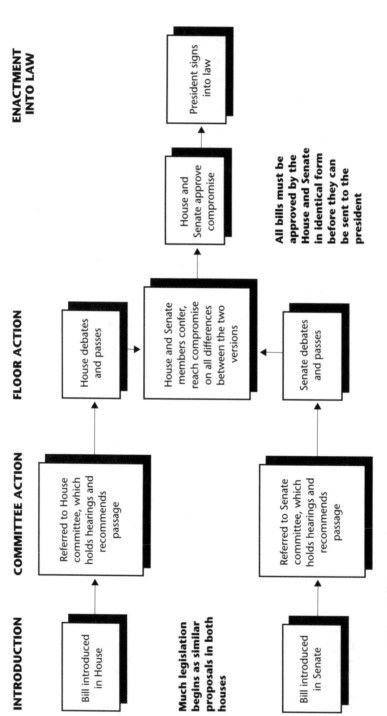

INTRODUCTION

Bill introduced in House

Much legislation begins as similar proposals in both houses

Bill introduced in Senate

COMMITTEE ACTION

Referred to House committee, which holds hearings and recommends passage

Referred to Senate committee, which holds hearings and recommends passage

FLOOR ACTION

House debates and passes

House and Senate members confer, reach compromise on all differences between the two versions

Senate debates and passes

All bills must be approved by the House and Senate in identical form before they can be sent to the president

ENACTMENT INTO LAW

President signs into law

FIGURE 1-1 How a Bill Becomes Law

strategic maneuvers. For instance, scholars talk about the surge of filibusters, or the threat of filibusters, in today's Senate. Why? The past two decades have witnessed the rise of a more partisan and individualistic Senate, and senators have more incentives to push their procedural prerogatives to the limit. Omnibus bills came into prominence during the 1980s and 1990s (even though they were used in earlier decades, too). Why? In part because fiscal deficits dominated Congress's attention and the main way to force unwanted cuts in federal programs and agencies was to use the reconciliation process, which involved packaging the program reductions together in one massive bill to be voted up or down. Party leaders bypass the standing committees more commonly today than previously, in large measure because the partisan stakes are high, and they want to avoid having major bills get bogged down in committee. Is this a novel practice? Recall that Senate Majority Leader Mike Mansfield, D-Mont., deliberately bypassed the Senate Judiciary Committee (headed by a segregationist chairman) and placed the Civil Rights Act of 1964 directly on the legislative calendar.

Procedural change is a persistent feature of the House and Senate. Lawmaking expectations in the early 2000s are different in many ways from those of the 1970s. In one of Congress's most dramatic legislative sessions, for example, the House in early 1995 reviewed, debated, and voted on virtually everything associated with the GOP's Contract with America. The contract had served as a 1994 campaign document for Republicans, who promised to enact it within the first hundred days of the 104th Congress if the electorate gave them majority control, and as a governing document around which GOP House members rallied and focused from January 4 to April 7, 1995. Reflecting the accelerated pace, the House was in session 528 hours during the contract period—more than double the session hours of the first thirteen weeks of the 103d Congress and almost triple those of the 102d. About twelve hundred hearings and markups were held during the hundred days— one-third more than the eight hundred held in the comparable period of the previous Congress.[17] "I'm on the [Judiciary] constitutional subcommittee," said Democratic Rep. Jose E. Serrano, N.Y., "and we're amending the Constitution every week. This should not be happening this way, but [Republicans] have a deadline, and we have no choice."[18]

Several recent House Speakers, such as Thomas P. "Tip" O'Neill Jr., D-Mass., employed partisan or bipartisan task forces to facilitate passage of legislation and to draft legislation. However, Speaker Gingrich accelerated the creation of task forces, most comprised only of GOP lawmakers. A Capitol Hill newspaper suggested that Gingrich was "implementing a new House structure that relies heavily on task forces to carry out responsibilities handled by committees."[19] This was an overstatement, but Gingrich did create a large number of these ad hoc groups, several of which exercised important policy influence. For instance, Gingrich created a so-called Design Group, composed of the principal Republican lawmakers with expertise in health issues, to craft Medicare reform legislation. "This bill, right from the start, was written in the Speaker's office," said Commerce Chairman Thomas Bliley, R-Va.[20]

Although Speaker J. Dennis Hastert, R-Ill., who succeeded Gingrich, deemphasized the use of task forces, they are still created but on a more selective basis. For example, "to blunt Democratic momentum on the issue of Medicare coverage for prescription drugs," Hastert established a GOP task force to devise a drug prescription plan for elderly citizens.[21] Similarly, Senate Majority Leader Trent Lott, R-Miss., employs partisan task forces to advance GOP priorities. Lott named a GOP Health Care Task Force, headed by Majority Whip Don Nickles of Oklahoma, to write legislation regulating the practices of health maintenance organizations.[22]

Ideas can become law with little or no committee or floor debate in either the House or Senate. No statistics have been kept on the number of instances of this occurring, but congressional insiders suggest that it is on the increase. A convenient venue for this practice is the conference stage. A major budget revision bill bypassed the House and Senate committee stages entirely with initial House consideration of the bill occurring at the end of the bill-enacting process, when representatives debated the conference report. With no committee hearings or floor debate in either chamber, a one-sentence, forty-six-word, $50 billion tobacco tax break was quietly inserted into a budget conference report, which the president signed into law. When word leaked out about the tax break, it was later repealed in another law.[23]

Precedents and Folkways

Congress is regulated not only by formal rules but also by informal ones that influence legislative procedure and member behavior. Two types of informal rules are precedents and folkways. Precedents, the accumulated past decisions on matters of procedure, represent a blend of the formal and informal. They are the common law of Congress and govern many procedures not explicitly covered in the formal rules. As a noted House parliamentarian wrote, the great majority of the "rules of all parliamentary bodies are unwritten law; they spring up by precedent and custom; these precedents and customs are this day the chief law of both Houses of Congress."[24] For example, formal rules prescribe the order of business in the House and Senate, but precedents permit variations through the unanimous consent of the members. The rulings of the Speaker of the House and presiding officer of the Senate form a large body of precedents. They are given formal status by the parliamentarians in each chamber and then become part of the accepted rules and procedures.

Folkways are unwritten norms of behavior that members are expected to observe. Like rules and precedents, folkways evolve in response to new times, demands, and lawmakers. During the 1950s, for instance, scholars wrote about norms of "apprenticeship" (junior lawmakers should listen and learn from their more seasoned colleagues before actively getting involved in policy making), "courtesy" (members should be solicitous toward their colleagues and avoid personal attacks on them), or "specialization" (a member should master a few policy areas and not try to impress colleagues as being a jack-of-all-trades). Today, these norms no longer apply. In both chambers, lawmakers enter an "entrepreneurial" environment where the incentives—both inside and outside Congress—are to get quickly involved in lawmaking, publicity seeking, and campaign fund raising. "You don't have to wait around to have influence," noted then representative Schumer. "Entrepreneurs do very well." [25]

The to-get-along, go-along culture of the 1950s and 1960s Congresses is mainly a thing of the past. Newcomers who quietly sit back and defer to their elders are likely to be viewed as unusual, especially in the Senate where norms of individualism pervade the institution. In today's Senate, wrote a noted scholar, a member "feels minimally constrained by consensual codes of behavior. The relevant distinction in his life is not between the Senate and the rest of the political world but between himself (plus his staff) and everything else. . . . With the help of the Senate's formal rules, he knows he can bring the collective business to a halt. He can be a force to be reckoned with whenever he wants to be." [26] Congressional decision making, then, is shaped by each chamber's formal and informal structure of rules, precedents, traditions, goals, and expectations.

CONGRESSIONAL DECISION MAKING

The congressional decision-making process is constantly evolving, but it has certain enduring features that affect consideration of all legislation. The first is the decentralized power structure of Congress, characterized by numerous specialized committees and a central party leadership that struggles to promote party and policy coherence. A second feature is the existence of multiple decision points for every piece of legislation. The many decision points mean that at each step of a bill's progress a majority coalition must be formed to move the measure along. This leads to the third important feature of the process: the need for bargaining and compromise to form a winning coalition. Finally, each Congress has only a two-year life cycle in which to pass legislation once it has been introduced. The pressure of time is an ever-present force underlying the process.

Decentralized Power Structure

Congress's decentralized character reflects both political and structural realities. Politically, legislators owe their reelection to voters in widely differing states and localities; structurally, the legislative branch has an elaborate division of labor to help it manage its immense workload. Responsibility for specific subject areas is dispersed among some two hundred committees and subcommittees.

Structural decentralization means that policy making is subject to various disintegrative processes. Broad issues are divided into smaller subissues for

BOX 1-2   Leadership Structure of Congress

The party leadership in the House and Senate is crucial to the smooth functioning of the legislative process. In the House, the formal leadership consists of the Speaker, the majority and minority leaders, whips from each party, assistants to the whips, and various partisan committees. In the Senate, the vice president of the United States serves as president; in his absence, the president pro tempore or, more commonly, a temporary presiding officer of the majority party presides. The Senate also has majority and minority leaders, whips, assistant whips, and party committees.

The Speaker's fundamental power is to set the agenda of the House. He achieves his influence largely through personal prestige, mastery of the art of persuasion, legislative expertise, and the support of members. Among his formal powers are presiding over the House, deciding points of order, referring bills and resolutions to committee, scheduling legislation for floor action, and appointing House members to select, joint, and House-Senate conference committees. The Speaker seldom participates in debate and usually votes only to break a tie. The Speaker's institutional prerogatives are buttressed by his role as leader of the majority party. For example, the Speaker chairs his party's committee assignment panel and can expedite or delay floor action on legislation.

---

consideration by the committees. Overlapping and fragmented committee responsibilities can impede the development of comprehensive and coordinated national policies. Many House and Senate committees, for example, consider some aspect of health, trade, or energy policy.[27] Jurisdictional controversies occur as committees fight to protect or expand their turf. Finally, committees develop special relationships with pressure groups, executive agencies, and scores of other interested participants. These alliances, often called *subgovernments, issue networks,* or *sloppy large hexagons,* influence numerous policy areas. Committees, then, become advocates of policies and not simply impartial instruments of the House or Senate.[28]

In theory, political parties are supposed to provide the cohesive force to balance the centrifugal influences of a fragmented committee system. The reality is often much different. Parties serve to organize their members and elect the formal leaders of Congress. Democrats and Republicans regularly meet in policy committees and caucuses to discuss substantive and political issues. Neither party, however, commands the consistent support of all its members. Too great a spread of ideological convictions exists within each party. Too many countervailing pressures (constituency, region, individual conscience, career considerations, or committee loyalty) also influence the actions of representatives and senators. "I'll fight for my district even though it may be contrary to my national goals," declared a former House majority whip.[29] As a

The majority and minority parties of the House and Senate elect, respectively, majority and minority leaders. The House majority leader has considerable influence over the scheduling of bills and day-to-day management of the floor. He ranks just below the Speaker in importance. The minority leader heads his party in the House. Among other things, he develops policy alternatives to majority initiatives, serves as party spokesperson, and devises strategies to win back majority control of the House.

In the Senate, the majority leader is the most influential officer because neither the vice president nor the president pro tempore holds substantive powers over the chamber's proceedings. Everyday duties of the minority leader correspond to those of the majority leader, except that the minority leader has little authority over scheduling legislation. Agenda-setting is the prime prerogative of the majority leader. The minority leader speaks for his party and acts as field general on the floor, promoting partisan cohesion and searching for votes on the majority side.

Each party in the House and Senate elects a whip and appoints a number of deputy, assistant, or regional whips to aid the floor leader in implementing the party's legislative program. The diversity of whips provides greater geographical, ideological, and seniority balance in the party leadership structure. At its core, the whips' job is to know where the votes are and to produce the votes on behalf of party objectives.

result, public policies usually are enacted because diverse elements of both parties temporarily coalesce to achieve common goals.

The usual lack of disciplined parties, in or out of Congress, underscores the difficult and delicate role of congressional party leaders (see Box 1-2). They cannot dictate policy because they lack the means to force agreement among competing party factions or autonomous committees and subcommittees. "What influence I have is based upon . . . respect and reasoned persuasion and some sensitivity to the political and other concerns of individual Senators," said Majority Leader George J. Mitchell, D-Maine, in 1994. "I don't have a large bag of goodies to hand out to Senators nor do I have any mechanism for disciplining Senators."[30] A number of legislators, too, are not particularly dependent on their state or local parties for reelection. This means that party leaders cannot count on automatic party support but must rely heavily on their skills as bargainers and negotiators to influence legislative decisions. In addition, the power and style of any party leader depend on several factors, some outside the leader's control. Among them are personality, intellectual and political talent, the leader's view of the job, the size of the majority or minority party in the chamber, whether the White House is controlled by the opposition party, the expectations of colleagues, and the institutional complexion of the House or Senate during a particular historical era.

Many of these factors were clearly evident when the Gingrich-led House completed action on the Contract with America even before the promised hundred-day period ended (see Table 1-1). The House approved nine of the ten contract items (rejecting only term limits for lawmakers) with most GOP lawmakers, unlike the Democrats, marching in lockstep to enact their plan. "A total of 141 of the 230 Republicans" had party unity scores of 100 percent; the lowest GOP score was by Constance A. Morella, Md., "who voted with the party on 73 percent of the contract items."[31] Moreover, Speaker Gingrich took steps to centralize authority in his own hands and to weaken the power of committee chairs to block action on legislation. He bypassed the seniority custom in naming loyalists to head three standing committees (Appropriations, Commerce, and Judiciary); he also approved a new House rule limiting committee and subcommittee chairmen to three consecutive terms. (The Speaker's own length of service was restricted to four consecutive terms, or eight years, to be consistent with the constitutional amendment limiting presidential service.) The "Newt Deal," then, represented an unusual period when the Speaker exercised top-down control over what some commentators previously called the ungovernable and gridlocked House.

Multiple Decision Points

Although Congress can on occasion act quickly, normally legislation works its way slowly through multiple decision points. One congressional report identified more than a hundred specific steps that might mark a "bill's progress through the Congress from introduction to possible enactment into law."[32]

After a bill is introduced, it usually is referred to committee and then frequently to a subcommittee. The views of executive departments and agencies often are solicited. "Almost every bill that is moving in Congress is sent to my office . . . by the committees for a reaction," remarked the head of the Justice Department's office of legislative affairs.[33] Hearings are held and reports on the bill are issued by the subcommittee and full committee. The bill then is reported out of the full committee and scheduled for consideration by the majority party leadership. After floor debate and final action in one chamber, the same steps generally are repeated in the other house. At any point in this sequential process, the bill is subject to delay, defeat, or modification. "It is very easy to defeat a bill in Congress," President John F. Kennedy once noted. "It is much more difficult to pass one."[34]

Congressional procedures require bills to overcome numerous hurdles. At each stage, measures and procedures must receive majority approval. All along the procedural route, therefore, strategically located committees, groups, or individuals can delay, block, or change proposals if they can form majority coalitions. Bargaining may be necessary at each juncture to build the majority coalition that advances the bill to the next step in the legislative process. Thus, advocates of a piece of legislation must attract not just one

TABLE 1-1 Contract with America Scorecard at One Hundred Days

Legislative proposal	Passed by House	Passed by Senate	Signed by President
Balanced-budget amendment and	•	Defeated	
line-item veto	•	•	
Anticrime package	•		
Welfare reform	•		
Family and children	•		
Defense package	•		
Unfunded mandate	•	•	•
Social Security reform	•		
Litigation reform	•		
Tax cuts	•		
Term limits	Defeated		

majority but several successive majorities at each of the critical intersections along the legislative route.

Bargaining and Coalition Building

Three principal forms of bargaining are used to build majority coalitions: logrolling, compromise, and nonlegislative favors.

Logrolling is an exchange of voting support on different bills by different members of Congress. It is an effective means of coalition building because members rarely are equally concerned about all the measures before Congress. For example, representatives A, B, and C strongly support a bill that increases government aid to farmers. A, B, and C are indifferent toward a second bill that increases the minimum wage, which is strongly supported by representatives D, E, and F. Because D, E, and F do not have strong feelings about the farm bill, a bargain is struck: A, B, and C agree to vote for the minimum wage bill, and D, E, and F agree to vote for the farm bill. Thus both bills are helped on their way past the key decision points at which A, B, C, D, E, and F have influence. Logrolling may be either explicit or implicit. A, B, and C may have negotiated directly with D, E, and F. Alternatively, A, B, and C may have voted for the minimum wage bill, letting it be known through the press or in other informal ways that they anticipate similar treatment on the farm bill from D, E, and F. The expectation is that D, E, and F will honor the tacit agreement because at a later date they may again need the support of A, B, and C.

Compromise, unlike logrolling, builds coalitions through negotiation over the content of legislation. Each side agrees to modify policy goals on a given bill in a way that generally is acceptable to the other. A middle ground often is found—particularly with bills involving money. A, B, and C, for example, support a $50 million education bill; D, E, and F want to increase the funding to $100 million. The six meet and compromise on a $75 million bill they all can support.

Note the distinction between logrolling and compromise. In the logrolling example, the participants did not modify their objectives on the bills that mattered to them; each side traded voting support on a bill that meant little in return for support on a bill in which they were keenly interested. In a compromise, both sides modify their positions. "Anyone who thinks that compromise is a dirty word," remarked Rep. Charles W. Stenholm, D-Texas, "should go back and read one of the fascinating accounts of all that happened in Philadelphia in 1787" when the Constitution was drafted.[35] As Sen. Alan K. Simpson, R-Wyo., put it: "In politics there are no right answers, only a continuing flow of compromises between groups resulting in a changing, cloudy, and ambiguous series of public decisions where appetite and ambition compete openly with knowledge and wisdom." [36]

Nonlegislative favors are useful because policy goals are only one of the many objectives of members of Congress. Other objectives include assignment to a prestigious committee, getting reelected, running for higher office, obtaining larger office space and staff, or being selected to attend a conference abroad. The wide variety of these nonpolicy objectives creates numerous bargaining opportunities—particularly for party leaders, who can dispense many favors—from which coalitions can be built. As Senate majority leader from 1955 to 1961, Lyndon B. Johnson of Texas was known for his skill in using his powers to satisfy the personal needs of senators to build support for legislation Johnson wanted.

> For Johnson, each one of these assignments contained a potential opportunity for bargaining, for creating obligations, provided that he knew his fellow senators well enough to determine which invitations would matter the most to whom. If he knew that the wife of the senator from Idaho had been dreaming of a trip to Paris for ten years, or that the advisers to another senator had warned him about his slipping popularity with Italian voters, Johnson could increase the potential usefulness of assignments to the Parliamentary Conference in Paris or to the dedication of the cemeteries in Italy.[37]

In this way, Johnson made his colleagues understand that there was a debt to be repaid.

The Congressional Cycle

Every bill introduced in Congress faces the two-year deadline of the congressional term. (The term of the 107th Congress, elected in November 2000, begins at noon on January 3, 2001, and expires at noon on January 3, 2003.) Legislation introduced must be passed by both the House and the Senate in identical form within the two-year term to become law. Congress normally adjourns prior to the end of the two-year term; thus bills usually have less than two full years. Bills that have not completed the required procedural journey before final adjournment of a Congress automatically die and must be reintroduced in a new Congress to start the legislative process anew. Inaction or postponement at any stage of the process can mean the defeat of a bill.

Many measures considered by Congress come up in cycles. Much of Congress's annual agenda is filled with legislation required each year to continue and finance the activities of federal agencies and programs. Generally, this kind of legislation appears regularly on the congressional agenda at about the same time each year. Other legislation comes up for renewal every few years. Emergencies demand immediate attention. Other issues become timely because public interest, international events, or the president has focused on them; health care, trade with China, national missile defense, and Social Security reform are examples of such issues in the early 2000s.

Complex legislation often is introduced early because it takes longer to process than a simple bill. A disproportionately large number of major bills are enacted during the last few weeks of a Congress. Compromises that were not possible in July can be made in December. By this time—with the two-year term about to expire—the pressures on members of the House and Senate are intense, and lawmaking can become frantic and furious. "It is a time when legislators pass dozens of bills without debate or recorded votes, a time when a canny legislator can slip in special favors for the folks back home or for special interest lobbyists roaming Capitol corridors."[38] Members plan purposefully to take advantage of the end game in lawmaking.

Finally, many ideas require years or even decades of germination before they are enacted into law. Controversial proposals—reintroduced in successive Congresses—may need a four-, six-, or eight-year period before they win enactment. Many of the 1960s policies of Presidents Kennedy and Johnson, for example, first were considered during the Congresses of the 1950s. Landmark immigration reform legislation required the action of three 1980s Congresses before it eventually surmounted hurdles and roadblocks to become public law. While health care reform efforts began in the mid-1990s, substantive legislation to revise, refine, or revamp the health care system will likely occupy center stage in the twenty-first century.

THE HOUSE AND SENATE COMPARED

The "House and Senate are naturally unlike," observed Woodrow Wilson.[39] Each chamber has its own rules, precedents, and customs; different terms of office; varying constitutional responsibilities; and differing constituencies. "We are constituted differently, we serve different purposes in the representative system, we operate differently, why should [the House and Senate] not have different rules," said Sen. Wayne Morse, D-Ore. (1945–1969).[40] Table 1-2 lists the major differences between the chambers.

Probably the three most important differences are (1) the House is more than four times the size of the Senate, (2) senators represent a broader constituency than do representatives, and (3) senators serve longer terms of of-

TABLE 1-2 Major Differences between the House and Senate

House	Senate
Shorter term of office (two years)	Longer term of office (six years)
Adheres closely to procedural rules on floor activity	Operates mostly by unanimous consent
Narrower constituency	Broader, more varied constituency
Originates all revenue bills	Sole power to ratify treaties and advise and consent to presidential nominations
Policy specialists	Policy generalists
Less press and media coverage	More press and media coverage
Power less evenly distributed	Power more evenly distributed
Less prestigious	More prestigious
More expeditious in floor debate	Less expeditious in floor debate
Strict germaneness requirement for floor amendments	No general germaneness rule for floor amendments
Less reliance on staff	More reliance on staff
More partisan	Somewhat less partisan
Strict limits on debate	Unlimited debate on nearly every measure
Method of operation stresses majority rule	Traditions and practices emphasize minority rights

fice. These differences affect the way the two houses operate in a number of ways.

Complexity of the Rules

The factor of size explains much about why the two chambers differ. Because it is larger, the House is a more structured body than the Senate. The restraints imposed on representatives by rules and precedents are far more severe than those affecting senators. House rules for the 106th Congress take 1,335 pages to describe. Its precedents from 1789 to 1936 are in eleven huge volumes; those from 1936 on are recorded in the multivolume *Deschler's Precedents of the United States House of Representatives* and *Deschler-Brown Precedents of the United States House of Representatives*. In contrast, the Senate's rules and standing orders are contained in 1,038 pages and its precedents in one volume.

Where Senate rules maximize freedom of expression, House rules "show a constant subordination of the individual to the necessities of the whole House as the voice of the national will."[41] Furthermore, House and Senate rules differ fundamentally in their basic purpose. House rules are designed to permit a determined majority to work its will. Senate rules are intended to slow down, or even defer, action on legislation by granting inordinate parliamentary power (through the filibuster, for example) to individual members and determined minorities. "Senate rules are tilted toward not doing things," remarked Jim Wright, D-Texas, who served as Speaker from 1987 to 1989. "House rules, if you know how to use them, are tilted toward allowing the majority to get its will done."[42] Ironically, moving legislation is easier in the larger House than the smaller Senate because of differences in their rules. A simple majority is sufficient to pass major and controversial legislation in the House. In the Senate, at least sixty votes (necessary to break a filibuster) might be needed—sometimes more than once—to move legislation to final passage. The House acts on the basis of majority rule; the Senate emphasizes minority rule and often functions as a supermajoritarian institution where sixty votes are crucial to the enactment of legislation.

The Senate, as a result, is more personal and individualistic. "The Senate is run for the convenience of one Senator, to the inconvenience of 99," said one senator.[43] It functions to a large extent by unanimous consent, in effect adjusting or disregarding its rules as it goes along. It is not uncommon for votes on a bill to be rescheduled or delayed until an interested senator can be present. Senate party leaders are careful to consult all senators who have expressed an interest in the pending legislation, because "under the rules of the Senate any one Senator can hold up the works here," said Senator Byrd, an acknowledged expert in Senate procedure.[44] In the House, the leadership can consult only key members—usually committee leaders—about upcoming floor action. No wonder bills often take longer to complete in the smaller Senate than the larger House. All senators can participate actively in shaping decisions on the floor given their unique prerogatives: unlimited debate and unlimited opportunities to offer floor amendments to virtually any bill. House members typically get involved on the floor only on measures reported from the committees on which they serve. To be sure, far-reaching issues (such as major health reform or education proposals) will trigger floor participation by many representatives.

Policy Incubation

Incubation entails "keeping a proposal alive, while it picks up support, or waits for a better climate, or while the problem to which it is addressed grows."[45] Both houses fulfill this role, but it is promoted in the Senate particularly because of that body's flexible rules, more varied constituent pressures on senators, and greater press and media coverage. As the chamber of greater prestige, lesser complexity, longer term of office, and smaller size, the Senate is simply easier for the media to cover than the House.[46] The Senate is more involved than the House with cultivating national constituencies, formulating questions for national debate, and gaining general public support for policy proposals. The policy-generating role is particularly characteristic of senators having presidential ambitions, who need to capture headlines and national constituencies.[47]

However, when the House began televising its floor sessions in 1979 over C-SPAN (Cable-Satellite Public Affairs Network)—the Senate began gavel-to-gavel coverage in mid-1986—many activist representatives recognized the technology's bully-pulpit potential. For example, when Newt Gingrich was elected to the House in 1978, he quickly saw C-SPAN as a means for mobilizing grass-roots support behind the GOP's agenda and for attacking Democrats and their decades-long control of the House. He organized floor debates and speeches, even when there was hardly anyone in the chamber, to highlight Republican ideas to the C-SPAN viewing audience and to persuade them that they ought to put the House in Republican hands. He was successful.

As Speaker of the 104th and 105th Congresses (1995–1999), Gingrich took the public role of the Speakership to new heights.[48] For instance, he went on prime-time national television after the House successfully completed action on the Contract with America, emulating presidents who address the nation. By contrast, Dennis Hastert plays a less visible public role, sharing the spotlight with other party members. A Gallup poll in 2000 found that only 6 percent of Americans could name Hastert as the House Speaker. "Three years ago, 53 percent knew that Newt Gingrich had that job."[49]

Many Senate Republicans who had previously served in the House with Gingrich began to emulate their former colleague in certain ways by conducting organized, often early morning, speeches to a largely empty chamber. These orchestrated speeches are designed to bolster their party's image and agenda. For example, the eleven Senate Republican freshmen elected to the 104th Congress (seven of whom had served in the House) organized a Freshman Focus to emphasize their commitment to changing the way Washington works. The GOP freshmen began presenting twice-weekly speeches, aimed at C-SPAN viewers, on timely and major issues—mindful that, as freshman senator James M. Inhofe, R-Okla., stated, "a lot of people out there are watching what's going on here."[50] Senate Democrats have their own informal message group, which takes the floor periodically to highlight ideas and party priorities to the C-SPAN viewing public.

Specialists versus Generalists

Another difference between the chambers is that representatives tend to be known as subject matter specialists while senators tend to be generalists. "If the Senate has been the nation's great forum," a representative said, then the "House has been its workshop."[51] The House's greater work force and division of labor facilitate policy specialization. "Senators do not specialize as intensively or as exclusively in their committee work as House members do" because senators must spread their "efforts over a greater span of subjects than the average representative."[52] During the 106th Congress, for example, the average senator served on about ten committees and subcommittees, compared with about five for the average representative.

One reason for the specialist-generalist distinction is that most senators represent a more heterogeneous constituency than House members. This compels the former to generalize as they attempt to be conversant on numerous national and international issues that affect their state. With their six-year term, senators are less vulnerable to immediate constituency pressures. Therefore, they can afford to be more cosmopolitan in their viewpoints than House members. Journalists tend to expect senators, more than representatives, to have an informed opinion on almost every important public issue. Senators, too, suffer from what Senator Byrd called "fractured attention."[53] They are often away from the Senate raising campaign funds, appearing on television, giving speeches, or engaging in other activities that limit their ability to participate in floor deliberations.

A result of the generalist role is greater reliance by senators on knowledgeable personal and committee staff aides for advice in decision making. House members are more likely to be experts themselves on particular policy issues. If not, they often go to informed colleagues rather than staff aides for advice on legislation. "House members rely most heavily upon their colleagues for all information," one study concluded, while senators "will often turn to other sources, especially their own staffs, for their immediate information needs."[54] Consequently, Senate staff aides generally have more influence over the laws and programs of the nation than do their House counterparts. Some senators, however, certainly can hold their own with knowledgeable House members.

The House in 1995 adopted rules that limit members to six consecutive years of service as committee or subcommittee chairs. The purpose of this change, besides allowing additional majority party lawmakers to assume leadership posts, was "more importantly to prevent stagnation or too close a relationship to develop between committee leaders and the interests they oversee."[55] Rotating committee leadership also limits the ability of the chairs to master the work of being a leader (such as negotiating compromises, setting the agenda, and managing the committee), fosters short-term thinking when long-range planning may be necessary, and undermines the panel leaders' bargaining potency with the White House, the executive branch, and other groups and entities. If Republicans maintain control of the House following the November 2000 elections, the six-year limit will mean that about a dozen standing committees will have new committee leaders. Democrats have indicated they will drop the term-limit rule if they retake the House. (Senate Republicans also imposed a six-year term limit on committee chairmen, but it was in the form of a party rule that took effect in January 1997.)

Distribution of Power

Another difference between the two chambers is that power to influence policy is more evenly distributed in the Senate than in the House. Unlike most representatives, senators can readily exercise initiative in legislation and oversight, get floor amendments incorporated in measures reported from committees on which they are not members, influence the scheduling of bills, and, in general, participate more widely and equally in all Senate and party activities. Witness the ability of Sen. Bill Bradley, D-N.J., then a relatively junior member of the Finance Committee, to become known as the father of the landmark tax reform package of 1986 even though the chamber was in Republican hands. Every senator, too, of the majority party typically chairs at least one committee or subcommittee.

This ability to make a difference quickly is one reason that the Senate is so politically attractive to House members. "I've found the Senate to be a very liberating experience," said former representative and now senator Robert Torricelli, D-N.J. "The House is so structured by its rules, and Members are so compartmentalized by ideologies or interests. Sometimes it's hard to make an impact." [56] In the 106th Congress, forty-six senators were former House members; by contrast, no representative served previously in the Senate. House procedures, in short, emphasize the mobilization of voting blocs to make policy; deference to individual prerogatives is the hallmark of senatorial decision making. Sen. Pat Roberts, R-Kan., a former House member, noted that a House member must legislate by coalition, but a senator has to "work with each individual senator." [57]

Similarities

The House and Senate have many similarities. Both chambers are essentially equal in power and share similar responsibilities in lawmaking, oversight, and representation. Both have heavy workloads, decentralized committee and party structures, and somewhat parallel committee jurisdictions. The roles and responsibilities of one chamber interact with those of the other. House and Senate party leaders often cooperate to coordinate action on legislation. Cooperation generally is made easier when both houses are controlled by the same party.

In recent years, the two chambers have become more similar in some unexpected areas. Today's House members are more dependent on staff than were their colleagues of a few decades ago, in part because issues are more complex and because more informed constituents look to Capitol Hill for assistance and information. Senators are much more involved in constituency service than ever before. Like House members, they travel frequently to their states to meet in diverse forums with their constituents. In fact, small-state senators "have even more contact with their constituents than the House members in those states do." [58]

Many senators, too, emulate their House colleagues by preparing to run for reelection almost immediately after being sworn into office. This situation reflects contemporary electoral developments unforeseen by the framers—the escalating costs of election races, the professionalization of campaigns (the need to hire consultants, pollsters, and the like), and the emphasis on videopolitics—that make senatorial races more competitive than most House contests. Sen. Frank Lautenberg, D-N.J., decided not to seek a fourth term in 2000 in part because of the strain of raising campaign funds. "To run an effective campaign I would have to ask literally thousands of people for money. I would have to raise $125,000 a week, or $25,000 every working day," he said.[59]

House members enjoy more incumbent protection than senators because they attract fewer effective, well-known, or politically experienced challengers (in part by scaring off opponents with their money-raising ability), receive more favorable press and media attention, represent more homogeneous areas, and court their constituents assiduously. Thus, representatives are more likely than senators to survive periodic electoral tides that oust numerous incumbents. But not always.

The mid-term election of 1994 was nationalized (instead of being a series of local elections), largely by Newt Gingrich's Contract with America, which activated segments of the attentive public dismayed with the economy, the president, the government, and the direction of the country. The result was severe losses for the Democrats, among incumbents as well as candidates in formerly Democratic open districts. An electorate angry at the party that had controlled the House for forty years and the Senate for thirty-four of those years produced a nationwide surge of votes for Republicans with only Democrats targeted for defeat. Many incumbent Democrats, including Speaker Thomas S. Foley, Wash., were unable to insulate themselves from this electoral tide. "The combination of shrinking vote totals for the Democrats with an exploding GOP vote (nearly one-third larger than 1990) was unparalleled since the Democrats' own growth spurt during the Depression and early days of the New Deal."[60] The GOP triumph shifted party control from Democrats to Republicans in both chambers—something that had not occurred since the election of 1952—and transformed Congress's policy agenda. By contrast, the November 2000 elections for the House were another banner year for incumbents, most of whom ran in uncompetitive contests dominated by local issues.

A whole range of institutional, partisan, and policy connections makes bicameralism a force that shapes member behavior and policy outcomes. Along with traditional interchamber jealousies and rivalries, evident even when the same party controls both chambers, House members sometimes hold intense negative feelings against what they perceive as Senate obstructionism. As House members sometimes say: "The other party is only the opposition, the Senate is the enemy!" Part of the explanation is House frustration and exasperation with the ability of even one senator to block legislation through extended debate, to place a hold on legislation, or to force votes on unwanted nongermane amendments. Senators have their own complaints about House procedures and policy making. The within-chamber procedures of each body influence the policy-making activities of the other. The two are interlocked with national policies fundamentally shaped by the interchamber connection.[61]

PRESSURES ON MEMBERS

In making their legislative decisions, members of Congress are influenced by numerous pressures—the White House, the news media, constituents, lobbyists and interest groups, and their own party leadership and colleagues on Capitol Hill. These pressures are a central feature of the congressional environment; they affect the formal procedures and rules of Congress. All of these pressures are present in varying degrees at every step of the legislative process. The interests and influence of groups and individuals outside Congress have a considerable impact on the fate of legislation.

The President and the Executive Branch

The president and executive branch are among the most important sources of external pressure exerted on Congress. Many of the president's legislative functions and activities are not mentioned in the Constitution. The president is able to influence congressional action through the manipulation of patronage, the allocation of federal funds and projects that may be vital to the reelection of certain members of Congress, and the handling of constituents' cases in which senators and representatives are interested.

For example, President Clinton worked feverishly to win a come-from-behind victory for congressional approval of the North American Free Trade Agreement (NAFTA). Clinton bartered for votes on such a grand scale that Olympia J. Snowe, R-Maine, an anti-NAFTA House member (now a senator) said, "They have practically given away the family silver." Another NAFTA opponent, consumer activist and 2000 Green Party presidential nominee Ralph Nader, established a "NAFTA Pork Patrol" to calculate "the cost of the deals to U.S. taxpayers."[62]

As leader of the Democratic or Republican Party, the president is his party's chief election campaigner. The president also has ready access to the news media for promoting his administration's policies and commanding headlines. This bully-pulpit role, as Theodore Roosevelt described it, enables presidents to mold public opinion and build popular backing for White House proposals. With advances in communications technology and the amplifying power of the media, the bully-pulpit role is arguably the president's most significant resource. Teledemocracy (satellite press conferences, cable TV, interactive technology, talk show formats, 800 telephone numbers, televised town hall meetings, the Internet, and more) enables public officials to bypass traditional news outlets and communicate directly with the electorate. As a Clinton pollster put it, to enact the president's agenda "is not simply a matter of presenting a policy proposal, sending it to Congress and letting

Congress do its work. Now you need an effort to keep the American public with you." [63]

The president's role as legislative leader derives from the Constitution. While the Constitution vests "all legislative Powers" in Congress, it also directs the president to "give to the Congress Information of the State of the Union, and recommend to their Consideration such Measures as he shall judge necessary and expedient." This function has been broadened over the years. The president presents to Congress each year, in addition to his State of the Union message, two other general statements of presidential aims: an economic report, including proposals directed to the maintenance of maximum employment, and a budget message outlining his appropriations requests and policy proposals. During a typical session, the president transmits to Congress scores of other legislative proposals and ensures that his White House and executive agency liaison offices keep tabs on legislative activities and lobby for administration policies. The president's constitutional power to veto acts passed by Congress, which requires a two-thirds vote in each house to override, often promotes legislative-executive accommodations.

The Media

Of all the pressures on Congress, none is such a two-way proposition as the relationship between legislators and the media.

While senators and representatives must contend with the peculiarities of the news-gathering business, such as deadlines and limited space or time to describe events, and with constant media scrutiny of their actions, they also must rely on news organizations to inform the public of their legislative interests and accomplishments. At the same time, reporters must depend to some extent on inside information from members, a condition that makes many of them reluctant to displease their sources lest the pipeline of information be shut off.

But Congress basically is an open organization. Information flows freely on Capitol Hill and secrets rarely remain secret for long. An enterprising reporter usually can find out what is newsworthy. Moreover, Congress has taken a variety of actions during the past two decades to further open its proceedings to public observation. It has allowed nationwide, gavel-to-gavel coverage over C-SPAN of House and Senate floor proceedings. Instead of relying on press accounts of congressional actions, many citizens now have an opportunity to watch the floor sessions via the electronic gallery and make their own legislative judgments.

The Congress-media connection has undergone recent changes that significantly affect individual lawmakers, the two parties, and the legislative branch itself. From an individual perspective, lawmakers are exploiting a large array of technologies to communicate with their constituents, generate favorable publicity, and promote their policy proposals. As Rep. David E. Price, D-N.C., described this aspect of his legislative experience:

We send a weekly five-minute radio program, in which I discuss an issue before Congress, to fifteen stations in the district. We may also send radio feeds and, occasionally, satellite television feeds to local stations from Washington, offering commentary about matters of current interest, and we arrange interviews on these topics when I am home. In addition, we provide a steady stream of press releases to newspaper, radio, and television outlets; most of these either offer news about my own initiatives or give some interpretation of major items of congressional business, often relating to North Carolina. We furnish copies of my statements and speeches and let stations know when they can pick up my floor appearances on C-SPAN. I also do a monthly call-in show on cable television, which is then distributed and rebroadcast on most cable systems in the district.[64]

Lawmakers employ a variety of high-tech devices—faxes, computers, electronic mail, teleconferencing (meeting constituents in their states or districts without ever leaving Capitol Hill), and more—in addition to their traditional means (newsletters, franked mail, radio and television) of contacting constituents or promoting issues. As a sign of the times, Sen. Larry E. Craig, R-Idaho, and Rep. Charles W. Stenholm, D-Texas, fielded questions from users of the CompuServe computer network as part of their effort "to be armed with favorable comment [on their legislation] from beyond the Beltway sent to them over the information superhighway."[65]

From a party perspective, Democratic and Republican leaders devote considerable attention to ways of using the media to frame the terms of public debate on substantive and political issues so as to promote the outcome they want. Regularly, House GOP leaders employ sophisticated high-tech and communications strategies to highlight their goals and message to the American public. Opinion polling, televised ads, the mobilization and coordination of interest groups, town meetings, airport rallies, radio and television interviews, op-ed articles, and more are employed to muster public support. Daily and weekly "theme team" meetings also are held "to plan the message of the [day or] week for the speeches at the beginning and end of each legislative day" (see Figure 1-2).[66] Similarly, when Democrats lost control of the House, Minority Leader Richard A. Gephardt of Missouri created a new communications team to accomplish several goals: to plan and coordinate the daily themes the party wants to emphasize, "to stay ahead of the news curve, rather than continually playing catch-up to Republicans," and to assemble the best technology available to get their message out to the public.

The politics of message-sending are also employed by both parties in the Senate as a way to project a favorable public image and to activate and energize their core electoral supporters. For instance, the Senate Republican Conference provides a number of communication services to GOP lawmakers, such as graphic design, Internet support, radio, and television. Senate Democrats under the leadership of Tom Daschle, S.D., established a Technology and Communications Committee, headed by Sen. John D. Rockefeller IV, W.Va. "Rockefeller's job is to examine the growing selection of communica-

TALKING POINTS

January 26, 2000

GOP Agenda: Pay Off Debt, Provide Retirement Security, Tax Relief

• This Republican Congress has stopped the Raid on Social Security. New CBO estimates released Wednesday show that we did exactly what we said we would do: Preserved every dime of the Social Security Trust Fund to provide retirement security for every working American.

• We will now take the next step to preserve our nation's prosperity and improve the personal wealth of every American by paying off the public debt by 2013. This will result in lower interest rates on houses, cars, loans and credit cards for everyone, allowing families to keep more of their own money to make their dreams come true.

• More than 40 million working Americans are being punished by our tax code simply because they are married. This is unfair and unacceptable. We will pass legislation by mid-February that provides marriage penalty relief to working couples struggling to provide for their families.

• Republicans have worked hard these last five years to balance the budget and slow the growth of government. We have created an era of unprecedented revenue surpluses. We will not let those surpluses be frittered away by the Clinton/Gore Administration's long laundry list of spending proposals. Instead, we will use the surpluses to pay off the public debt, provide much-deserved tax relief to American families and ensure retirement security for every single working American.

FIGURE 1-2 A Daily Message for House Republicans

tions technology available in an effort to improve the Democrats' ability to get their message out to the general public—and to receive feedback." [67] Minority Leader Daschle emphasized the importance of keeping pace with the latest in telecommunications developments. "It's inevitable, or equally inevitable that we won't win." [68]

From an institutional perspective, scholarly research has shown "that press coverage of Congress has declined in volume and increased sharply in negativity, while moving from coverage of what the institution does as a legislature to increased emphasis on reports, rumors, and allegations of scandal, individual and institutional." [69] The implications that flow from this development are several, including heightened public disrespect for the legislative branch. Citizens seem so turned off by Congress that they are skeptical about whatever it does. In the judgment of Senator Lautenberg:

> Democracy simply cannot function in an atmosphere of distrust. After all, when citizens view everything the Congress does in the worst possible light, they are similarly skeptical about the legislation we propose. That makes it extremely difficult to build public support. And without public support, it becomes almost impossible to address major social problems in a meaningful way. [70]

Congress and the media are interdependent institutions. As broadcast journalist Walter Cronkite said: "Newspapers and broadcasting stations are to politicians as heavy guns to generals—weapons to be used or neutralized in the continuing battle for favorable public opinion." [71]

Constituent Pressures

Although many pressures compete for influence on Capitol Hill, the constituents, not the president or the party or the congressional leadership, still grant and take away a member's job. [72] A member who is popular back home can defy all three in a way unthinkable in a country such as Great Britain, where the leadership of the legislature, the executive, and the party are the same.

The extent to which a member of Congress seeks to follow the wishes of his constituents is determined to a considerable degree by the issue at stake. Few members would actively oppose issues deemed vital by most constituents. A farm-state legislator, for instance, is unlikely to push policies designed to lower the price of foods grown by those who elect him. Likewise, few members would follow locally popular policies that would endanger the nation. Between these extremes lies a wide spectrum of different blends of pressure from constituents and from conscience. And members must make most of their decisions in this gray area. (It is no coincidence that the committees on which senators and representatives seek membership often are determined by the type of constituency served.)

A fundamental change from a generation ago is the increased amount of time that lawmakers spend with the people they represent. Today, most members travel virtually weekly to their states or districts to meet with constituents. Technology, too, enables members to maintain a constant presence in their state or district even when they are not physically present. With the advent of the cyber-Congress, lawmakers exchange e-mails with constituents from anywhere in the world. Some lawmakers even use video e-mail. "The messages feature a 30-second to 40-second video next to a list of options that constituents can click, sending them to a lawmaker's Web site or allowing them to send a reply."[73]

Lawmakers not only are in close and constant touch with voter sentiments back home, but also they may be even too hypersensitive to constituency opinion. From a member's perspective, doing a good job on constituency service is understandably the road to electoral success. However, it tends to push lawmakers toward more of an ombudsmen role than a leadership role where citizens are educated about major problems and solutions and about the unpopular decisions and difficult choices that may be required to serve the national interest. As Walter Mondale (former senator, vice president, and ambassador to Japan) told the Joint Committee on the Organization of Congress in 1993:

> Good constituent service is, of course, necessary—and honorable—work for any member of Congress and his staff. Citizens must have somewhere to turn for help when they become victims of government bureaucracy. But constituent service can also be a bottomless pit. The danger is that a member of Congress will end up as little more than an ombudsman between citizens and government agencies. As important as this work is, it takes precious time away from Congress' central responsibilities as both a deliberative and a law-making body.[74]

Members, then, regularly confront the dilemma of how to maintain a rough balance between serving the often contradictory impulses of their constituents (provide more government services without raising taxes, for instance) and the larger national interest.

Washington Lobbyists

Lobbyists and lobby groups play an active part in the legislative process. The corps of Washington lobbyists has grown markedly in number and diversity since the 1930s, in line with the expansion of federal authority and its spread into new areas. The federal government has become a tremendous force in the life of the nation, and the number of fields in which changes in federal policy may spell success or failure for special interest groups has been greatly enlarged. Thus commercial and industrial interests; labor unions; ethnic, ideological, health, education, environmental, and racial groups; professional organizations; state and local governments; citizen groups; and representatives of foreign interests—all from time to time and some continuously—have sought by one method or another to exert pressure on Congress to attain their legislative goals.

Pressure groups, whether operating at the grass-roots level to influence public opinion or through direct contacts with members of Congress, perform some important and indispensable functions. These include helping to inform both Congress and the public about problems and issues, stimulating public debate, opening a path to Congress for the wronged and needy, and making known to Congress the practical aspects of proposed legislation: whom it would help, whom it would hurt, who is for it, and who is against it.

Lobbyists also work closely with sympathetic legislators and their staffs drafting legislation, developing strategy, or preparing speeches. Majority Whip Tom DeLay, R-Texas, for instance, is the key liaison for House Republicans with business and conservative groups and has organized them into a de facto extension of his own whip organization. Meeting in DeLay's Capitol office on Wednesday mornings, they are brought "together in clusters based on common interests, the lobbyists are deployed from the very beginning of a legislative push, and they are used both to identify members' positions and to pressure them to vote the leadership's way."[75] "Electronic advocacy" by way of the Internet and other means is also being used today to generate grass-roots campaigns for or against legislation.[76]

Interest groups may, in pursuing their own objectives, lead the legislature into decisions that benefit a particular pressure group but do not necessarily serve other segments of the public. A group's ability to influence legislation is based on a variety of factors: the quality of its arguments; the size, cohesion, and intensity of the organization's membership; the group's ability to augment its political power by forming ad hoc coalitions with other associations; its financial and staff resources; and the shrewdness of its leadership.

These groups understand the potency of grass-roots lobbying, mobilizing constituents to pressure lawmakers by phone calls, faxes and telegrams, letters, or personal visits. Efforts also are made to build global grass-roots campaigns via the Internet on behalf, for instance, of the inclusion of labor and environmental standards in international trade agreements. Even if grass-roots activity is manufactured, members realize they cannot simply ignore these expressions of voter opinion. Hence, a crucial phase in determining whether a bill is passed, defeated, or amended on Capitol Hill is the struggle among contending interests in members' states or districts.

The proliferation of interest groups and their sophistication in using campaign funds, expert information, and technology to affect legislative decisions has, on the one hand, added to the demands on lawmakers and created difficulties in organizing winning coalitions. The very proliferation of these groups, on the other hand, often enables lawmakers to play one against another. "The power of interest groups is not, of course, exercised without opposition," wrote several scholars. "The typical issue has some interest groups on one side and some on the other, or many interest groups on many sides, not necessarily with an equal balance of power."[77] Although lawmakers must contend with more interest groups, no single one is likely to exercise dominant influence over policy formation as sometimes occurred in the past. For example, where tobacco interests once held sway on Capitol Hill, their efforts at avoiding smoking bans, regulation, and higher cigarette taxes are being undermined by legal threats, antismoking campaigns, and a variety of antismoking interests that have stressed the health perils of both directly inhaled smoke and so-called secondhand smoke.

NOTES

1. Eric Pianin and Juliet Eilperin, "House GOP to Split Bill on Violence," *Washington Post,* June 15, 1999, A1.
2. Margaret Kriz, "Still Charging," *National Journal,* December 6, 1997, 2462.
3. Paul L. Ford, ed., *The Federalist: A Commentary on the Constitution of the United States by Alexander Hamilton, James Madison and John Jay* (New York: Henry Holt, 1898), 319 (Federalist No. 47). James Madison wrote the commentary "Separation of the Departments of Power."
4. Thomas Jefferson, "Notes on Virginia," in *Free Government in the Making,* ed. Alpheus Thomas Mason (New York: Oxford University Press, 1965), 164.
5. *Constitution, Jefferson's Manual, and Rules of the House of Representatives,* 102d Cong., 2d sess., H Doc 102-405, 121–122.
6. *Congressional Record,* April 8, 1981, S3615.
7. Statement of Rep. Earl Pomeroy, D-N.D., on the application of laws to Congress, Hearing before the House Rules Subcommittee on Rules, March 24, 1994, 1.
8. *Congressional Record,* September 16, 1982, H7097.
9. Adam Clymer, "In House and Senate, 2 Kinds of G.O.P.," *New York Times,* November 15, 1994, B8.
10. Clarence Cannon, *Cannon's Procedure in the House of Representatives,* 86th Cong., 1st sess., H Doc 86-122, iii.
11. John M. Barry, "The Man of the House," *New York Times Magazine,* November 23, 1986, 109.
12. "Lawmakers Were Warned of Abuses at H.U.D.," *New York Times,* July 3, 1989, 9.
13. Testimony before the GOP Task Force on Congressional Reform, House Republican Research Committee, December 16, 1987, 3.
14. *National Review,* February 27, 1987, 24.
15. *Los Angeles Times,* February 7, 1977, sec. 1, 5.
16. *Congressional Record,* March 9, 1976, 5909.
17. *CQ Daily Monitor,* April 17, 1995, 1.
18. *Washington Post,* March 7, 1995, A1, A6.
19. Deborah Kalb, "Government by Task Force: The Gingrich Model," *The Hill,* February 22, 1995, 3.
20. Eric Pianin and John Yang, "House Passes Medicare Reform Bill," *Washington Post,* October 20, 1995, A4.
21. *CQ Daily Monitor,* January 27, 2000, 5. See Juliet Eilperin, "House GOP to Name Task Force on Drug Coverage for Elderly," *Washington Post,* January 27, 2000, A4.
22. *Congressional Record,* July 12, 1999, S8224–S8225.
23. Edwin Chen, "'$50-Billion Tobacco Tax Break Rejected by Senate, 95-3,'" *Los Angeles Times,* September 11, 1997, B5; the budget law was the 1985 emergency deficit reduction act sponsored by Sens. Phil Gramm, R-Texas, Warren B. Rudman, R-N.H., and Ernest F. Hollings, D-S.C., and adopted as a Senate amendment to a House-passed bill raising the national debt ceiling.
24. Quoted in *Deschler-Brown Precedents of the United States House of Representatives,* vol. 1, 94th Cong., 2d sess., H Doc 94-661, iv.
25. *Wall Street Journal,* June 29, 1987, 54.

26. Richard F. Fenno Jr., "Adjusting to the Senate," in *Congress and Policy Change,* ed. Gerald C. Wright Jr., Leroy N. Rieselbach, and Lawrence C. Dodd (New York: Agathon Press, 1986), 134–136. See also Edward V. Schneier, "Norms and Folkways in Congress: How Much Has Already Changed?" *Congress & the Presidency* (Autumn 1988): 117–138; David W. Rohde, "Studying Congressional Norms: Concepts and Evidence," *Congress & the Presidency* (Autumn 1988): 139–145; and Chester W. Rogers, "New Member Socialization in the House of Representatives," *Congress & the Presidency* (Spring 1992): 47–63.

27. During the 96th Congress (1979–1981), a House reorganization panel found that eighty-three committees and subcommittees exercised some jurisdiction over energy issues in the House alone. See *Final Report of the Select Committee on Committees, U.S. House of Representatives,* 96th Cong., 2d sess., H Rept 96-866, 334–355.

28. Roger H. Davidson and Walter J. Oleszek, *Congress against Itself* (Bloomington: Indiana University Press, 1977); Roger H. Davidson, "Breaking Up Those 'Cozy Triangles': An Impossible Dream?" in *Legislative Reform and Public Policy,* ed. Susan Welch and John G. Peters (New York: Praeger, 1977), 30–53; Hugh Heclo, "Issue Networks and the Executive Establishment," in *The New American Political System,* ed. Anthony King (Washington, D.C.: American Enterprise Institute for Public Policy Research, 1978), 87–124; and Charles O. Jones, *The United States Congress: People, Place, and Policy* (Homewood, Ill.: Dorsey Press, 1982), 360. "Sloppy large hexagons," a phrase coined by Jones, refers to the large number of participants who shape policyissues.

29. Jeff Rainmundo, "Cool Whip," *California Magazine,* April 1987, 64.

30. Richard E. Cohen, "Sen. Mitchell, A Lame Duck, Sizes Up '94," *National Journal,* March 12, 1994, 598.

31. David S. Cloud, "Shakeup Time," *Congressional Quarterly Weekly Report,* March 25, 1995, 10.

32. *The Bill Status System for the United States House of Representatives,* Committee on House Administration, July 1, 1975, 19.

33. *New York Times,* October 31, 1984, B6.

34. Donald Bruce Johnson and Jack L. Walker, "President John Kennedy Discusses the Presidency," in *The Dynamics of the American Presidency* (New York: Wiley, 1964), 144.

35. *Congressional Record,* March 17, 1994, H1483.

36. *Congressional Record,* May 20, 1987, S6798.

37. Doris Kearns, *Lyndon Johnson and the American Dream* (New York: Harper & Row, 1976), 11.

38. *Los Angeles Times,* October 6, 1982, sec. 1, 1.

39. Woodrow Wilson, *Constitutional Government in the United States* (New York: Columbia University Press, 1911), 87.

40. *Congressional Record,* February 7, 1967, 2838.

41. Asher C. Hinds, *Hinds' Precedents of the House of Representatives* ,vol. 1, v.

42. Janet Hook, "Speaker Jim Wright Takes Charge in the House," *Congressional Quarterly Weekly Report,* July 11, 1987, 1486.

43. *New York Times,* November 22, 1985, B8.

44. *Congressional Record,* September 10, 1987, S11944.
45. Nelson W. Polsby, "Policy Analysis and Congress," *Public Policy* (Fall 1969): 67.
46. Michael Green, "Obstacles to Reform: Nobody Covers the House," *Washington Monthly,* June 1970, 62–70.
47. See Robert L. Peabody, Norman J. Ornstein, and David W. Rohde, "The United States Senate as a Presidential Incubator: Many Are Called But Few Are Chosen," *Political Science Quarterly* (Summer 1976): 236–258.
48. See Douglas Harris, "The Rise of the Public Speakership," *Political Science Quarterly* (Summer 1998): 193–212.
49. August Gribbin, "Education, Health Top Issues in Poll," *Wall Street Journal,* February 6, 2000, C5.
50. *National Journal,* April 15, 1995, 938. See also, for instance, *Congressional Record,* April 6, 1995, S5277.
51. Charles Clapp, *The Congressman* (Garden City, N.Y.: Doubleday, 1963), 39.
52. Richard F. Fenno Jr., *Congressmen in Committees* (Boston: Little, Brown, 1973), 172.
53. Robert C. Byrd, "Operations of Congress," Hearing before the Joint Committee on the Organization of Congress, February 2, 1993, 4.
54. Norman J. Ornstein, "Legislative Behavior and Legislative Structure: A Comparative Look at House and Senate Resource Utilization," in *Legislative Staffing,* ed. James J. Heaphey and Alan B. Balutis (New York: John Wiley & Sons, 1975), 175.
55. *Congressional Record,* January 4, 1995, H34.
56. Ed Henry, "The Senate's Freshman Firestorm: Torricelli 'Liberated' by His Move to Upper Chamber," *Roll Call,* June 2, 1997, 24.
57. Lindsay Sobel, "From House Chairman to Senate Freshman, Pat Roberts Rides in Smaller Farm Pasture," *The Hill,* June 11, 1997, 20.
58. Francis Lee and Bruce Oppenheimer, *Sizing Up the Senate* (Chicago, Ill.: University of Chicago Press, 1999), 56.
59. *National Journal's CongressDaily/PM,* February 17, 1999, 1.
60. Rhodes Cook, "Rare Combination of Forces May Make History of '94," *Congressional Quarterly Weekly Report,* April 15, 1995, 1076.
61. See, for example, Lawrence Longley and Walter J. Oleszek, *Bicameral Politics: Conference Committees in Congress* (New Haven, Conn.: Yale University Press, 1989).
62. Both quotations are from Jackie Calmes, "How a Sense of Clinton's Commitment and a Series of Deals Clinched the Vote," *Wall Street Journal,* November 19, 1993, A7.
63. Thomas B. Rosenstiel, "Presidents' Pollsters: Who Follows Whom?" *Los Angeles Times,* December 28, 1993, A5.
64. David E. Price, *The Congressional Experience* (San Francisco, Calif.: Westview Press, 1992), 115–116.
65. Andrew Mollison, "Lawmakers for Balanced Budget Take Case to Computer Network," *Washington Times,* February 15, 1994, A8.
66. Robin Toner, "G.O.P. Mobilizes for Contract Deadline," *New York Times,* March 30, 1995, A21.
67. *The Hill,* March 8, 1995, 15.
68. *Washington Post,* April 24, 1995, A4.

69. Norman J. Ornstein, "If Congress Played a Better Host to Guests, Maybe It Would Improve a Crummy Image," *Roll Call,* March 31, 1994, 15.

70. *Congressional Record,* March 25, 1994, S4025.

71. Quoted in Mammes F. Fixx, ed., *The Mass Media and Politics* (New York: Arno Press, 1972), ix.

72. For a valuable discussion of constituent pressures, see David Mayhew, *The Electoral Connection* (New Haven, Conn.: Yale University Press, 1974).

73. Glenn Simpson, "Now Showing on an E-Mail Screen Near You: Your Congressman, Produced by Joe Taxpayer," *Wall Street Journal,* January 7, 2000, A16.

74. Testimony of Walter F. Mondale, Hearing before the Joint Commmittee on the Organization of Congress, July 1, 1993, 33.

75. Gebe Martinez with Jackie Koszczuk, "Tom DeLay: 'The Hammer' That Drives the House GOP," *Congressional Quarterly Weekly Report,* June 5, 1999, 1323.

76. Alice Love, "The Age of CyberLobbying," *Roll Call,* March 13, 1995, 3.

77. John P. Heinz, Edward O. Laumann, Robert L. Nelson, and Robert H. Salisbury, *The Hollow Core: Private Interests in National Policy Making* (Cambridge, Mass.: Harvard University Press, 1993), 391. See also Allan J. Cigler and Burdett A. Loomis, *Interest Group Politics,* 5th ed. (Washington, D.C.: CQ Press, 1998).

CHAPTER 2

The Congressional Budget Process

A REMARKABLE change transformed the character of congressional budgeting at the end of the twentieth century. In 1998, for the first time since 1969, the federal government ran a surplus. Deficit financing had defined the federal budget for almost thirty years. Annual deficits (the shortfall between revenues and expenditures) led to a skyrocketing national debt (the annual deficit accumulated over time). The high deficits resulted from such factors as the growth of entitlements and the policy decisions of the Reagan White House and Congress, with each protecting or expanding its spending priorities despite revenue shortfalls. The debt went from about $900 billion in 1979 to about $5.5 trillion twenty years later.

Several important developments contributed to the fiscal turnaround. First, the end of the cold war in 1989 led to significant reductions in defense expenditures. Second, the Federal Reserve devised an effective monetary policy that promoted economic expansion. Third, the American economy experienced a record-setting nine years (and counting) of expansion, the longest in U.S. history. A booming stock market flooded the federal Treasury with tax and capital gains dollars. Fourth, the fiscal decisions of Congress and the White House during the 1990s, such as passage of the Budget and Enforcement Act of 1990, encouraged fiscal restraint and led to budgetary savings. Finally, luck and timing contributed to the optimistic fiscal outlook. "Just about everything broke right that could have broken right," said Robert D. Reischauer, a former director of the Congressional Budget Office.[1]

No one can predict with certainty that the huge projected budgetary surpluses—estimated by the Clinton administration in June 2000 to total $4.2 trillion ($2.3 trillion in Social Security surpluses and $1.9 trillion for general governmental activities) by 2010—will materialize. An economic recession, international crises, domestic emergencies, or other unexpected contingencies could erode the projected surpluses. Regardless, the question before today's Congress is no longer how to reduce the deficit but what should be done with the surplus. Lawmakers from each chamber and party differ, often sharply, as to what is the best use of the surplus revenues. "We haven't quite figured out the politics of surplus," exclaimed Sen. Joseph I. Lieberman, D-Conn.[2]

OVERVIEW

The framers of the Constitution deliberately lodged the power of the purse in Congress because it is the branch of government closest to the people. "This power of the purse," wrote James Madison in *The Federalist* (No. 58), "may, in fact, be regarded as the most complete and effectual weapon with which any constitution can arm the immediate representatives of the people, for obtaining a redress of every grievance, and for carrying into effect every just and salutary measure." Under Article I of the Constitution, only Congress is empowered to collect taxes, borrow money, and authorize expenditures. The executive branch can spend money only for the purposes and in the amounts specified by Congress. As Section 9 of Article I proclaims: "No Money shall be drawn from the Treasury, but in Consequence of Appropriations made by Law." The Sixteenth Amendment to the Constitution also permits Congress "to lay and collect" income taxes.

The Constitution, however, did not prescribe a budget system for the legislative branch. Instead, it evolved over time to reflect new demands and pressures, such as the huge increase in the size and cost of government from the Great Depression through the Vietnam War, congressional traditions and practices, and statutory developments. In the U.S. system of separate institutions sharing power, the president exercises significant fiscal authority through his constitutional veto power and his wide-ranging ability to influence the lawmaking process. Congress, too, recognizes the value of the president's role in budgeting and delegated him statutory responsibility for preparing an annual national budget in the Budget and Accounting Act of 1921. With this responsibility, the president has been able to spotlight his priorities, frame the budgetary debate, and require Congress to respond to the chief executive's budgetary proposals.

If Madison and the other constitutional framers returned today, they might wonder about the overall effectiveness of the congressional purse strings when about 70 percent of federal expenditures are relatively uncontrollable under existing law. That is, the government is required to spend money automatically for certain purposes because of laws previously enacted by Congress. Uncontrollables include interest on the public debt ($208 billion in fiscal 2001), entitlements (laws that require mandatory payments to all eligible individuals, such as Social Security, Medicare, and government pension programs), and contract obligations that must be paid when due (such as the Defense Department's procurement arrangements with various businesses).

One consequence of uncontrollables is clear. If the 107th Congress adjourns on the day it convenes in January 2001, without passing any laws, federal government spending for that year still would be more than $1 trillion. Further, spending each year thereafter would continue—and increase—because many federal programs are indexed to the cost of living. Congress can convert uncontrollables into controllables by changing the basic law that establishes governmental obligations and that authorizes automatic funding without regular legislative review. (There are different degrees of controllability, however. Interest on the national debt and the interest rates to finance that debt are largely beyond Congress's control.) But members who want to subject uncontrollables to annual budgetary scrutiny can incur serious political risks.

Congress chooses to place programs in the uncontrollable category for a variety of reasons. Stability, certainty, and preferred status are among the values that accrue to such programs. Retired persons, for instance, would have "to live under a great deal of financial uncertainty" if Congress subjected Social Security to annual review.[3] The federal budget itself reflects the president's and Congress's choices among competing national priorities and identifies where the nation has been, where it is now, and where the administration plans to make future fiscal as well as policy commitments. Thus, the nation's budget is both an economic and a political document. As the ranking Democrat on the Senate Budget Committee stated: "By their nature, debates on the budget tend to be more partisan than other debates. After all, setting a broad plan for allocating resources necessarily depends on judgments based on established principles we bring with us from our views and priorities influenced by our respective partisan affiliations."[4]

In broad terms, federal budgeting is composed of four main phases:

1. Preparation and submission of the budget by the president to Congress.
2. Congressional review of the president's budget and action on required budgetary matters.
3. Execution of budget-related laws by federal departments and agencies.
4. Audits of agency spending.

The first and third steps are controlled primarily by the executive branch; the fourth is conducted largely by the General Accounting Office, a legislative support agency of Congress. The focus of this chapter is on the second stage, the basic elements and features of Congress's budgetary process.

AUTHORIZATION-APPROPRIATIONS PROCESS

Fundamental to the congressional budget process is the distinction between authorizations and appropriations. This two-step, sequential process was created by House and Senate rules. Authorizations establish programs or policies; appropriations fund authorized programs and policies. Both authorizations and appropriations bills must be approved by both houses and presented to the president for his signature or veto.

Congress first passes an authorization bill that establishes or continues—a reauthorization—an agency or program and provides it with the legal authority to operate. Authorizations may be for one or more years, and such legislation typically recommends funding levels for programs and agencies. The bills also include statutory language (such as "hereby authorized to be appropriated") that permits the enactment of appropriations. The basic purposes of an authorization are highlighted in Box 2-1. Notice that the sea grant program is authorized for five years (with recommended funding levels for each year), after which Congress decides whether to reauthorize the program. Today,

BOX 2-1   Basic Purposes of Authorizations Acts

Below are excerpts from the National Sea Grant College Program Reauthorization Act of 1998 (PL 105-16) that illustrate some of the basic purposes of authorizations: to establish federal agencies or programs and to set forth their duties and functions (Section 5) and to provide an authorization of appropriations (Section 9). Because this reauthorization specifically covers fiscal years 1999 to 2003, Congress will have to pass a new authorization for fiscal year 2004 and beyond so that the consideration of appropriations for those years will be in order. The funds mentioned in the law can be spent only to the extent provided in appropriations.

An Act
To reauthorize the Sea Grant Program
* * * * * *

Sec. 5. National Sea Grant College Program.

Section 204 (33 U.S.C. 1123) is amended to read as follows:
Sec. 204. National Sea Grant College Program.
(a) Program Maintenance.—The Secretary shall maintain within the Administration a program to be known as the national sea grant college program. The national sea grant college program shall be administered by a national sea grant office within the Administration.
(c) Responsibilities of the Secretary.—
(1) The Secretary, in consultation with the panel, sea grant colleges, and sea grant institutes, shall develop a long-range strategic plan which establishes priorities for the national sea grant college program and which provides an appropriately balanced response to local, regional, and national needs. . . .
(d) Director of the National Sea Grant College Program.—
(1) The Secretary shall appoint, as the Director of the National Sea Grant College Program, a qualified individual. . . . The Director shall be appointed and compensated . . . at a rate payable under section 5376 of title 5, United States Code. . . .

Sec. 9. Authorization of Appropriations.

(a) Grants, Contracts, and Fellowships.—Section 212(a) (33 U.S.C. 1131(a)) is amended to read as follows:
(a) Authorization.—
(1) In General.—There is authorized to be appropriated to carry out this Act—
　　(A) $56,000,000 for fiscal year 1999;
　　(B) $57,000,000 for fiscal year 2000;
　　(C) $58,000,000 for fiscal year 2001;
　　(D) $59,000,000 for fiscal year 2002; and
　　(E) $60,000,000 for fiscal year 2003.

SOURCE: Adapted from Robert Keith and Allen Schick, *Manual on the Federal Budget Process*, CRS Report 98-720, August 28, 1998, 100.

most authorizations are multiyear with a few exceptions, such as defense, that are annual.

Until the 1950s, most federal programs were permanently authorized. Permanent authorizations remain in effect until changed by Congress and provide continuing statutory authority for ongoing federal programs and agencies. The authorizing committees won enactment of laws that converted many permanent authorizations into temporary authorizations. Two major factors precipitated this change. First, the authorizing committees wanted greater control and oversight of executive and presidential activities, especially given interbranch tensions that stemmed from the Vietnam War and Watergate. Second, short-term authorizations put pressure on the appropriating committees to fund programs at levels recommended by the authorizing panels.

Today, much of the federal government is funded through the annual enactment of thirteen general appropriations bills. No constitutional requirement exists for annual appropriations, but the practice since the First Congress has been to appropriate for a single year. Another long-standing precedent is that the House originates appropriations bills based on its constitutional authority to initiate revenue-raising measures.

Appropriations bills are of three main types: (1) annual—also called regular or general; (2) supplemental—to address unexpected contingencies, such as emergency funding for natural disasters; and (3) continuing—often called continuing resolutions or CRs—to provide stop-gap or full-year funding for agencies that did not receive an annual appropriation by the start of the fiscal year, which runs from October 1 to September 30. Congress enacts about fifteen or so appropriations bills every fiscal year: the thirteen regular bills; one or more supplementals; and one or more continuing appropriations. The structure of a regular appropriations act is depicted in Box 2-2.

Although most activities that individuals usually associate with the federal government—the FBI, the Coast Guard, the national park system, defense, space exploration, housing, foreign aid, research and development, and so on—are funded through the annual enactment of the thirteen general appropriations bills, only roughly one-half of federal spending each year is subject to the authorization-appropriations process. The other half gets its legal basis from laws that provide spending either automatically, such as entitlement programs (Social Security and Medicare are the largest), which make monies continuously available to eligible beneficiaries under the terms of previously enacted statutes, or annually through appropriated entitlements, such as food stamps and unemployment compensation, which are funded through the regular appropriations process. However, any shortfall in appropriated entitlement programs must be covered by supplemental appropriations.

The fiscal reality is that the annual appropriations process controls only about 30 percent of all federal spending. This controllable side of congressional budgeting is referred to as discretionary spending, and it funds most

Box 2-2 Structure of a Regular Appropriations Act

An appropriations act has three main components: (1) the enacting clause, which specifies the fiscal year for which the appropriations are made, (2) appropriations to specified accounts, and (3) general provisions. Below are excerpts from the Department of Transportation Appropriations Act for Fiscal Year 1998 (PL 105-66). Each unnumbered paragraph is a separate appropriation account, and the provisions in the paragraph pertain only to the account. The general provisions, which may limit the use of funds or contain new legislation, are numbered sections. These provisions apply to all accounts in the title or in the entire act, as specified.

An Act

Making appropriations for the Department of Transportation and related agencies for the fiscal year ending September 30, 1998, and for other purposes.

Enacting Clause

Be it enacted by the Senate and House of Representatives of the United States of America in Congress assembled, That the following sums are appropriated, out of any money in the Treasury not otherwise appropriated, for the Department of Transportation and related agencies for the fiscal year ending September 30, 1998, and for other purposes, namely:

Appropriations to Specified Accounts

DEPARTMENT OF TRANSPORTATION
OFFICE OF THE SECRETARY
Salaries and Expenses

For necessary expenses of the Office of the Secretary, $61,000,000, of which not to exceed $40,000 shall be available as the Secretary may determine for allocation within the Department for official reception and representation expenses: *Provided,* That notwithstanding any other provision of law, there may be credited to this appropriation up to $1,000,000 in funds received in user fees: *Provided further,* That none of the funds appropriated in the Act or otherwise made available may be used to maintain custody of airline tariffs that are already available for public and departmental access at no cost; to secure them against detection, alteration, or tampering; and open to inspection by the Department.

General Provision

Sec. 307. None of the funds appropriated in this Act shall remain available for obligation beyond the current fiscal year, nor may any be transferred to other appropriations, unless expressly so provided herein.

SOURCE: Adapted from Robert Keith and Allen Schick, *Manual on the Federal Budget Process,* CRS Report 98-720, August 28, 1998, 130.

domestic and defense programs. The other 70 percent or so of federal spending consists of automatic payments for either interest on the national debt or entitlements. "Entitlement spending [in 2000] represents 55 percent of all Federal spending," remarked Senate Budget Committee Chairman Pete V. Domenici, R-N.M. "If we add paying the interest on the national debt as another entitlement . . . then 77 percent of what we spend every year" is mandatory (also called direct) spending.[5]

Congressional analysts distinguish between *discretionary spending,* which is controlled through the appropriations process, and *direct spending,* which is primarily used to fund entitlement programs that are provided for in authorization laws. Direct spending is under the jurisdiction of the authorizing, not the appropriating, committees. Discretionary spending has borne the brunt of reductions over the years, because politicians have been keen on reducing the size of government. However, the direct spending side of the budget has escalated, because Congress cannot control mandatory expenditure levels for the entitlement programs established by permanent law. Congress can modify those statutes, but doing so is an electorally risky venture. The elderly, who are well organized and who turn out to vote, are not reluctant to tell lawmakers: "Keep your hands off my Social Security!" (In 1996 Congress converted welfare—Aid to Families with Dependent Children—from an entitlement program to a fixed block grant program.)

Another budgetary distinction to bear in mind is that between *budget authority* and *budget outlays.* Appropriations approved by Congress provide budget authority, which allows government agencies to make financial commitments, up to a specified amount, that eventually result in budget outlays—that is, the spending of dollars. As one budget analyst explains it:

> Congress does not directly control the level of federal spending that will occur in a particular year. Rather, it grants the executive branch authority (referred to as *budget authority*) to enter into *obligations,* which are legally binding agreements with suppliers of goods or services or with a beneficiary. When those obligations come due, the Treasury Department issues a payment. The amount of payments, called *outlays,* over an accounting period called the fiscal year (running from October 1 to September 30) equals federal expenditures for that fiscal year. Federal spending (outlays) in any given year, therefore, results from the spending authority (budget authority) granted by Congress in the current and in prior fiscal years.[6]

To state it differently, budget authority occurs when you put money in your checking account; budget outlays take place when you write a check.

The conversion of budget authority to budget outlays depends on a variety of factors, including the character of the program or activity. Budget authority granted annually to pay federal salaries is typically converted to budget outlays that same year. Budget authority to build a highway is converted to budget outlays at a variable rate over several years as highway planning costs give way to construction costs. Lawmakers require both figures so they can assess the projected total cost of a multiyear program or project compared with what will be spent on it annually. Legislators are mindful of budget authority figures for these—instead of the outlay numbers—are the better predictors of an agency's growth or decline. Outlays, however, are reflected in each year's national deficit or surplus levels.

Authorizing and Appropriating Committees

Whether agencies receive all the budget authority they request depends in part on the recommendations of the authorizing and appropriating committees. Each chamber has authorizing committees (Agriculture, Banking, Commerce, Small Business, and many others) with responsibilities that differ from those of the two appropriating committees—the House and Senate Appropriations committees. The authorizing committees are the policy-making centers on Capitol Hill. As the substantive legislative panels, they propose solutions to public problems and advocate what they believe to be the necessary level of appropriations for new and existing federal programs.

Each house's Appropriations Committee and its thirteen subcommittees (covering agriculture, defense, transportation, and so on) recommend how much federal agencies and programs will receive in relation to available fiscal resources and economic conditions. The twenty-six subcommittee chairs are collectively known in their respective chambers as the "College of Cardinals" because of their large influence over spending issues. These chairmen often include earmarks in their bills or committee reports—recommendations that agencies should dedicate funds for a particular purpose.

For each program and agency subject to the annual appropriations process, the Appropriations committees have three main options: (1) provide all the funds recommended in the previously approved authorization bill, (2) propose reductions in the amounts authorized, or (3) refuse to provide any funds.[7] A newspaper headline declaring that Congress has just authorized, for example, a new $3 billion antidrug program means that the program officially exists on paper. However, it still lacks money to operate until it receives an appropriation, and even then the program might be appropriated only a portion of the amount authorized.

Congress requires authorizations to precede appropriations to ensure that substantive and financial issues are subject to separate and independent analysis. This procedure also permits almost every member and committee to participate in Congress's constitutional power of the purse. Numerous exceptions are made to this two-step model, despite House and Senate rules that encourage separation of the authorization-appropriations stages.

Constitutional Underpinning

The authorization-appropriation dichotomy is not required by the Constitution. It is a process that has been institutionalized by the rules of the House and Senate and in some cases by statute. Of the two steps, the appropriations stage is on firmer legal ground because it is rooted in the Constitution.

An appropriations measure, which provides departments and agencies with authority to commit funds, may be approved even if the authorization bill has not been enacted. As long as "appropriations are enacted," wrote a budget scholar, "funds may be obligated by agencies, regardless of whether. . . . authorizations have been enacted."[8] Or, as one House Appropriations subcommittee chairman put it, "It's not the end of the world if we postpone the Clean Air Act or a tax measure. But the entire government will shut down if . . . appropriations" are not enacted annually.[9]

Informally, Congress has employed this division of labor since the beginning of the Republic, as did the British Parliament in 1789 as well as the colonial legislatures. As Sen. William Plumer of New Hampshire noted in 1806: "Tis a good provision in the constitution of Maryland that prohibits their Legislature from adding any thing to an appropriation law."[10] Generally called supply bills in the early Congresses, appropriations measures had narrow purposes: to provide specific sums of money for fixed periods and stated objectives. Such bills were not to contain matters of policy.

There were exceptions to this informal rule even during the early days, but the practice of adding riders, or extraneous policy provisos, to appropriations bills mushroomed in the 1830s. This practice often provoked sharp controversy in Congress and delayed the enactment of supply bills. "By 1835," wrote a parliamentary expert, the "delays caused by injecting legislation [policy] into these [appropriations] bills had become serious, and [then representative] John Quincy Adams . . . suggested that they be stripped of everything save appropriations."[11] Two years later the House adopted a rule requiring authorization bills to precede appropriations. The Senate later followed suit.

Separate Policy and Fiscal Decisions

Several major implications flow from Congress's efforts to separate policy from fiscal decision making—matters that usually are inextricably intertwined with each other. Among the major implications are flexibility, bicameral differences, and committee rivalries.

Flexibility. The authorization-appropriations rules, like almost all congressional rules, are not self-enforcing. Either chamber can choose to waive, ignore, or circumvent them or establish precedents and practices that obviate distinctions between the two. As one scholar has written:

> The real world of the legislative process differs considerably from the idealized model of the two-step authorization-appropriation procedure. Authorization bills contain appropriations, appropriation bills contain authorizations, and the order of their enactment is sometimes reversed. The Appropriations Committees, acting through various kinds of limitations, riders, and nonstatutory controls, are able to establish policy and act in a substantive manner. Authorization Committees have considerable power to force the hand of the Appropriations Committees and, in some cases, even to appropriate.[12]

Flexibility in the authorization-appropriations procedure allows it to accommodate stresses and strains. A failure to enact authorization bills does not bring the appropriations process to a halt. For example, 118 authorization laws that expired in fiscal year 1999 nevertheless received more than $102 billion in appropriations.[13] The must-pass annual appropriations bills often become the vehicle for extending or revamping existing laws that did not make it through the authorization process. As Rep. David R. Obey, D-Wis., the ranking member on the Appropriations Committee, stated:

> It seems to me what has happened in our system is that the authorization process has been jammed up many times, sometimes because of committee incompetence, sometimes because the issues are just . . . tough and we have issues that aren't resolvable over the short haul, and sometimes because the White House has chosen to simply stiff the authorizing committee because they think they can get a better deal from us on appropriations.14

It is not uncommon for authorizers to ask appropriators to include policy proposals or legislation in annual appropriations bill.

Bicameral Differences. Because the House and Senate are dissimilar, they have different rules governing the authorization-appropriations process. These differences reflect each chamber's fundamental nature: the smaller Senate permits greater procedural flexibility than the larger House (see Table 2-1).

The rules affect each chamber's legislative behavior and policy deliberations. The Senate, for example, sometimes gets off to a slower start on appropriations measures because, by tradition, it waits for the House to originate those bills. Moreover, the multistage process creates numerous opportunities to shape issues. Policy debates may be resurrected again and again in different contexts in either chamber.

An issue of some concern to the House involves the committee assignment practices of the Senate. In the House, for both parties, service on the Appropriations Committee is, with few exceptions, an exclusive assignment. Senators, by contrast, may serve simultaneously on both authorizing and appropriating committees. In some instances, the same senator chaired both the authorizing committee (or relevant subcommittee) and the comparable appropriations subcommittee. Fundamental bicameral imbalances are created, said a House Science chairman, when senators "are permitted to serve on both Committees. Inevitably, Members will prefer to legislate in appropriations bills (or the accompanying reports), which by their nature and by the rules of both Houses, are more protected from debate, amendment, and perfection than are corresponding authorization bills."[15] Or as another House chairman stated:

> What we have seen happening is that, because the [Senate] appropriators find that it is easy to just throw everything into the appropriation bill, very often the authorizing bills simply don't get passed, and therefore authorization bills that pass the House are left sitting in the Senate. And we will sometimes go one, two,

TABLE 2-1 Authorization-Appropriations Rules Compared

House	Senate
No unauthorized appropriations are permitted except for public works in progress. The Appropriations Committee generally cannot report a general appropriations bill unless there is an authorization law.	Unauthorized appropriations are not permitted. Exceptions are if the Senate has passed an authorization during that session; if an authorization is reported by any Senate standing committee, including Appropriations; or if an authorization is requested in the president's annual budget.
No legislation (policy) is permitted in an appropriations bill.	No legislation is permitted in an appropriations bill unless it is germane to the House-passed bill.
No appropriation is permitted in an authorization bill. Floor amendments that propose appropriations are not in order in authorization bills.	There is no equivalent rule. By custom, the House initiates appropriations bills and objects to Senate efforts aimed at circumventing this arrangement.

three, four years before we get an authorization bill passed in a very important policy area.[16]

Committee Rivalries

Another consequence of the two-step system is that it breeds continuing conflict between the authorizing and appropriating committees. The authorizing committees generally support high levels of spending for the programs they recommend and seek ways to bypass Appropriations Committee domination. The appropriating panels, meanwhile, often view themselves as guardians of the purse. It is their job, they believe, to say no to many funding requests. Occasions arise, however, when maximum funding is the preferred objective of the Appropriations committees.

The traditional tension between authorizers and appropriators is illustrated by the periodic clashes between Transportation Committee Chairman Bud Shuster, R-Pa., and the Appropriations Committee (and other committees, too). Shuster, who heads the largest committee in the history of Congress with seventy-five members, attempted in 1999 to take the aviation trust fund off-budget, just as he did the year before with the transportation trust fund. (A trust fund is a legally created account that receives revenues from earmarked sources to be used for specific purposes.) The distinction between off-budget and on-budget involves the federal government's use since 1968 of a unified budget, which is a comprehensive accounting of all the government's financial activities. Taking programs off-budget means they are outside the control of the appropriators and the budget-writers. In effect, trust funds constitute a dedicated funding stream exempt from budgetary constraints and whose funds are reserved exclusively for mandatory spending on specific projects.

In 1998 Chairman Shuster rolled over opposition from the appropriators and took the highway trust fund (federal gasoline taxes are earmarked for this fund) off-budget. He even wrote a new House rule in the Transportation Equity Act of the 21st Century (TEA-21), that declares "out of order any attempt to lower the obligational limits for highway and transit spending spelled out in the authorizing law. If a transportation appropriations bill drops below the figures for highways and transit in the surface transportation law, a House member can raise a point of order against it." [17] The upshot was that Shuster's committee, and not the appropriations panel, makes highway spending decisions. Not only did TEA-21 arouse the ire and tie the hands of the appropriators, it also angered the Rules Committee, which has jurisdiction over changes in the House's rulebook.

A year later Shuster attempted to take the Airport and Airway Trust Fund (which receives money from airline fuel and passenger taxes) off-budget, arguing the need to improve and modernize airport facilities. His Aviation Investment and Reform Act for the 21st Century (AIR-21) was strongly opposed by the Appropriations chairman as well as other influential committee and party leaders. They feared that taking popular programs off-budget was becoming a trend, and they objected to slighting other transportation modes, such as railroads. Chairman Shuster easily prevailed in the House in large part because lawmakers find it hard to vote against bills that provide money and projects for their districts. However, Shuster compromised with the Senate, agreeing not to take the aviation trust fund off-budget but winning guarantees that for the next three years appropriators would be obligated to spend all the revenue and interest (estimated to be $33 billion) from the aviation trust fund on airport and flight safety improvements. [18]

More generally, authorizers devise ways to circumvent the annual appropriations process. These backdoor authorization measures (avoiding the appropriators' front door) blur the distinction between authorizations and appropriations because they permit spending by the federal government. Three common forms are (1) borrowing authority (a federal agency, for instance, is authorized by law to borrow specific sums of money from the Treasury or the public, through commercial channels, to build low-cost homes or make student loans); (2) contract authority (for example, a federal agency is statutorily permitted to enter into contractual agreements with private companies for the construction of municipal sewage treatment plants; appropriations must be provided in the future to honor these commitments); and (3) entitlement authority (federal programs such as Social Security, Medicare, and Medicaid that allow eligible recipients to be automatically entitled to federal payments). Entitlements constitute the fastest growing part of the federal budget. Appropriators often suggest that various entitlement programs be taken off automatic pilot and be subjected to annual appropriations review.

Exceptions to the Rules

There are many exceptions to the authorization-appropriations rules. Legislative (or policy) provisions find their way into appropriations bills notwithstanding the strictures of the rules—for instance, if no member raises a point of order against the practice or if either chamber waives its rules. The House by precedent also permits unauthorized programs to be included in continuing resolutions that provide interim funding for agencies whose general appropriations bills have not been enacted by the start of the fiscal year.

Senate rules, unlike those for the House, grant wide leeway to appropriators to authorize projects, programs, or activities. "I'm not about to start hunkering down and running like a scared rabbit because somebody says it's got to be authorized," said Sen. Robert C. Byrd, D-W.Va., when he headed Appropriations. "If this committee wants to authorize demonstration grants, it has the authority." [19]

Limitation Riders. Limitation riders are provisions in general appropriations bills or floor amendments to those measures that prohibit the spending of funds for specific purposes. Always phrased in the negative ("None of the funds provided in this Act shall be used for . . . ."), limitations are based on scores of House precedents that collectively uphold the position that because the House can refuse to appropriate funds for programs that have been authorized, it also can prohibit the use of funds for any part of a program or activity.

House members and staff aides may devote endless hours to carefully drafting provisions that make policy in the guise of limitations. For guidance they turn to the House rulebook, which is replete with precedents that have interpreted permissible from impermissible limitations. There are three basic criteria. Limitations cannot (1) impose additional duties or burdens on executive branch officials, (2) interfere with their discretionary authority, or (3) require officials to make judgments or determinations not required by existing law.

The 1977 antiabortion amendment remains a classic example of a limitation and the impact that procedure can exert on policy. The appropriations bill for the Department of Labor and the Department of Health, Education, and Welfare (HEW, now the Department of Health and Human Services) contained a limitation on the use of funds "to perform abortions except where the life of the mother would be endangered if the fetus were carried to term." A point of order was raised and sustained against that amendment on the ground that it was legislation in an appropriations bill. The limitation required officials in the executive branch to determine when the life of a pregnant woman would be endangered. The language then was amended to read: "None of the funds appropriated by this Act shall be used to pay for abortions or to promote or encourage abortions, except when a physician has certified the abortion is necessary to save the life of the mother." Again, a point of order was raised that the amendment was legislation in an appropriations bill. And again the chair ruled in favor of the parliamentary objection, this time on the ground that the federal government employed many physicians and that they would be required to make life-deciding judgments. Finally, the sponsor of the proposal, Rep. Henry J. Hyde, R-Ill., said he had no choice but to offer the following language: "None of the funds appropriated under this Act shall be used to pay for abortions or to promote or encourage abortions." There was no point of order because the amendment required no judgments by executive officials. The Hyde amendment then was adopted.[20]

When the Labor-HEW bill, containing the Hyde amendment, reached the Senate, Edward W. Brooke, R-Mass., offered an amendment that permitted abortions "where the life of the mother would be endangered if the fetus were carried to term, or where medically necessary, or for the treatment of rape or incest." Barry Goldwater, R-Ariz., said the amendment was legislation in an appropriations bill and raised a point of order. The Senate has its own procedural devices to obviate such points of order, however, and Senator Brooke used them successfully on the abortion issue. He raised what is called the defense of germaneness before the presiding officer had ruled on the Goldwater point of order.

Germaneness. Senate rules require that amendments be germane to general appropriations bills. Once the question of germaneness is raised, those rules require that the issue be submitted to the entire membership for resolution by majority vote and without debate. If the Senate decides that the proposed amendment is germane, the point of order automatically falls. In the abortion case, the Senate declared Brooke's amendment germane by a 74–21 vote. In such situations senators typically vote on the policy issue and not on the procedural question. As Ted Stevens, R-Alaska, noted, Senate rules prohibit legislation on appropriations, but if senators raise the defense of germaneness on their amendments, "we will have a vote on germaneness, and that will be equivalent to adopting the amendment."[21] Technical objections, in short, can be waived to achieve preferred policy outcomes. (A 1979 Senate precedent states that the defense of germaneness is applicable when there is arguably House legislative language—recall that the House originates appropriations bills—to which the Senate amendment at issue might conceivably be germane.)

On March 16, 1995, the Senate opened the floodgates on adding policy riders to appropriations bills. It voted to overturn the correct ruling by the presiding officer that an amendment offered by Sen. Kay Bailey Hutchison, R-Texas, dealing with the Endangered Species Act, constituted legislation on an appropriations bill and violated Senate Rule XVI. (A precedent established in this manner trumps Senate rules.) Thus was born the Hutchison precedent and with it came a greater proliferation of riders to appropriations bills, many of them sponsored to highlight partisan agendas. One result was that the change made it difficult to enact appropriations bills in a timely manner. Finally, the Senate voted on July 26, 1999, to, as Majority Leader Trent Lott, R-Miss., noted, "reinstate rule XVI which would make a point of order in order against legislation on an appropriations bill." [22]

Riders are sometimes added to appropriations bills because they would be unlikely to survive as freestanding bills. Controversial riders also make it difficult to pass appropriations measures by triggering partisan disputes, bicameral controversies, lobbying battles, or veto threats. When the fiscal 2000 Interior Department appropriations bill became the magnet for numerous riders that environmental groups opposed, they launched a coordinated campaign to eliminate "extremely ugly" riders on topics ranging from forests to oil royalties to grazing.[23] The president declared that if the Interior appropriations bill landed on his desk with the objectionable riders, "I will give it a good environmental response—I will send it straight to the recycling bin." [24]

The House experienced a rapid increase in the number of limitation amendments—from eleven in 1965 to eighty-six in 1980. Many of those dealt with so-called social issues, particularly school busing, school prayer, and abortion. These controversial issues were repeatedly bottled up in the authorizing committees, and members wanting action on them turned increasingly to limitations as a vehicle to force House consideration. Frustrated by the sharp controversies and long delays these limitations were causing, the House changed its rules in 1983 to restrict the opportunities for members to offer limitation riders to appropriations bills.[25] The change authorized limitation amendments only if the motion to rise from the Committee of the Whole was either rejected or not offered after the regular amendment process was completed on an appropriations bill.

When Republicans took control of the House in the mid-1990s, they again changed House rules by allowing the majority leader or a designee to have precedence in offering the motion to rise. "The intent of the new rule is to permit the offering of limitation amendments at the end of the reading [for amendment], subject only to a motion to rise offered by the majority leader or a designee." [26] The effect of this change is to enhance the majority leadership's control over the offering of limitation amendments.

Another House rule designed to preserve committees' jurisdictional prerogatives stipulates that no committee except Ways and Means may report tax or tariff proposals. This rule was first used on October 27, 1983, when Ways and Means Chairman Dan Rostenkowski, D-Ill., raised a point of order against a proposition in a general appropriations bill that concerned the duty-free entry of certain products from the Caribbean countries. The chair sustained the point of order by ruling that the provision "is a tariff measure in violation" of House rules. Just as authorizing committees may not report appropriations, appropriating and authorizing panels may not report tax and tariff proposals.

PRELUDE TO BUDGET REFORM

Congress's continuing struggle to control expenditures precipitated a comprehensive overhaul of its budgetary process. Titled the Congressional Budget and Impoundment Control Act of 1974, the law came about largely for three reasons. First, the congressional Appropriations committees gradually lost control of budget expenditures as the legislative, or authorizing, committees turned to backdoor financing techniques to accomplish their policy objectives. Congress thus lacked a central body to coordinate budgetary decisions, relate governmental revenue to expenditures, or calculate the effect of individual spending actions on the national economy. National fiscal policy reflected whatever emerged from Congress's excessively fragmented budget process. Second, the annual deficit had been on an upward spiral, and many lawmakers believed that a revamped budgetary process would enable Congress to gain better control of fiscal decisions. Third, presidents sometimes took advantage of Congress's piecemeal process. President Richard M. Nixon clashed with Congress over national spending priorities and impounded (refused to spend) monies at unprecedented levels for programs initiated by Democrats in Congress. "Far from administrative routine," wrote a budget scholar, "Nixon's impoundments in late 1972 and 1973 were designed to rewrite national policy at the expense of congressional power and intent." [27]

The combination of these three factors, along with growing public concern about the state of the national economy, led to enactment of the landmark 1974 budget law. That act established a congressional budget process that encouraged coordination and centralization. However, it did not institute this fiscal reorganization by abolishing the traditional authorization-appropriations process. Such an attempt would have pitted the most powerful committees and members against one another and jeopardized any chance of realizing substantive budgetary changes. Instead, Congress added another budget layer to "the existing revenue and appropriations process" of the House and Senate.[28]

THE 1974 BUDGET ACT

Passage of the 1974 budget act had a major institutional and procedural effect on the legislative branch. Many of the act's original requirements have been modified in response to new developments. However, almost three decades later, it is still worthwhile to describe the main features of the act, because they remain generally intact—the institutional entities, the timetable for budget decisions, the concurrent budget resolution, controls on backdoors and impoundments, reconciliation and the Byrd Rule, and enforcement of the budget resolution.

New Entities

The budget act created three new entities: the House Budget Committee, the Senate Budget Committee, and the Congressional Budget Office (CBO). The two budget committees have essentially the same functions, which include preparing annually a concurrent budget resolution, reviewing the impact of existing or proposed legislation on federal expenditures, overseeing the Congressional Budget Office, and monitoring throughout the year the revenue and spending actions of the House and Senate.

The two panels, however, are constituted differently. The House Budget Committee is required to have a rotating membership; most members may not serve more than eight years during a period of six consecutive Congresses. The committee must be composed of members drawn mainly from other standing committees, including five each from Appropriations and Ways and Means, and a leadership member from each of the two parties. While rotation allows many lawmakers over time to serve on this panel, it also has the effect of inhibiting cohesion (members' loyalty is to other committees), thus making it difficult at times for committee members to reach consensus on issues. Further, although the jurisdiction of the House Budget Committee was expanded somewhat in 1995 and 1997 to include, for instance, budget legislation generally and measures affecting budget totals and controls over the federal budget, the committee's fundamental task remains focused on one critical, visible, and often sharply partisan function: producing a concurrent budget resolution that reflects differing Democratic and Republican views on the role and priorities of the national government.

By contrast, the Senate Budget Committee has no restrictions on tenure, and its members are not required to come from other designated committees. The Senate Budget Committee "has standing on a par with any other committee in the institution." [29] The Congressional Budget Office is Congress's principal informational and analytical resource for budget, tax, and spending proposals. With about two hundred thirty aides, CBO performs important services—analyzing budget, economic, and policy issues and making fiscal projections are examples—for the House and Senate Budget committees and other congressional panels.

With budgetary issues dominating much Capitol Hill activity, CBO's role in providing scoring reports to the House and Senate Budget committees is especially significant. CBO has a scorekeeping unit, a small staff of number-crunchers who measure the budgetary effects of the spending and tax plans of appropriators, authorizers, party leaders, and presidents. The unit tracks pending and enacted spending and revenue measures to ensure that they are within the budgetary limits set by the concurrent budget resolution or other budget laws. CBO evaluates budget proposals against a baseline, which is an estimate of future spending and revenue projections for a fiscal year assuming no change in existing budget policies. Scoring can be controversial and opens CBO to criticism from lawmakers who do not like the results. For instance, if CBO calculates that bills of top priority to either party cost more than expected, Democrats or Republicans can be subject to partisan political attacks for sponsoring such legislation. (The director of the nonpartisan CBO is appointed to a four-year term.)

Timetable

To promote order and coordination in the budget process, Congress established a budgetary schedule (see Box 2-3). The timetable has been periodically changed, and Congress commonly misses some of the target dates. For example, Congress is supposed to enact its concurrent budget resolution on or before April 15 of each year, but that does not always happen. Disagreements over priorities and between the chambers, parties, and branches are among the considerations that account for the missed deadlines. Only once, for fiscal year 1999, did Congress fail to adopt a budget resolution. The House and Senate passed dramatically different resolutions, and the GOP leaders of each chamber could not agree on how to allocate funding. The 1974 budget act prohibits the House and Senate from taking up budgetary measures prior to the adoption of the budget resolution for the upcoming fiscal year. However, the House permits appropriations bills to be taken up after May 15 if a budget resolution has not been agreed to. Both chambers, too, can waive the requirement by unanimous consent or majority vote.

Whenever Congress cannot complete action on one or more of the thirteen regular appropriations bills by the start of the fiscal year, it provides temporary funding for the affected federal agencies through a joint resolution called a continuing resolution or a continuing appropriation. In 1999 Congress passed seven continuing resolutions. Traditionally, continuing resolutions are employed to keep a few government agencies in operation for short periods, typically one to three months. Continuing resolutions, however, have sometimes become major policy-making instruments of massive size and scope. In 1986 and 1987, for example, Congress packaged all thirteen regular appropriations bills into continuing resolutions. Such measures are often called megabills; they authorize and appropriate money to operate the federal government and make national policy in scores of diverse areas. These kinds of omnibus bills grant large powers to the small number of people who put these packages together—party and committee leaders and top executive officials. Omnibus measures usually arouse the ire of the rank and file, because typically little time is available in the final days of a session to debate these massive measures or to know what is in them.

Concurrent Budget Resolution

The core of Congress's annual budget process centers on the adoption of a concurrent budget resolution. This measure is formulated by the Budget committees, which consider the views and estimates of the other panels and hears the testimony of numerous witnesses. The budget resolution is composed of two basic parts. The first deals with fiscal aggregates: total federal spending (budget authority and outlays), total federal revenue, and the public debt (or

---

Box 2-3   Congressional Budget Process Timetable

Deadline	Action to Be Completed
Between the first Monday in January and the first Monday in February	President submits budget to Congress
February 15	Congressional Budget Office submits report on economic and budget outlook to Budget committees
Six weeks after president's budget is submitted	House and Senate committees submit reports on views and estimates to respective Budget Committee
April 1	Senate Budget Committee reports budget resolution
April 15	Congress completes action on budget resolution
June 10	House Appropriations Committee reports last regular appropriation bill
June 30	House completes action on regular appropriations bills and any required reconciliation legislation
July 15	President submits midsession review of his budget to Congress
October 1	Fiscal year begins

SOURCE: Robert Keith and Allen Schick, *Manual on the Federal Budget Process*, CRS Report 98-720, August 28, 1998, 64.

---

surplus) for the upcoming fiscal year. (The budget resolution also sets multiyear targets for these fiscal aggregates.) The second subdivides the budget aggregates among twenty functional categories, such as national defense, energy, and agriculture, and establishes spending levels for each. In effect, the budget resolution sets the overall level of discretionary spending for the upcoming fiscal year.

An optional process that the resolution may call for is reconciliation, which can require changes in tax policy or entitlement programs. Congress develops reconciliation legislation to ensure that its spending and revenue decisions comport with the policies set forth in the budget resolution. The budget resolution is a fiscal blueprint that establishes the context of congressional budgeting; guides the budgetary actions of the authorizing, appropriating, and taxing committees; and represents Congress's spending priorities. It is not submitted to the president; thus, it cannot be vetoed and does not carry legal effect. Sen. Bob Graham, D-Fla., explained the purposes of a budget resolution this way:

> [The budget] resolution would be analogous to an architect's set of plans for constructing a building. It gives the general direction, framework, and prioritization of Federal fiscal policy each year. Those priorities then drive the individual appropriations and tax measures which will support that architectural plan.[30]

The House and Senate Budget committees and individual lawmakers can enforce the terms of the budget resolution through points of order.

The budget resolution is considered in the House under a rule issued by the Rules Committee. For instance, in 1995 the GOP-controlled Rules Committee permitted House action on several alternative budget plans with the added requirement that each had to balance the budget by the year 2002 to be eligible for floor consideration. First to be acted upon was a plan put forward by conservative Democrats, then another by a group of Republicans, and then a budget drafted by the Congressional Black Caucus. The Rules chairman pointed out that the order of consideration is important, "because if any one of these pass, then the debate immediately ceases and we go right to final passage." [31] (Parliamentary principles stipulate that it is not in order to re-amend something that has already been amended. A substitute budget plan, if adopted, would amend the entire text of the concurrent budget resolution leaving nothing left to further amend.) In the end, the House rejected all three fiscal alternatives and agreed to the GOP-crafted budget blueprint.

Senate procedure for considering budget resolutions is different from other legislation in four major ways. First, floor action is regulated by the statutory requirements of the 1974 act as well as unanimous consent agreements negotiated by the party leadership. Second, concurrent budget resolutions are privileged, which means that they can be taken up easily either by unanimous consent or by a nondebatable motion to proceed to their consideration. (Motions to proceed for most legislation are subject to extended debate.) Third, budget resolutions carry a fifty-hour statutory debate limitation (twenty hours for reconciliation bills), which means that they cannot be filibustered to death. Amendments are subject to a two-hour debate limit. Fourth, the 1974 act imposes a germaneness requirement on amendments to budget resolutions. The act permits the germaneness standard to be set aside, but it requires at least sixty votes, instead of a simple majority, to obtain the waiver. The Senate, unlike the House, has no general germaneness rule.

When the House and Senate pass budget resolutions that contain different aggregate and functional totals, which is normal practice, the disagreements usually have to be resolved by a conference committee. The conferees prepare a report that provides a bank account for the various House and

Senate committees. This account distributes the total agreed-upon spending for the year among twenty functional categories.

This allocation procedure, called a budget crosswalk, involves two steps. First, section 302a of the 1974 budget act requires the joint statement that accompanies the conference report to divide the budget totals among the House and Senate committees with budgetary jurisdiction for the programs reflected in the various functional categories. The crosswalk is necessary because Congress chooses to employ functional category designations developed by the White House's Office of Management and Budget. These designations do not correspond exactly to many House and Senate committees, with their overlapping jurisdictions.

Second, under section 302b, the House and Senate Appropriations committees each subdivide their spending allocations among its subcommittees. (If the concurrent budget resolution is not passed by the required April 15 date, then to avoid delays in the appropriations process the allocation to committees is based on the discretionary spending amounts included in the president's budget.) The suballocations are reported by the Appropriations committees to their respective chambers, and they are enforceable by members raising points of order against bills that exceed a committee's total allocation and the suballocations assigned its subcommittees. And in the Senate, such points of order can be overturned only by a 60 percent supermajority vote.

The whole section 302b process is important because it is employed by committees and members to ensure compliance with the financial totals specified in the budget resolution. Further, the suballocation process among the thirteen Appropriations subcommittees in each chamber is crucial in influencing funding for various policy priorities. Little is known about how the Appropriations committees divide their spending pie among the subunits. "The allocation of the [discretionary] federal budget among the thirteen Appropriations subcommittees is the most closed, the least understood, and the most consequential annual process within the Congress," wrote a congressional budget analyst.[32] No doubt hard bargaining permeates the activities of the College of Cardinals as each subcommittee chair strives to maximize his or her share of spending authority. A public report is made available once the appropriators have made their allocation decisions for each of the thirteen subcommittees. These allocations are enforceable by points of order against an appropriations bill or amendment that breaches a subcommittee's allotted spending level.

Reconciliation

Reconciliation is an optional procedure that enables Congress to implement its comprehensive fiscal policy (as reflected in the budget resolution) by changing tax and entitlement laws. It is a two-step process designed to reconcile the parts with the whole or, put differently, to bring existing law into conformity with the current budget resolution. In practice, reconciliation is used to reduce spending, primarily through entitlement savings, and either to increase revenues or cut taxes. It does not address funding that is established in annual appropriations bills. The Appropriations committees are bound by the discretionary spending limits set forth in the budget resolution. First used in 1980, reconciliation through fiscal year 2001 has been employed sixteen times because it has proven to be an effective device for making budgetary savings.

The first step in reconciliation calls for congressional approval of a budget resolution that instructs House and Senate committees to report legislation making cuts in spending, increases in revenue, or both on programs and agency operations by a certain date. (An example of Senate reconciliation directives is presented in Box 2-4.) The panels' recommended budget savings, which are supposed to meet or exceed the amounts designated for each committee in the resolution, are transmitted to the respective House and Senate Budget committees. The second step involves the packaging of the recommendations into an omnibus reconciliation bill, followed by floor action in each chamber. The Budget committees cannot make substantive changes in the savings proposals received from each instructed committee.

In 1981 President Ronald Reagan persuaded Congress to employ reconciliation to achieve massive cuts in domestic programs (totaling about $130 billion over three years). Never before had reconciliation been employed on such a grand scale. The entire process was expedited and in a manner that short-circuited regular legislative procedures. A highly charged atmosphere produced a legislative result, wrote Howard H. Baker Jr., R-Tenn., then Senate majority leader, "that would have been impossible to achieve if each committee had reported an individual bill on subject matter solely within its jurisdiction." [33] Reconciliation forced nearly all House and Senate committees to make unwanted cuts in programs under their jurisdiction. Given their policy-making significance, these bills, not surprisingly, are shepherded through Congress by party leaders.

The irony was that Congress's budget process, designed in 1974 to advance and reassert the legislative branch's power of the purse, was captured by the White House in 1981 and used to achieve President Reagan's objectives. However, reconciliation can be used by either branch or party provided it has the votes to implement its objectives. In 1995 the GOP Congress employed reconciliation to try to scale back the size of government, cut taxes, and balance the budget in seven years. "Its efforts," in the judgment of an attorney, "led to two historic federal government shutdowns, thirteen stopgap measures, several presidential vetoes, and ultimately failed to produce a meaningful fiscal agreement with the White House." [34]

On a few occasions, reconciliation directives provided for more than one reconciliation bill. In 1996, for instance, the directive provided for a three-stage process with a tax cut bill to be considered in conjunction with two measures drafted to achieve savings in Medicare, welfare, and other entitlement programs. Four years later the budget resolution instructed the House Ways and Means Committee and the Senate Finance Committee to produce two tax cut bills by the end of the year. In the lead-up to the November 2000

BOX 2-4   Senate Reconciliation Directives

Below are excerpts from the Concurrent Resolution on the Budget for Fiscal Year 1998 conference report (H Con Res 84—H Rept 105-116) stipulating reconciliation directives to the Senate. The directives assumed that the recommendations for spending reductions would be incorporated into an omnibus bill that the Senate Budget Committee would report (without any substantive revision), but that the Senate Finance Committee would report its recommendations for the $85 billion tax cut directly to the Senate as a separate bill. Like the House reconciliation directives, the Senate directives provided a deadline for the submission by committees of their recommendations. In the case of the omnibus bill, the instructed committees had to submit both legislative language (for incorporation into the omnibus bill) and report language (for incorporation into the accompanying report).

Sec. 104. Reconciliation in the Senate

(a) Reconciliation of Spending Reductions.—Not later than June 13, 1997, the committees named in this subsection shall submit their recommendations to the Committee on the Budget of the Senate. After receiving those recommendations, the Committee on the Budget shall report to the Senate a reconciliation bill carrying out all such recommendations without any substantive revision.

(1) Committee on Agriculture, Nutrition, and Forestry.—The Senate Committee on Agriculture, Nutrition, and Forestry shall report changes in laws within its jurisdiction that provide direct spending . . . to increase outlays by not more than $300,000,000 in fiscal year 2002 and by not more than $1,500,000,000 for the period of fiscal years 1998 through 2002.

(2) Committee on Banking, Housing, and Urban Affairs.—The Senate Committee on Banking, Housing, and Urban Affairs shall report changes in laws within its jurisdiction that reduce the deficit $434,000,000 in fiscal year 2002 and $1,590,000,000 for the period of years 1998 through 2002.

✳ ✳ ✳ ✳ ✳ ✳

(b) Reconciliation of Revenue Reductions.—Not later than June 20, 1997, the Senate Committee on Finance shall report to the Senate a reconciliation bill proposing changes in laws within its jurisdiction necessary to reduce revenues by not more than $20,500,000,000 in fiscal year 2002 and $85,000,000,000 for the period of fiscal years 1998 through 2002.

SOURCE: Adapted from Robert Keith and Allen Schick, *Manual on the Federal Budget Process*, CRS Report 98-720, August 28, 1998, 81.

elections, congressional Republicans wanted to spotlight tax relief as a GOP priority.

Reconciliation is a powerful procedure for fiscal retrenchment, and it was employed extensively during the deficit era. Now, with surpluses projected for the next several years, reconciliation is likely to be downplayed as a procedure. What role does a procedure designed exclusively for deficit reduction play during a surplus period? For two years running (1999 and 2000), reconciliation involved only the tax-writing committees, and they were instructed to report tax reduction bills directly to the House and Senate floors. Like the budget resolution, reconciliation legislation is accorded major procedural protections in the Senate against nongermane amendments and filibusters. In the House, reconciliation is considered under the terms of a rule from the Rules Committee.

The Byrd Rule

The Byrd Rule, named after Senator Byrd of West Virginia and initiated in 1985 (it has been modified several times since), fundamentally states that reconciliation provisions must reduce the deficit. Because reconciliation requires committees with policy-making responsibilities—the tax-writing and authorizing committees—to either raise revenues or cut mandatory spending programs, these panels sometimes report policy provisions that have no bearing on reducing any deficit, and which may even increase its size. Reconciliation has been used, for example, to expand Medicaid coverage, reinstate the broadcast fairness doctrine, and provide funds for the trade adjustment assistance program. Such provisions are inserted in reconciliation bills in part "because the budget committees are specifically prohibited from making any substantive changes in the recommendations from each committee." [35]

The addition of extraneous matter to reconciliation bills has proven to be more of a problem in the Senate than in the House. The House has the Rules Committee, which can, for example, permit members to offer motions to strike extraneous matter from these bills. In the Senate, reconciliation measures are taken up under procedures that limit the normally unfettered debate and amendment process. Committees, as a result, may deliberately add new initiatives to reconciliation bills to gain procedural protections for proposals that if taken up separately would be subjected to unlimited debate and amendment, including the offering of nongermane amendments.

The Byrd Rule's objective, then, is to exclude extraneous (unrelated to deficit reduction) matter in reconciliation bills. To maximize its potency, the rule can be waived only by a three-fifths vote of the Senate. Similarly, sixty votes are required to overturn a ruling of the Senate's presiding officer that a provision in a reconciliation bill (or a floor amendment to it) is extraneous. What is extraneous, however, is not always easy to determine.

> The application of the [Byrd] rule can be tortuous. Take food stamps, for example. The House [in 1993] approved $7.3 billion in extra spending for food stamps in its reconciliation bill; the Senate did not. Conferees . . . agreed to include up to the House amount in the conference report, but [Senate] Republicans hope to strip it out, arguing that it violates the Byrd rule because it would force the [Senate Agriculture] committee to miss its deficit-cutting target. The Senate Agriculture Committee's target was $3.2 billion. [Senate] Democrats argued behind the scenes that it was impossible to apply the Byrd rule to a

conference report. What was the relevant "committee"? House Agriculture? Senate Agriculture? The conference committee? The House's Committee of the Whole? [The Senate] parliamentarian agreed that the rule could not properly apply [in this case], clearing the way for the food stamps provision to remain [in the conference report].[36]

Because the Byrd Rule also applies to House-Senate conference reports, it has become a source of heightened conflict between the chambers. House committee chairmen charge that the Byrd Rule, "by allowing Senators to rise on points of order and strike extraneous provisions [from conference reports], gives the Senate the power to dictate House actions."[37] Where House members may recommend the elimination of the Byrd Rule insofar as it applies to conference committees, senators have recommended that the rule be strengthened.

Controls on Impoundments

Title X of the 1974 budget act permits Congress to review executive impoundments of appropriated funds. The act divides impoundments into two categories—deferrals (a temporary delay in the expenditure of funds to achieve savings made possible through greater efficiencies or to provide for contingencies) and rescissions (the permanent cancellation of budget authority)—which are considered under separate procedures. Presidents are obligated to inform Congress of their proposed deferrals and rescissions and to set forth the reasons for them. The General Accounting Office is authorized to review these special messages to ensure that impoundments are not misclassified and to challenge misclassifications in federal court.

To rescind budget authority, the president submits a message to Congress indicating the reasons for the rescission. Congress then has forty-five days of continuous session (days when Congress is in session, not calendar days) to pass a rescission bill that either cancels all, part, or none of the amount requested by the president. If both houses fail to pass a rescission bill before the expiration of the forty-five-day period, the president must make the funds available for obligation. Inaction, in short, produces action: the release of appropriated funds.

To strengthen the president's ability to control spending, the GOP-controlled Congress passed the Line-Item Veto Act of 1996. Although some Republicans expressed concern that President Clinton would use the new authority to cancel GOP-sponsored riders or pork, they passed it anyway as part of their Contract with America. The act permitted the president to cancel any dollar amount of discretionary budget authority, any new entitlement spending, and any limited tax benefit. The statute, an amendment to the 1974 budget act, required the president to first sign a bill; then he could exercise his cancellation authority provided it would reduce the budget deficit and not impair governmental functions or the national interest.

The line-item veto law also obligated the president to submit a list of his cancellations to Congress within five calendar days (excluding Sunday) after he signed a measure into law. Congress could then pass a disapproval bill, which the president could veto subject to Congress's ability to override by two-thirds vote of each house. The line-item veto law stacked the deck in favor of the president. Unlike a rescission, which takes effect only if it is approved by Congress, cancellations under the legislative line-item veto occur if Congress fails to act.

In practice, President Clinton made little use of the new veto authority, in part because he did not want to anger lawmakers whose support he might need to pass administration priorities. Two years after the law was enacted, the Supreme Court declared it unconstitutional *(Clinton v. City of New York)* on the grounds that it permitted the president to unilaterally amend or repeal a law. Subsequently, lawmakers introduced line-item veto alternatives, including a constitutional amendment. Rep. Charles W. Stenholm, D-Texas, proposed an "expedited rescission" alternative under which the president "would be able to single out individual items in tax or spending legislation and send a rescission package to Congress which would then be required [by a certain time] to vote up or down on the package."[38] Congress has yet to approve any of these alternatives.

Enforcement of the Budget Resolution

The House and Senate enforce the goals and policies set forth in the budget resolution through devices such as scorekeeping, spending allocations to committees and subcommittees, reconciliation, budgetary information provided by CBO, and the monitoring role of the budget committees as well as through points of order such as the Byrd Rule raised on the House or Senate floor. Points of order under the budget act are either substantive or procedural in character. Substantive points of order are raised to ensure compliance with the budget resolution. For example, a lawmaker can challenge a floor amendment that would cause a standing committee to exceed its allocation of new discretionary spending authority. Procedural points of order are raised to ensure compliance with features of the 1974 budget act and companion legislation. The House and Senate permit waivers of any points of order. The House usually does this in a rule issued by the Rules Committee. The Senate, by contrast, must waive most points of order by a three-fifths vote of all senators. A common feature of Senate floor activity is efforts by senators to attract sixty votes to waive some feature of the budget act so as to accomplish a policy objective, especially when a broad consensus exists to pass a bill or amendment.

EVOLUTION OF THE BUDGET PROCESS

Change is ever-present in congressional procedures and politics. This is certainly the case with the congressional budget process. In the mid-1980s and later, Congress enacted significant statutory changes to its budget process. These changes emerged from a new political climate: the politics of deficit reduction. A dramatic upsurge in the size of the annual deficits took place when Ronald Reagan took office in 1981. His objectives were clear and threefold: slash domestic spending, increase defense expenditures, and cut taxes. However, the revenue losses caused by the tax cuts, combined with rising defense expenditures and insufficient reductions in other areas, soon produced deficits in the $200 billion to $300 billion range. Never before had the nation seen such huge deficits during peacetime and during an economic expansion (following the 1982 economic recession).

The escalating growth of entitlement spending, then and today, remains an outstanding issue of budgetary control. As House Appropriations Chairman C. W. Bill Young, R-Fla., stated in 2000:

> Since 1995, mandatory spending . . . has increased nearly $214 billion; Social Security increased $70 billion. That is a mandatory entitlement. Medicare increased $42.6 billion. Medicaid increased $27 billion. Agriculture programs increased $21 billion. Deposit insurance increased $16.5 billion. Federal employment retirement programs increased $11.8 billion. Supplemental security income increased $7 billion. Veterans' benefits and services increased $6.4 billion. Since enactment of TEA-21, funding for highways and mass transit will increase by $37.1 billion through fiscal year 2000. Aviation programs will increase $10 billion over three years. These last two are now, in effect, treated as mandatory programs.[39]

In general, the public wants more governmental services than it is willing to pay for and individuals are not happy with suggestions to reduce their benefits. As Sen. Russell B. Long, D-La., quipped, when he was Senate Finance Committee chairman: "Don't tax me. Don't tax thee. Tax that fellow behind the tree."

Entitlements

Until the mid-1960s Great Society era, few entitlement programs existed other than Social Security and veterans' pensions. As a result, the Appropriations committees were well situated to balance competing program claims against available financial resources. For example, in 1932 "the Appropriations Committee in each chamber was responsible for 90 percent of federal spending."[40] Today, that share has fallen to around 30 percent, with entitlements consuming more than 50 percent of current federal expenditures and interest on the debt constituting the remainder. The dominant role of the federal budget, as one scholar wrote, has now become "transferring money to recipients outside the government rather than financing the operations of the government."[41] To be sure, appropriators are strong supporters of gaining more control over these open-ended mandatory spending programs. Skyrocketing entitlement expenditures constrict their share of available monies, and their annual bills become handy targets for lawmakers who want to offer floor amendments cutting discretionary spending programs.

A dramatic reversal clearly has taken place between the amount of money controlled through yearly appropriations and that subject to mandatory spending. Social Security and Medicare are the largest entitlements and are expanding (see Figure 2-1). They are growing rapidly for two interconnected reasons: the aging of the population and medical advances that extend the longevity of life. Even with a robust economy, fiscal projections indicate that once the baby boomer population (those born between 1946 and 1964) start to retire early in the twenty-first century, only a few decades will pass before these two programs run short of funds to cover eligible beneficiaries. For example, estimates made in 2000 about Social Security project that "by 2015 the tidal wave of baby boomer retirements will leave too few workers ponying up payroll taxes to fund all the promised benefits." [42] Other analysts suggest that the size of the projected shortfall is overstated and that future generations are likely to earn substantially more in incomes and hence their payroll taxes will ensure the continued solvency of Social Security.

Regularly, Washington decision makers discuss entitlement reforms, such as establishing private retirement accounts for workers or introducing more competitive and cost-effective health coverage for the elderly. The challenge to curb entitlement costs, as well as discretionary spending, precipitated enactment of a significant budgetary reform: the Budget Enforcement Act (BEA) of 1990. This act, and the 1993 and 1997 amendments to it, contributed to the elimination of the deficit and the projected start of a new surplus era.

The Budget Enforcement Act

In October 1990, Congress and the White House negotiated a five-year budget agreement entitled the Budget Enforcement Act. (The BEA was Title XIII of an omnibus reconciliation bill.) Once again Congress changed its fiscal procedures. The legislation outlined a binding, multiyear deficit-reduction

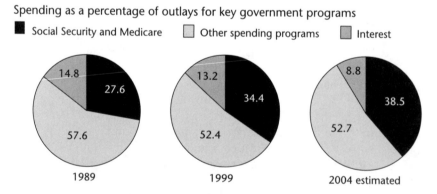

Spending as a percentage of outlays for key government programs

■ Social Security and Medicare   ▢ Other spending programs   ▨ Interest

14.8	13.2	8.8
27.6	34.4	38.5
57.6	52.4	52.7
1989	1999	2004 estimated

SOURCE: Adapted from Howard Gleckman, "The Baby Boom That Ate the Budget," *Business Week*, February 15, 1999, 33.

FIGURE 2-1 The Graying of the Budget

plan (almost $500 billion over five years) and established complex procedural controls to restrain federal spending. When President Clinton signed the Omnibus Reconciliation Act of 1993 into law, which passed the House and Senate without a single Republican vote, the BEA was extended through 1998; the Budget Enforcement Act of 1997 extended it through 2002.

The BEA's fundamental focus was on spending and revenue controls. Two enforcement mechanisms undergird the BEA. First, the BEA set spending caps for discretionary programs. For example, for fiscal year 2001 discretionary spending is limited to $600.4 billion ($310.9 billion for defense and $289.5 billion for nondefense programs), which is less than required to account for inflation. On occasion, Congress prohibits the shifting of money from one category (defense) to another (nondefense). This prohibition (called a firewall) is designed to prevent Congress from raiding the defense category to fund domestic programs. At other times, the categories have been merged into one pot of discretionary money with all programs competing for scarce dollars. With the spending caps, any increase for one program has to be offset by decreases in another—a case of zero-sum budgeting. Under BEA, Congress is prohibited from breaching the spending caps. Otherwise, a sequestration (automatic spending reductions) could occur in all discretionary programs. The caps can be changed, but Congress and the president would have to agree to modify the law. In 1997, when both branches signed onto a balanced budget plan, they also agreed to impose even stricter caps than those set out in the 1990 BEA.

Second, BEA makes taxes and entitlements subject to a pay-as-you-go (PAYGO) procedure, which requires that any tax reductions or increases in mandatory spending programs must be offset by tax hikes or reductions in other mandatory spending programs. Otherwise, there would be a sequester of those mandatory spending programs not exempt under the terms of the BEA. (Existing entitlements are not subject to PAYGO requirements; only new ones are.) As the chief counsel of the Senate Budget Committee put it, "The 'pay-as-you-go' label implies that Congress and the President may cut taxes or create new programs—that is 'go'—if they also agree to provide offsetting increased revenues or spending reductions—that is 'pay.' "[43] An indirect effect of PAYGO is to limit the Senate's ability to adorn (or Christmas tree) tax bills with "revenue-losing provisions as bargaining chips" for the conference committee, because all "revenue losses must be offset, even if the revenue loss is incidental to the bill's main objective."[44]

THE SURPLUS ERA

Procedurally and politically, the surplus era has created new strains in budgeting. As Rep. Gary A. Condit, D-Calif., observed, "No matter what the surplus is, it won't be enough to do what everyone wants to do."[45] Procedurally, lawmakers face the prospect of large surpluses, but their budget rules are designed for deficit reduction. The tax and spending plans of many lawmakers are frustrated by budgetary rules that lock them in a fiscal straightjacket. For example, many lawmakers want to increase spending for defense as well as many domestic programs. Unless the caps or revenues are raised, spending hikes for defense or education need to be paid for by making cuts in other agencies and programs that also enjoy popular backing inside and outside the Congress.

Reluctant to change the tight caps statutorily at a time of heightened partisanship, when charges of fiscal irresponsibility could be used by either party against the other, Congress and the president have resorted to budgetary gimmicks to comply with the fiscal limits while still increasing spending for various programs. A favorite technique is for Congress and the president to declare something an emergency, which exempts it from the caps imposed by the BEA. They are aided by the lack of a specific definition for what constitutes an emergency. Instead, broad and vague criteria (for example, an essential or vital item or an urgent need) are used for emergency spending designations.[46] The emergency designation, for example, was used to fund Operation Desert Storm (the military rollback of Iraq's 1990 invasion of Kuwait) and to provide money for various domestic disasters. Congress has also used the emergency designation to finance the constitutionally required decennial census and to cover routine maintenance costs at the Pentagon. The emergency designation became a huge loophole for providing new spending. (In 2000, as part of the concurrent budget resolution, the Senate established a sixty-vote point of order—the number needed to waive the objection—against all emergency designations except for discretionary defense spending. If the point of order is sustained, the emergency designation is deleted from any legislation, including conference reports.)

When Congress and the White House agreed to tighter caps as part of the 1997 budget agreement, they had no idea that a booming economy would soon help erase the deficit era and generate heightened pressures to spend more on various programs. The president simply ignored the spending caps when he submitted his fiscal 2001 budget to Congress.[47] In its concurrent budget resolution for fiscal 2001, Congress adhered to the caps set forth in the 1997 budget agreement but adjusted them upward to more realistic levels. Still, an issue before Congress and the president is whether spending caps matter in a surplus era.

Like spending caps, the focus of PAYGO is also deficit reduction. Tax cuts or entitlement increases need to be offset by an equivalent tax hike or entitlement reduction. Budget rules, for instance, forbid the use of the surplus to pay for tax reductions. "We have surpluses and the [PAYGO] rules ought to be updated to meet the current situation," declared the Senate Finance Committee chairman.[48] (PAYGO rules do not apply if the surplus occurs in the non-Social Security part of the budget.) Some in both parties and chambers oppose changing the caps and PAYGO rules on the grounds that maintaining fiscal discipline is important. They argue that any fiscal surplus is short-term and will quickly evaporate when the baby boom generation begins to retire and Medicare costs escalate. These issues remain the nation's long-term financial problems.

Politically, both parties strive to position themselves advantageously with the electorate as to how to spend the surplus while maintaining a balanced budget. Both, too, are internally divided in large part because the surplus question reflects partisan differences about the role of the federal government. Many Republicans, for instance, advocate large tax cuts to starve the national government of fiscal resources. Other Republicans want to use most of the money to pay down the national debt. For their part, many Democrats favor an activist governmental role and advocate new spending to address the nation's unmet needs in education, health, or research and development. Others counsel the need to avoid being tagged as big spenders and recommend a more frugal approach to the surplus, such as using some of the money for targeted tax cuts, a portion for new investments, and a part for paying down the debt. Congress and the president have little experience in handling the possibilities and opportunities created by the surplus, and the outstanding question remains: What should be done with the surplus?

The budget wars of the 1990s between the GOP-controlled Congress and the Democratic president did eventually produce a bipartisan agreement of large significance. For decades the government used the large surpluses accumulating in the Social Security Trust Fund to help finance other federal programs and agencies. Doing so masked the true size of the deficit, and few thought much about it. The on-budget or non-Social Security surplus refers to money the federal government derives from income and other taxes to run the government. This was the part of the nation's budget that for years was in the red. Today, the on-budget portion has started to show surpluses. In 2000, for instance, the total on-budget surplus was projected by the Office of Management and Budget to be $76 billion.

To stymie GOP plans for large tax cuts, President Clinton in 1998 told the nation that the budget surplus ought to be used to "save Social Security first." No longer should the government borrow from Social Security to pay for spending or tax cuts. Quickly, Republicans one-upped the president and promised to lock up all the revenues flowing into Social Security. The GOP embraced this notion as a way to ward off Democratic charges that Republicans wanted to raid Social Security to pass tax cuts for the wealthy and to demonstrate their backing of the nation's most popular social program. The effect of this newfound bipartisan consensus meant that each party had checkmated the other. "We said 'save the surplus to stop tax cuts,'" stated a senior Senate Democratic staff aide. "They used it to stop spending programs. So it came out a draw."[49]

Political competition between the two parties produced an informal agreement whose implications for balanced budgets are huge. No longer would elected officials raid the surpluses in Social Security (estimated to continue until 2015 when benefit payments start to exceed tax receipts) to fund other government programs. As former CBO director Reischauer explained,

"[P]oliticians changed the aim of fiscal policy from balancing the unified budget to balancing the budget without counting the Social Security surplus. It is the most profound fiscal policy shift we have seen for years." [50]

No one can predict the longevity of this bipartisan pledge, but its indirect effect is to pay down the national debt. Money that flows into the federal Treasury that is not spent automatically goes for debt reduction. If the huge Social Security surpluses are not used to fund general governmental operations, some predict that the national debt could be paid off by 2015. With Social Security locked up, and if the on-budget surplus continues to accumulate, then lawmakers will battle over whether the non-Social Security surplus should be used for tax cuts, new spending, or some combination of both, all the while keeping the budget in balance.

Politics on Capitol Hill is shifting with the demise of the deficit, but its direction is unclear because there are so many uncertainties, including the continued health of the economy within the globalized marketplace. What does seem clear, however, is that the government appears to face in the short term a bright surplus future but in the long term a looming fiscal challenge given the retirement and health needs of the aging baby boomers. As former CBO director Reischauer predicted: "The deficit dragon has not been slain. It's just locked in a closet—for the time being." [51]

NOTES

1. Elizabeth Shogren and Janet Hook, "Clinton Hails First Fiscal Year in Surplus in Three Decades," *Los Angeles Times,* October 1, 1998, A7.
2. Lawrence Goodrich, "A Season of Stalemate on Hill," *Christian Science Monitor,* June 30, 1998, 10.
3. *Congressional Control of Expenditures,* House Committee on the Budget, January 1977, 6. The study was prepared by Allen Schick.
4. *Congressional Record,* April 4, 2000, S2055.
5. *Congressional Record,* February 24, 2000, S782.
6. John William Ellwood, ed., *Reductions in U.S. Domestic Spending* (New Brunswick, N.J.: Transaction Books, 1982), 21.
7. Absent an authorization law, the Appropriations committees typically base their financial recommendations on the president's budget requests.
8. Roy T. Meyers, "Biennial Budgeting," staff working paper, Congressional Budget Office, November 1987, 42.
9. Richard Munson, *The Cardinals of Capitol Hill* (New York: Grove Press, 1993), 6.
10. Everett Somerville Brown, ed., *William Plumer's Memorandum of Proceedings in the United States Senate, 1803–1807* (New York: Macmillan, 1923), 490.
11. Robert Luce, *Legislative Problems* (Boston: Houghton Mifflin, 1935), 425–426.

12. Louis Fisher, "The Authorization-Appropriation Process in Congress: Formal Rules and Informal Practices," *Catholic University Law Review* (Fall 1979): 53.

13. Congressional Budget Office, *Unauthorized Appropriations and Expired Authorizations,* January 8, 1999.

14. *Operations of the Congress: Testimony of House and Senate Leaders,* Hearing before the Joint Committee on the Organization of Congress, 103d Cong., 1st sess. (January 26, 1993), 75–76.

15. *Budget Process,* Hearing before the Joint Committee on the Organization of Congress, 103d Cong., 1st sess. (March 16, 1993), 52.

16. *Operations of the Congress,* 70.

17. Jeff Plungis, "Shuster's Use of Budgetary 'Firewalls' Takes Other Chairman by Surprise," *Congressional Quarterly Weekly Report,* August 7, 1999, 1917.

18. *CQ Daily Monitor,* March 2, 2000, 1.

19. Jon Healey, "Lautenberg Moves to Reduce Transportation Earmarks," *Congressional Quarterly Weekly Report,* October 2, 1993, 2625.

20. Fisher, "The Authorization-Appropriation Process in Congress," 74–75. The House considered the issue on June 17, 1977, and the Senate on June 29, 1977. See Roger H. Davidson, "Procedures and Politics in Congress," in *The Abortion Dispute and the American System,* ed. Gilbert Y. Steiner (Washington, D.C.: Brookings Institution, 1982), 30–46.

21. *Congressional Record,* October 20, 1993, S13966.

22. *Congressional Record,* July 26, 1999, S9171.

23. Charles Pope, "Senate Takes Little Action on Interior Spending Bill Laden with Environmental Riders," *Congressional Quarterly Weekly Report,* August 7, 1999, 1945.

24. Charles Pope, "Clinton Condemns Interior Bill for Environmental Riders," *Congressional Quarterly Weekly Report,* October 16, 1999, 2457.

25. *Congressional Record,* January 3, 1983, H5–H22.

26. *Congressional Record,* January 4, 1995, H37.

27. Allen Schick, *Congress and Money* (Washington, D.C.: Urban Institute Press, 1980), 46.

28. Schick, *Congress and Money,* 59.

29. Daniel P. Franklin, *Making Ends Meet: Congressional Budgeting in the Age of Deficits* (Washington, D.C.: CQ Press, 1993), 40.

30. *Congressional Record,* March 2, 2000, S1050.

31. *Congressional Record,* May 17, 1995, H5107.

32. Munson, *The Cardinals of Capitol Hill,* 19.

33. Howard H. Baker Jr., "An Introduction to the Politics of Reconciliation," *Harvard Journal on Legislation* (Winter 1983): 2.

34. Anita Krishnakumar, "Reconciliation and the Fiscal Constitution: The Anatomy of the 1995–96 Budget 'Train Wreck,' " *Harvard Journal on Legislation* (Summer 1998): 489.

35. Stanley E. Collender, *The Guide to the Federal Budget, Fiscal 1995* (Washington, D.C.: Urban Institute Press, 1994), 60.

36. George Hager, "The Byrd Rule: Not an Easy Call," *Congressional Quarterly Weekly Report,* July 31, 1993, 2027.

37. Karen Foerstel, "Byrd Rule War Erupts Once Again," *Roll Call,* February 24, 1994, 13.

38. *Congressional Record,* November 17, 1999, H12112.

39. *Congressional Record,* March 29, 2000, H1517.

40. John F. Cogan, *Federal Budget Deficits: What's Wrong with the Congressional Budget Process* (Palo Alto, Calif.: Stanford University, Hoover Institution, 1992), 14.

41. Allen Schick, *The Capacity to Budget* (Washington, D.C.: Urban Institute Press, 1990), 37.

42. *USA Today,* April 10, 2000, 26A.

43. William G. Dauster, "Budget Process Issues for 1993," *Journal of Laws & Politics,* vol. 9, no. 9 (1992): 26.

44. Allen Schick, *The Federal Budget: Politics, Policy, Process,* rev. ed. (Washington, D.C.: Brookings Institution, 2000), 147.

45. Matthew Miller, "It's Party Time," *U.S. News and World Report,* January 12, 1998, 20.

46. See, for example, *Conference Report, Concurrent Resolution on the Budget for Fiscal Year 2001,* 106 Cong., 2d sess., H. Rept. 106-577 (April 12, 2000), 16.

47. Charles Babington and Eric Pianin, "Clinton Plan Ignores '97 Budget Pact," *Washington Post,* January 14, 2000, A1.

48. Jacob Schlesinger, "Senate Leaders Call for Easing of Rules Limiting Tax Cuts and Spending Increases," *Wall Street Journal,* December 7, 1998, A3.

49. Alison Mitchell, "On Budget, Everything in Moderation," *New York Times,* November 19, 1999, A29.

50. "Budget Making: Another Paradigm Shift," *The Economist,* November 20, 1999, 30.

51. Donald Lambro, "Politics on Hill Will Change When Budget Surpluses Loom," *Washington Times,* August 10, 1997, A4.

CHAPTER 3

Preliminary Legislative Action

THE INTRODUCTION of a bill in Congress is a deceptively simple procedure. House members drop their bills into the hopper, a mahogany box near the clerk's desk at the front of the chamber. Senators generally submit their proposals and accompanying statements to clerks, or they may introduce their bills from the floor.

However, lawmakers contemplate a variety of pre-introductory considerations, especially for major bills—those subject to the most scrutiny and debate. Timing is important. Should a controversial bill be introduced early or late in a legislative session? For example, a bill likely to be filibustered in the Senate might be introduced early to allow plenty of time to overcome any talkathon. The naming of the legislation also could be an issue. An attractive title, such as the Freedom of Information Act or the American Dream Restoration Act, could garner a bill useful media attention. Opponents, meanwhile, could play on the name in an attempt to attach an unattractive label to a particular measure. For example, Education Secretary Richard W. Riley dubbed an educational block grant bill called "Straight A's" (the Academic Achievement for All Act), which the Clinton administration opposed, the "straight F's" act.[1] Should companion bills (identical legislation) be introduced in the House and Senate to expedite legislative action? How many cosponsors (members who join together to introduce a bill) should be sought and who should they be? As Sen. Edward M. Kennedy, D-Mass., said about Sen. Strom Thurmond, R-S.C., "Whenever Strom and I introduce a bill together, it is either an idea whose time has come or one of us has not read the bill."[2]

Considerable pre-introductory jockeying on major bills also could go on behind the scenes as committees battle to assert jurisdiction over measures before they are introduced formally. Given the overlapping nature of committees' jurisdictional mandates, they understandably want to lay claim to significant topics, such as health care or communications technology, because doing so boosts the political clout of members who serve on the winning committees and garners them campaign contributions as well. As one scholar explained: "Committee jurisdictions are akin to property rights [over issues], and few things in Washington are more closely guarded or as fervently pursued."[3]

The complexity and interconnectedness of many contemporary issues almost guarantees that more than one committee will share jurisdiction over legislation. Furthermore, lawmakers recently have made wider use of so-called megabills, measures that are hundreds of pages long. The average

TABLE 3-1 From Bill to Law, 1979–1999

Congress		Bills Introduced		Bills Passed		Public Laws	Average Page Per Statute
		House	Senate	House	Senate		
96th	(1979–1981)	9,103	3,480	929	977	613	8.1
97th	(1981–1983)	8,094	3,396	704	803	473	9.2
98th	(1983–1985)	7,105	3,454	978	936	623	7.8
99th	(1985–1987)	6,499	3,386	973	940	664	10.8
100th	(1987–1989)	6,263	3,325	1,061	1,002	713	6.8
101st	(1989–1991)	6,683	3,669	968	980	650	8.9
102d	(1991–1993)	7,771	4,245	932	947	590	12.8
103d	(1993–1995)	6,647	3,177	749	682	465	16.2
104th	(1995–1997)	4,542	2,266	611	518	333	19.1
105th	(1997–1999)	5,014	2,718	710	586	394	18.4

SOURCE: Norman Ornstein, Thomas Mann, and Michael Malbin, *Vital Statistics on Congress, 1999–2000* (Washington, D.C.: AEI Press, 2000), 155, 157, 160.

number of pages per law has increased from two and a half in the 1950s to more than eighteen in the late 1990s (see Table 3-1). The contemporary Congress may pass fewer laws than before, but they are considerably larger.

The act of introducing a bill sets off a complex and variable chain of events that may or may not result in final passage. Although thousands of pieces of legislation are introduced in every Congress, a relatively small number become law. For example, of the 7,732 bills and joint resolutions introduced during the 105th Congress (1997–1999), only 394 (5.1 percent) became public law. Committees are the primary graveyard for most bills that die in Congress. Committees select from the vast number of bills introduced those that they feel merit further consideration.

CATEGORIES OF LEGISLATION

The winnowing process that occurs in committee suggests that the thousands of bills introduced in each Congress may be broken down roughly into three categories: bills having so little support that they are ignored and die in committee; noncontroversial bills that are expedited through Congress; and major bills that generate so much debate that they occupy the major portion of Congress's time. Legislative proposals take four forms: bill, joint resolution, concurrent resolution, and resolution. (See Glossary.)

Bills Lacking Wide Support

Bills having little support usually are introduced with no expectation that they will be enacted into law. Members introduce such bills for a variety of reasons: to go on record in support of a given proposal, to satisfy individual constituents or interest groups from the member's district or state, to convey a message to executive agencies, to publicize an issue, to attract media attention, or to fend off criticism during political campaigns. Once a member has introduced a bill, he or she can claim action on the issue and can blame the committee to which the bill has been referred for its failure to win enactment. Most of the bills introduced in each Congress fall into this category.

Noncontroversial Bills

Noncontroversial bills make up another large segment of the measures introduced. Examples are bills that authorize construction of statues of public figures, establish university programs in the memory of a senator, rename a national park, or name federal buildings after former members of Congress. Committees in both chambers have developed rapid procedures for dealing with such measures. These bills generally are passed on the floor without debate in a matter of minutes.

Major Legislation

Bills taking up the largest percentage of a committee's time have some or all of the following characteristics: they are prepared and drafted by executive agencies or by major pressure groups; they are initiated by committee chairmen or other influential members of Congress; they are supported by the majority party leadership; or they deal with issues on which a significant segment of public opinion and the membership of Congress believe some sort of legislation is necessary.

Bills having such characteristics do not necessarily become law. They also are unlikely to become law in the form in which they originally were introduced. Sentiment may be so sharply divided that they do not even emerge from committee. Nevertheless, these are the major bills before Congress each year. They may affect the wage earner's paycheck (taxes and Social Security) and the consumer's pocketbook (health insurance and electricity deregulation); they may be brought up repeatedly at presidential news conferences and covered in the electronic and print media. They are the bills on which Congress devotes the largest portion of its committee and floor time. These bills account for perhaps only a hundred or so of the thousands introduced in each Congress.

Executive Branch Bills. The president's leadership in the initial stages of the legislative process is pronounced. The administration's major legislative proposals are outlined in the president's annual State of the Union address, which is televised nationally during prime time and delivered before a joint session of Congress. In the weeks and months following the address, the president sends to Congress special messages detailing his proposals in specific areas, such as defense, education, and health. Bills containing the administration's programs are drafted in the executive agencies, and members of Congress, usually committee chairmen, are asked to introduce them simultaneously as companion bills in both chambers. It is customary in both chambers for the words "by request" to be printed in the *Congressional Record* by the sponsor's name to flag the measure as an administration initiative. Only representatives and senators, not the president or executive officials, may introduce legislation in Congress.

Influential Members' Bills. Bills supported by influential members stand a good chance of receiving attention in committee and at the other lawmaking stages. For example, Congress in 1999 modernized a sixty-six-year-old banking law—enacted during the Great Depression to create a wall between the banking and securities industry—to reflect technological and marketplace changes. The chairman of the Senate Banking Committee, Phil Gramm, R-Texas, was determined to move legislation to end this separation and permit businesses to provide banking, insurance, and securities services. Throughout the legislative process, Senator Gramm was instrumental in forging compromises among House and Senate members, executive officials, and rival industry groups. Sometimes the services of Speaker J. Dennis Hastert, R-Ill., and Senate Majority Leader Trent Lott, R-Miss., were required to get Gramm, House Banking Chairman Jim Leach, R-Iowa, and House

Commerce Chairman Tom Bliley, R-Va., to strike a deal during their bargaining sessions. But in the end, by many press accounts, it was Gramm's bulldog determination that enabled Congress to pass this landmark legislation after years of failure by other lawmakers who tried to do it.

Must-Pass Legislation. As lawmakers, members of Congress may not want to deal with controversial no-win public issues such as abortion or gun control. As politicians answering constituent mail, responding to inquiring journalists, and facing reelection, they may not be able to ignore them. Hence, members who are in basic agreement that legislation must be enacted to deal with a given problem often are in sharp disagreement over the solution. Under these circumstances, most members seek a compromise because they realize that some type of legislation is desirable or unavoidable. Money bills also fall into the category of must-pass legislation, as did the measures associated with the House Republicans' Contract with America.

BILL REFERRAL PROCEDURE

Once a bill is introduced it receives an identifying number. Measures introduced in the House are identified by the letters "HR" (for House of Representatives) and an accompanying number (see Box 3-1); Senate bills are identified by the letter "S" and a number. Usually, bills are assigned numbers according to the chronological order in which they are introduced. Occasionally, however, members will request the bill clerk to reserve a particular number. H.J. Res. 51 would admit the District of Columbia as the fifty-first state. S. 25 would ban .25 caliber bullets. S. 24 would exempt people with acquired immune deficiency syndrome (AIDS) from a mandated twenty-four-month waiting period before receiving benefits under Medicare.[4]

Bill numbers also may be assigned for political and symbolic purposes. Customarily, party leaders of the House and Senate reserve the first several numbers for measures that are important party initiatives. When the 103d Congress began, with a Democrat in the White House for the first time in a dozen years, the Senate Democratic leadership introduced as their first five priority bills (S. 1, S. 2, and so on), such as the family and medical leave act, legislation that had been vetoed by GOP president George Bush. Every measure in the Contract with America received top billing during the 104th Congress, starting with H.R. 1, the Congressional Accountability Act (to apply federal workplace safety and other laws to Congress). When the 106th Congress (1999–2001) began, the House amended its rules to state: "The first ten numbers for bills (H.R. 1 through H.R. 10) shall be reserved for assignment by the Speaker when introduced on or before March 1, 1999." These top bill numbers reflect the majority party's priority agenda items.

Some measures are assigned the same number for several Congresses. This is often done to avoid confusion among legislators and others who have grown accustomed to referring to a proposal by its bill number. Informally,

---

BOX 3-1 **For the Record**

Under clause 2 of Rule XII, public bills and resolutions were introduced and severally referred, as follows:

By MR. CAMPBELL:
H.R. 4291. A bill to amend title 13, United States Code, to provide that decennial census questionnaires be limited to the basic questions needed to allow for an enumeration of the population, as required by the Constitution of the United States; to the Committee on Government Reform.

By MR. CANADY of Florida:
H.R. 4292. A bill to protect infants who are born alive; to the Committee on the Judiciary.

By MR. CANNON (for himself, MR. TALENT, and MR. THOMPSON of California):
H.R. 4293. A bill to amend title 18, United States Code, with respect to the employment of persons with criminal backgrounds by nursing homes; to the Committee on the Judiciary, and in addition to the Committee on Commerce, and Ways and Means, for a period to be subsequently determined by the Speaker, in each case for consideration of such provisions as fall within the jurisdiction of the committee concerned.

By MR. CARDIN:
H.R. 4294. A bill to amend the Internal Revenue Code of 1986 to modify the alternative minimum tax for estates in bankruptcy; to the Committee on Ways and Means.

By MS. CARSON (for herself and MR. BURTON of Indiana):
H.R. 4295. A bill to suspend temporarily the duty on Fluridone aquatic herbicide; to the Committee on Ways and Means.

SOURCE: *Congressional Record,* April 13, 2000, H2337.

---

many bills also come to be known by the names of their sponsors, such as Kennedy-Kassebaum (after Senators Edward Kennedy and Nancy Landon Kassebaum, R-Kan.)—a 1996 law permitting workers to take their health insurance with them from job to job. The name game also can be influenced by political considerations. In the lead-up to the November 2000 presidential contest, GOP representative H. James Saxon, N.J., introduced a bill to create the "Albert Gore Jr. Mud Dump Site" as a way to criticize Gore's environmental record.

With few exceptions, bills are referred to the appropriate standing committees.[5] The job of referral formally is the responsibility of the Speaker of the House and the presiding officer of the Senate, but usually this task is carried out on their behalf by the parliamentarians of the House and Senate.[6]

Precedent, public laws, turf battles, and the jurisdictional mandates of the committees as set forth in the rules of the House and Senate determine which committees receive what kinds of bills. As an example, the jurisdiction of the House Education and the Workforce Committee is listed in Table 3-2.

The vast majority of referrals are routine. Bills dealing with farm crops are sent to the House Agriculture Committee and the Senate Agriculture, Nutrition, and Forestry Committee; tax bills are sent to the House Ways and Means Committee and the Senate Finance Committee; and bills dealing with veterans benefits are sent to the Veterans' Affairs committees of each chamber.[7] Thus, referrals generally are cut-and-dried decisions. (House and Senate standing committees are listed in Box 3-2.)

Yet committees can and do clash over their jurisdictional prerogatives. Irate that the Ways and Means Committee chairman objected on turf grounds to a provision in an appropriations bill, the ranking Democrat on the Appropriations Committee, David R. Obey of Wisconsin, declared: "Ways and Means is the biggest octopus not only in this Capitol, but any capital in the world. Once in a while, something ought to escape its jurisdiction."[8] Or as Sen. Ernest F. Hollings, S.C., the ranking Democrat on the Commerce Committee, said about Banking Chairman Gramm's expansionist instincts: "He does everything in the world to come in on our jurisdiction."[9] Jurisdictional border wars influence the expansion or contraction of committees' authority. Some committees even have "staffers called 'border cops,' whose jobs involve protecting turf and looking for new areas to conquer."[10]

There are even cases of reverse turf wars. The House International Relations Committee and the House Appropriations Committee each fought to

---

TABLE 3-2 Jurisdiction of House Committee on Education and the Workforce

1. Child labor.
2. Columbia Institution for the Deaf, Dumb, and Blind; Howard University; Freedmen's Hospital.
3. Convict labor and the entry of goods made by convicts into interstate commerce.
4. Food programs for children in schools.
5. Labor standards and statistics.
6. Measures relating to education or labor generally.
7. Mediation and arbitration of labor disputes.
8. Regulation or prevention of importation of foreign laborers under contract.
9. United States Employees' Compensation Commission.
10. Vocational rehabilitation.
11. Wages and hours of labor.
12. Welfare of miners.
13. Work incentive programs.

SOURCE: *Constitution, Jefferson's Manual, and Rules of the House of Representatives of the United States, One Hundred Sixth Congress.*

BOX 3-2 **Standing Committees, 106th Congress**

Senate

Agriculture, Nutrition, and Forestry
Appropriations
Armed Services
Banking, Housing, and Urban
  Affairs
Budget
Commerce, Science, and
  Transportation
Energy and Natural
  Resources

Environment and Public Works
Finance
Foreign Relations
Governmental Affairs
Health, Education, Labor,
  and Pensions
Judiciary
Rules and Administration
Small Business
Veterans' Affairs

House

Agriculture
Appropriations
Armed Services
Banking and Financial Services
Budget
Commerce
Education and the Workforce
Government Reform
House Administration
International Relations

Judiciary
Resources
Rules
Science
Small Business
Standards of Official Conduct
Transportation and
  Infrastructure
Veterans' Affairs
Ways and Means

---

make a controversial proposal on international family planning the other panel's responsibility and not its own. Neither committee wanted to handle the nettlesome issue, "in part because of the [president's] veto threat but also because it creates conditions for a seemingly intractable battle between the House and Senate. While the House has repeatedly backed the abortion restrictions, the Senate has rejected them and kept them from becoming law." [11]

In the House, a member is not permitted to appeal referral decisions to the entire membership except in rare instances of erroneous referral. In the Senate, the rules allow an appeal to the full Senate by majority vote, but in practice such appeals do not take place. Disputes over referral in the Senate may be resolved informally through negotiation prior to the introduction of the bill in question. Senate (and House) party leaders sometimes request committees with overlapping responsibility to work together and reach a consensus on how their respective issues should be addressed in draft legislation. Party leaders may then assume responsibility for putting the different pieces together. Senate Majority Whip Don Nickles, R-Okla., for example, asked the chairmen with jurisdiction over tobacco—Agriculture, Commerce, Finance, Health, and Judiciary—to "develop consensus positions in legislative form" on how to reduce teen smoking.[12]

Legislative Drafting, Referral Strategy

Bill sponsors often consider how to draft legislation in such a fashion that it will be referred to a committee likely to act favorably on it instead of one where members are known to be less sympathetic. One technique is to word the measure ambiguously so that it can legitimately fall within the jurisdiction of more than one committee, thus presenting the Speaker or the presiding officer with some options in making the referral. (Both the House and Senate have full-time professional staff in their respective Office of Legislative Counsel who are skilled in converting members' ideas for laws into legislative language.)[13] Another technique is for members to introduce legislation that amends statutes over which their committees have jurisdiction. To lay claim to Internet legislation and avoid referral of their bill to the Commerce Committee, two House Judiciary Committee members drafted their measure to amend the Sherman Anti-Trust Act, which is within their panel's exclusive jurisdiction, and not the Telecommunications Act of 1996, which falls under the Commerce Committee. In the Senate, the Finance and the Health, Education, Labor, and Pensions (HELPS) committees claim jurisdiction in the area of health. Finance members can obtain health legislation by addressing health care in the context of changing relevant provisions of the tax code; HELPS members could write bills that focus on employer-sponsored health plans.

Knowledge of precedents is also important in influencing the referral of legislation. Typically, references to taxes in bills mean that they will be sent to the tax-writing committee (House Ways and Means or Senate Finance). To avoid referral of his bill (barring taxation of Internet commerce) to the Ways and Means Committee, Commerce Committee member Christopher Cox, R-Calif., took advantage of precedents stating that "so long as the bill is limited to the taxing powers of state and local governments, it is the domain of the Judiciary or Commerce Committees."[14]

The House and Senate parliamentarians regularly meet with congressional staffers (and even receive briefs from lobbyists regarding bill referrals) who are interested in having their measures referred to particular committees. The parliamentarians provide general advice on what language or terms to include in legislation so it will be referred to preferred committees. "A great deal of our time in the office is spent dealing with drafts of bills," stated the Senate parliamentarian, "the committee to which they would be referred, advising staff on what to include and what to delete if in fact they have a preference in terms of committee referral."[15]

These bill drafting techniques and others are the exceptions and not the rule. Committees guard their jurisdictional turfs closely, and the parliamentarians know and follow the precedents. Only instances of genuine jurisdictional ambiguity provide opportunities for the legislative draftsman and referral options for the Speaker and the presiding officer of the Senate to bypass one committee in favor of another.

Referral to Several Committees

The contents of many bills cut across the jurisdiction of several committees so that deciding where to refer a bill sometimes is difficult. Committees' jurisdictional mandates often are ambiguous or overlap in various issue areas. For example, House rules assign the Committee on International Relations jurisdiction over international economic policy; Commerce handles foreign commerce generally; and Ways and Means considers reciprocal trade agreements. Committees often share jurisdiction—formally or informally. For instance, to minimize clashes on referrals, the chairmen of the House Armed Services and the House Transportation and Infrastructure Committees developed a memorandum of understanding explaining their agreement as to how matters involving the merchant marine would be divided between them. As the chairmen wrote: "In general, matters relating to merchant marine activities will be referred to the [Armed Services] Committee if the national security aspects of the matter predominate over transportation and other merchant marine aspects." [16] This type of informal intercommittee referral agreement will be honored by the parliamentarian.

The Senate has long permitted the practice of multiple referral, assigning legislation to two or more committees. There are three types of multiple referral: joint referral of a bill concurrently to two or more committees; sequential referral successively to one committee, then a second, and so on; and split referral of various parts of a bill to different committees. Sometimes multiple referrals are used in combination—after committees report a multireferred bill another panel might obtain a sequential referral, typically for a designated time period.

The Senate makes infrequent use of multiple referrals. Measures normally are sent to a single committee as determined by the panel that has jurisdiction over the "subject matter which predominates," the referral criterion specified for the Senate in the Legislative Reorganization Act of 1946. However, multiple referrals can be implemented either by unanimous consent or upon a joint motion made by the majority and minority leaders (to date never employed). An example of the unanimous consent method occurred on February 2, 2000, upon a request made by Sen. George V. Voinovich, R-Ohio:

> Mr. President, I ask unanimous consent that when the Governmental Affairs Committee reports S. 1977, the bill then be sequentially referred to the Committee on Finance for a period of up to 45 days during which the Senate is in session. I further ask unanimous consent that if the bill is not reported by the end of that period, it be discharged from the Finance Committee and placed back on the calendar.

No senator objected to this sequential referral. The Senate normally grants such requests because senators who offer them usually have worked out an agreement previously with all interested parties—committee chairmen, party leaders, and other members concerned about the bill. By the time the bill is introduced the appropriate bases have been touched; thus no senator is likely to object to the multiple referral. On a major tobacco bill, Senate Majority Leader Lott won the unanimous consent of the Senate to permit the Finance Committee to have a one-day sequential referral of the measure, which had been reported by the Commerce Committee. Finance members wanted a brief opportunity to review tobacco-related issues that fell within their jurisdiction.[17]

Until 1975 House precedents dictated that the Speaker could refer a bill to only one committee. That year, flexibility was injected into the bill-referral process by two changes in the rules. First, the Speaker was permitted to refer a bill to more than one committee through joint, sequential, or split referral. (Split referrals have been used infrequently because the interlocking character of bills makes them difficult to divide into parts.) This authority augments the Speaker's power by enabling him to delay (sending a bill to several panels) or expedite (fixing committee reporting deadlines) action on legislation. Second, the Speaker, subject to approval of the House, was permitted to create ad hoc committees to consider measures that overlap the jurisdictions of several committees.

Speaker Thomas P. "Tip" O'Neill Jr., D-Mass., exercised this option in 1977 by creating an Ad Hoc Energy Committee to expedite action on the Carter administration's complex energy proposals. The ad hoc committee was composed of members selected from the five committees to which various parts of the energy proposal initially had been referred.[18] In the Senate, the administration's 1977 energy proposals were referred to the Finance Committee and the Energy and Natural Resources Committee. The Senate has no formal rule providing for the creation of ad hoc committees by party leaders. (House and Senate party leaders may create on their own authority partisan or bipartisan task forces or other ad hoc devices for considering legislation.)

In 1977 House rules were amended to permit the Speaker to impose committee-reporting deadlines during the initial referral of measures. Further, the Speaker announced on January 3, 1983, his intention "in particular situations to designate a primary committee among those to whom a bill may be jointly referred, and may impose time limits on committees having a secondary interest following the report of the primary committee."

In 1995 the majority Republicans abolished joint referrals (retaining sequential and split references) and added to House rules the requirement that the Speaker shall "designate a committee of primary jurisdiction upon the initial referral of a measure to a committee."[19] This change was designed in part to achieve greater committee accountability for legislation while retaining significant flexibility for the Speaker in determining whether, when, and how long additional panels will receive the legislation. The House parliamentarian refers to this new form of multiple referral as an additional initial referral. Such referrals occur in this way:

> H.R. 3897. A bill to provide for digital empowerment, and for other purposes; to the Committee on Education and the Workforce, and in addition to the

Committees on Commerce, Banking and Financial Services, and Ways and Means, for a period to be subsequently determined by the Speaker, in each case for consideration of such provisions as fall within the jurisdiction of the committee concerned.[20]

For H.R. 3897, the Committee on Education and the Workforce is the primary committee of jurisdiction; the other committees obtain the measure on an additional initial basis. Secondary panels can consider measures before the primary committee, but their action does not force action on the part of the primary committee. However, once the primary committee files its report on a bill, the Speaker imposes time limits for action on the other panels. (During the period of joint referrals, it was the practice that all committees that simultaneously received a measure had to report it before the bill was eligible for floor consideration. At times, this was a formula for stalemate.) Committees may also waive their right to consider a measure, or particular sections, via a sequential referral in the interest of expediting legislation and without their decision constituting a referral precedent when comparable measures are subsequently introduced on the topic (see Box 3-3).

Several observations may be made about multiple referral. First, contemporary problems tend to have repercussions in many areas; thus more and more of the major bills coming before Congress—particularly those in new problem areas—will be candidates for multiple referral. Second, to the extent that multiple referral is chosen as an option, the decentralized nature of congressional decision making is reinforced. Third, every time another committee is added to the legislative process, additional opportunities arise for delay, negotiation, compromise, and bargaining. Fourth, multiple referrals may promote effective problem solving as several committees bring their expertise to bear on complex issues. Fifth, on the one hand, when the Speaker designates a panel as primary, he knows which committee to call to get action. On the other hand, multiple referrals sometimes require the Speaker to get involved in mediating and resolving jurisdictional claims or disputes between or among committees. Finally, multiple referrals are a growth area in the House. From 6 percent of all House measures introduced during the 94th Congress (1975–1977), multiple referrals climbed to 18 percent of all measures introduced by the 102d Congress (1991–1993). Even with the multiple referral change instituted during the 104th Congress, about 23 percent (347 of 1,510) of the measures introduced during the first one hundred days were assigned to two or more committees. "One bill, one committee" no longer applies to the extent that it once did. With growing frequency, the processing of legislation has become "one bill, many committees," including multiple subcommittee review within the parent committees.

CONSIDERATION IN COMMITTEE

Once a bill has been referred, the receiving committee has several options. It may, for example, consider and report (approve) the bill, with or without

---

BOX 3-3   A Jurisdictional Accommodation

Following is a letter written from House Commerce Committee Chairman Thomas J. Bliley Jr., R-Va., to House Judiciary Committee Chairman Henry J. Hyde, R-Ill., pertaining to the sequential committee referral of H.R. 775.

HOUSE OF REPRESENTATIVES,
COMMITTEE ON COMMERCE,
Washington, DC, May 10, 1999.

Hon. HENRY J. HYDE,
Chairman, Committee on the Judiciary,
Washington, DC

DEAR HENRY: I am writing with regard to H.R. 775, the Year 2000 Readiness and Responsibility Act.

Although the Committee on Commerce did not receive a named additional referral of H.R. 775 upon introduction, the Speaker has nevertheless granted my Committee a sequential referral of the bill. This sequential referral results from provisions in the introduced legislation within the Commerce Committee's jurisdiction pursuant to Rule X of the Rules of the House of Representatives. As you know, during the markup of H.R. 775, your Committee adopted amendments which eliminate the Commerce Committee's jurisdictional concerns over these provisions.

Because of the importance of this legislation, I recognize your desire to bring it before the House in an expeditious manner. I will therefore agree to discharge the Commerce Committee from further consideration of H.R. 775. By agreeing to waive its consideration of the bill, however, the Commerce Committee does not waive its jurisdiction over H.R. 775. In addition, the Commerce Committee reserves its right to seek conferees during any House-Senate conference that may be convened on Y2K legislation. I ask for your commitment to support any such request with respect to matters within the Rule X jurisdiction of the Commerce Committee.

I request that a copy of this letter be included as part of the record during consideration of the legislation on the House floor.

Sincerely,
TOM BLILEY,
Chairman

SOURCE: *Congressional Record,* May 12, 1999, H3014.

---

amendments or recommendation, and send it to the full House or Senate. It may rewrite the bill entirely, reject it, or simply refuse to consider it. Failure of a committee to act on a bill usually is equivalent to killing it. When a committee does report a bill, the House or Senate often accepts its main thrust even when the chamber amends the bill on the floor.

There are several reasons for this general deference to the committee's decisions. Committee members and their staffs have a high degree of expertise on the subjects within their jurisdiction, and a bill comes under its sharpest congressional scrutiny at the committee stage. Therefore, a bill that has survived the scrutiny of the experts likely will be given serious consideration on the floor by the generalists of the House and Senate.

A committee's decision not to report a bill generally will be respected by the chamber as a whole. After all, if the experts have decided not to approve a bill, why should their decision be second-guessed? Furthermore, the general impact of the rules in both chambers—particularly those of the House—is to "protect the power and prerogatives of the . . . committees . . . by making it very difficult for a bill that does not have committee approval to come to the floor."[21] Formal procedures are in place for overturning committee decisions or even bypassing committees, but these procedures are employed infrequently and are seldom successful. In addition, other ways are available to circumvent committees.

When a committee decides to take up a major bill, the full committee may consider it immediately. But more often the chairman assigns the bill to a subcommittee for study and hearings. The subcommittee usually schedules public hearings on the bill, inviting testimony from interested public and private witnesses. Or the subcommittee may decide not to schedule hearings if executive branch officials or interest groups strongly oppose the legislation. After the hearings have concluded, the subcommittee meets to mark up the bill; that is, to consider line by line and section by section the bill's specific language before sending it to the full committee. The subcommittee may approve the bill unaltered, amend it, rewrite it, or block it altogether. The panel then reports its recommendations to the full committee.

When the full committee receives the bill, it may repeat the subcommittee's procedures, in whole or in part, or it may simply ratify the subcommittee action. If the committee decides to send the bill to the House or Senate, it justifies its actions in a written statement called a report, which must accompany the bill.

On a major legislative proposal the entire committee process may stretch over several Congresses, with a new bill (containing identical or similar provisions) introduced at the beginning of each Congress. For example, the struggle to enact controversial legislation dealing with immigration reform, clean air, gun control, or health care can take several consecutive Congresses. Decades may pass before some bills become public law. For other legislation, the process can be compressed into a very short time. In less than twenty-four hours, both houses passed and the president signed into law legislation stopping a nationwide rail strike in 1991 "by mandating further mediations between labor and management."[22]

THE COMMITTEE CHAIRMAN'S ROLE

To a large extent, the options available to a committee in dealing with a bill are exercised by the chairman, who has wide discretion in establishing the committee's legislative priorities. The chair's sources of authority include control of the committee's legislative agenda, control over referral of legislation to the subcommittees, management of committee funds, control of the committee staff and committee facilities, and the designation of majority party conferees. As a House Banking chairman said, the "real power" of the chairmen is "to set the agenda, mark the course and lead."[23]

The chairman usually has had a long period of service on the committee and is likely to be better informed than most other members on the myriad of issues coming before the committee. The chairman often is privy to the leadership's plans and policies, especially the Speaker's or the Senate majority leader's legislative objectives. Chairmen can use these and other resources to delay, expedite, or modify legislation.

A chairman who opposes a bill may simply refuse to schedule hearings on it until it is too late to finish action on the bill during the session. The same result can be achieved by allowing the hearings to drag on. A chairman having strong negative feelings about a bill can instruct the committee staff to stack the witnesses testifying against it. He also may ask witnesses holding favorable views to submit statements instead of having them appear in person.[24] In the case of welfare reform hearings during the mid-1990s, some opponents of the legislation were almost excluded from the process. "We had to fight to testify," remarked a staff aide for Catholic Charities, "and when we did it was 8 o'clock at night after almost all the members and all the press had gone."[25]

Committee members who are likely to raise dilatory questions or employ obstructive tactics may be recognized before others. Through control of committee funds and the power to hire and fire most staffers, the chairman can block action on a bill by directing the staff to disregard it.[26]

A chairman who favors a bill can give it top priority by mobilizing staff resources, compressing the time for hearings and markups, and, in general, encouraging expeditious action by committee members. Chairmen sometimes bypass the public hearing stage entirely and proceed directly to full committee markup. Chairmen are typically the chief agenda-setters of committees. They employ this prerogative to powerfully influence the form in which bills are reported to the House or Senate as well as the timing of floor action on their bills.

The ranking minority party member on a committee also has certain prerogatives. He or she controls the hiring and firing of minority staff aides; recommends minority party conferees; acts as the minority side's spokesperson to the press and media; influences, depending on his or her relationship with the committee leader, the panel's agenda of activities; and designates the minority floor manager for legislation reported by the committee. Like committee chairmen, ranking members devise parliamentary strategy, anticipate amendments, ensure the attendance of their members, mobilize winning coalitions, and coordinate their approach to markups with the central party leadership.

The Chairmen in Perspective

The general picture of a committee chairman as an almost omnipotent figure underwent modification during the 1970s. Until then, the chairmen were the central figures in the legislative process, holding power equaled only by a few party leaders of great influence, such as House Speaker Sam Rayburn, D-Texas (1913–1961; Speaker 1940–1947, 1949–1953, 1955–1961), or Senate Majority Leader Lyndon B. Johnson, D-Texas (Senate 1949–1961; majority leader 1955–1961). The chairmen's power was gradually trimmed under pressure from newly elected members and from some senior members who wanted to equalize the distribution of power. During the 1970s, Congress approved several fundamental changes that ended the nearly absolute authority enjoyed by committee chairmen.

The most significant change came when both parties modified the seniority system, specifically the practice of automatically selecting as chairman the majority party member with the longest continuous service on the committee. Seniority meant that chairmen normally came from safe congressional districts, were repeatedly reelected, and served until their retirement or death. Because many safe districts during the 1950s and 1960s were in the conservative Democratic South, chairmen often were sharply at odds with Democratic presidents, congressional leaders, and northern Democrats. Nevertheless, as seniority then was practiced, the chairmen could not be removed. They were able to use their entrenched positions to block civil rights and social welfare legislation proposed by Democratic administrations.

Today, because of party rule changes made by Democrats and Republicans in each chamber, all committee chairmen (and ranking minority committee members) are subject to secret ballot election within the confines of their party caucus or conference. Chairmen and ranking minority committee members are now accountable for their actions to at least a majority of their party's caucus or conference. When Democrats were in charge of the House, they even deposed committee and subcommittee chairmen and elected other party members in their stead. With the GOP takeover of Congress following the 104th Congress, the House amended its rules to impose a six-year term limit on committee and subcommittee chairmen. Thus, regardless of whether Republicans or Democrats win control of the House following the November 2000 elections, many committee leadership changes will take place in the 107th Congress (2001–2003). (Senate Republicans imposed via a party rule, starting in 1997, a six-year term limit for their committee and subcommittee chairmanships.) Speaker Newt Gingrich, R-Ga., ignored seniority and named several committee chairmen who were ideologically in sync with the leadership's views and agenda.

The one-person rule that previously characterized many House and Senate committees has evolved toward greater bargaining and negotiation among the chairman, other members of the committee, and party leaders. Nevertheless, committee chairmen remain crucial figures in the legislative process. As House Commerce Chairman Thomas J. Bliley Jr., R-Va., stated, "The chairman controls the staff, the chairman has the right to name the subcommittee chairmen and has much more power than the . . . Democratic chairmen [had] when they were in the majority."[27] (Bliley, who faced the six-year limit on his chairmanship, retired at the end of the 106th Congress.) Because Congress functions primarily through its committees, the person who heads one has considerable influence over the advancement or defeat of legislation.

HEARINGS

Ostensibly, hearings are important primarily as fact-finding instruments. Witnesses from the executive branch, concerned members of Congress, interest group spokesmen, academic experts, and knowledgeable citizens appear before the committee to give it their opinions as to the merits or pitfalls of a given piece of legislation. From this encounter the committee members gather the information needed to act as informed lawmakers. Hearings also aid members in determining whether new laws are needed or whether changes in the administration of existing laws will be sufficient to resolve problems. "Legislation need not always be the answer," remarked then senator Al Gore, D-Tenn. "In many areas, the most important missing ingredient is attention, and an elevated awareness of the problem can be a very successful outcome of hearings."[28] Committee members are sometimes more interested in making opening statements or engaging colleagues in discussions, especially at high-profile hearings, than listening to witnesses.

Much information is available to committee members long before the hearings take place. Major bills usually have been the subject of public debate and media coverage. The positions of the administration and the special interest groups are well known, and, in all likelihood, executive branch officials and pressure group lobbyists have already presented their views to committee members and staff aides. The members themselves often have strong partisan positions on the legislation and thus may have little interest in whatever additional information emerges from the hearings.[29] Hearings often are poorly attended by committee members, and interruptions are common because of floor votes or quorum calls.

Hearing Formats

Committees regularly utilize five hearing formats—traditional, panel, joint, field, and high-tech—when they conduct legislative (focusing on a particular bill or set of related measures), oversight, investigative, or confirmation hearings. For each type, staff research and preparatory work precede the committee hearings. Committee aides, for example, may interview witnesses in advance, compile research and documentary materials, and prepare notebooks for committee members to use at the hearings. These notebooks may list the questions—and the answers—used in probing the witnesses. Explained a committee staff director:

> We write the question. Under the question we write the answer. This is the answer we expect to get on the basis of the staff research that has gone before. The Member who asks the question knows what the witness has told us in the weeks and weeks of preparation; and he knows he should get the same information. If he does not get that information, then he has the answer in front of him and he can ad lib the questions that solicit that information or refute it.[30]

Sometimes hearings can be perfunctory, particularly where similar legislation has been before the committee for several years in succession. Witnesses usually read or summarize from prepared texts, while the committee members present often feign interest or simply look bored until the statement has been presented. Once the formal testimony is completed, each committee member, usually in order of seniority, will ask the witness questions. House rules allot at least five minutes per member to question witnesses. House rules also provide that the chairman or ranking minority member may designate specific committee members or staff to conduct extended questioning of up to thirty minutes per side per witness. Senate rules have no such provisions. Instead, each committee establishes its own rules governing internal procedures. For example, the rules of the Senate Energy and Natural Resources Committee give each member five minutes to question witnesses until all members have had an opportunity to ask questions. (Several comparable House and Senate rules that govern the hearings process for most committees are presented in Box 3-4.)

Committees also conduct joint hearings (with other panels or with the other body), field hearings (away from Capitol Hill), and panel sessions where two or more witnesses of similar or divergent views are arrayed at a table in front of the committee members. Microsoft's Bill Gates in 1998 testified before the Senate Judiciary Committee in a panel setting with other computer chief executive officers who were hostile to Gates's alleged monopolistic practices. To foment some rhetorical fireworks, the committee staff deliberately placed Gates next to his chief antagonist. Congress is also increasing its use of high-tech or interactive hearings, during which witnesses located around the United States or around the world can testify before House or Senate committees via, for example, video teleconferencing. The House Agriculture Committee became "the first congressional panel to broadcast its proceedings in live audio format over the Internet."[31] (A House rule requires committees to "make [their] publications available in electronic form to the maximum extent feasible.") Committees even hold prehearings to assess privately issues that witnesses will discuss later during the public sessions.

Box 3-4   Selected Formal Rules Governing Hearing Procedures

Although House and Senate committees have wide latitude in how they organize and conduct hearings, formal rules in each chamber regulate these proceedings. Several of the most important rules for committee hearings are identified below.

Notice. The committee chairman shall publicly announce the date, place, and subject matter of a committee hearing at least one week before the commencement of the hearing. House rules permit this rule to be waived either with the concurrence of the chairman and ranking minority member or by majority vote of the committee. Senate rules permit the notice rule to be waived if the committee determines that good cause exists to begin a hearing at an earlier date.

Openness. Hearings shall be open to the public and the media. Each chamber has provisions that enable committees or subcommittees to close the hearings but only for certain enumerated reasons, such as endangering national security, compromising sensitive law enforcement information, or defaming or disgracing an individual.

Quorum. House rules stipulate that committees may fix the number of members who must be present to take testimony, but it may not be less than two. Senate rules allow committees to set any number who may be present to take testimony, including just one senator.

Witness Requirements. Witnesses are required, unless there is good cause for noncompliance, to submit in advance copies of their written testimony to the committee. House rules also require nongovernmental witnesses to file a curriculum vitae and to disclose the amount and source of any federal grant or contract they might have received during the current and two preceding years.

Broadcasting. House rules state that whenever any committee or subcommittee hearing is open to the public, those proceedings shall be open to coverage by radio or television or both. Senate rules provide that any public hearing of a committee or subcommittee may be broadcast under the terms specified in committee rules.

Minority Party's Right to Call Witnesses. The minority party on a committee is entitled, upon request made to the chairman by a majority of the minority members before the completion of the hearing, to call witnesses of its choosing to testify on the subject of the hearing for at least one day.

Purposes of Hearings

Despite their limitations, hearings remain an integral part of the legislative process. They provide a permanent public record of the position of committee members and the various interested groups on a legislative proposal.

Preparation of congressional testimony is regarded as an important function by executive agencies and interest groups. Above all, hearings are important because members of Congress believe them to be important. The decision to hold hearings is often a critical point in the life of a bill. Measures brought to the floor without first being the subject of hearings are likely to be the targets of sharp criticism. (Policies not subject to hearings often become public law, however. Offering legislative proposals as floor amendments, incorporating them into conference reports, or burying them in megabills are among the techniques for bypassing committee hearings.) The sanctity of the committee stage is based on the assumption that the experts—the committee members—carefully scrutinize a proposal, and hearings provide a demonstrable record of that scrutiny.

Hearings are perhaps the most orchestrated phase of policy making and usually are part of any overall strategy to get bills enacted into law. Committee members and staff typically plan with care who should testify, when, and on what issues. Ralph Nader's testimony before several congressional committees on his 1965 best-selling book, *Unsafe at Any Speed,* led to passage of the Traffic Safety Act of 1966. The testimony of celebrity witnesses, such as movie stars, television personalities, or professional athletes, is a sure-fire way to attract national attention to issues. "I haven't seen anything like this in the 30 days we have had hearings," declared a Senate subcommittee chairman about the extensive press coverage when actress Elizabeth Taylor testified on the need for more money for AIDS research.[32] Or as Sen. Arlen Specter, R-Pa., put it: "Quite candidly, when Hollywood speaks, the world listens. Sometimes when Washington speaks, the world snoozes."[33]

Witnesses who have experienced issues or problems firsthand and can tell their stories to lawmakers are especially sought after, because they put a human face on public problems.

> Speaking to a congressional committee [considering the issue of child care], a 10-year-old girl whose parents could no longer afford day care said, "Some things scare me when I'm alone—like the wind, the door creaking, and the sky getting dark fast." "This may not seem scary to you," she told the committee of adults, "but it is to young people who are alone."[34]

During Senate Finance Committee hearings in 1998 about the abuses of taxpayers by the Internal Revenue Service (IRS), not only did ordinary taxpayers recount their "horror stories" of tax collection efforts by the IRS, but IRS employees "disguised behind screens, with altered voices for some witnesses," provided high drama to the proceedings.[35] Committees often want witnesses who will provide a broad coalition of endorsements for their predetermined position and promote political and public support for this course of action.

Hearings serve other functions as well. They may be used to assess the intensity of support or opposition to a bill, to gauge the capabilities of an executive agency official, to publicize the role of politically ambitious committee chairmen and members, to allow citizens to express their views to their representatives, to promote new ideas or agendas, to assert the jurisdictional reach of committees, or to build public support for an issue. The Senate's constitutional duties mean that it holds hearings on advising and consenting to treaties and nominations. The Judiciary Committee's televised hearings on controversial Supreme Court nominations—Robert H. Bork in 1987 and Clarence Thomas in 1991—involve extensive preparation on both the nominee's and chairman's part. The nominees often participate in mock hearings called "murder boards" to get ready for the tough questions they may face. Similarly, the Judiciary chairman may also prep by having himself videotaped during mock questioning of someone playing the role of the nominee to assess the clarity and value of his questions.

Congress also uses oversight and investigative hearings to explore problems and issues and assess program performance. These hearings serve several purposes. They promote efficient program administration, secure information needed to legislate, and inform public opinion. Millions of American households watched on television the unfolding drama of the 1954 Army-McCarthy hearings, the 1957 hearings into corruption of the Teamsters Union, the Senate Foreign Relations Committee's hearings during the 1960s on the Vietnam War, the Watergate hearings of the 1970s, the 1987 Iran-contra hearings, and the late 1990s presidential impeachment hearings. Investigative hearings often prompted the drafting of legislation to deal with the problems that were uncovered and subsequently led to more hearings on the legislation itself. On occasion, individual members conduct ad hoc, or informal, investigative hearings of their own.

Importance of Timing

The chairman's control over the timing and duration of hearings is an important factor in deciding a bill's fate. Postponing or dragging out hearings is an obvious ploy if the chairman is opposed to a bill or wants it extensively modified. Sometimes a delay will help the bill's chances. This might be true if sentiment in favor of the bill is much stronger in the other chamber than in the chairman's. Another possibility is that both House and Senate chairmen supporting a bill may want to expedite hearings because of time pressures.

Committee chairmen take into account a variety of factors when scheduling hearings. Among the more important are the positions of the White House, pressure groups, executive agencies, the other chamber, party leaders, and principal legislators; the climate of public opinion; the intensity of feeling of the major participants; and the mix of witnesses who can create momentum and support for legislation.

THE MARKUP

Some time after the conclusion of the hearings, the committee or subcommittee may meet to mark up the bill. (The origin of the word *markup* probably stems from lawmakers making marks on the bill—changing its terminology and phraseology.) Here committee members decide whether the legislation should be rewritten, either in whole or in part. The chairman's task is to keep the committee moving, getting unanimous agreement on as many sections of the bill as possible, trying to resolve differences through compromise, and sensing when to delay or speed up matters. Committee chairmen regularly line up leadership backing for their committee's bill, insert special provisions in legislation to win members' support, or accommodate interest group or agency officials by permitting them to make presentations during committee markup. Because the chairman is likely to be responsible for managing the bill on the floor, he or she will try throughout the markup to gather as much support within the committee as possible. A sharp split among the committee members may seriously damage chances of passing the bill in the House or Senate.

Overview. As with the different kinds of hearings, committees utilize different kinds of markups that reflect their traditions and customs as well as the controversialism of the legislation. Chairmen sometimes schedule pre-markup sessions for the committee members, either on a partisan or bipartisan basis, to discuss possible revisions of the legislation and to develop a consensus on the bill. These informal and private sessions on major legislation are common for many congressional committees. On an overhaul of the Clean Air Act, for instance, the Senate Environment and Public Works Committee chairman "scheduled several seminars prior to the formal markup, to educate the members on the major issues and to try to develop a consensus among the members on the issues." [36] Other preparatory actions of chairmen or ranking minority members are to develop markup summaries (analyses of the bill, a list of which members or outside groups are for it or against it, and so on), to organize briefings for the legislative staff of individual committee members, to anticipate possible amendments and develop responses to them, to devise party strategy, and to know which members will be in attendance and where absent members can be reached.

Some committees closely adhere to formal parliamentary procedures; others conduct conceptual markups, where committee members agree generally on broad ideas or principles, and staff then draft the legal language for later review by the membership; and still other panels operate informally, largely by consensus, and in a bipartisan manner. Rules of the Senate Foreign Relations Committee even state: "Insofar as possible, [markup] proceedings of the Committee will be conducted without resort to the formalities of parliamentary procedure and with due regard for the views of all members." Some markups are sedate affairs while others are riven by partisan or substantive controversies.

Senate markups typically occur at the full committee level rather than in subcommittees. By contrast, House markups commonly occur at both the subcommittee and full committee level. A key reason for this bicameral difference is that senators are subject to greater workload and time pressures than the average House member. (Senators serve on about a dozen committees and subcommittees; House members sit on about a half-dozen panels.)

Whether in the House or Senate, markups are generally characterized by a greater degree of personal and parliamentary informality than proceedings in the chamber. As smaller entities, committees simply need less formality in their markup meetings. Moreover, in neither chamber are official parliamentarians assigned to the committees to assist in interpreting the rules. Committee and subcommittee chairmen often use their own experience and judgment in enforcing the rules or, if a particularly knotty procedural issue arises, they may request the advice of a majority committee staff aide knowledgeable in parliamentary matters or telephone the House or Senate parliamentarian and seek his counsel.

Rarely are points of order made on the floor against a bill's consideration on the grounds of defective committee procedure. For instance, unless a committee violated an explicit House rule, House precedents stipulate that the rules or procedures of committees are for those committees to interpret. Even if a committee directly violates a House rule, the Rules Committee can obviate points of order by waiving the relevant chamber rule. The more flexible Senate has a rule (the clean-up rule) that states if a committee follows proper procedure in reporting a bill to the floor—a quorum of panel members who vote in open session and in person—then challenges against consideration of the bill for violating other markup rules (holding secret sessions as a matter of convenience, for instance) will not be upheld. The markup, then, is where committee members redraft portions of the bill, attempt to insert new provisions and delete others, bargain over final language, and generally determine the final committee product.

Committee Markup Procedures.   House and Senate rules each distinguish between a quorum for markups and a quorum to report legislation. A quorum for markups consists of one-third of the membership; a majority quorum is required to report measures. Several other procedural issues suffuse House and Senate markups, such as the choice of vehicle, or document, to be used for markup purposes; the amendment process; the openness of markup sessions; and the conduct of votes.

Committee and subcommittee chairmen typically decide what document will be used for markup purposes. The choices include the bill as introduced and referred to the committee, a subcommittee-prepared product, the administration's proposal, a staff draft, or a legislative draft that is commonly called the chair's mark (his or her idea of what the committee members should focus upon). The selection is important for both substantive and procedural reasons. Substantively, the markup vehicle frames and shapes the policy discussion among the committee members. Procedurally, keeping items in the markup document often is easier than amending it, which can arouse public debate and controversy. As Sen. Ted Stevens, R-Alaska, phrased it:

"Everybody knows that . . . it is much more difficult to get something out of a committee bill than it is to put something into the committee bill." [37] Some committees make their markup document available on their panel's Internet home page.

Once the markup vehicle is before the committee and after the chair and members make brief opening statements, the committee is ready to consider amendments that it will recommend to either the House or Senate. (Only the full House or Senate has the authority to amend the text of legislation; thus, committee amendments are recommendations presented to each chamber.) In the House, the committee amendment process tracks closely the amendment process in the chamber at large. For example, the markup vehicle is commonly read (the reading is usually waived by unanimous consent) section by section with members recognized to offer their amendments after each section is pending before the panel. Members are accorded five-minutes to discuss amendments, and the chair alternates between the majority and minority side in recognizing members to offer amendments or to debate the pending proposals. In the Senate, committee members can offer amendments to any part of the bill, and few restrictions are made on debate. Dilatory actions in Senate markups are often harder to stop than in the House because senators in most committees can filibuster either by talking at length or by offering scores of amendments, even requiring that they be read in full. Further, to stop markups from continuing, senators sometimes invoke a Senate rule, which is usually routinely waived, that forbids markups after the Senate has been in session for two hours.

Most markups are conducted in open session. House and Senate rules also require committee reports accompanying legislation to contain the names of members voting for and against any amendments and motions to report the bill. However, important measures (tax or appropriations, for example) may still be discussed in private without much protest from the press, media, or others. Even proponents of openness admit that members can reach compromises and make tough decisions more easily when they are away from the glare of lobbyists sitting in the audience. Moreover, with scores of journalists and media representatives covering Capitol Hill, the results of closed sessions become quickly known once the committee opens its doors. "Closed sessions don't necessarily mean bad legislation and sunshine doesn't guarantee good laws," remarked a journalist. "Openness just makes the process and the results slightly easier to discern." [38]

During markups, House and Senate committees decide issues by voice vote, a show of hands, or roll-call votes. Senate chairmen may collect proxy votes to win key issues—often to the chagrin of the minority committee members who are in attendance. Proxy voting permits a committee member to cast a vote for an absent colleague. (Proxy voting is prohibited on the House or Senate floor.) As one account of a Senate markup noted:

> [The subcommittee chairman's] preparation paid off. The committee had been in session for more than five hours and about half the members had left. But

when the vote was taken, [the chairman] could supplement the eight votes he had in the room with nine proxies. The vote was 17-12.[39]

In 1995 the GOP-controlled House banned proxy voting in committees and subcommittees. During their forty consecutive years in the minority, Republicans long chafed under a system where their members attended committee markups yet were always outvoted by the handful of Democrats present because the chairman voted the proxies of absent colleagues. Abolishing proxy voting was designed to promote member participation in markups. However, many lawmakers with multiple committee assignments often have to sprint back and forth to cast votes in committees marking up bills simultaneously or run back and forth from committee markup sessions and the floor to cast votes. Their participation in markups is minimal. Further, some GOP chairmen have discovered midway "through a markup that they have suddenly lost control of the proceedings." For example, twenty Republican absences in the Banking Committee "allowed Democrats to win adoption of a GOP-opposed amendment."[40] Chairmen stall the proceedings while staff work furiously to round up enough majority committee members to carry the day.

Strategies during Markup. Committee chairmen and members use various strategies during the markup. To accelerate action on major legislation, chairmen can, for instance, schedule marathon markups that go on for weeks and that meet daily from early morning to late at night. Or chairmen might hold abbreviated markups to speed legislation to the floor. One ploy, sometimes used by opponents of a bill, is to add amendments to strengthen the measure. During markup of a gun control measure by the House Judiciary Committee, the National Rifle Association (NRA), the major lobbying group opposed to gun control, told its supporters in Congress that it would be easier to defeat a strong firearms proposal. "The way we look at it," said an NRA lobbyist, "the stronger the bill that comes out of committee, the less chance it has of passing on the floor."[41] Conversely, proponents of a strong bill might try to weaken it in committee so that it stands a better chance of winning majority support on the floor. Supporters then can try to persuade the other chamber or the House-Senate conference committee to strengthen the measure.

Another approach used by a bill's opponent is to offer a flurry of amendments to make a bill complicated, confusing, and unworkable for the executive branch agencies that would have responsibility for administering the law. Moreover, offering scores of amendments, or offering one huge amendment and insisting that it be read—slowly—in full, may stall the markup and grant opponents additional time to lobby against the legislation. For example, Sen. William V. Roth Jr., R-Del., sought to delay markup of a federal employees bill "by reading—slowly and deliberately—a lengthy statement explaining his opposition. He then offered seven amendments" and launched into a long explanation of each.[42] To prevent Republicans from conducting committee markups, minority House Democrats sometimes boycotted the meetings to delay or prevent drafting sessions from proceeding.

Mobilizing grass-roots support and targeting the states or districts of key committee members is often critical to the outcome of markups. During markup by Congress's tax-writing panels, special interests work diligently to shape the thinking of these committees. As one account noted:

> For several months, the lobbyists have been working behind the scenes trying to influence the outcome by personally talking with members and aides of the tax committees in both chambers and getting members of their lobbying coalitions to write and phone their Congressmen. To bolster their arguments, the lobbyists have hired independent research firms to produce analyses that show the impact of the proposed tax changes, and they have tried to mold public opinion through press releases and advertising campaigns.[43]

To win over opponents or skeptics, chairmen often willingly accept numerous amendments from their committee colleagues. In this way, these members develop a stake in the legislation and may stand united behind it on the House or Senate floor. The reverse strategy is to load down a bill with scores of costly add-ons so the legislation might sink of its own weight. "We might just as well kill the president's [health reform] bill with kindness" by adding costly and untenable amendments, said Rep. Marge Roukema, R-N.J., during a markup of the House Education Committee.[44]

Another tactic of committee chairmen who want to avoid votes on unfriendly or politically tailored amendments is to offer their own substitute proposal. Senate Democrats on the Budget Committee, for instance, wanted to force committee Republicans to vote on a tax cut plan put forward by 2000 GOP presidential hopeful Texas governor George W. Bush that many Republicans on the panel did not support. To avoid this embarrassing vote, Budget Chairman Pete V. Domenici, R-N.M., offered "his own substitute [amendment to negate the Democratic initiative], which would ask the new president to search for waste, fraud and abuse within the federal government and then apply such savings to a big tax cut."[45] Senator Domenici's parliamentary maneuver was successful.

An important factor affecting markup strategies in the Senate is the smaller size of its panels. "To get an amendment adopted [on my Senate subcommittee]," wrote Sen. Paul Simon, D-Ill., in 1985, "I need only two other votes of the five-member subcommittee. In the House, subcommittees with more than 20 members are common," which means greater effort in forging winning coalitions.[46]

Compromise during the committee markup—or at any stage of the legislative process—is more likely when the members recognize that some sort of legislation is necessary. The outcome of markups, with their tradeoffs, compromises, and complexities, may not be perfect, but it does reflect what attracted at least a majority vote of the panel members. As House Ways and Means Chairman Dan Rostenkowski, D-Ill., said after a tax markup: "We have not written perfect law. Perhaps a faculty of scholars could do a better job. A group of ideologues could have provided greater consistency. But

TABLE 3-3 Procedural Differences at Preliminary Stages of the Legislative Process

House	Senate
Bills are usually introduced before committee or floor action can proceed.	Committees may originate their own bills without first having measures sent to them.
No effective way to challenge the Speaker's (parliamentarian's) referral decisions.	Referrals are subject to appeals from the floor.
The Speaker is granted authority by House rules to refer bills to more than one committee.	Multiple referrals occur by unanimous consent, although the majority leader and minority leader can jointly offer a motion to that effect.
The Speaker is authorized, subject to House approval, to create ad hoc panels to consider legislation.	Neither the majority leader nor the presiding officer has authority under Senate rules to create ad hoc panels to process legislation.
Generally difficult to bypass committee consideration of measures.	Bypassing committee consideration of measures occurs more easily.
Floor action is sometimes less important for shaping policies than committee action.	Floor action is as important as committee action in decision making.

politics is an imperfect process."[47] Rep. Barney Frank, D-Mass., emphasized this point in describing coalition building on a controversial measure: "Our goal is to find something that's 60 percent acceptable to 52 percent of the members and I think we have a 75 percent chance of doing that."[48] Once committees conclude their markups, members often mobilize to achieve their objectives, such as lobbying colleagues and organizing pep rallies on Capitol Hill. Table 3-3 lists several major House-Senate differences regarding the introduction, referral, and committee consideration of legislation.

THE REPORT

Assuming that major differences have been ironed out in the markup, the committee then meets to vote on reporting the bill out of committee. House and Senate rules require a committee majority to be present for this purpose; otherwise, a point of order may be made on the floor that will force the bill to be returned to committee.

Bills voted out of committee unanimously stand a good chance on the floor. A sharply divided committee vote presages an equally sharp dispute on the floor. A bill is rejected if the committee vote is a tie.

Committees have several options when they vote to report, or approve, a bill. They may report the bill without any changes or with various amendments. Or a committee that has extensively amended a bill may instruct the chairman to incorporate the modifications in a new measure, known as a clean bill. This bill will be reintroduced, assigned a new bill number, referred back to the committee, and reported by the panel.

The clean-bill procedure is employed for various reasons, such as expediting floor consideration of legislation. Another factor involves germaneness. Provisions already in a bill are ipso facto considered to be germane; hence they are protected in the House against points of order. (Germaneness rules apply to proposed floor amendments and not to provisions in the bill itself.) Finally, a clean bill may reflect negotiated agreements between key committee members and executive officials.

Committees may take other actions besides favorably reporting a bill. They may report out a bill adversely (unfavorably), recommending that the bill not be passed by the full chamber, or they may report legislation without a formal recommendation, allowing the chamber to decide the bill's merits. In either case, the bill may be sent to the full chamber and scheduled for floor action. Committees adamantly opposed to a measure may decide not to take any action at all, thus blocking further consideration except through special procedures.

After the bill is reported, the chairman instructs the staff to prepare a written report. (House rules require a written report to accompany legislation; Senate rules do not impose that requirement, but it is informally observed in most cases.) The report describes the purposes and scope of the bill, explains the committee revisions, notes proposed changes in existing law, and, usually, includes the views of the executive branch agencies consulted. Committee members opposing the bill often submit dissenting, or minority, views. Any committee member may file minority, supplemental, or additional views, which are printed in the committee report. House and Senate rules also require committee reports to contain certain information, such as five-year cost estimates, oversight findings, and regulatory impact statements. Measures are open to points of order on the floor if their committee report fails to contain this material. A report may be more than a thousand pages long.

Reports are directed primarily at House and Senate members and seek to persuade them to endorse the committee's recommendations when the bill comes up for a floor vote. The reports are the principal official means of communicating a committee decision to the entire chamber. Committee reports are also used by executive officials to fathom legislative intent when they are interpreting ambiguous statutory phrases. Federal judges, too, examine committee reports and other aspects of legislative history (hearings, floor debates, and conference reports) when laws are challenged in court.

Some federal justices, most notably Supreme Court Justice Antonin Scalia, argue that legislative history should be minimized in the interpretation of ambiguous statutes. Instead of examining staff-written committee reports to determine what Congress intended, Justice Scalia argues, judges should consider only the exact text of the statute because it is that and not legislative history that lawmakers vote on. Justice Stephen G. Breyer, by contrast, answers "that no one claims that legislative history is in any strong sense 'the law,' but rather that it is useful in ascertaining the meaning of words in the statute." [49]

Reports are numbered, by Congress and chamber, in the order in which they are filed with the clerk of the House or Senate. (Thus, in the 106th Congress the first House report was designated as H. Rept. 106-1 and the first Senate report as S. Rept. 106-1. The first page of a report is shown in Figure 3-1.) Both the committee-reported bill and its accompanying report are then assigned to the appropriate House or Senate calendar to await scheduling for floor action.

BYPASSING COMMITTEES

A recent article by a well-known congressional journalist was titled the "Crackup of Committees." The author's lead sentence declared: "The congressional committees have lost their long-standing pre-eminence as the center of legislative ideas and debate." [50] Certainly many of today's committees are not as influential as they once were, such as during the 1950s and 1960s, when committee chairmen were independent powers who could usually mobilize winning coalitions behind their proposals. (See Box 3-5 on p. 105 with respect to the House Judiciary Committee.) Today, committee review of legislation is problematic on many key issues, partly because of partisan strife, narrow majorities, and independent-minded lawmakers. Committee power has diminished compared with party power.

Party leaders or individual members are not reluctant to employ a number of techniques to circumvent committee consideration of legislation, such as the use of partisan task forces to craft legislation or to propose changes in legislation after committees report their handiwork. Speaker Hastert and Senate Majority Leader Lott, for example, each appointed partisan task forces during the 106th Congress to produce legislation (the so-called patients' bill of rights) regulating health maintenance organizations. There are a number of other ways that committees may be bypassed in the House or Senate, such as attaching legislative riders to appropriations bills, having the House Rules Committee bring bills to the floor without committee hearings or markups, offering to pending legislation on the Senate floor nongermane amendments that embody the bills pigeonholed in committee, or adding new propositions to conference reports during bicameral negotiations on legislation.

Various overlapping reasons account for the tendency to circumvent committees, but five are among the most important. The first is time. A good example is the mid-1990s House Republican Contract with America. GOP leaders believed that committees had insufficient time to conduct hearings and markups and issue reports on the contract bills before the promised time period (one hundred days) for action ticked away. Thus, many of the contract

106TH CONGRESS *2d Session*	HOUSE OF REPRESENTATIVES	REPORT 106–563

HMONG VETERANS' NATURALIZATION ACT OF 2000

APRIL 6, 2000.—Committed to the Committee of the Whole House on the State of the Union and ordered to be printed

Mr. HYDE, from the Committee on the Judiciary,
submitted the following

R E P O R T

[To accompany H.R. 371]

[Including cost estimate of the Congressional Budget Office]

The Committee on the Judiciary, to whom was referred the bill (H.R. 371) to expedite the naturalization of aliens who served with special guerrilla units in Laos, having considered the same, reports favorably thereon with amendments and recommends that the bill as amended do pass.

TABLE OF CONTENTS

	Page
The Amendment	2
Purpose and Summary	3
Background and Need for the Legislation	3
Hearings	6
Committee Consideration	6
Vote of the Committee	6
Committee Oversight Findings	6
Committee on Government Reform Findings	6
New Budget Authority and Tax Expenditures	6
Congressional Budget Office Cost Estimate	7
Constitutional Authority Statement	8
Section-by-Section Analysis and Discussion	8
Agency Views	9

79–006

FIGURE 3-1 House Committee Report

BOX 3-5   Judicial Bypass

Taking a detour around the House Judiciary Committee, as GOP leaders did with gun control in 1999, has happened relatively often since 1995. Among the major instances:

- *Assault Weapons Ban.* In 1996 House Rules Committee Chairman Gerald B. H. Solomon, R-N.Y., ushered to the floor a bill to repeal the 1994 ban on certain dangerous weaponry.
- *Tax Increase Supermajority.* Although Judiciary has jurisdiction over constitutional amendments, it was skipped in a 1996 effort to require a two-thirds majority vote to increase taxes.
- *Term Limits.* The Contract with America plank regarding congressional term limits was written in Judiciary in 1995, but the panel's action was ignored when House leaders sent a new version to the floor.
- *Product Liability.* Judiciary Chairman Henry J. Hyde, R-Ohio, agreed that the Commerce Committee's version of a product liability bill should go to the floor in 1995.

On the biggest issue of recent years—the impeachment of President Bill Clinton in 1998–1999—Judiciary got full display, defeating proposals to set up a special committee.

SOURCE: Adapted from Mark Hankerson, "Judicial Bypass," *Congressional Quarterly Weekly Report,* June 12, 1999, 1354.

---

bills went to the floor without prior subcommittee or committee hearings and markups. Party leaders, too, may rush measures to the floor that are popular with the public or that lawmakers want to consider quickly. For instance, to provide immediate relief to consumers angry with the sharp increase in gasoline prices, Senate Majority Leader Lott on March 28, 2000, brought a bill to the floor temporarily cutting the federal gas tax. The legislation had not been reviewed by any committee.

A second reason is partisanship. Majority party leaders may want to avoid review by a committee divided by sharp partisan disagreements. In their estimation, the minority party should not be provided two opportunities—in committee and on the floor—to frustrate the majority and to showcase its agenda. The partisan infighting associated with committee consideration of a politically potent issue and the negative media coverage it will generate are something the majority leadership prefers to avoid.

A third factor involves committee gridlock. Factional disputes within the majority party, combined with strong resistance from the minority party, may prevent committees from reaching agreement on measures deemed important to the majority party. As a result, party leaders will intervene to bypass the stalled committee stage and bring the legislation to the floor. Occasions may arise, too, when committees are substantively out-of-sync with the policy preferences of their party or with political imperatives that require the House or Senate to act expeditiously on legislation.

A fourth reason is electoral salience. Certain compelling issues are of such political importance to the majority party in terms of their appeal to the general public or to their party's core supporters that the leadership will circumvent the committee process to keep tight control of them. The Speaker, for instance, could use his authority over the House Rules Committee to have his preferred version of a bill sent to the floor under debate and amendment procedures that advantage the majority party. The Senate majority leader might convene closed door drafting sessions or invoke a procedure (Rule XIV) that places a measure directly on the legislative calendar, preventing it from being referred to committee.

A fifth factor is consensus: the relevant committee of jurisdiction, and perhaps a majority of the membership or at least the majority party, supports circumvention. Committees may waive consideration on the grounds that they have conducted hearings and markups on the legislation for several successive Congresses. Some proposals, too, may be debated year after year by the House and Senate so that lawmakers are familiar with the pros and cons of the legislation. "This bill [heading directly to the floor] is pretty straightforward," remarked Rep. Clay Shaw, R-Fla. "I don't know that it needs much scrubbing by a committee."[51]

When a bill has been reported from committee, it is ready to be scheduled for floor action. Like the winnowing process that occurs in committee, scheduling involves the budgeting of congressional time. Important political choices must be made in determining the order in which bills will be considered on the floor, how much time will be devoted to each measure, and to what extent the full chamber will be permitted to reexamine a committee decision.

NOTES

1. June Kronholz, "GOP, Democrats Spar Over Education, As Law Comes Up for Reauthorization," *Wall Street Journal,* August 16, 1999, A16.
2. Julie Rovner, "Senate Committee Approves Health Warnings on Alcohol," *Congressional Quarterly Weekly Report,* May 24, 1986, 1175.
3. David C. King, *Turf Wars: How Congressional Committees Claim Jurisdiction* (Chicago, Ill.: University of Chicago Press, 1997), 11.
4. Philippe Shepnick, "Moynihan Is Champion Bill Writer," *The Hill,* March 10, 1999, 6.
5. On rare occasions a member introducing a bill may ask unanimous consent that it be passed. Unanimous consent is more likely to be granted in the Senate than in the House and only on a noncontroversial measure or one on which all members agree that immediate action is required.
6. Article I, Section 3 of the Constitution provides that the vice president is president of the Senate, but he infrequently presides over that body. The Constitution also provides for a president pro tempore, a largely honorary position elected by the majority party. By custom, that position is held by the most se-

nior member of the majority party. Usually, however, junior members designated by the majority leader preside over the daily sessions of the Senate. Each chamber has a parliamentarian, who is an expert on rules of procedure. During a session, the parliamentarians or one of their assistants are present to advise the chair on all points of order and parliamentary inquiries. They also provide technical assistance to members in drafting bills or motions.

7. Committee structure and jurisdiction are not identical in the House and Senate. The House has nineteen standing (permanent) committees; the Senate, sixteen.

8. *National Journal's CongressDaily/PM,* May 4, 1998, 6.

9. *CQ Daily Monitor,* March 1, 2000, 8.

10. David C. King, "The Nature of Congressional Committee Jurisdictions," *American Political Science Review* (March 1994): 49.

11. Carroll Doherty, "Abortion Controversy Stymies Two Foreign-Policy Bills," *Congressional Quarterly Weekly Report,* July 26, 1997, 1800.

12. *National Journal's CongressDaily/AM,* November 7, 1997, 8.

13. Lawrence E. Filson, *The Legislative Drafter's Desk Reference* (Washington, D.C.: CQ Press, 1992).

14. *National Journal's CongressDaily/PM,* April 24, 1998, 6.

15. "Senate Parliamentarian Can Control Course of Bills," *C-Span Update,* January 14, 1990, 6.

16. *Congressional Record,* January 30, 1995, H849.

17. *CQ Daily Monitor,* May 14, 1998, 15.

18. See Bruce I. Oppenheimer, "Policy Effects of U.S. House Reform: Decentralization and the Capacity to Resolve Energy Issues," *Legislative Studies Quarterly* (February 1980): 5–30; and David J. Vogler, "Ad Hoc Committees in the House of Representatives and Purposive Models of Legislative Behavior," *Polity* (Fall 1981): 89–109.

19. *Congressional Record,* January 4, 1995, H36.

20. *Congressional Record,* March 9, 2000, H921.

21. Randall B. Ripley, *Congress: Process and Policy* (New York: W.W. Norton, 1975), 75.

22. Mike Mills, "Hill Moves with Alacrity to End Rail Strike," *Congressional Quarterly Weekly Report,* April 20, 1991, 981.

23. *Congressional Record,* May 9, 1994, H3181.

24. Stacking was modified somewhat by the Legislative Reorganization Act of 1970, which gave the minority party on a committee at least one day in which to call witnesses. On issues where the committee members of both parties share similar views, however, opposing witnesses have limited opportunities to testify.

25. *Washington Post,* May 21, 1995, A4.

26. Members of Congress rely heavily on committee staff for assistance in organizing hearings, selecting witnesses, and drafting bills, as well as for many other key support functions. The chairman's control of committee staff therefore is an important resource in his control of the legislative process.

27. Kirk Victor, "Mr. Smooth," *National Journal,* July 8, 1995, 1759.

28. *Wall Street Journal,* April 11, 1986, 54.

29. Members unable to attend a committee session frequently assign committee staffers to attend the meeting and brief them later. Staff aides can ask questions of witnesses if authorized by committee rules or by the chairman.

30. *Workshop on Congressional Oversight and Investigations,* 96th Cong., 1st sess., H. Doc. 96-217, 25.

31. *Washington Post,* September 23, 1998, A23.

32. *Washington Post,* May 9, 1986, D8.

33. Bob Pool, "Survivors Take Stock of Gains against Cancer," *Los Angeles Times,* May 30, 1997, B1.

34. *Christian Science Monitor,* November 27, 1985, 28. See also Barbara Vobejda, "Children Show Congress Scars of Gun Violence," *Washington Post,* March 11, 1993, A16.

35. Jackie Calmes, "New Round of Senate Hearings on IRS Risks Overkill," *Wall Street Journal,* March 31, 1998, A24.

36. *State Government News,* April 1982, 4.

37. *Congressional Record,* July 20, 1983, S10430.

38. *Washington Post,* May 6, 1984, F5.

39. Ronald Elving, "Smoking Ban for Short Flights Likely to Ignite Senate Scrap," *Congressional Quarterly Weekly Report,* October 3, 1987, 2409.

40. *CQ Daily Monitor,* March 21, 2000, 1.

41. *Washington Post,* February 6, 1976, A6.

42. Elizabeth Palmer, "Roth's Parliamentary Moves Halt Hatch Act Reform," *Congressional Quarterly Weekly Report,* March 7, 1992, 534.

43. *New York Times,* October 15, 1985, D25.

44. Dana Priest and Spencer Rich, "Key Hill Committees Take Up Health Care Legislation," *Washington Post,* May 19, 1994, A23.

45. *National Journal's CongressDaily/AM,* March 30, 2000, 13.

46. Paul Simon, "Trying on the Senate for Size," *Chicago,* November 1985, 150.

47. *Washington Post,* November 25, 1985, A4.

48. *Washington Post,* February 24, 1988, A22.

49. Robert A. Katzmann, "Justice Breyer: A Rival for Scalia on the Hill's Intent," *Roll Call,* May 30, 1994, 5. See Joan Biskupic, "Congress Keeps Eye on Justices as Court Watches Hill's Words," *Congressional Quarterly Weekly Report,* October 5, 1991, 2863–2867; and Joan Biskupic, "Listening In on the 'Conversation' between Court and Congress," *Washington Post,* May 1, 1994, A4. See also Michael Koby, "The Supreme Court's Declining Reliance on Legislative History: The Impact of Justice Scalia's Critique," *Harvard Journal on Legislation* (Summer 1999): 369–395; and Michael Slade, "Democracy in the Details: A Plea for Substance over Form in Statutory Interpretation," *Harvard Journal on Legislation* (Winter 2000): 187–236.

50. Richard Cohen, "Crackup of Committees," *National Journal,* July 31, 1999, 2210.

51. *National Journal's CongressDaily/AM,* May 12, 1999, 11.

CHAPTER 4

Scheduling Legislation in the House

THE POWER of the Speaker of the House is the power of scheduling," stated Thomas P. "Tip" O'Neill Jr., D-Mass., who served more consecutive years as Speaker (1977–1987) than anyone else.[1] Scheduling floor activities in the House is fundamentally the prerogative of the Speaker and the majority party leadership. Consequently, the politics of scheduling can strongly influence a bill's fate. Determining when (if at all), what, how, and in which order measures are brought to the floor is part of the arsenal of legislative tools that the leadership uses to produce winning coalitions, provide political protection to members, mobilize bipartisan support, engineer a record of accomplishment, or advance its own partisan agenda.

Scheduling legislation for House floor debate may be simple or complex. Priorities for floor consideration of the bills reported from committee are established by the majority leadership (the Speaker, the majority leader, and the majority whip), sometimes in consultation with the minority leader. Numerous factors influence their decisions: House rules, budgetary timetables, bicameral considerations, election-year activities, the pressure of national and international events, the administration's programs, the leadership's policy and political preferences, and the actions of the House Rules Committee. All these elements interact as legislators, pressure groups, and executive agencies maneuver to get favored legislation on the floor.

Scheduling involves advance planning of annual recesses and adjournments, coordinating committee and floor action, providing a steady and predictable weekly agenda of business, anticipating legislative priorities during the end-game rush to adjourn, regulating the flow of bills to the floor during slack or peak periods, and devising a workload that takes into account members' family needs, such as scheduling recesses around school vacations. Scheduling even has some mystery as majority party leaders assess the political climate. As Jim Wright, D-Texas, who served as Speaker from 1987 to June 1989, once noted:

> In scheduling the program for the Congress one must be constantly aware of the importance of maintaining a little suspense. I learned this from Agatha Christie. Always hold something back and keep people guessing a little bit. And that is what we are doing with this bill, quite frankly. We are maintaining a little suspense in the schedule [while we determine the best time for taking up this legislation].[2]

The procedures for managing the flow of bills to the floor have evolved throughout the history of Congress and still undergo frequent change. At first glance, they may appear needlessly complex and cumbersome, but they have an internal logic and serve the needs of the House.

THE HOUSE LEGISLATIVE CALENDARS

The House maintains five legislative calendars, which aid in the scheduling of floor action. All measures reported from committee are assigned, in chronological order, by the clerk of the House to either Union, House, or Private calendars. In addition, measures may be placed on the Corrections or Discharge calendars.

Legislation dealing with raising, authorizing, or spending money is assigned to the Union Calendar (technically, the Calendar of the Committee of the Whole House on the State of the Union). Non-money measures, such as proposals to amend the Constitution, are put on the House Calendar. Bills of a private nature ("for the relief of"), those not of general application and usually dealing with individuals or specific entities, are assigned to the Private Calendar. The Speaker may assign bills on the Union or House Calendars to the Corrections Calendar. The Discharge Calendar lists bills removed from committees through special, and infrequently successful, procedures.

When the House is in session, members receive a daily document, the *Calendars of the United States House of Representatives and History of Legislation,* which lists all House as well as Senate measures that have been reported from committee (see Figure 4-1). Not every measure listed is called up and considered by the House.

Regardless of the legislative calendars, any lawmaker can ask unanimous consent at almost any time the House is in session to pass legislation. However, the Speaker in 1984

> established a policy of conferring recognition ["For what purpose does the gentleman (or gentlelady) rise?"] upon Members to permit consideration of bills and resolutions by unanimous consent only when assured that the majority and minority floor leadership and committee and subcommittee chairmen and ranking minority members have no objection.[3]

This policy still remains in effect. The Speaker's power of recognition is an unchallengeable prerogative of the chair.

MINOR AND NONCONTROVERSIAL BILLS

Legislation on the Corrections and Private calendars is in order only during special calendar days. The House also processes noncontroversial measures that are on the Union or House calendars under procedures that grant them privileged access to the floor during certain designated days of the month. These include measures brought to the floor under suspension of the rules and bills dealing with the District of Columbia.

ONE HUNDRED SIXTH CONGRESS

FIRST SESSION { CONVENED JANUARY 6, 1999
ADJOURNED NOVEMBER 22, 1999

SECOND SESSION { CONVENED JANUARY 24, 2000

CALENDARS

OF THE UNITED STATES
HOUSE OF REPRESENTATIVES
————————————AND————————————
HISTORY OF LEGISLATION

LEGISLATIVE DAY 40   CALENDAR DAY 41

Tuesday, May 2, 2000

PRIVATE CALENDAR—SUSPENSIONS

HOUSE MEETS AT 12:30 P.M.

SPECIAL ORDERS

(SEE NEXT PAGE)

PREPARED UNDER THE DIRECTION OF JEFF TRANDAHL, CLERK OF THE HOUSE OF REPRESENTATIVES:
By the Office of Legislative Operations

The Clerk shall cause the calendars of the House to be printed and distributed each legislative day. Rule II, clause 2(e)   *Index to the Calendars will be printed the first legislative day of each week the House is in session*

U.S. GOVERNMENT PRINTING OFFICE: 2000 79-038

FIGURE 4-1 *Calendars of the United States House of Representatives and History of Legislation*

Corrections Calendar

On June 20, 1995, the House abolished the Consent Calendar and replaced it with the Corrections Calendar.[4] The Consent Calendar originated in 1909 as a way to expedite action on noncontroverial measures. Legislation on this calendar was in order on the first and third Mondays of the month and adopted quickly without amendment by unanimous consent. However, during several Congresses (the 102d and 103d, for instance), the Consent Calendar was never used; instead, the House relied increasingly on unanimous consent and suspension of the rules to process noncontroversial or relatively noncontroversial measures.

Crediting the concept to Republican governor John Engler of Michigan, Speaker Newt Gingrich, R-Ga., in 1995 stated that he wanted to establish a "Corrections Day" procedure for repealing "the dumbest things the federal government is currently doing."[5] After the idea was considered and refined by a party task force and two standing committees, the House voted 271 to 146 on June 20, 1995, to accept the Corrections Day concept.

The Corrections Calendar is in order the second and fourth Tuesdays of the month, at the Speaker's discretion. Only bills that have been favorably reported by committee and assigned to either the House or Union calendars are eligible for placement on the Corrections Calendar. The Speaker has sole authority to determine whether a bill is to be on the agenda for Corrections Day. Bills are debated for one hour, equally divided between the majority and minority; no amendments are permitted except if proposed by the committee or chairman of the primary committee of jurisdiction; a motion to recommit, with or without instructions, may be offered by a minority member; and a three-fifths vote (261 if all 435 members are present and voting) is required to pass corrections legislation. A bipartisan advisory group of seven Republicans (named by the Speaker) and five Democrats (named by the minority leader) assists the Speaker in determining which corrections bills are to be taken up. During the 104th Congress (1995–1997), fourteen corrections measures became law; during the 105th Congress (1997–1999), four. In 1999, only one measure was considered via the Corrections Day procedure: adding the Martin Luther King Jr. federal holiday to the list of days on which the American flag should especially be displayed.

Despite limited use of this procedure, the idea for a Corrections Day spotlighted the GOP's public commitment to repeal overly burdensome or unnecessary rules. The policy-political goals of Republicans were publicly advertised by amending the House rulebook. Measures introduced by all lawmakers could make their way onto the Corrections Calendar, but GOP members were able to claim credit for being responsive to citizen concerns about the "regulatory state."

Suspension of the Rules

Another legislative shortcut and increasingly utilized source of agenda control by the Speaker—for important as well as minor public bills, resolutions,

TABLE 4-1 The Corrections Calendar and Suspension of the Rules

Corrections Calendar	Suspension of the Rules
Second and fourth Tuesdays	Every Monday and Tuesday, and during the last six days of the session
Bills must be on the Corrections Calendar for three legislative days before House consideration	No deadline
Bills may not be amended unless offered by the primary committee jurisdiction	No floor amendments; forty minutes of debate
Bipartisan advisory group to advise Speaker	No such group
For bills repealing laws or regulations viewed as unnecessary, obsolete, or overly burdensome	No restrictions on substance of bills; $100 million limit
Three-fifths vote required for passage	Two-thirds of the members voting, a quorum being present, is required for passage

and conference reports—is suspension of the rules ("I move to suspend the rules and pass H.R. 1234."). The rules of the House stipulate that this procedure is in order every Monday and Tuesday and during the last six days of a session of Congress. Informally, lawmakers often refer to measures on the "suspension calendar" even though there is no formal calendar for this purpose.

Debate on suspension bills is limited to forty minutes, evenly divided between proponents and opponents. The motion to suspend the rules and pass a bill may include amendments, but only if they are stipulated in the motion offered by the majority floor manager ("I move to suspend the rules and pass H.R. 1234, as amended."); otherwise, amendments from the floor are not permitted. The final and only vote on the measure is both to suspend the rules and pass the bill—by a two-thirds vote. Bills that fail to gain the necessary two-thirds support may be considered again under regular House procedures. The House rules that govern legislation considered under the Corrections Calendar and suspension procedure are summarized in Table 4-1.

To accommodate lawmakers' constituency activities—many members travel to their district on Friday and return late the following Monday—the House instituted a cluster voting rule. The Speaker announces that recorded votes on a group of bills considered under the suspension procedure will be postponed until later that day or until the next day. The bills then are brought up in sequence and disposed of without further debate. On the first clustered vote in a series, members have a minimum of fifteen minutes in which to vote;

on the remaining votes the Speaker may reduce the time on each one to a minimum of five minutes.

The Speaker is in complete charge of the measures considered under the suspension procedure. Committee chairmen, usually with the concurrence of their ranking minority colleagues, write the Speaker requesting that certain bills be taken up via the suspension route. (By custom, veterans bills are brought to the House floor under suspension procedure.) Typically, these bills were reported by committee. But any measure—reported or not, previously introduced or not, including conference reports and constitutional amendments—can be brought to the floor under suspension of the rules if the Speaker chooses to recognize the representative offering the suspension motion. Speaker O'Neill, for example, brought a constitutional amendment, the Equal Rights Amendment (ERA), to the House floor in 1983 under suspension procedure to prevent opponents from offering controversial floor amendments on abortion and the military draft. However, the ERA failed to attract the required two-thirds vote, in part because even its supporters objected to taking up such a significant issue under procedures that limited debate and prevented amendments.

When Republicans won control of the House in the mid-1990s, they adopted guidelines governing the consideration of measures under the suspension method. Under GOP Conference rules, the Speaker "shall not schedule any bill or resolution for consideration under suspension of the Rules which fails to include a cost estimate, has not been cleared by the minority, was opposed by more than one-third of the committee members [who] reported the bill, and exceeds $100,000,000." The leadership "does not ordinarily schedule bills for suspensions unless confident of a two-thirds vote." [6]

The suspension procedure enables the House to bypass normal floor procedures and quickly approve legislation that can attract an overwhelming voting majority. Committee chairmen generally support the suspension of the rules because the procedure protects their bills from floor amendments and points of order. Party leaders, too, use the suspension route to expedite emergency legislation or to move their issue agenda. Table 4-2 highlights the use of suspension procedure from the 100th through the 105th Congresses.

During the hectic last days of a congressional session, suspension of the rules is used more frequently and even on important measures. Dozens of bills may be scheduled daily for suspension votes. The parliamentary situation also is somewhat different during this period. Members who at an earlier time in the session might have voted against a bill brought up under suspension, because they had no opportunity to offer amendments to it or because it was a major bill, might have voted for the legislation during the end-of-the-session crunch on the argument that it was that version or nothing. The minority party's role is also enhanced during this pressure-packed, rush-to-adjourn time, because suspension votes virtually always require some bipartisan support.

Most of the legislation that goes before the House is passed by either unanimous consent requests or the suspension procedure. These types of bills are

TABLE 4-2 Motions to Suspend the Rules in the House, by Party of Sponsor, 100th to 105th Congresses

| | Measure Sponsored by | | | | |
| | Democrat | | Republican | | |
Congress	Number	Percent	Number	Percent	Total
100th (1987–1989)	512	83.4	102	16.6	614
101st (1989–1991)	468	80.3	115	19.7	583
102d (1991–1993)	513	83.4	102	16.6	615
103d (1993–1995)	412	88.2	55	11.8	467
104th (1995–1997)	69	17.2	332	82.8	401
105th (1997–1999)	126	20.4	491	79.6	617

SOURCE: Richard Beth, Jennifer Manning, and Faye Bullock, "Suspension of the Rules in the House: Measure Sponsorship by Party." CRS Report 97-901, February 11, 1998. Additional data for the 105th Congress was provided by Faye Bullock.

typically neither controversial nor complex. Measures that fail under suspension may pass the House under a rule granted by the Rules Committee.

District of Columbia Legislation

The federal capital is a unique governmental unit. Residents of the District of Columbia have no voting representation in Congress. (They have a nonvoting delegate in the House and no representation in the Senate.)

In a rules change initiated by D.C. delegate Eleanor Holmes Norton, the 103d Congress (1993–1995) permitted Norton, the three territorial delegates, and the one resident commissioner—all Democrats—to vote in the Committee of the Whole. (The Committee of the Whole is a special forum into which the House transforms itself to consider most important measures. General debate on legislation is not permitted, but debate and amendment may occur under the five-minute rule.) However, if their votes determined the outcome of an amendment, an automatic revote would be taken without their participation. Republicans vehemently protested granting the delegates and resident commissioner the right to vote in the Committee of the Whole. In a good example of the majority rule principle in action, they dropped this provision from the House's rulebook when they took control of the House in the 104th Congress.

Despite home rule for the capital, the House exercises control over the District principally through two committees, Appropriations and Government Reform. Both have a District of Columbia subcommittee.

House rules set aside the second and fourth Mondays of each month for District legislation reported by the Government Reform Committee. Appropriations bills for the District, however, do not come up during those special days. Instead, they are considered under the privilege given all legislation reported by the Appropriations Committee. If District bills are referred to the

Union Calendar, they are considered in the Committee of the Whole under the five-minute rule. If District bills are placed on the House Calendar, they are considered in the House under the one-hour rule, meaning no amendments unless the House rejects the previous question.

The Private Calendar

Private bills are designed to provide legal relief to specified persons or entities adversely affected by laws of general applicability. Most deal with immigration and naturalization cases and claims against the federal government. For example, general immigration requirements may be waived or expedited to permit foreign-born athletes to be part of the U.S. Olympic team or to allow a Philadelphia woman to marry a Greek man. In January 2000, several lawmakers introduced private bills to grant permanent residency or citizenship status to Elian Gonzalez, the six-year-old Cuban boy who was rescued after his mother and several other Cubans drowned when their boat sank off the coast of Florida. Most private bills are referred to the House and Senate Judiciary committees for review, and, like other bills, private bills passed by both chambers are sent to the president for signature or veto.

Under House procedures, the Speaker is required to call private bills on the first Tuesday of each month (unless the rule is dispensed with by a two-thirds vote or unanimous consent is obtained to transfer the call to some other day of the month) and, at his discretion, on the third Tuesday as well. Because few lawmakers have the time to review private bills, the Private Calendar Objectors Committee is assigned that task. The panel is composed of three members from each party appointed by the majority and minority leaders.

Bills must be placed on the Private Calendar seven days before being called up to give the objectors time to screen them for controversial provisions. (Committee reports on private measures must also be available to the objectors for three calendar days.) The objectors attend House sessions on Private Calendar days to answer any questions about the pending measures. If two or more members of the House object to a bill on the first Tuesday, it automatically is sent back to the committee that reported it, although at the request of a member it may at this time be "passed over without prejudice" for later consideration. Generally, private bills are not subject to lengthy consideration and are disposed of by voice vote.

The number of private bills introduced each Congress has been in sharp decline. From 1,269 private claims bills introduced during the 80th Congress (1947–1949), the number fell to fewer than two hundred during the 105th Congress (1997–1999). In the 82d Congress (1951–1953), Congress cleared 1,023 private bills; the 103d Congress (1993–1995), 8; the 104th, only 4. Several factors account for the drop-off. First, scandals associated with the introduction of private bills for pay (in the so-called Abscam scandal of 1980, for example, FBI agents dressed as Arab sheiks paid a number of lawmakers to introduce private immigration bills for them) led to stricter procedures for

TABLE 4-3 Committees with Direct Access to the Floor for Selected Legislation

Committee	Legislation
Appropriations	General appropriations bills; continuing appropriations resolutions if reported after September 15
Budget	Budget resolutions and reconciliation bills under the Congressional Budget and Impoundment Control Act of 1974
House Administration	Matters relating to enrolled bills, contested elections, and House expenditures, including committee funding resolutions
Rules	Rules and the order of business
Standards of Official Conduct	Resolutions recommending action with respect to the conduct of a member, officer, or employee of the House

their consideration. Second, Congress authorized administrative agencies and the U.S. Court of Claims to handle the bulk of these cases. Third, private bills often require an enormous amount of time to handle and in the end the claims can prove to be incorrect or fraudulent. Finally, congressional staff aides suggest that "legislators [are] uncomfortable passing [private claims] bills that [pay] money to a few individuals when so many other programs affecting larger numbers [are] being cut." [7]

PRIVILEGED LEGISLATION

Under House rules, five standing committees have direct access to the floor for selected bills. The Appropriations and Budget panels report measures to finance the operations of the government; the Standards of Official Conduct Committee is concerned with matters involving the public reputation of the House; the House Administration panel handles necessary housekeeping proposals; and the Rules Committee plays a major role in determining which measures the House considers. The committees and types of legislation eligible to be called up for immediate debate are listed in Table 4-3.

Unlike the other standing committees, which act only on legislation referred to them, these panels have the authority to originate, or initiate, specific measures. The bills may be called up when other matters are not already pending on the House floor. Despite the privilege, consideration of most of these bills must wait at least three days to give members time to read the committee reports. Special rules from the Rules Committee, however, must lay over only one day, while reports on budget resolutions must be available to members for ten days. (A few other matters, such as declarations of war, are exempt from the three-day layover rule.) Privileged measures are matters of special import to the House as an institution or to the federal government.

Even privileged measures are subject to points of order (parliamentary objections that any member may raise at an appropriate time) on the grounds that they violate certain rules of the House. If upheld, such points of order return the measure to the committee that considered it. Committees with privileged access therefore will usually ask the Rules Committee to waive points of order against their bills. The Appropriations Committee, for example, may violate House rules banning unauthorized appropriations or legislative provisions (policy provisos) in general appropriations bills and will protect the panel's bills from points of order by persuading the Rules Committee to issue waivers.

MAJOR LEGISLATION

Most major bills do not go directly from committee to a calendar and then to the House floor. Because they are important and usually controversial, they cannot reach the House floor by way of the Corrections Calendar, unanimous consent requests, or suspension procedure. Instead, such measures are given special review by the Rules Committee.

Brief Overview

The Rules Committee is among the oldest of House panels. The First Congress in April 1789 appointed an eleven-member rules body to draw up its procedures. With a few early exceptions, each succeeding Congress has done the same, although for nearly a century the Rules panel was a select (temporary) committee that prepared procedures for the incoming Congress and then went out of existence.

In 1858 the Speaker became a member and leader of the Rules Committee. In 1880 the Rules Committee became a standing (permanent) committee, and in 1883 it initiated the practice of reporting special orders, or rules, which, when agreed to by majority votes of the House, controlled the amount of time allowed for debate on major bills and the extent to which they could be amended from the floor.

Speakers during and after the 1880s permitted the Rules Committee to acquire authority over the House's agenda and the order of business. Speaker Joseph G. Cannon, a Republican from Illinois who was Speaker from 1903 to 1911, abused these and other powers, with the result that the House revolted in 1910 and removed the Speaker from the Rules Committee. The House majority leadership, however, retained—and still retains, in cooperation with the Rules Committee—fundamental control over the flow of legislation reaching the floor.

A notable exception was maverick Rules Chairman Howard W. Smith, D-Va. (1931–1967), who presided over the committee with an iron hand from 1955 to 1967. Smith was no traffic cop simply regulating the flow of bills to the floor. He firmly believed the committee should "consider the substance and merits of the bills," and he often blocked measures he disapproved of and advanced those he favored, sometimes thwarting the will of the majority.[8]

The Rules Committee lacks authority to amend bills, but it can bargain for changes in return for granting rules. In an attempt to lessen the power of the conservative coalition of southern Democrats and Republicans that controlled the committee from the mid-1930s to the early 1960s, House liberals succeeded in adopting a series of rules changes beginning in the late 1940s. But the independent power of the chairman was not substantially curbed until the membership of the committee was expanded in 1961.[9] (This resulted from a titanic battle between Speaker Sam Rayburn, D-Texas, and Rules Chairman Smith. Newly elected president John F. Kennedy directly intervened in an internal matter affecting House rules—a rare event for any president. Kennedy supported Rayburn's successful effort to enlarge Rules to change its ideological complexion so conservative members could not kill the president's New Frontier program.)

The committee's composition in the 106th Congress (1999–2001) was nine Republicans and four Democrats. Traditionally, the panel has had a disproportionate partisan ratio to ensure majority control. Today, the committee is one of the few centralizing panels in a decentralized House. Hence the importance of its rule-writing responsibilities.

By the 95th Congress (1977–1979), the Rules Committee had become closely linked to the Speaker. In 1975 the Democratic Speaker was authorized by his party caucus to appoint, subject to party ratification, all majority party members of the Rules Committee. In 1989 House Republicans authorized their leader to name all the GOP members of the Rules Committee. Thus, in the 106th Congress, Speaker J. Dennis Hastert, R-Ill., named the chairman and the other eight GOP members, and Minority Leader Richard A. Gephardt, D-Mo., appointed the four Democratic members.

This type of party change has reduced the Rules panel's independence and transformed it into "the Speaker's committee." As Jim Wright stated:

> The Rules Committee is an agent of the leadership. It is what distinguishes us from the Senate, where the rules deliberately favor those who would delay. The rules of the House, if one understands how to employ them, permit a majority to work its will on legislation rather than allow it to be bottled up and stymied.

Or as the GOP Rules vice chairman, Porter J. Goss of Florida, said about the panel's relations with the Speaker: "How much is the Rules Committee the handmaiden of the Speaker? The answer is, totally."[10]

Still, the Rules Committee's power should not be underestimated. The Speaker cannot track every major and minor bill or issue instructions constantly to the panel. The history of the Rules Committee is "one of the committee's accommodating the leadership on the one hand and seeking independent status on the other."[11] For the time being, at least, the emphasis is on sharing power with the Speaker.

Role of the Rules Committee

The power of the Rules Committee lies in its scheduling responsibilities: its traffic cop or police chief role. Besides deciding whether to grant a rule, the committee must craft rules to accomplish diverse purposes, such as providing for orderly review of major policy alternatives on the floor, protecting partisan objectives, focusing House debate on the main proposals in contention, and expediting consideration of priority measures.

As public bills are reported out of committee, they are entered in chronological order on one of the two main calendars, the Union Calendar or the House Calendar. All revenue bills, general appropriations bills, and measures that directly or indirectly appropriate money or property (including all authorization measures) are placed on the former; all remaining public bills, which generally deal with administrative and procedural matters, go on the latter. If all measures had to be taken up in the order in which they were listed on the calendars, as was the practice in the early nineteenth century, many major bills would not reach the House floor before Congress adjourned. Instead, major legislation reaches the floor in most instances by being granted precedence through a special order (rule) obtained from the Rules Committee. A rule is a simple resolution (H. Res.). A written request for a rule usually is made to the Rules chairman by the chairman of the committee reporting the bill.

The Rules Committee holds a hearing on the request with witnesses limited to members of Congress and debates it in the same manner that other committees consider legislative matters. One congressional scholar called hearings the "dress rehearsal" function of the Rules Committee.

> Rules members comprise the first audience for a piece of legislation outside the narrow confines of the committee and subcommittee that reported it. As such, the hearing on a rule request serves as a "dress rehearsal" for bill managers before they take the legislation to the House floor. The hearing on a rule is an opportunity for them to present their case and test the reaction from Rules members.[12]

Following the hearings, Rules members (particularly of the majority party) craft their rule and vote it out of committee. Once reported by the panel, the rule is considered on the House floor as privileged matter, which essentially means it is subject to one hour of debate and no amendments, and it is voted on in the same fashion as regular bills. In effect, a rule provides a tailor-made process for floor consideration of a bill that constitutes a departure from the procedures provided in the standing rules of the House. A rule, then, serves several important purposes:

1. It bumps a bill up the ladder of precedence, eliminating the waiting time that would be needed if chronological order were observed. The Rules Committee, in effect, shuffles the Union and House calendars by holding back rules for some bills and reporting them for others.

2. It governs the length of general debate on the bill as opposed to allowing any member to speak for up to one hour on it.

3. It usually dispenses with the first reading of the bill and the reading of amendments that are preprinted in the *Congressional Record* or in the report of the Rules Committee accompanying the rule.

4. It usually limits the number of amendments that may be offered and the time for debate on any amendment, as opposed to allowing any member to offer and debate as many germane amendments as he or she wants.

5. It orders the previous question as opposed to allowing the House to further amend and debate the bill after it has been reported from the Committee of the Whole.

In blocking or delaying legislation from reaching the floor, the Rules Committee is not necessarily playing an obstructionist role. It may be providing political cover by drawing fire away from the leadership, certain committees, and individual members. Representatives sometimes request that the Rules Committee prevent unwanted bills or amendments from reaching the floor. As former Speaker O'Neill once said, "It takes the heat for the rest of the Congress, there is no question about that." [13]

The committee also acts as an informal mediator of disputes among other House committees and members. Because of overlapping jurisdictions, one committee may report a measure that trespasses on the authority of another. In such a case, the Rules Committee may resolve the dispute by authorizing the second committee to offer amendments or by refusing to waive points of order on the floor, thus giving members of the second committee an opportunity to attempt to delete the offending matter. Intraparty conflicts are mediated, too, by Rules so majority party members are not hanging their dirty linen in public when contentious issues reach the floor. Interparty differences are reconciled to the extent that bills enjoy cross-party support.

The Rules Committee also plays a jurisdictional arbitration role on multiply referred legislation. As a precondition for a rule, the committee may urge or require competing committees to agree on the vehicle—one of the committee's reported bills, some consensus product, or something else—for floor debate and amendment. This practice limits floor fights among rival committees, simplifies floor decision making, expedites the processing of legislation, and avoids putting Rules in the position of deciding which panel's bill to use for floor discussion.

The Rules Committee also has substantive (or original jurisdiction) responsibilities. It reported out such major measures as the Legislative Reorganization Act of 1970, the Congressional Budget and Impoundment Control Act of 1974, and resolutions providing for the creation of a permanent Select Intelligence Committee and the televising of House floor sessions. As part of its jurisdiction over the House rulebook, the panel in 1995 supported the creation of new points of order, which it cannot waive, against the imposition of unfunded mandates on states and localities and the private sector. For example, a member can raise a point of order against consideration of a rule if it permits consideration of measures that contain unfunded mandates on states and localities in excess of $50 million annually. If a lawmaker makes that point of order, and specifies the precise violation, the Speaker does not rule but puts the question ("Will the House now consider the resolution?") to the membership. Twenty minutes of debate are permitted (ten per side), and then the House votes on whether it will take up the rule.[14] In 2000 the panel held hearings on whether Congress should switch from an annual budget and appropriations process to a biennial one.

Traditional Types of Special Rules

The Rules Committee traditionally grants three basic kinds of rules: open, closed, and modified. The distinction among them goes solely to the question of the amendment process. All three types almost always provide a fixed number of hours for general debate. In addition, any of these types also may contain waivers of points of order. An example of a rule from the Rules Committee, with an explanation of its basic features, is shown in Box 4-1 on pp. 124 and 125.

Open Rule. Open rules were common for most bills until about the 95th Congress, when restrictive rules began to increase in number (see Table 4-4). As Robert H. Michel, R-Ill., wrote at the end of his thirty-eight-year career in the House, the last fourteen (1981–1995) as GOP leader: When Democrats controlled the House, they "clamped down on the granting of open rules, making it more and more difficult for Members to offer amendments to legislation."[15] Given their frustrating and even embittering experience with rules that often restricted their right to offer amendments, Republicans, when they took control of the House in the 104th Congress, allowed the Rules Committee to provide more amendment opportunities for all lawmakers.

Under an open rule, any germane amendment to a bill may be offered from the floor. Amendments may be simple or complex. For example, an amendment may extend the funding of a program from two to four years or it may rewrite whole sections of a bill. Some committees, such as Science, customarily request the Rules Committee to grant an open rule for their legislation.

Although open rules permit any and all germane amendments, they do have a downside in the length of time it may take to complete action on legislation and in the unpredictable character of the many amendments that might be offered. After two weeks of debate and with nearly 170 amendments still pending to one of their Contract with America measures, Republicans began to have some doubts about open rules. They believed Democrats were offering scores of amendments to an unfunded mandates bill to prevent Republicans from considering all their contract bills within the first one hundred days of the 104th Congress, as promised. Hence, the GOP voted to limit debate to ten minutes for each of the pending amendments. Rules Chairman

Gerald B. H. Solomon, R-N.Y., then added, "It looks like we're going to have to increasingly restrict rules if the Democrats won't cooperate."[16]

Open rules raise the important question of where the fundamental deliberations on legislation should take place: in the committee setting among a relatively small number of lawmakers who specialize in the subject area or on the House floor with the entire membership having a say in policy formulation?

Closed Rule. A closed rule prohibits floor amendments, but rarely are such pure closed rules reported by the Rules Committee. Instead, closed rules in the contemporary House usually forbid floor amendments except those offered by the reporting committee or committees. On occasion, a closed rule will be reported that requires a bill to be considered in the House and not in the Committee of the Whole under procedures that limit debate to one hour and prohibit amendments because the rule automatically orders the previous question on the bill. Critics say closed rules (also called "gag" rules) hamper the legislative process and violate democratic norms. Rep. Charles W. Stenholm, D-Texas, put it this way:

> In most cases, closed rules say that we as individual Members are willing to allow a small portion of the whole to decide what information we need to consider, what complexities our minds are able to master, and from what alternatives we should choose. Furthermore, many times closed rules indicate either an arrogance on the part of the proponents of a bill or an insecurity about the bill's merits or abilities to stand up against competing ideas.[17]

Supporters of closed rules say they are necessary in the case of complex measures subject to intense lobbying. In addition, national emergency legislation sometimes needs to be expedited by the closed rule procedure.

Tax bills provide a good illustration of the pressures surrounding closed rules. For decades and still today the House considers tax measures under closed rules, agreeing with the argument of Wilbur D. Mills, D-Ark. (1939–1977), chairman of the Ways and Means Committee from 1958 to 1975, that tax legislation was too complex and technical to be tampered with on the floor. If unlimited floor amendments were allowed, Mills argued, the internal revenue code soon would be in shambles and at the mercy of pressure groups.

Closed rules are also used when the majority leadership wants to expedite action on its legislative priorities and to activate its electoral base. For instance, a bill to ban so-called partial-birth abortions was brought to the floor on April 5, 2000, without subcommittee or committee markup and under a closed rule that permitted two hours of debate, no amendments, and one motion to recommit (to return the bill to committee). In addition, the rule contained a provision that expedited the convening of a conference committee with the Senate on its version of the legislation. (The sole purpose of some rules is to facilitate the creation of a conference committee, such as having the

BOX 4-1 Reading a Special Rule

H. Res. 289

[Report No. 106-317]

Original Text of the Resolution

Resolved, That at any time after the adoption of this resolution the Speaker may, pursuant to clause 2(b) of the rule XVIII, declare the House resolved into the Committee of the Whole House on the state of the Union for consideration of the bill (H.R. 1655) to authorize appropriations for fiscal years 2000 and 2001 for the civilian energy and scientific research, development, and demonstration and related commercial application of energy technology programs, projects, and activities of the Department of Energy, and for other purposes.

EXPLANATION: *Authorizes the Speaker to transform ("resolve") the House into the Committee of the Whole House to consider the measure after adoption of the special rule.*

The first reading of the bill shall be dispensed with. General debate shall be confined to the bill and shall not exceed one hour equally divided and controlled by the chairman and ranking minority member of the Committee on Science.

EXPLANATION: *Dispenses with the first reading of the bill. (Bills must be read three times before being passed.) Sets the amount of general debate time—one hour—and specifies which members control that time—in this instance, the chair and ranking minority member of the Committee on Science. Specifies that debate should be relevant to the bill.*

After general debate the bill shall be considered for amendment under the five-minute rule.

EXPLANATION: *Sets reading for amendment one section at a time (or one paragraph at a time for appropriations bills), and provides that each member can speak for five minutes on each amendment. Because this special rule sets no limitations on amendments that can be offered, it is an open rule. Nonetheless, amendments still must comply with the House's standing rules, such as germaneness.*

It shall be in order to consider as an original bill for purposes of amendment under the five-minute rule the amendment in the nature of a substitute recommended by the Committee on Science now printed in the bill. Each section of the committee amendment in the nature of a substitute shall be considered as read.

EXPLANATION: *Identifies text to be open to amendment in the Committee of the Whole. A special rule can provide that a committee-reported substitute be considered as an original bill for the purpose of amendment. Allowing a full-text substitute to be considered as an original bill is usually done to permit second-degree amendments to be offered.*

During consideration of the bill for amendment, the Chairman of the Committee of the Whole may accord priority in recognition on the basis of whether the Member offering an amendment has caused it to be printed in the portion of the Congressional Record designated for that purpose in clause 8 of rule XVIII. Amendments so printed shall be considered as read.

EXPLANATION: *Determines recognition order for offering amendments. Open rules customarily grant the chair of the Committee of the Whole discretion to give priority recognition to members who submitted their amendments for preprinting in the* Congressional Record. *Absent this provision, the chair would follow the custom of giving preferential recognition to members, based on seniority, who serve on the reporting committee, alternating between the parties.*

The Chairman of the Committee of the Whole may: (1) postpone until a time during further consideration in the Committee of the Whole a request for a recorded vote on any amendment; and (2) reduce to five minutes time for electronic voting on any postponed question that follows another electronic vote without intervening business, provided that the minimum time for electronic voting on the first in any series of questions shall be 15 minutes.

EXPLANATION: *A special rule that allows amendments to be offered might allow the chair of the Committee of the Whole to postpone votes on amendments, as shown here. The chair may reduce to five minutes the time for electronic voting on a postponed question, provided that the voting time on the first in any series of questions is not less than fifteen minutes.*

At the conclusion of consideration of the bill for amendment the Committee shall rise and report the bill to the House with such amendments as may have been adopted.

EXPLANATION: *Provides for transformation ("to rise") back to the House from the Committee of the Whole. This provision eliminates the need for a separate vote on a motion to rise and report.*

Any Members may demand a separate vote in the House on any amendment adopted in the Committee of the Whole to the bill or to the committee amendment in the nature of a substitute.

EXPLANATION: *Enables separate votes to occur in the House on each first-degree amendment approved by the Committee of the Whole. House rules require the House to vote on each first-degree amendment approved by the Committee of the Whole.*

The previous question shall be considered as ordered on the bill and amendments thereto to final passage without intervening motion except one motion to recommit with or without instructions.

EXPLANATION: *Expedites final passage. By automatically imposing the "previous question," intervening debate and the offering of motions is precluded. The only motion allowed is a motion to recommit.*

SOURCE: Michael L. Koempel and Judy Schneider, *Congressional Deskbook 2000* (Alexandria, Va.: TheCapitol.Net, 2000), 250–251. www.CongressionalDeskbook.com. Reprinted with permission.

TABLE 4-4 Open versus Restrictive Rules, 95th to 105th Congresses

Congress		Open Rules		Restrictive Rules	
		Number	Percent	Number	Percent
95th	(1977–1979)	179	85	32	15
96th	(1979–1981)	161	75	53	25
97th	(1981–1983)	90	75	30	25
98th	(1983–1985)	105	68	50	32
99th	(1985–1987)	65	57	50	43
100th	(1987–1989)	66	54	57	46
101st	(1989–1991)	47	45	57	55
102d	(1991–1993)	37	34	72	66
103d	(1993–1995)	31	30	71	70
104th	(1995–1997)	68	46	80	54
105th	(1997–1999)	58	42	81	58

SOURCE: *Congressional Record*, October 5, 1994, H10862. Data for the 104th and 105th Congresses provided by Donald Wolfensberger, former staff director, House Rules Committee, and director, Congress Project, Woodrow Wilson Center.

House disagree to the Senate's amendment to its bill and agree to the conference requested by the Senate.)

Modified Rule. A third category of special orders is the modified rule. There are two versions of this rule: modified open and modified closed, designations that are somewhat subjective. A modified open rule might indicate that all parts of a bill are open to amendment except a specific title or section. A modified closed rule could state that an entire bill is closed to amendment except a certain title or section. Or the distinction between the two is sometimes based on the number of amendments made in order by the Rules Committee: ten or more is modified open, fewer than ten is modified closed. Fundamentally, modified open rules provide more amendment opportunities than modified closed rules.

Waiver Rules. Finally, there are rules waiving points of order. Under these rules, which appear in open, closed, and modified rules, specific House procedures are temporarily set aside. Without such waivers, measures in technical violation of House procedures could not be dealt with rapidly, and important parts of bills could be deleted for technical reasons during floor debate. "If we went strictly by the House rules," remarked a House member, "I am sure this body would have a very difficult time operating."[18] The sole purpose of some rules is to waive points of order against the consideration of legislation that is privileged (it has a right-of-way to the floor), such as conference reports, but which has also violated various House rules. The panel, too, may issue a martial law rule. The purpose of this special rule—typically employed when the House is trying to quickly wrap up its end-of-session business—is to allow the

Rules Committee to bring priority legislation to the floor on the same day the panel approves a special rule. The House rulebook specifies that special rules brought to the floor on the same day they are approved by the panel require a two-thirds vote for adoption instead of the usual majority vote. Martial law rules set aside, or waive, the two-thirds requirement.

Generally, waivers are of two types: exemptions from specific House rules and procedures or blanket waivers of all points of order against pending legislation. A surge of blanket and specific waivers has been evident in recent Congresses. For example, from the 96th Congress (1979–1981) to the 102d Congress (1991–1993) a jump from 8 percent to 14 percent was seen in the number of times the Rules Committee waived the House rule requiring committee reports on legislation to be available to lawmakers for at least three calendar days (excluding Saturdays, Sundays, and legal holidays) before the House can take up a measure. The Republicans, then the minority, objected strenuously to the increase of waivers. When they assumed majority control of the House in the mid-1990s, Republicans amended the rules of the House to require the Rules Committee, to the maximum extent possible, "to specify in any special rule providing for the consideration of a measure any provisions of House rules being waived."[19] Today, waivers are routinely granted to advance party and substantive objectives (see Box 4-2).

Lawmakers understand that blanket waivers are sometimes essential to lawmaking.[20] Unsurprisingly, minority Democrats complain when Republicans bring legislation to the floor with blanket waivers. "They have," stated Rep. Barney Frank, D-Mass., "exactly the same view of rules and waivers that we had."[21] (Sometimes members refer to open plus rules, which means an open amendment process with the plus of having waivers that provide protection for certain amendments against valid points of order.)

The Rules Committee may establish its own informal practices with respect to waivers. General appropriations bills are privileged under House rules. However, these measures are commonly regulated by special rules that waive appropriate points of order. When Republicans took control of the House in 1995, the GOP leadership established a protocol relating to waivers of unauthorized programs and legisl-ative language (policy) in general appropriations bills. As the Rules chairman explained:

> Under this protocol, the Committee on Rules would provide the necessary waivers to enable the bill to come to the floor if the authorizing committee chairmen did not object to them. If the authorizing chairmen objected to the waivers, then under the leadership's protocol, the Committee on Rules would leave the specific language in question exposed to a point of order on the floor.[22]

This informal policy can be loosely applied depending on the circumstances (conflict between the authorizing chairman and one of his subcommittee leaders, for example), but it is still in effect.

BOX 4-2 **Tax-Hike Rule Waiver**

The Rules Committee routinely anticipates and waives points of order when House rules stand in the way of legislation backed by the leadership. The rules usually pushed aside include those prohibiting policy language in appropriations bills or requiring that conference reports season for three days before adoption.

But not even a special hurdle the GOP added to the rulebook in 1995 to discourage tax increases, requiring a three-fifths majority to pass any bill that would hike income tax rates, was beyond the reach of waivers. The rule was part of the effort by Speaker Newt Gingrich, Ga., and the new 104th Congress Republican majority to change how Washington does business. In reality, it served largely as a reminder of Republican intentions. The leadership-controlled Rules panel set it aside just as routinely as other House regulations.

The three-fifths requirement was diluted as part of a rules package adopted at the beginning of the 106th Congress (1999–2001). The change narrowed the definition of a rate increase triggering the supermajority requirement. The majority's maneuvering around the rule took a new twist in August 1999. And the resulting awkwardness delighted House Democrats opposed to the tax bill under consideration.

The three-fifths majority had to be waived to protect the tax-cut package from a point of order that it contained a massive tax increase. The problem was the bill's across-the-board income tax rate cuts would expire after 2008, leaving tax rates to jump back up to their current levels. "I thought it was funny. I also thought it was sad," said a Democratic aide. "They weakened that rule at the beginning of this Congress and they still had to waive it. That was really good."

SOURCE: Adapted from Russ Freyman, "Tax Cut Bill Needed Waiver of Tax-Hike Rule," *CQ Daily Monitor*, August 9, 1999, 4.

Creative Rules for the House

Fundamental changes in the workings of the House that began during the 1970s and continue into the 2000s triggered the rise of so-called creative rules. The House witnessed a dramatic redistribution of internal influence from powerful, seniority-chosen committee chairmen to scores of individual lawmakers, including subcommittee chairmen, factional leaders, and rank-and-file members. Party leaders and caucuses gained influence, too, as with the Speaker's multiple referral authority and the role of party caucuses in approving (or disapproving) committee chairmen (or ranking minority members). Partisan polarization also enveloped the House as did the intensity of outside pressures, such as press and media coverage of congressional affairs.

In addition, substantive and procedural complexity triggered the need for creative rules. Not only did measures become bigger and more complex, but also new procedures—multiple referrals, the requirements of the 1974 budget act, and various statutory provisions providing special procedures for certain bills—required the Rules Committee to sort through the complications and devise an orderly procedure for debating and amending legislation. The House also amended its rules in ways that encouraged lawmakers to ask for more recorded votes. The House permitted recorded votes in the Committee of the Whole in 1971 (votes had been unrecorded in this main amending forum), and electronic voting was authorized two years later.

All these changes produced a basic shift in the political culture of the House. It went from the to-get-along, go-along spirit of Speaker Rayburn's era to an entrepreneurial and participatory style where even freshmen lawmakers have wide opportunities to voice their views and exert their influence in all phases of lawmaking. The Rules Committee responded to the new climate during most of the 1970s by providing members with wide-open amending opportunities on the floor. As one scholar pointed out:

> Fewer than 900 amendments were offered in the 91st Congress (1969–1970) and fewer than 800 were offered in the 92d Congress (1971–1972), but over 1,400 were offered in the 93d Congress (1973–1974) and nearly 1,400 were offered in the 94th (1975–1976). In the 95th, floor amendments peaked at nearly 1,700. Clearly, the incentive to put oneself or one's opponents on the record helped to stimulate more amending activity. . . . [Further, a] group of Republicans—John Ashbrook of Ohio, Robert Bauman of Maryland, and John Rousselot of California—deliberately badgered Democrats with many amendments and requests for recorded votes.[23]

By the end of the 1970s, Democratic leaders and lawmakers wanted the Rules Committee to exert greater control over floor procedures. Members wanted greater certainty in an environment grown more conflict-ridden and unpredictable. The open amendment process produced longer sessions, disruptions in members' schedules, more dilatory tactics, and numerous challenges to committee-reported measures that often undercut carefully crafted compromises that had been negotiated in advance of floor consideration. For example, when President Jimmy Carter's proposal to create a Department of Education went to the floor in June 1979, "Republican opponents prepared nearly 200 amendments, for the express purpose of delaying a final vote and blocking passage."[24]

Other factors, too, contributed to the need for creative rules and the procedural crackdown that limited members' amendment opportunities. They included the use of multiple referrals, which required Rules to play a larger coordinative role in arranging floor action on legislation reported by several committees; the rise of megabills hundreds of pages in length that contained priorities that the Speaker did not want picked apart on the floor; and the escalation of sharp partisanship, especially in the aftermath of Republican Ronald Reagan's election as president in November 1980 while the House remained in Democratic hands. GOP lawmakers, for example, sponsored floor amendments designed to embarrass Democrats and to supply Republican House challengers with campaign ammunition.

In response to these diverse circumstances, the Democratically controlled Rules Committee tightened opportunities for floor amendment and devised a variety of innovative and procedurally creative rules, which remain available today to the GOP-controlled House. Their primary objectives are to expedite floor decision making, focus member attention on the major policy alternatives, enhance partisan goals, and strengthen committee prerogatives. Among these creative procedures are structured, self-executing, king-of-the-hill, and multiple-stage rules.

Structured Rules. Structured rules limit the number of floor amendments, establish a specific order in which those amendments are to be offered, frequently identifying the member who can offer each amendment, and typically prohibit any change in the amendments made in order. These rules may also prescribe debate limits on the entire amendment process or on each amendment made in order. Structured rules may require that all amendments be published in the *Congressional Record* prior to floor action on the legislation. This requirement aids the floor managers. "Newer chairmen are kind of unsure of themselves," said Rep. Joe Moakley, D-Mass., who served as Rules chairman from 1989 to 1995. "They ask for amendments to be printed [in advance, in the *Record*] so they can be ready for anything." [25]

On the one hand, the thrust of these rules is to restrict members' general right to offer floor amendments. This result frequently arouses the ire of minority party members. On the other hand, structured rules can expand the range of policy options put before the membership. Issues that are not eligible under normal parliamentary procedures can be made eligible for floor consideration. The Rules Committee can allow consideration of nongermane amendments, legislation stuck in committee, or even measures that have never been introduced.

Whether restrictive, expansive, or both, a fundamental purpose of structured rules is to define the sequence in which specific amendments are to be voted upon—sometimes to benefit the committee that reported the legislation, sometimes to grant other members an opportunity to revamp the reporting committee's priorities. The Rules Committee's ability to determine the sequence of action can influence the ultimate outcome. For example, the majority leadership may support a less costly initiative over an expensive one advocated by the minority leadership. The Rules Committee could fashion a rule that permits votes on only three policy alternatives: the costly version; the less costly version; and a compromise midway between the other two, advanced by the majority leadership and designed to attract broad support. Members can then explain to constituents who opposed both the budget-buster and inadequate alternative that they voted for the reasonable option.

Self-Executing Rules.   This kind of rule embodies a two-for-one procedure. That is, when the House adopts a rule it also simultaneously agrees to dispose of a separate matter, which is specified in the rule itself. For instance, a self-executing rule may stipulate that a discrete policy proposal is deemed to have passed the House and been incorporated in the bill to be taken up. The effect is that neither in the House nor in the Committee of the Whole will lawmakers have the opportunity to amend or to vote separately on the self-executed provision. For example, on August 2, 1989, the House adopted a rule (H.Res. 221) that automatically incorporated into the text of the bill made in order for consideration a provision that prohibited smoking on domestic airline flights of two hours or less duration. On May 7, 1998, an intelligence authorization bill was made in order by H.Res. 420, which dropped a section from the intelligence legislation that would have permitted the Central Intelligence Agency (CIA) to offer its employees an early-out retirement program.

A self-executing rule "saves the House time by avoiding multiple subsequent votes that can be taken care of by the rule," and it allows members to escape a direct recorded vote on a controversial issue. By way of comparison, Democrats used thirty-five self-executing rules in the 103d Congress while Republicans employed twenty-seven in the 104th and forty-five in the 105th Congresses.[26]

King-of-the-Hill Rules.   The early 1980s witnessed another procedural innovation: the king-of-the-hill (or king-of-the-mountain) rule. "As far as I know," said Rules Chairman Richard W. Bolling, D-Mo., during May 1982 debate on a rule governing consideration of the concurrent budget resolution, this procedure is "unique."[27] The rule is unusual in a parliamentary sense for two major reasons. First, it permits the House to vote on an array of major policy alternatives—so-called substitutes that are the equal of new bills—one after the other. Significantly, no matter the outcome—yea or nay—on any of the substitutes, the king-of-the-hill rule typically stipulates that the vote on the last substitute is the only one that counts for purposes of accepting or rejecting a national policy.

Speaker Gingrich, then House minority leader, highlighted the partisan importance of structuring the sequence of amendments for lawmakers. "[If] you are the Democratic leadership, what you do is you set up the bills and you say to your Members, vote for anything you want to, but when you get to the last one, vote for ours."[28] The king-of-the-hill rule has advantages. First, it provides political cover to legislators who can cast votes on several policy alternatives and explain their actions to constituents in any manner they choose. Second, the rule limits criticism of the Rules Committee. The panel can allow votes on major policy alternatives advocated by different House factions without taking sides among them.

Third, the king-of-the-hill rule waives scores of procedures and precedents. For instance, parliamentary principles state that once part of a bill is amended, re-amending it is generally not in order unless another amendment, broader in scope, changes the part by taking a bigger bite of the legislation. The massive substitutes made in order by the king-of-the-hill rule amend everything in the pending legislation. Technically, nothing is left to be changed and the amending process automatically terminates under traditional House procedures. Traditional procedures, however, are not followed when this type of rule is used, because political and policy objectives are of overriding concern.

Multiple-Stage Rules. The Rules Committee will sometimes issue several rules for the same bill (multiple-stage rules) to facilitate coherent consideration of issues or to expedite action on legislation. Defense legislation, for instance, has been considered with a series of rules that separates general debate from the amendment process. For example, the initial rule on a defense bill will govern the terms for general debate. The objectives are to focus House deliberation on the major issues and to apportion debate fairly among the interested parties. Then a second rule will be granted to govern the amendment process on the principal military issues. All related amendments might be grouped together and be debated under specific time limits. A third or even fourth rule might then regulate how all the remaining amendments will be considered by the membership. (The time lapse among multiple-stage rules can be hours, days, or even weeks.)

A variation of the multiple stage rule is the "shutdown" rule, which is issued when a bill has become bogged down in a filibuster by amendments under an open rule. Failing unanimous consent or a series of motions to limit debate on amendments, the committee in charge of the bill, with the support of the majority leadership, will ask the Rules Committee to issue a new rule to limit the number of remaining amendments or the time for consideration of further amendments.

GOP Innovations

When Republicans assumed majority control of the House in 1995, they promised to provide a fair and open amendment process. This goal, however, sometimes clashed with a fundamental objective of any majority party: passage of priority measures even if that means restricting lawmakers' amendment opportunities. Democrats, trying to hold the GOP firmly to the new openness they promised, regularly chastised Republicans for providing anything less than a completely open and unrestricted amendment process. Republicans returned the rhetorical fire, as the following exchange between ranking Democrat Moakley and Rules Chairman (1995–1999) Solomon demonstrates.

> MR. MOAKLEY. [Y]ou said you were going to come forward with open rules so everybody could fully participate. I say to the gentleman, if you want to emulate our Congress, fine, but I thought you were coming in with a new broom, that you were going to sweep clean and give all open rules.

MR. SOLOMON. I say to the gentleman, you never had it so good. We are treating you twice as fairly as you treated us. Never in the history of this Congress has a minority been treated as fairly as we are treating you.[29]

Throughout the 104th Congress, Republicans and Democrats prepared dueling statistics on the number of open versus restrictive rules.[30] During the period when the Contract with America was considered by the House, Republicans said they reported open rules 72 percent of the time; Democrats claimed that it was only 26 percent. Their differences stemmed from how each defined an open rule and what measures were included in their calculations. Republicans, for instance, included three noncontroversial bills brought to the floor with open rules. Democrats deleted those from their count. They argued that Republicans granted open rules to the bills solely to pad their figures and that the measures were so noncontroversial they should have been brought up under suspension of the rules.[31] (A cease-fire took hold in the 105th Congress, when neither party argued publicly about the number of open versus other kinds of rules. This change occurred in part because the Rules Committee generally permitted more floor amendment opportunities, including a guaranteed motion to recommit with instructions, than took place during some of the Democratic years.)

There is little question, however, that change has characterized the GOP-run Rules Committee. Speaker Gingrich, for instance, appointed one freshman, two women, and three sophomores to the committee. Not since 1915 had a GOP freshman been assigned to this influential panel.[32] Speaker Hastert also appointed a freshman to Rules at the start of the 106th Congress. At least three creative rules employed by the GOP-controlled panel are of note: queen-of-the-hill, time-structured, and bifurcated (also called MIRVs by Capitol Hill insiders—multiple independent reentry vehicles) rules.

Queen-of-the-Hill Rules. When they were in the minority, Republicans regularly lambasted Democrats for use of the king-of-the-hill procedure. Once in the majority, GOP Rules Chairman Solomon objected to this rule because it "allowed lawmakers to be on both sides of an issue and violated the democratic principle that the position with the strongest support should prevail."[33] As a result, Republicans rejected the king-of-the-hill rule in favor of the queen-of-the-hill rule, which stipulates that whichever substitute amendment wins the most votes in the Committee of the Whole is forwarded to the full House for a vote on final passage. In the event that two or more amendments receive the same number of affirmative votes, then the last one voted on is considered as finally approved.

The Rules Committee employed the queen-of-the-hill (or "most votes win") rule on a proposed constitutional amendment to establish term limits for lawmakers. (As part of their Contract with America, Republicans wanted to replace career politicians with citizen legislators.) The rule made in order two GOP substitutes (each imposed a limit of twelve years for senatorial service but differed on the length of House service) and one Democratic alternative (applying any new term limits to current members) to the base bill (a six-term limit for House service) supported by the GOP leadership. None of the substitute amendments even attracted minority support, and, in an outright rejection of a contract item, the congressional term limits proposal failed to attract the two-thirds vote required to enact constitutional amendments.[34] (On May 22, 1995, in *U.S. Term Limits Inc. v. Thornton,* the Supreme Court ruled 5-4 that states could not impose term limits on federal lawmakers.)

In 1998 the GOP leadership devised a queen-of-the-hill rule to frustrate House approval of campaign reform legislation that would prohibit the parties from receiving or spending soft money (unregulated campaign contributions used for party-building and get-out-the-vote drives but not for advocating the election or defeat of specific candidates). To kill this proposal, sponsored by Reps. Christopher Shays, R-Conn., and Martin T. Meehan, D-Mass., the Rules Committee made in order eleven substitute amendments, forcing the soft money ban to compete against all the other recommendations. For instance, one of the substitutes proposed the creation of a bipartisan commission on campaign finance reform. GOP leaders generally expected this noncontroversial proposal to receive an overwhelming number of "yes" votes and easily trump the soft money alternative. However, Representatives Shays and Meehan persuaded many who supported the commission idea to vote either "no" or "present," fully mindful that under the queen-of-the-hill procedure the amendment receiving the most votes becomes the House bill (see Box 4-3). In the end, the strategy worked, and their proposal was agreed to by the House. It later died in the Senate.

Time-Structured Rules. To accommodate the GOP leadership's pledge for open rules with its need to act on priority bills, the Rules Committee issued rules that established debate limits on the entire amendment process. A ten-hour cap for debating and voting on amendments is an example of such a rule. (These rules, too, commonly include the stipulation that members who preprint their amendments in the *Congressional Record* should be accorded priority recognition for offering those amendments by the chair.) As Rules Chairman David Dreier, R-Calif., explained:

> The [GOP] majority . . . on the Committee on Rules has reported a large number of rules in which a time cap has been used. The reason is very simple, Mr. Speaker. After years in the minority, during which time the 9 to 4 [Democratic] majority structured rules to stack the deck politically for the majority, we learned how unfairly structured rules can be. Time limits, I will acknowledge, are not perfect. However, it is possible with time limits for the chairman and ranking member of a bill's committee of jurisdiction to minimize the drawbacks of those time limits. They are recognized for amendments before other Members . . . . [and they can] largely set the course of debate.[35]

BOX 4-3   Open Debate and Political Maneuvering

The House Rules Committee in June 1998 appeared to have found the magic bullet that the Republican leadership had been searching for to kill campaign finance legislation in the 105th Congress.

After a growing group of GOP rebels joined most Democrats in signing a discharge petition, which would have forced the issue to the floor and threatened the leadership's control over the chamber, the GOP leadership in April had agreed to bring a comprehensive campaign finance bill to the floor. Speaker Newt Gingrich, R-Ga., even promised in writing that it would be "fully debated under an open rule, permitting substitutes and amendments." The Republican hierarchy strategy was to try to turn that promise to its advantage.

The Rules Committee, by design an agent of the Speaker, permitted an unusual number of substitutes—eleven in all—to be considered to the underlying campaign finance measure under a queen-of-the-hill rule. On a voice vote, the panel June 4 approved a rule under which each substitute would face dozens of amendments, thus guaranteeing that the debate would be long, drawn-out, and confusing. The rule specifically allowed 258 amendments, although it permitted an unlimited number as long as they were germane to the bill.

"We don't have a right to complain because we asked for an open rule," said Christopher Shays, R-Conn., the author of one of the major campaign finance proposals to be considered. But cosponsor Martin T. Meehan, D-Mass., insisted that the GOP maneuver would backfire. "Every time they put up this kind of strategy, support for our bills grows," he said.

A maze-like parliamentary situation faced members who wanted to see the House pass campaign finance legislation. The first substitute permitted under the rule would create a commission to study changes to campaign laws and then report its recommendations back to Congress. Second in line was the Shays-Meehan proposal. Under the rule, only the proposal with the largest number of "yes" votes would advance. And a significant number who supported the commission also supported Shays-Meehan and did not want to see the former trump the latter. Carolyn B. Maloney, D-N.Y., one of the original sponsors of the commission bill, subsequently announced that she would vote present on the commission proposal to prevent it from winning more votes than the Shays-Meehan substitute.

SOURCE: Adapted from Elizabeth A. Palmer, "You Want an Open Debate? Fine, GOP Says," *CQ Daily Monitor*, June 5, 1998, 7.

Democrats criticize these rules as not being genuinely open. Because the time for voting on amendments is counted against the cap, a ten-hour restriction may leave, for example, only seven hours for debating amendments. Limits, they say, encourage dilatory tactics. Recorded votes may be called on amendments that could pass by voice vote "in order to consume time allotted for considering amendments."[36] Republicans respond, as noted by

Representative Dreier, that Democrats should consult in advance with their leaders to identify priority amendments that need to be offered inside the cap. On occasion GOP lawmakers get upset with caps, too, because they may be foreclosed from offering their amendments.[37]

Bifurcated Rules. An innovation of Rules Chairman Dreier, bifurcated rules make at least two separate bills in order for back-to-back consideration in the chamber. Under bifurcated (or MIRV) rules, the House first debates, amends, and passes one bill and then it proceeds to consider another related but different bill. These actions can occur on a separate day. Once the second measure is agreed to, the rule provides that the two bills will be joined together into one measure and sent to the Senate. A separate vote is not taken on the combined legislation. The basic purpose of this rule is to provide political cover to Republicans on issues on which Democrats have the momentum. These issues in the 106th Congress included gun control, managed health care, and raising the minimum wage.

The GOP leadership opposed the idea of raising the minimum wage—a key priority of nearly every House Democrat. However, the Republican leadership recognized that some moderate Republicans strongly supported raising the minimum wage and that the combination of the two blocs—Democrats and moderate Republicans—made it a winning coalition. The GOP leaders thus faced a potential revolt within their ranks if they did not bring minimum wage to a vote on the floor. They also realized that without a vote on minimum wage some of their vulnerable moderates could be hurt electorally in the November 2000 elections. Hence, the Rules Committee crafted a bifurcated rule designed to neutralize the issue's campaign potency in Republican-held districts where organized labor's influence remains strong.

The rule first permitted consideration of a bill providing $122 billion in tax cuts over ten years, which appealed to both GOP moderates and conservatives and which took the sting out of the wage hike for the Republican-leaning business community. No amendments were permitted to the tax bill—a closed rule process. The second bill, raising the minimum wage, was then taken up and debated under a modified closed rule procedure (two amendments were made in order). The House passed both bills by a separate vote. Then, under the MIRV rule, they were combined into one measure (in this instance the wage hike was added to the tax cut bill) and sent to the Senate without ever having been voted upon as a single piece of legislation. Combing two bills into a single package raises a potential problem when it is sent to the president, because if the chief executive favors one proposal but not the other, his veto ends up killing both.

Creative rules affect House operations in important ways. They enable the majority party to advance its policy and political agenda and to cope effectively with today's substantive and procedural complexities. They exacerbate partisan tensions when minority lawmakers are shut out from proposing their favorite amendments. They promote greater certainty and predictability in floor decision making and in the overall scheduling of House activities. And, in this era of video or message politics and partisan polarization, creative rules may protect many lawmakers from casting politically troublesome votes.

Adoption of the Rule

All rules must be approved by a majority of the House. Rules are reported to the House by the Rules Committee and are debated for a maximum of one hour, with the time equally divided by custom between the Rules chair, or a designee, and the ranking minority member of the committee, or a designee. The hour rule is the basic rule of floor debate in the House. Theoretically, it permits each member one hour of debate on any question. The hour rule is never followed in practice, however. A member who controls the debate time under the hour rule, in this case the Rules chairman or his designee, always moves the previous question at the end of this hour (or before the full hour is used if no member seeks time for debate). Adoption of this motion by majority vote stops all debate, prevents the offering of amendments, and brings the House to an immediate vote on the main question, the rule itself in this context.

The main strategy, then, for a member wishing to amend a rule is to defeat the previous question. "I am urging my colleagues to vote against the previous question on this rule so that we can offer a substitute rule" is a common refrain from members who oppose the rule. Under House precedents, the member who led the fight against approval of the previous question is recognized by the Speaker to propose a substitute rule. The significant vote here often is not on adoption of the rule but on approval of the previous question.

If there is no controversy, rules are adopted routinely by voice vote after a brief discussion. Under a 1977 procedural change, the Speaker may postpone votes on rules and permit them to be voted on at five-minute intervals later in the day or any time within the next two days. The procedure is similar to cluster voting under suspension of the rules.

The House seldom rejects a rule proposed by the Rules Committee. Speaker O'Neill once remarked, "Defeat of the rule on the House floor is considered an affront both to the Committee and to the Speaker." [38] The Rules Committee generally understands the conditions the House will accept for debating and amending important bills. Further, it is an expectation within the majority party that support for rules is a given and that deviations from this behavioral norm could be held against a lawmaker when, for example, plum committee assignments are handed out. The record number of rules defeated during the 103d Congress—seven—highlighted the fissures within Democratic ranks that doubtlessly contributed to their loss of the House in November 1994 after forty years of continuous control. (Six rules were rejected in the 100th Congress, three in the 101st, none in the 102d, one in the GOP-run 104th, and five in the 105th.)

LEGISLATION BLOCKED IN COMMITTEE

What happens when a standing committee refuses to report a bill that many members support, or when the Rules Committee fails to grant a rule to legislation having substantial support? Several procedures are available to bring such legislation to the floor. Which procedure to use depends on the nature of the legislation. Suspension of the rules is appropriate if the measure is relatively noncontroversial or minor. If a major bill is being blocked, extraordinary procedures can be employed to spring the bill from committee. These procedures are difficult to implement, but if the House is determined, committees can be compelled to yield legislation.

The Discharge Petition

The discharge procedure, adopted in 1910, provides that if a bill has been before a standing committee for thirty legislative (a day on which the House meets) days, any member can introduce a motion to relieve the panel of the measure. A clerk of the House then prepares a discharge petition, which is made available for members to sign when the House is in session. If the requisite number of members (218) sign the petition, this procedure permits a majority of the House to bring a bill to the floor even if it is opposed by the committee that has jurisdiction over the measure, the majority leadership, and the Rules Committee. This procedure is difficult to use in part because majority party leaders often urge their partisan colleagues not to sign petitions.

Until 1993, House precedents prohibited public disclosure of the names of lawmakers who signed discharge petitions until the required 218 signatures had been obtained. Then the names were published in the *Congressional Record.* Critics of this procedure successfully changed House rules to require the signers' names to be made public as soon as a discharge petition is introduced instead of when a majority is achieved. The sponsor, James M. Inhofe, R-Okla. (House 1987–1994; Senate 1994), and backers such as 1992 Reform Party presidential candidate Ross Perot, conservative talk show hosts, the *Wall Street Journal,* and freshmen lawmakers, including Democrats, argued that the change would help eliminate secrecy and hypocrisy by ending the practice whereby House members introduce, cosponsor, or publicly proclaim support for bills but then refuse to sign discharge petitions that might facilitate getting those same measures to the floor. Without public disclosure, they said, party and committee leaders could pressure members either not to sign or to remove their name if they had signed a discharge petition.

Opponents contended, unsuccessfully, that disclosure would permit lobbyists to pressure lawmakers to sign discharge petitions on their pet bills, encourage the filing of frivolous petitions, and encourage orchestrated public campaigns to expedite action on emotionally charged but unrealistic legislation, bypassing the scrutiny provided by the committee system. The House was not persuaded by these arguments. As a minority member of the Rules

Committee put it, the "sunshine rule for discharging committees of popular legislation will make the House more responsive to the people."[39] (The House amended its rules in 1995 to require weekly publication in the *Congressional Record* of members who have signed a discharge petition and daily availability in the clerk's office of the cumulative list of signers.)

When 218 members have signed the petition, the motion to discharge is put on the Discharge Calendar. After seven legislative days on the calendar, it becomes privileged business on the second and fourth Mondays of the month (but not during the last six days of a session). Any member who signed the petition may be recognized to offer the discharge motion. When the motion is called up, debate is limited to twenty minutes, divided between proponents and opponents. If the discharge motion is rejected, the bill is not eligible again for discharge during that session. If the discharge motion prevails, any member who signed the petition can make a motion to call up the bill for immediate consideration. It then becomes the business of the House until it is disposed of. A vote against immediate consideration assigns the bill to the appropriate calendar, with the same rights as any bill reported from committee.

Few measures are discharged from committee. From 1931 through 1994 (approximately the period during which the modern version of the rule has been in effect), more than five hundred discharge petitions were filed, but only forty-six attracted the required signatures and only nineteen bills were discharged and passed by the House.[40] Of those, only two became law: the Fair Labor Standards Act of 1938 and the Federal Pay Raise Act of 1960.

Several factors account for the general failure of the discharge procedure. Members are reluctant to second-guess a committee's right to consider a bill. The discharge rule violates normal legislative routine, and even members who support a bill blocked in committee may refuse to sign a discharge petition for this reason. Committees, too, may nullify the discharge attempt by reporting the bill. Because it no longer has the measure, the committee cannot be discharged.

Legislators also are reluctant to write legislation on the House floor without the guidance and information provided in committee hearings and reports. Particularly in the case of complicated legislation, many members feel the need for committee interpretation. Then, too, obtaining 218 signatures is not easy. Attempts to reduce the existing requirement occasionally are made, but none has been successful. Finally, members are hesitant to employ a procedure that one day may be used against committees on which they serve.

For all its limitations, the discharge rule serves important purposes. It focuses attention on particular legislative issues, and the threat of using it may stimulate a committee to hold hearings or report a bill. Discharge petitions also provide a way for the minority party to gain some visibility for its key agenda items. Democrats in the 106th House, for instance, launched petition drives on such matters as a minimum wage hike, campaign finance reform, school construction, gun control, the patients' bill of rights, and a prescription drug bill for senior citizens.[41] However, if the minority party fails to attract sufficient discharge signatures for its priority items, it can undermine any message of party unity. "How do you say the [Democratic] Caucus is united—that we want this [bill] on the floor—with only 140 signatures?" said an exasperated Democratic aide.[42]

Rules Committee's Extraction Power

The Rules Committee has an extraordinary authority that it seldom exercises: it can introduce rules for bills that the committee of jurisdiction does not want to report. The power of extraction is based on an 1895 precedent, which the committee has invoked rarely. Extraction is a highly controversial procedure and evokes charges of usurpation of other committees' rights.

One of the rare occasions when extraction was used occurred on February 9, 1972. The Education and Labor (now Education and the Workforce) Committee refused to approve a dock strike measure, but the Rules Committee reported a rule for floor action on the bill. Despite the vigorous opposition of Speaker Carl Albert, D-Okla. (1947–1977), the House adopted the rule by a 203-170 vote, thus springing the bill from the committee. The House then proceeded to pass the bill.

The threat of extraction by the Rules panel in itself can break legislative logjams. In 1967 the Judiciary Committee balked at reporting an anti-riot bill. Rules Chairman William M. Colmer, D-Miss., announced that his committee would soon hold hearings on a rule for the bill. This was enough to prompt the Judiciary Committee to report the legislation.[43]

A Rules Committee chairman can try to make any measure in order for floor action, even if it has not received committee consideration. Chairman Claude Pepper, D-Fla., in 1988 "used his position to circumvent Ways and Means and clear his home-care health bill for floor action without hearings, debate, or markup in the committee of jurisdiction—a rare use of the Rules Committee's chairman's power."[44]

In 1995, when the GOP-controlled Government Reform Committee rejected legislation changing the federal retirement system, the Rules Committee included the change as part of a major tax bill. "In what is clearly an extraordinary departure from usual procedures," declaimed the ranking minority member on the Government Reform panel, "the Rules Committee has chosen to take a course of action which negates the very existence of the authorizing committees."[45] Despite her protest and that of others, the House agreed with the action of the Rules Committee.

Discharging the Rules Committee

The discharge rule also applies to the Rules Committee. The main reason a discharge petition is sometimes filed on a special rule is to control the terms of debate and amendment on the bill the special rule would make in order. The bill itself must still have been pending for at least thirty legislative days before a standing committee. A motion to discharge the Rules Committee is in order seven legislative days—instead of thirty—after a special rule has been referred to the panel.

Because the Rules Committee reports rules as a matter of original jurisdiction, members who wish to discharge a rule (making the stalled bill in order) have to draft and introduce one of their own so there will be something to discharge. (This introduced rule, according to the House rulebook, can neither allow for nongermane amendments nor make more than one bill in order.) Then, once the rule has been pending before the Rules Committee for seven legislative days, House precedents state it is in order to bring before the House "a measure pending before a standing committee for 30 legislative days." If the Rules Committee determines that a discharge attempt might be successful, it can report its own special rule for considering the bill on which discharge is sought.

Calendar Wednesday

Under House procedures, every Wednesday is reserved for standing committees to call up measures (except privileged bills) that have been reported but not granted rules by the Rules Committee. The Speaker calls the roll of standing committees in alphabetical order. Each chairman (or designated committee member) then decides whether to bring up for House debate a measure pending on the House or Union calendars. The rule may be dispensed with by unanimous consent—that is, without objection—or by a two-thirds vote of the House. The Rules Committee may not report a rule setting aside Calendar Wednesday.

The Calendar Wednesday rule was adopted to circumvent Speaker Cannon's control of the legislative agenda. Today it is seldom employed and usually is dispensed with by unanimous consent. During the 98th Congress (1983–1985), however, a group of Republicans led by Representative Gingrich objected regularly to dispensing with Calendar Wednesday proceedings. Their purpose was to generate political heat on the majority leadership to schedule nonprivileged measures (a constitutional balanced budget amendment, school prayer measures, criminal code reform, and so on). Republicans called their list of priority measures the Agenda of the American People (precursor of the Contract with America). The House even adopted an agriculture bill under its Calendar Wednesday procedure.[46] Objections to dispensing with Calendar Wednesday gradually diminished because of inherent limitations with the procedure.

Since 1943, fewer than fifteen measures have become law under Calendar Wednesday proceedings.[47] House consideration of the 1984 agricultural measure was the first time the procedure had been used in a quarter-century. Five factors account for the limited use of this procedure: (1) Only two hours of debate are permitted, one for proponents and one for opponents. This may not be enough to debate complex bills. (2) A committee far down in the alphabet may have to wait weeks before its turn is reached. (3) A bill that is not completed on one Wednesday is not in order the following Wednesday, unless two-thirds of the members agree. (4) The procedure is subject to dilatory tactics because the House must complete action on the same day. (5) Only the chairman or a member authorized by the committee may bring up a bill under Calendar Wednesday.

FINAL SCHEDULING STEPS

After a bill has been granted a rule, the final decision on when the measure is to be debated is made by the majority party leaders. The leadership prepares daily and weekly schedules of floor business and adjusts them according to shifting legislative situations and demands. A bill the majority has scheduled for consideration may be withdrawn if it appears to lack sufficient support. Nothing in the House rules requires the majority leadership to provide advance notice of the daily or weekly legislative program. However, as a matter of long-standing custom, majority party leaders make announcements about floor action, often in response to a query from the minority leader. The legislative program for the following day for both chambers also is published in each issue of the *Congressional Record*, in a section called the Daily Digest. The Friday *Record* contains a section called the Congressional Program Ahead, which lists the following week's legislative agenda and the dates on which floor action has been scheduled.

The majority (and minority) leadership also sends whip notices to its members at the end of each week or more frequently, if necessary. The whip notices contain information concerning the daily program for the following week. Although sent under the majority whip's signature, the agenda is developed mainly by the Speaker and majority leader. The schedule often is changed in response to unforeseen events or new circumstances. A whip notice is reproduced in Figure 4-2.

The majority and minority whip's offices have several phone recordings that announce the daily and weekly programs, legislative actions taken on the floor, and changes in the schedule. Democratic and Republican members obtain similar information from their respective cloakrooms (located just off the chamber floor), from various partisan entities, and from various House Web sites. The GOP Conference, for instance, publishes daily summaries of bills and amendments to be considered on the floor.

Two other agenda-setting actions are fast-track procedures and the politics of scheduling. Fast-track procedures are specified in some statutes to expedite the processing of certain legislation. Known as rule-making provisions, these statutory procedures are enacted under Congress's constitutional authority to "determine the rules of its proceedings." They are equivalent to the formal rules of each chamber, which also means they can be set aside if either body chooses to follow another procedure. Examples of fast-track procedures are timetables established in law for committees to report measures; legislation granted privileged access to the floor; prohibition of floor amendments of any type; imposition of strict debate

One Hundred Sixth Congress
U.S. House of Representatives
Office of the Majority Whip

Floor Information: 57430
Legislative Program: 52020

WHIP NOTICE
WEEK OF MAY 8, 2000

MONDAY, MAY 8
ON MONDAY, THE HOUSE WILL MEET AT 12:30 P.M. FOR MORNING HOUR AND
2:00 P.M.FOR LEGISLATIVE BUSINESS. NO RECORDED VOTES ARE EXPECTED
BEFORE 6:00 P.M.

Suspensions (6 Bills):

H.R. 3577	-	To increase the amount authorized to be appropriated for the north side pumping division of the Minidoka reclamation project, Idaho.
H.Con.Res. 89	-	Recognizing the Hermann Monument and Hermann Heights Park in New Ulm, Minnesota, as a national symbol of the contributions of Americans of German heritage.
H.Con.Res. 296	-	Expressing the sense of the Congress regarding the necessity to expedite the settlement process for discrimination claims against the Department of Agriculture brought by African-American farmers.
H.R. 1237	-	To amend the Federal Water Pollution Control Act to permit grants for the national estuary program to be used for the development and implementation of a comprehensive conservation and management plan, to reauthorize appropriations to carry out the program, and for other purposes.
H.R. 3069	-	Southeast Federal Center Public-Private Development Act of 2000
H.R. 3313	-	Long Island Sound Restoration Act

TUESDAY, MAY 9
ON TUESDAY, THE HOUSE WILL MEET AT 9:30 A.M. FOR MORNING HOUR AND
11:00 A.M. FOR LEGISLATIVE BUSINESS.

Suspensions (5 Bills):

H.R. 2647	-	To amend the Act entitled 'An Act relating to the water rights of the Ak-Chin Indian Community' to clarify certain provisions concerning the leasing of such water rights, and for other purposes.
H.R. 3293	-	To amend the law that authorized the Vietnam Veterans Memorial to authorize the placement within the site of the memorial of a plaque to honor those Vietnam veterans who died after their service in the Vietnam war, but as a direct result of that service.
H.R. 4040	-	Long-Term Care Security Act
H.R. 3244	-	Trafficking Victims Protection Act
H.R. 4386	-	Breast and Cervical Cancer Treatment Act

WEDNESDAY, MAY 10 AND THURSDAY, MAY 11
THE HOUSE WILL MEET AT 10:00 A.M. FOR LEGISLATIVE BUSINESS. ON THURSDAY,
NO VOTES ARE EXPECTED PAST 6:00 P.M.

H.R. 3709	-	Internet Nondiscrimination Act (Subject to a Rule)
H.R. 701	-	Conservation and Reinvestment Act (Subject to a Rule)
H.R. 863	-	Comprehensive Budget Process Reform Act (Subject to a Rule)

FRIDAY, MAY 12
NO VOTES

Sincerely,

Tom DeLay
Majority Whip

The Whip Notice is available on the Home Page of the Majority Whip at http://majoritywhip.house.gov and is available for e-mail delivery each week it is published by subscribing at http://majoritywhip.house.gov/mail.

FIGURE 4-2 House Whip Notice

limits; and counterpart legislation from the other chamber acted on promptly with little or no debate.

Traditionally, trade laws contain fast-track provisions. They are designed to expedite House and Senate committee and floor consideration of trade agreements negotiated by the president and follow-on implementing legislation. Under these laws, Congress delegates trade negotiating authority to the president with the explicit understanding that he must consult with Congress during the negotiations. When the trade agreement and implementing legislation are submitted to Congress, fast-track procedures prohibit any amendments by the House or Senate and impose a timetable for committee and floor action. "The goal of fast track," wrote an analyst, "is to prevent U.S. trade agreements from being amended in Congress in ways that might be unacceptable to the other nation or nations that are parties to the agreements."[48]

As for the politics of scheduling, party leaders consider numerous factors and circumstances to advance their objectives. Three examples will make the point. First, to maximize public attention and visibility, certain kinds of bills are brought to the floor to correspond with well-known dates: tax measures on or near April 15, flag-burning bills or constitutional amendments around July 4, or family values legislation around Mother's Day. Second, the House (and Senate) floor is used as a campaign platform to highlight partisan agenda items (message politics), especially as the November elections get nearer. House Republicans, for instance, brought several politically attractive tax cut proposals to the floor during 2000 "to keep pressure on Democrats in this pivotal election year and give Republicans popular campaign issues."[49] Or the two parties might advocate agendas of interest to selected groups or communities. To appeal to the high-tech community, for example, Republicans developed their E-Contract 2000; Democrats had their E-Agenda.[50]

Third, party leaders practice deadline lawmaking; that is, they take advantage of various work or electoral cycles to facilitate action on legislation. For instance, with a Democrat in the White House, Minority Leader Gephardt and others considered a one-issue strategy going into the November 2000 elections. The plan involved having President Bill Clinton "isolate one major legislative priority [prescription drugs for the elderly] that Congress must pass before it leaves, pressuring Republicans to get on board or risk the reproach of the voters."[51] Congressional Republicans, for their part, recognize the importance of enacting the must-pass appropriations bill on a timely basis, otherwise the president has leverage through his veto power to win eleventh hour spending decisions—and close to election day—that advantage Democrats over Republicans. "We do not want to be like we were the last couple of years—spending our way out of Washington," declared Rep. Fred Upton, R-Mich. "The public will see right through that."[52]

NOTES

1. *Congressional Record,* November 15, 1983, H9856.
2. *Congressional Record,* July 2, 1980, H6106.
3. *Congressional Record,* January 5, 1993, H59. See also *Congressional Record,* January 4, 1995, H111.
4. *Congressional Record,* June 20, 1995, H6104–H6116.
5. *Washington Post,* January 31, 1995, A13.
6. Martin Gold, Michael Hugo, Hyde Murray, Peter Robinson, and A. L. "Pete" Singleton, *The Book on Congress* (Washington, D.C.: Big Eagle Publishing Co., 1992), 124.
7. Jeffrey S. Hill and Kenneth C. Williams, "The Decline of Private Bills: Resource Allocation, Credit Claiming, and the Decision to Delegate," *American Journal of Political Science* (November 1993): 1017.
8. *Nation's Business,* February 1956, 103.
9. See, for example, James A. Robinson, *The House Rules Committee* (Indianapolis, Ind.: Bobbs-Merrill, 1963); Charles O. Jones, "Joseph G. Cannon and Howard W. Smith: An Essay on the Limits of Leadership in the House of Representatives," *Journal of Politics* (September 1968): 617–646; and Robert L. Peabody, "The Enlarged Rules Committee," in *New Perspectives on the House of Representatives,* 2d ed., ed. Robert L. Peabody and Nelson W. Polsby (Chicago, Ill.: Rand McNally, 1969).
10. *New York Times,* April 2, 1995, 20.
11. *New York Times,* December 18, 1987, A34.
12. *A History of the Committee on Rules,* 97th Cong., 2d sess. (Washington, D.C.: Government Printing Office, 1983). See also Bruce I. Oppenheimer, "The Changing Relationship between House Leadership and the Committee on Rules," in *Understanding Congressional Leadership,* ed. Frank H. Mackaman (Washington, D.C.: CQ Press, 1981).
13. Spark M. Matsunaga and Ping Chen, *Rulemakers of the House* (Urbana, Ill.: University of Illinois Press, 1976), 21. See also Alan Ehrenhalt, "The Unfashionable House Rules Committee," *Congressional Quarterly Weekly Report,* January 15, 1983, 151.
14. For an example of the use of this procedure, see *Congressional Record,* June 10, 1998, H4338–H4343.
15. Bob Michel, "Beyond the Political Wilderness: Reforming 40 Years of One-Party Rule," *Commonsense,* Fall 1994, 56.
16. Jonathan Salant, "Under Open Rules, Discord Rules," *Congressional Quarterly Weekly Report,* January 28, 1995, 277.
17. *Congressional Record,* December 15, 1987, H11436.
18. *Congressional Record,* July 14, 1987, H6282.
19. *Congressional Record,* January 4, 1995, H32.
20. Implicitly, all special rules waive certain House rules and therefore potential points of order under them, such as the daily order of business rule. Explicitly, waivers are generally of two kinds: those waiving points of order that would prevent consideration of a bill and those waiving points of order against specific provisions in a bill or amendments to the bill that otherwise might be ruled out of order.
21. *CQ's Daily Monitor,* March 2, 1995, 3.

22. *Congressional Record,* July 10, 1997, H5049.
23. *Floor Deliberations and Scheduling, Hearings before the Joint Committee on the Organization of Congress* (Washington, D.C.: Government Printing Office, 1993), 216–217.
24. Alan Ehrenhalt, "O'Neill Studying Moves to Counter GOP 'Obstructionism,' " *Washington Star,* August 5, 1979, A3.
25. Janet Hook, "GOP Chafes under Restrictive House Rules," *Congressional Quarterly Weekly Report,* October 10, 1987, 2452.
26. Data gathered by Donald Wolfensberger, former staff director, House Rules Committee, and director, Congress Project, Woodrow Wilson Center. The Rules Committee maintains a well-organized Web site (www.house.gov/rules) replete with procedural information about the panel's role in the House.
27. *Congressional Record,* May 21, 1982, H2519.
28. *Congressional Record,* August 8, 1994, H7181.
29. *Congressional Record,* February 27, 1995, H2239. The order of this dialogue was reversed to make the partisan viewpoints stand out clearly.
30. See, for example, *Congressional Record,* May 23, 1995, H5390–H5394.
31. Mary Jacoby, "Three-Quarters 'Open,' or Two-Thirds 'Closed'? Parties Can't Agree on How to Define Rules," *Roll Call,* April 13, 1995, 7.
32. *Roll Call,* December 8, 1994, 10.
33. *National Journal,* January 21, 1995, 183.
34. Jennifer Babson, "House Rejects Term Limits; GOP Blames Democrats," *Congressional Quarterly Weekly Report,* April 1, 1995, 918.
35. *Congressional Record,* May 23, 1995, H5395.
36. *Congressional Record,* February 27, 1995, H2235.
37. See, for example, *Congressional Record,* February 24, 1995, H2211.
38. "Switched Votes for Gas Bill," *Congressional Quarterly Weekly Report,* February 14, 1976, 313.
39. *Washington Times,* September 29, 1993, A4. See *Congressional Record,* September 28, 1993, for the debate and vote on the new discharge rule.
40. Figures were made available to the author by Richard Beth, congressional specialist, Government Division, Congressional Research Service, Library of Congress.
41. See, for example, Ethan Wallison, "Gephardt Plans Petition Strategy," *Roll Call,* May 17, 1999, 1.
42. Ethan Wallison, "House Democrats Split on Strategy," *Roll Call,* February 17, 2000, 28.
43. Matsunaga and Chen, *Rulemakers of the House,* 25.
44. Julie Kosterlitz, "Still Going Strong," *National Journal,* January 2, 1988, 15.
45. *Congressional Record,* April 5, 1995, H4204.
46. *Congressional Record,* January 25, 1984, H126–H139.
47. Information compiled by Richard Beth, congressional specialist, Government Division, Congressional Research Service, Library of Congress.
48. Bob Benenson, "Removal of 'Fast Track' May Put GATT in the Fast Lane," *Congressional Quarterly Weekly Report,* September 17, 1994, 2561. Also see I. M. Destler, *American Trade Politics,* 2d ed. (Washington, D.C.: Institute for International Economics, 1992), 71–76.
49. Dave Boyer and John Godfrey, "Republicans Set to Move Forward on 3 Tax-Cut Bills," *Washington Times,* May 4, 2000, A1.

50. Jim VandeHei, "GOP Drafts 'E-Contract' with America in Pitch for Community's Support," *Wall Street Journal,* May 9, 2000, A28.
51. Ethan Wallison, "Democrats Mull New Drug Bill," *Roll Call,* May 1, 2000, 1.
52. David Bauman, "A Republican Resurgence," *National Journal,* May 6, 2000, 1417.

CHAPTER 5

House Floor Procedure

VISITORS to the House gallery may be surprised by what they observe on the House floor. On the one hand, floor activity appears hopelessly disorganized. People come and go in an endless stream. Motions are offered, amendments are proposed, and points of order are raised. On the other hand, representatives on the floor display little interest in what is going on. Legislators talk in small groups or read newspapers while their colleagues make speeches. Furthermore, attendance is often sparse during floor debates. Members may be in committee sessions, meeting with constituents, or attending to numerous other tasks. Members can reach the floor quickly, however, to respond to quorum calls, participate in debate, or vote.

The House chamber has two levels. Above the floor are the galleries for visitors, diplomats, reporters, and other observers. Visitors sit on either side or facing the Speaker's rostrum; the press sits above and behind the rostrum. Unlike senators, representatives have no desks in the chamber. Seats, which are unassigned, are arranged in semicircular rows in front of the Speaker. Aisles divide groups of seats, and a broad center aisle divides the majority and minority parties (see Figure 5-1).[1]

Normally, the House convenes daily at noon.[2] Buzzers ring in committee rooms, members' offices, and in the Capitol, summoning representatives to the floor. Rules and informal practices set the daily order of business: an opening prayer, approval of the *Journal* (a record of the previous day's proceedings), the Pledge of Allegiance, receipt of messages from the Senate or the president, one-minute speeches and insertions in the *Congressional Record,* and other routine business. A period of morning hour debate may occur prior to the start of formal legislative business. The House convenes from an hour to an hour and a half earlier to accommodate lawmakers who want to discuss various issues of the day. The time is equally divided between the two parties.[3] Today, with the escalation of partisanship, each party has its theme team or message group to orchestrate the daily speeches during the one-minute or other debate periods.

Under the rules, a majority of the House (218 of the 435 members) must be present for business to be conducted. Whether or not a quorum has been established, it is assumed to be present unless officially discovered otherwise. A member may ask for a quorum call provided he or she is recognized for that purpose by the Speaker. Any member, however, may make a point of no quorum whenever a vote is pending. Informally, the House frequently operates with far fewer members.

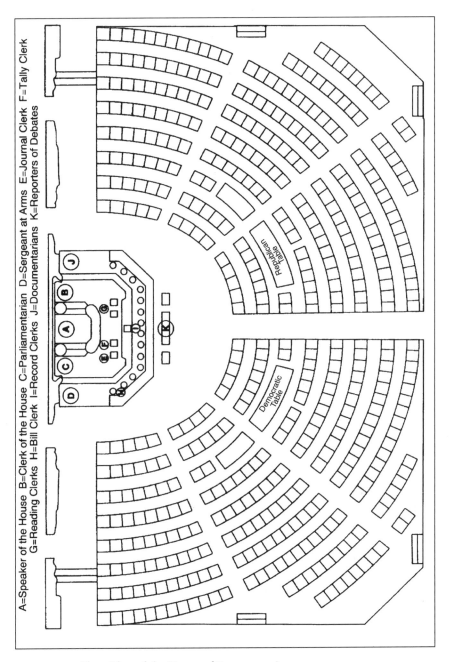

Figure 5-1 Floor Plan of the House of Representatives

A=Speaker of the House B=Clerk of the House C=Parliamentarian D=Sergeant at Arms E=Journal Clerk F=Tally Clerk G=Reading Clerks H=Bill Clerk I=Record Clerks J=Documentarians K=Reporters of Debates

The House usually is in session Monday through Friday. Mondays are reserved mainly for routine legislation. The workload on Fridays generally is light because many members want to return to their home districts on weekends. Most major business is conducted from Tuesday through Thursday. A three-day workweek sometimes makes it hard for lawmakers to carry out their many legislative and oversight responsibilities. (Other scheduling arrangements are sometimes employed at different times, such as providing for alternating four-day weekends with the House in session one week from Tuesday to Friday and the next from Monday to Thursday; five-day workweeks or more are common during the hectic last weeks of a legislative session.) The House has also tried for years to make its schedule more predictable and, thus, family friendly. Typically, the House meets less frequently during the second session (an election year) than the first session.

Although every day on the House floor is not the same—some are brief sessions while others go on all night, for example—a recurring pattern of daily activity has emerged. The basic steps in floor consideration for major bills are:

1. Adoption of the rule granted by the Rules Committee.
2. The act of resolving the House into the Committee of the Whole.
3. General debate.
4. The amending process.
5. The motion to recommit.
6. Final action by the full House.

ADOPTION OF THE RULE

The first step in bringing a major bill to the floor is adoption of a special rule issued by the Rules Committee. A rule sets the conditions under which a measure is to be considered, decreeing whether floor amendments will be permitted and how much debate will be allowed.

The House rarely rejects a rule. Challenging the Rules Committee is an uninviting task. House members in the future may need a rule from the committee for their own bills. Rejection of a rule usually reflects sharp divisions in the House; disagreements within the majority party (whose members are expected to support these procedural votes); heavy lobbying by pressure groups, the president, or federal agency officials; or general agreement that the reporting committee did a poor job of drafting the bill.

Voting down a rule is often a procedural kill. During the 99th Congress (1985–1987), in a particularly dramatic example, Republicans organized to defeat the rule on a landmark tax reform bill supported by President Ronald Reagan.

> The rule was a tempting target for the Republicans. Members were hesitant to vote against the bill itself, fearing they might be straddled with the blame for killing reform, but the rule offered a chance, as [GOP Whip—now Senate

majority leader—Trent] Lott put it, for members "to get rid of the bill without putting their fingerprints on the trigger." [4]

The defeat of the rule launched an intensive round of negotiations among the Speaker, party leaders, the Treasury secretary, and White House officials, as well as a private meeting of the president with all House Republicans, to bring a second rule on the tax bill to the floor. Speaker Thomas P. "Tip" O'Neill Jr., D-Mass., even took the floor and successfully urged members in a moving speech to vote for the second rule. This incident shows how procedural matters can have a critical impact on policy making. Without favorable action on the second rule, tax reform would have been dead.

In another example, the House rejected a rule on a major 1994 crime bill in part because of procedure (the rule contained controversial waivers), policy (the charge was made that the bill contained more money for social programs than prison construction), and politics (GOP anger at being shut out of substantive discussions by Democratic leaders). The comprehensive crime bill was a top priority of President Bill Clinton and House Democratic leaders, but the rule on the bill was defeated by an "odd alliance of conservative pro-gun Democrats, anti-death penalty liberals and Republicans of every stripe." [5] In the end, after extensive lobbying and marathon discussions by the president and Democratic leaders with discontented lawmakers, the House passed a second rule ten days later during a rare Sunday session.[6] Clinton subsequently signed the $30 billion anticrime measure into law.

On June 25, 1998, the House rejected by 125–291 a rule on a Treasury and Postal Service appropriations bill. Conservative Republicans and Democrats combined to defeat the rule. A group of GOP conservatives, who call themselves the Conservative Action Team, was angry that the rule protected a provision in the bill "that would require health plans for federal employees to cover a broad range of contraceptives. The rule protected the provision from being stripped from the bill on a point of order that could be raised under House rules that bar legislating on an appropriations bill." [7] In addition, 135 Democrats and Independent Bernard Sanders of Vermont opposed the rule, because the GOP leadership decided to delete from the bill emergency funding to address the anticipated problem of year 2000 computer glitches (Y2K) and deal with the issue in a separate bill. (Sometimes, prior to a vote, the majority leadership will yank a rule from floor consideration if adequate support to approve it is not evident.)

COMMITTEE OF THE WHOLE

After the House votes to adopt a rule, the Speaker declares the House resolved into the Committee of the Whole. The Committee of the Whole is the House in another form. Every legislator is a member. House rules require all revenue-raising or appropriations bills to be considered first in the Committee of the Whole. With its special authority for revenue and spending bills, wrote the staff director of the House Rules Committee, the Committee of the Whole "is the very essence of the House exercising its special [fiscal] powers and prerogatives under the Constitution." [8]

Technically, there are two such bodies. One is the Committee of the Whole House, which debates private bills. The other and more important is the Committee of the Whole House on the state of the Union, commonly shortened to Committee of the Whole, which considers public measures. The Committee of the Whole has its origins, like many congressional practices, in the British Parliament. During the seventeenth century, the Parliament and the Crown regularly clashed over finances and taxes. To ensure that all members of the House of Commons participated in debates involving the expenditure of money, Parliament established the Committee of the Whole to review and check the financial proposals made by parliamentary committees, which were sometimes stacked with the king's or queen's supporters. A further elaboration of the Committee of the Whole's origins is provided by a scholar and former member of the House of Representatives, De Alva Stanwood Alexander, R-N.Y. (1897–1911):

> It originated in the time of the Stuarts, when taxation arrayed the Crown against the Commons, and suspicion made the Speaker [of the House of Commons] a tale-bearer to the King. To avoid the Chair's espionage the Commons met in secret [in a Committee of the Whole], elected a chairman in whom it had confidence, and without fear of the King freely exchanged its views respecting [financial] supplies.[9]

The Committee of the Whole uses rules different from those of the House. They are designed to speed up floor action. A number of rules or customs distinguish the conduct of business in the full House from proceedings in the Committee of the Whole (see Table 5-1).

First, a quorum is only one hundred members in the Committee of the Whole (218 constitute a quorum in the House). Second, the Speaker does not preside over the Committee of the Whole but appoints a colleague, who is a member of his own party, to chair it (a practice that can be traced to English precedent). The Speaker is permitted to remain in the chamber and take part in debate, but he rarely participates except to make closing remarks on tightly contested major bills. By tradition, the Speaker seldom votes, except to break a tie. Third, it is in order in a Committee of the Whole to close or limit debate on sections of a bill by unanimous consent or majority vote of the members present. Fourth, various motions that are in order in the House are not permitted in the Committee of the Whole, such as the previous question motion or motions to recommit, adjourn, or reconsider the vote by which an amendment was agreed to or rejected. Fifth, amendments to bills are introduced and debated under the five-minute rule in the Committee of the Whole, not under the hour rule as in the House.[10] Sixth, in the Committee of the Whole, twenty-five members trigger a recorded vote; in the House, forty-four members (one-fifth of a quorum). Finally, the position of the mace, a forty-

TABLE 5-1 Major Characteristics, House and Committee of the Whole

House	Committee of the Whole
Mace raised	Mace lowered
Speaker presides	Chairman presides
More than half the House (218) is a quorum	One hundred is a quorum
One-hour rule for amendments	Five-minute rule for amendments
Previous question in order	Motion to limit debate on amendments, but not the previous question motion, in order
Forty-four members or one-fifth of the House trigger a recorded vote	Twenty-five members trigger a recorded vote
Motion to recommit in order	Motion to recommit not in order

SOURCE: Adapted from *Manual on Legislative Procedure in the U.S. House of Representatives,* 6th ed., 99th Cong., prepared under the auspices of the House Republican leader, May 1986.

six-inch column of ebony rods bound together by silver and topped by a silver eagle, indicates whether the House is in the Committee of the Whole. The mace, symbol of the authority of the sergeant at arms, is carried by him, if called upon, to enforce order on the floor. It rests on a pedestal on a table at the right of the Speaker's podium. It is taken down from the table when the Speaker hands the gavel to the chairman of the Committee of the Whole. When the committee rises and the Speaker resumes the chair, the mace is returned to its place.[11]

GENERAL DEBATE

The first order of business in the Committee of the Whole is general debate on the entire bill under consideration.[12] One hour of debate usually is allowed, equally divided between the minority and majority parties. For most bills, one hour is authorized; for complex legislation, as many as ten hours may be scheduled. The chairman of the Committee of the Whole presides over the proceedings and wields the gavel to maintain order and fairness. "It's an art form," said a lawmaker. "It takes an ability to sense the mood of the House, track the chemistry of what is going on in the floor, apply the gavel lightly or hard, depending on what is warranted."[13]

Each party has a floor manager from the committee of original jurisdiction who controls time, allotting segments to supporters or opponents, as the case may be. Almost without exception, the floor manager for the majority party is the spokesman for the bill. Sometimes both sides favor passage of a bill, and both floor managers rise in support. During debate on controversial legislation, both floor managers may declare their support for the bill's aims but reflect differences of opinion on specific sections or amendments.

The term *general debate* can be misleading, as most members deliver set speeches and engage in a minimum of give-and-take. Because committees and subcommittees shape the fundamental character of most legislation, only a limited number of representatives participate in debate, and those who do usually are members of the committee that drafted the legislation. Yet general debate has an intrinsic value that is recognized by most House members and experts on the legislative process. (The House experimented with three Oxford-style floor debates in 1994 on agreed-upon national issues—health, welfare, and trade—where teams of lawmakers engaged each other in sustained discussions of these topics. This British debating format has not been used since by the House.)

Purposes of General Debate

General debate is both symbolic and practical. It assures both legislators and the public that the House makes its decisions in a democratic fashion, with due respect for majority and minority opinion. "Congress is the only branch of government that can argue publicly," noted a House Republican. "Debate appropriately tests the conclusions of the majority." [14] General debate forces members to come to grips with the issues at hand; difficult and controversial sections of a bill are explained; constituents and interest groups are alerted to a measure's purpose through press coverage of the debate; member sentiment can be assessed by the floor leaders; a public record, or legislative history, for administrative agencies and the courts is built, indicating the intentions of proponents and opponents alike; legislators may take positions for reelection purposes; and, occasionally, fence-sitters may be influenced.

Some legislators doubt that debate can change views or affect the outcome of a vote. But debate, especially by party leaders just before a key vote, can change opinion. A 1983 speech by Speaker O'Neill on U.S. involvement in Lebanon, said a House Democrat, marked "one of the few times on the House floor when a speech changed a lot of votes." [15]

Robert H. Michel, R-Ill., House minority leader from 1981 to 1995, also highlighted the importance of having informed and persuasive speakers take part in floor debates.

> A classic example . . . occurred during our debate on the nuclear freeze in 1983. A Democratic colleague challenged my Illinois colleague, [Republican] Henry [J.] Hyde, who had just criticized a prominent woman advocate of the freeze. The Democrat said: "Yes, she is, as you say the mother of the freeze. But President Reagan, through his lack of arms control progress, is the father of the freeze." And, without missing a beat, Henry Hyde shot back: "And that makes you a son of a freeze." The debate went our way after that. [16]

Hyde's speech against a constitutional term limits proposal, which was reported from the Judiciary Committee that he chaired, contributed to House rejection of the proposal. In defending experience against ignorance, Hyde declaimed: "I just cannot be an accessory to the dumbing down of democracy." [17] A leader's exhortations may not be sufficiently persuasive, however. Speaker Newt Gingrich, R-Ga., appealed to lawmakers to back a GOP-sponsored effort to repeal the War Powers Resolution of 1973 but failed to garner enough support. [18]

Reasoned deliberation is important in decision making. Lawmaking consists of more than logrolling, compromises, or power plays. General debate enables members to gain a better understanding of complex issues, and it may influence the collective decisions of the House. The dilemma members often face, said a House member, "is to know what is right, and to make the right decisions" based upon skimpy, incomplete, or unavailable information. [19] This was certainly the case in 1991 when the House (and Senate) debated, before a nationwide Cable-Satellite Public Affairs Network (C-SPAN) audience, authorization for the president to use military force against Iraq following its invasion of Kuwait. The general debate on what amounted to a declaration of war, said Speaker Thomas S. Foley, D-Wash., was "the longest in the modern history of the House of Representatives, extending over 20 hours." [20]

Floor Managers' Role

Long-standing customs govern much of the action on the floor. But the floor managers direct the course of debate on each bill. The manager for the majority side often is the chairman of the committee that reported the bill or an appointed committee colleague. The ranking minority committee member, or an appointed surrogate, usually is the floor manager for the minority party. The floor managers are located during debate at long tables near the center of the chamber, with the main aisle separating the Democratic from the Republican side.

The floor managers guide their bills through final disposition by the House. Their principal tasks are to inform colleagues (and by inference the general public and media) of the contents of the bill; to explain the issues in controversy and why the committee made the decisions it did; and to provide lawmakers with reasons to vote for the legislation and to reject alternatives. In addition, they must:

1. Plan strategy and parliamentary maneuvers to meet changing floor situations;
2. Respond to points of order;
3. Attempt to protect the bill from amendments the majority considers undesirable;
4. Alert supporters to be on the floor to vote for or against closely contested amendments;

5. Advise colleagues on the meaning and importance of the amendments;
6. Judge when amendments of committee members should be offered or deferred;
7. Inform party leaders of member sentiment and the mood of the House toward their bill;
8. Control the time for general debate and, if necessary, act to limit debate on amendments, sections or titles of the bill, or on the entire measure;
9. Arrange the sequence of speakers on major amendments to ensure that the best supporting orators are matched against those of the opposition; and
10. Mobilize outside support to build winning coalitions on the floor.

The fate of much legislation depends on the skill of the floor managers. Effective floor management increases the chances for smooth passage. The enactment of the landmark Congressional Budget and Impoundment Control Act of 1974 was credited in large part to its skillful floor manager, Rep. Richard W. Bolling, D-Mo. (1949–1983).

Floor managers are given several advantages over their colleagues. They customarily lead off debate in the Committee of the Whole and have the first opportunity to appeal for support. During debate they receive priority recognition from the chair. Floor managers may take the floor at critical moments ahead of other legislators to defend or rebut attacks on the bill, or they may offer amendments to coalesce support for the measure. Floor managers also are entitled, by custom, to close the debate on an amendment, thus having the last chance to influence sentiment.

Floor managers generally can count on support from their party leadership. They also are permitted to have up to five of their committee's staff members on the floor during debate, ready to research rules and precedents, draft amendments, answer technical questions about the bill, or prepare statements. Finally, as a result of committee hearings, discussion, and markup, the managers have a reservoir of knowledge about the technical details of a measure and are in a good position to judge which amendments to accept and reject, and the best arguments to employ for or against them.

Delaying Tactics

Despite the generally tighter rules on debate in the House than in the Senate, representatives have many ways to prolong or delay proceedings. They may raise numerous points of order, make scores of parliamentary inquiries, or offer trivial amendments. For example, during consideration of a bill creating the Department of Education, an opponent offered two unsuccessful but dilatory amendments. One would have changed the department's name to the Department of Public Education (DOPE), the other to the Department of Public Education and Youth (DOPEY).[21] Members may also demand recorded votes on every amendment and motion, ask unanimous consent to speak for additional minutes on each amendment, make certain that all time for general debate is used, offer motions to adjourn the House, or move that the Committee of the Whole rise.

Until a 1971 rules change, a reading of the *Journal* was used as a delaying tactic. Before then, the reading could be dispensed with only by unanimous consent or by a motion to suspend the rules, requiring a two-thirds vote. Since then, the Speaker has been authorized to examine the *Journal,* although a vote is often demanded on its approval. That happens at the start of the day for various reasons: to determine which members are present, to break up committee meetings, or to vent partisan frustrations.

The purpose of delaying tactics is often to stall action on a measure to allow more time to gather support (if those using such tactics favor the bill) or to kill it (if they are opposed). Delay is intended sometimes to force action and other times to prevent it, or delay may be employed to protest actions of the majority. When Republicans were in the minority they used obstructionist tactics after a one-vote victory engineered, the GOP argued, by the unwarranted actions of Speaker Jim Wright, D-Texas, in permitting an extra ten minutes on a vote so that Democrats could lobby a partisan colleague to change his vote. To vent their anger and forge greater party rapport, Republicans retaliated by tying up the House for the next three days. The House found itself without a quorum (many legislators were in their districts) and could not conduct any business. The majority leader several times tried to adjourn the House but, because of Democratic absentees, Republicans kept voting against adjournment. Several hours elapsed before Democratic leaders rounded up enough partisan colleagues to adjourn the House.[22]

Minority Democrats since the mid-1990s have employed many of the parliamentary guerrilla warfare tactics used by Republicans when they were in the minority, such as raising parliamentary objections, clashing verbally with lawmakers on the other side of the aisle, demanding roll-call votes, forcing votes on the motion to adjourn the House, and offering floor amendments designed to foment reelection difficulties for members of the opposing party who must vote against them. "The job of the minority is to make trouble for the majority," remarked Majority Leader Dick Armey, R-Texas, "and they are doing a very good job of this."[23]

Democrats have also added to the repertoire of stalling tactics. In a coordinated effort, Democrats mobilized to end the House's investigation of a controversial contested election contest. The probe involved whether the 1996 election of Democratic representative Loretta Sanchez of California, who defeated the GOP incumbent Robert K. Dornan, was the result of illegal voting by noncitizens. Democrats argued that the yearlong GOP investigation had turned up no evidence that Sanchez had not been elected legally. Republicans countered that all the facts had not been uncovered and promised that the investigation would continue into 1998.

To pressure Republicans to end the Sanchez investigation, Democrats repeatedly raised what is called a question of privilege. Never before, so far as is known, has there been a systematic effort to use questions of privilege for partisan purposes. Questions of privilege involve the rights of the House collectively, its safety, dignity, and the integrity of its proceedings. This kind of question is brought before the House in the form of a resolution, and it has precedence over every other motion except a motion to adjourn. Any lawmaker may offer this privileged resolution after providing one-day's notice, and the resolution may layover two days before being called up. The majority leader and the minority leader are exempt from these requirements and may offer these privileged resolutions at any time.

During a two-week period from late October 1997 to early November, Democrats offered more than forty privileged resolutions to end the Sanchez investigation. (The Speaker acknowledged that the resolutions constituted a legitimate question involving the privileges of the House.) To compel as many votes as possible, each resolution had to be phrased differently. Not only did repeated use of the resolution irk Republicans, but the phraseology of some angered them as being frivolous and disrespectful of the House. For example, a Democratic lawmaker included the following "whereas" clauses in her resolution to differentiate it from the others: "Whereas Loretta Sanchez of the Golden State smiles brighter than Bob Dornan even on a cloudy day; and Whereas, many feel that the real bottom line in all of this is that Bob Dornan needs to get a life—and a job." [24]

Republicans did permit a privileged resolution offered on October 23, 1997, by Minority Leader Richard A. Gephardt, D-Mo., to be debated for the customary one hour. Then, instead of clouding the outcome by use of the motion to table (or kill) Gephardt's resolution, the GOP leaders mobilized their rank and file to kill it outright. A week later, however, Republicans tabled eight questions of privilege as soon as they were offered in the House. Finally, when GOP frustrations with the stalling tactics of Democrats reached their boiling point, the Rules Committee reported a rule, which the House adopted after sharp debate, that prohibited any lawmaker, except the majority and minority leaders, from offering a privileged resolution for the remainder of the session. The rule said that "the Speaker may not recognize a Member other than the majority leader or the minority leader to offer from the floor, or to announce an intention to offer, a resolution as a question of privileges of the House." [25] Much of the controversy over the Sanchez-Dornan case can be traced to a 1984 election, which Republicans contend that Democrats stole from them. With Democrats then in charge, Frank McCloskey, D-Ind., was declared the victor by the House by four votes over Republican Richard D. McIntyre. When the decision was announced, Republicans walked en masse from the House chamber.

THE AMENDING PROCESS

The amending process is the heart of decision making on the floor. Although amendment procedure can be complex, three distinctions can be made about amendments. First, amendments can be categorized by type. They add or insert language, take out or strike matter, or do both simultaneously—strike and insert. Second, amendments can be differentiated by their degrees (see p. 165). Third, amendments can be distinguished by how much they want to change the bill or a pending amendment: a little or substantially. A perfecting amending tends toward little change; a substitute leans toward more change. Under an open rule, amendments—which are policy alternatives—determine the final shape of bills passed by the House. At times, amendments become more important or controversial than the bills themselves.

The Five-Minute Rule

House rules require all bills and joint resolutions to be read three times to give members every opportunity to become familiar with the measures they are considering. In practice, bills are not read word for word. Verbatim readings generally are dispensed with by unanimous consent or by a rule that stipulates that each section of the bill is considered to have been read.

The first reading occurs when a measure is introduced and referred to committee. The bill is not read aloud; the bill's number and title are published in the *Congressional Record*. The second reading occurs in the Committee of the Whole. The third occurs by title (the name of the bill only) just before the vote on final passage.

Bills are considered, or read, as specified in the rule from the Rules Committee, usually section by section. The Rules Committee might specify a reading by title instead of by section, to permit larger, interrelated parts of the measure to be open to amendment.

At the end of general debate, a bill is read for amendment under the five-minute rule. Under this rule, "any Member shall be allowed five minutes to explain any amendment he may offer, after which the Member who shall first obtain the floor shall be allowed to speak five minutes in opposition to it, and there shall be no further debate thereon." [26]

Actual practice differs from the rule. Amendments are regularly debated for more than the ten minutes allowed. Members gain the floor by offering pro forma amendments, moving to strike the last word or to strike the requisite number of words. Technically, these also are amendments, although no alteration of the bill is contemplated by the sponsors; their purpose is to extend the debate. (Pro forma amendments are not in order under a closed rule.) In addition, members may ask for unanimous consent to speak longer than five minutes, and they may yield part of their time to other legislators.

Debate on amendments cannot extend forever, however, and the floor manager can move that discussion be terminated at a specified time. Time limits on amendments can be critical to the fate of legislation. For example, on a Labor-Health and Human Services (HHS) appropriations bill, a time limit on debate engineered by William H. Natcher, D-Ky., chairman of the Appropriations Subcommittee on Labor, HHS, and Education, in 1987 effectively prevented amendments from being offered on sensitive social topics (abortion, for example) that in years past mired the funding bill in controversy. [27]

Sometimes the rule itself imposes specific time limits on amendments, which can arouse sharp controversy. During 1996 debate on revamping the welfare system, the rule from the Rules Committee, to expedite floor action, allowed the majority floor manager, Ways and Means Chairman Bill Archer, R-Texas, to combine eleven individual amendments (each debatable for twenty minutes) into one en bloc (all together) amendment debatable for twenty minutes. When Chairman Archer proposed to do just that, his action infuriated the minority floor manager, Sam M. Gibbons, D-Fla., who asked unanimous consent that the en bloc amendment be debated for an hour. Republican Bill Emerson, Mo., objected. The following then occurred:

> MR. GIBBONS. Mr. Chairman, I ask unanimous consent for 59 minutes.
> MR. EMERSON. I object.
> MR. GIBBONS. Mr. Chairman, I ask unanimous consent for 58 minutes.
> MR. EMERSON. I object.
> MR. GIBBONS. Mr. Chairman, I ask unanimous consent for 57 minutes.
> MR. EMERSON. I object.

Minority floor manager Gibbons made several more attempts in this vein, and each time an objection arose. Gibbons was livid. He called the time limitation an "outrageous procedure." Chairman Archer stated that it was necessary "to expedite this debate." The discussion escalated into a frenzy of angry rhetoric. Gibbons, for instance, told Republicans: "You all sit down and shut up. Sit down and shut up." Finally, Archer asked and received unanimous consent to extend the time for debate for an additional thirty minutes.[28]

Amendments are in order as soon as the section to which they apply has been read, but they must be proposed before the clerk starts to read the next section. If the clerk has passed on to a succeeding section, a member must be granted unanimous consent to offer an amendment to the previous section. In addition to being timely, amendments must be germane to the bill and section under consideration. Reading by section or title helps structure rational consideration of complex bills, but on noncontroversial measures the floor manager usually asks unanimous consent that the entire bill be considered as read. In that case, the entire measure is open to amendment at any point. Thus, under the regular (customary) order, as explained by the Rules Committee,

> as each section is read, any amendments recommended by the reporting committee are automatically considered first without having to be offered from the floor. Quite often a special rule will provide that if the committee amendment is adopted, it becomes part of the base text for the purpose of further amendment so as not to block other members from amending that portion of the bill. Traditionally, the Chair next recognizes other members with amendments to that section. If two or more Members seek recognition, the Chair gives priority to Members of the committee(s) of jurisdiction over the bill, taking account of their seniority. Members of the primary committee of jurisdiction are recognized before secondary committee Members. The Chair will alternate between

the parties in recognizing Members to offer amendments. Special rules commonly authorize the chairman of the Committee of the Whole to give priority in recognition to Members who have pre-printed their amendments in the [*Congressional*] *Record*.[29]

Reading amendments can be used to delay or prolong proceedings. Any member can object to a unanimous consent request to dispense with the reading of amendments. Opponents of a bill may draft lengthy amendments, perhaps the size of the Manhattan telephone directory, not with the expectation that they will be adopted, but to cause delays by having them read in their entirety.

House rules, however, permit a nondebatable motion to be made in the Committee of the Whole to dispense with the reading of an amendment if it was either published in the *Congressional Record* or provided to the reporting committee at least one day prior to floor action on the bill. The Rules Committee, too, can obviate the reading requirement by requiring that amendments be published in advance in the *Record* or by specifying in its rules that amendments meet the terms of the House rule that dispenses with the reading of amendments.

The Rules Committee, too, often requests (or may require) that lawmakers have their proposed amendments to bills printed in advance in the amendment section of the *Congressional Record*. The special rule will then state that the "amendments so printed are to be considered as read." The prenotification of amendments strengthens the reporting committee's role on the floor by enabling it to prepare advance arguments, alternatives, or modifications to each prenoticed change. Advance notice of amendments also provides some degree of predictability in floor decision making, an objective favored by the floor managers and the majority leadership.[30]

Rationale for Amendments

Amendments serve diverse objectives. Some are offered in deference to pressure groups, executive branch officials, or constituents; others are designed to attract public notice, to stall the legislative process, to demonstrate concern for an issue, or to test sentiment for or against a bill; and still others are politically motivated. Amendments are designed to force controversial votes and thus provide electoral ammunition to congressional challengers. Some are more technical than substantive; they may renumber sections of a bill or correct typographical errors. One common strategy is to load down a bill with so many objectionable amendments that it will sink of its own weight. Declared Speaker Wright to proponents of an amendment he strongly opposed: "If that is your goal, if you just want to find a cynical way to burden down the committee bill and make it unpassable, then you might want to vote for this [amendment]."[31] Committee members may vote against a bill they originally reported if objectionable or irresistible, but inappropriate, amendments are added on the floor.

Committees do not have final authority to amend bills or measures during their markups. Only the full House has the authority to approve or disapprove of proposed changes to legislation. Committee amendments, then, are recommendations to the full House, where they are granted priority consideration ahead of amendments proposed by individual lawmakers. Committee amendments are usually subject to amendment.

Committee amendments, riders, and substitutes are different types of amendments that all propose to do one of three things: add or insert something into a bill, strike something from a bill, or both strike out and insert something that is not already in the measure.

Committee and Floor Amendments. House precedents grant priority to amendments recommended by the reporting committee(s). "Committee amendments to a pending section," these precedents state, "are normally considered prior to amendments offered from the floor." [32] This condition is another example of the parliamentary advantage accorded committees by House rules and precedents. Committees receive most of the bills introduced in the House, influence the kind of rule their bills receive from the Rules Committee, and control general debate on the floor.

In the past, the House was inclined to defer to the committees' recommendations. That is changing. "When I came here . . . [in 1965]," reflected Thomas Foley, then the majority leader, "most of the Members would follow the committee. Now . . . the committee's 'aye' or 'nay' isn't enough." [33] The former committee monopoly over policy making has diminished during the past few decades as the Capitol Hill environment has become more permeable to outside influences. Committees are bypassed in whole or in part by informal or leadership task forces established to draft legislation. The multiple referral of measures to several committees undercuts jurisdictional monopolies by involving several panels in the consideration of legislation. The trend away from committee autonomy has been reinforced by partisan actions that further consolidate power in the office of the Speaker and the majority party caucus.

With most committees being open to greater challenges on the floor (subject to the character of the rule), chairmen not surprisingly may look to the suspension procedure as a way to protect their measures from floor amendments. Or the Rules Committee will make clear that if legislation gets bogged down during an open amendment process, the panel will reconvene and report another shut-down rule that limits amendments and expedites action on the bill.

Riders. Riders are amendments that are extraneous to the subject matter of the bill. They are more common in the Senate because House rules, in theory at least, require amendments to be germane or relevant to the bill itself. Any member can question the relevance of a proposed amendment by raising a point of order, on which the chair must rule. Such questions are not always raised, however, either because the rule from the Rules Committee may waive them, through oversight, or because members are in general agreement with the provision. "I don't make points of order on all [riders]," a member once observed, "because some may be necessary due to changing conditions." [34] The House's strict rule requiring the germaneness of amendments is not self-enforcing.

A fundamental objective of the germaneness rule ("no motion or proposition on a subject different from that under consideration shall be admitted under color of amendment") is to focus the House's attention on one subject at a time. In addition, the rule facilitates majority party control of the agenda (by preventing, for example, the minority party from offering unrelated amendments) and bolsters the role of committees. Although brief, the germaneness rule, which applies to all amendments (committee and individual), is difficult and complex to apply. For example, if an amendment is proposed to a pending amendment, is the proposed change supposed to be germane to the pending amendment, to the bill, or to both? (The answer is to the pending amendment.) House members use scores of precedents and tests to defend their amendments from germaneness points of order (see Box 5-1). A dilemma for lawmakers is that these tests and "precedents do not set down perfectly distinct guidelines for analysis." [35]

For example, Rep. John Conyers Jr., D-Mich., in 1996 offered an amendment to add crimes of fraud and deception to a bill addressing crimes of violence against children, the elderly, and other vulnerable persons. A germaneness point of order was successfully lodged against Conyers's amendment on the grounds that it did not deal with crimes of violence. Immediately, Conyers offered another amendment—to add environmental crimes (the pollution of the environment) to the underlying bill. Again, a successful germaneness point of order was raised and sustained by the chair, which ruled that Conyers's amendment was "not confined to the subject of crimes of violence" as defined in the U.S. criminal code. Quickly, Conyers proposed a third amendment—to include environmental crimes as a subset of crimes of violence under the appropriate section of the U.S. criminal code. A germaneness point of order was raised, but the chair overruled it on the grounds that Conyers's amendment was confined to the subject of violent crimes against vulnerable persons. [36]

Riders often encompass proposals that are less likely to become law on their own merits (as separate bills), either because of resistance in the Senate or the probability of a presidential veto. The strategy on such issues is to draft them as riders to important legislation—must-pass bills that are almost certain to be enacted—such as appropriations measures funding the federal government. If the House is tenacious enough in clinging to its rider, the chances are good that it will be accepted—grudgingly—by the Senate and the president.

Substitute Amendments.   There are two kinds of substitutes: a substitute amendment and an amendment in the nature of a substitute. The first type is

---

Box 5-1　Some Tests of Germaneness

When a Representative raises a germaneness point of order, the burden of proof rests with the sponsor of the amendment to establish its germaneness.

1. *Fundamental Purpose.* A basic test of germaneness is that the fundamental purpose of an amendment must be germane to the fundamental purpose of the bill. In determining this purpose, substantial reliance should not be placed upon the title of the bill as the title need not state the fundamental purpose of the bill, either as introduced or later amended. One must look rather to the text of the bill as the principal tool in determining purpose.

2. *Subject Matter.* The amendment must relate to the subject matter under consideration. One must determine "what is the subject matter under consideration?" Once it is clear just what the subject matter is, the next element . . . is whether or not the amendment relates to that subject matter.

3. *Committee Jurisdiction.* The jurisdiction of a committee is not necessarily controlling as to the germaneness of an amendment. When an argument has been advanced that the subject matter of an amendment lies within the jurisdiction of a committee other than the committee reporting the bill, the Chair has ruled that the germaneness of an amendment is based upon its relation to the bill in its amended form. In short, the subject matter of the bill is the controlling factor, not the description in the Rules of the House of the various committees' jurisdiction.

Source: Excerpted from *Manual on Legislative Procedure in the U.S. House of Representatives,* 6th ed., 99th Cong., prepared under the auspices of the Republican leader, May 1986.

---

an amendment that deals with part of a bill. For instance, when an amendment is made to change part of a bill, a substitute amendment offers alternative language for the entirety of that pending amendment. (By contrast, a perfecting amendment seeks to change, but not replace completely, the language in the first offered amendment.) The second kind recommends new language for the entire bill. Amendments in the nature of substitutes have increased in importance in recent years, in part because of the complexity and interrelatedness of contemporary issues and also because of multiple referrals.

For example, committees that consider the same bill may report dissimilar versions of it. Sometimes, such differences are resolved through intercommittee cooperation. Members and staff from each panel might blend their products into a consensus bill that will be offered on the House floor as an amendment in the nature of a substitute for the bill as originally introduced. Usually, the Rules Committee will accommodate the committees by giving such an alternative substitute special status by making it, instead of the original bill, the vehicle for House debate and amendment. The rule typically states that the consensus or substitute text will be considered an "original bill for the purpose of amendment."

Degrees of Amendments

A basic parliamentary principle permits only two degrees of amendments: an amendment and an amendment to it. Any further motion to amend is a third-degree proposal (an amendment to an amendment to an amendment) and is out of order. "The line must be drawn somewhere," Thomas Jefferson wrote, "and usage has drawn it after the amendment to the amendment."[37]

When a bill is open to revision in the House, only four forms of amendments are usually pending simultaneously. They are (1) an amendment to the bill itself, (2) an amendment to the first amendment, (3) a substitute amendment, and (4) an amendment to the substitute amendment.

Once an amendment to a bill has been offered (the first degree), either an amendment to that amendment (the second degree) or a substitute amendment (another first-degree proposal under House rules) is in order.[38] Assuming that an amendment to the original amendment is offered, then members still may offer a substitute as well as an amendment to the substitute (second degree). A substitute amendment seeks not merely to modify the original first-degree amendment but also to substitute entirely new language for it. If a substitute is adopted, its effect is to replace the language of the original first-degree proposal and any second-degree changes to it that might have been adopted.

The four amendments, with the degrees that are permissible and the order of voting on each, are depicted in Figure 5-2. This representation of the common amendment tree has two first-degree amendments—the amendment to the text and the substitute amendment—and two amendments in the second degree. House Rule XVI states: "When a motion or proposition is under consideration a motion to amend and a motion to amend that amendment shall be in order, and it shall also be in order to offer a further amendment by way of a substitute, to which one amendment may be offered."

Second-degree amendments are voted on first, and the second-degree amendment to the original amendment to the bill is voted on before the second-degree amendment to the substitute. After consideration of the second-degree amendments, members face a choice between two policy alternatives, with voting occurring first on the perfected substitute and then on the perfected original amendment. (Perfected amendments—which do not mean improved per a dictionary definition—in this context are amendments that have been amended by the second-degree proposals.) The final vote occurs on the originally offered amendment as modified by any subsequent amendments.

Strategically, the amendment procedure can be critical to policy formulation. Either side of an issue may be aided by the voting sequence—whether the amendment is voted upon first or last. During House consideration of a nuclear freeze proposal, the proponents wanted the House to vote first on

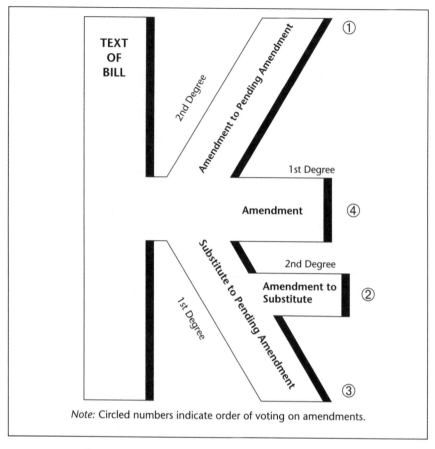

TEXT OF BILL

Amendment to Pending Amendment
2nd Degree
①

1st Degree

Amendment   ④

2nd Degree
Amendment to Substitute   ②

Substitute to Pending Amendment

1st Degree

③

Note: Circled numbers indicate order of voting on amendments.

FIGURE 5-2 The Basic Amendment Tree

their policy recommendation. As a result, they waited for opponents to offer a first-degree amendment before they countered with a second-degree amendment to their liking. This approach gave backers of the freeze the opportunity "to formulate the final version of any amendment." [39] The first vote, therefore, was on the freeze backers' alternative amendment to the opponents' amendment revising the text of the freeze resolution. The strategy of "fighting fire with fire" means that "threatening amendments by opponents are . . . met with counteramendments" by proponents. [40]

Maneuvering for Advantage: Common Tactics

Proponents and opponents of bills constantly seek to advance their policy objectives through the amending process. Skillful use of various motions, dilatory tactics, or shrewd drafting of the wording of amendments can influence which side carries the day. Customarily, the minority party has self-appointed floor watchdogs who seek to protect party interests and stymie majority steamrollers by raising points of order or making parliamentary inquiries. Timing, too, is all-important to the success of many floor maneuvers, especially preferential motions and amendments to sweeten bills.

Strike the Enacting Clause. Certain motions from the floor take preference over other House business. One is the motion to strike the enacting clause. This clause is the opening phrase of every House and Senate bill and makes it an operative law once the bill is approved by Congress and signed by the president: "Be it enacted by the Senate and House of Representatives of the United States of America in Congress assembled, ..." Under House rules, approval of a motion to strike the enacting clause is equivalent to rejecting the measure. A motion to strike the clause is in order at any time during the amending process. (The phrasing of the preferential motion is as follows: "I move that the Committee do now rise and report the bill to the House with the recommendation that the enacting clause be stricken out.") It is a privileged motion that must be disposed of before the House takes up any further business on the bill. The motion is in order only once, unless the bill is materially changed by adoption of major amendments, a determination the chair makes if a point of order is raised against a second motion to strike.

A motion to strike the enacting clause may cause considerable excitement in the chamber, and it may be used for psychological purposes by either opponents or proponents of a measure.[41] In 1974, for example, Representative Bolling, floor manager of a bitterly contested House committee reorganization bill, surprised foes of the plan by inviting them to offer a motion to strike the enacting clause. Bolling's plan was to defeat such a motion so resoundingly that it would be clear to all members that a committee reform plan was going to be considered in its entirety and adopted by the House.

Bolling gained an immediate psychological advantage when Rep. Joe D. Waggonner Jr., D-La. (1961–1979), one of the opposition leaders, observed that his side did not have the votes to pass the motion. It might be made, he said, "at a point in time when we think there is a chance for it to succeed." Ironically, a supporter of committee reorganization, disappointed by the course of the debate on the floor, later offered a motion to strike. It was turned down overwhelmingly because most members did not want the measure abruptly killed.

As another example, Rep. David R. Obey, D-Wis., the ranking minority member on Appropriations, offered the motion to make a political point. Immediately after the Speaker declared the House to be in the Committee of the Whole for the further consideration of an appropriations bill that reduced spending for many programs supported by Democrats, Obey made the preferential motion to rise. He said: "What I would simply say to you [Republicans] is this: We believe that this bill is warped and we believe there is no underlying sense of decency in the way the cuts are focused in this bill." The Appropriations chairman responded that the bill represents "the first step toward fiscal sanity and a balanced budget and it must be taken."[42] Obey's motion was rejected, 187–228.

Sweeteners. Measures considered unpalatable can be made more acceptable, or sweetened, by proposing changes to attract broader support. These might include amendments granting members more staff or additional office allowances, or pork-barrel provisions for construction of dams, highways, port facilities, airports, and the like in various congressional districts. Because lawmakers have criticized pork-barrel spending, amendment sweeteners may broaden their focus to address topics that have wide appeal with voters, such as spending reductions, streamlining federal regulations, or cutting bureaucratic red tape.

Pot-sweetening is the opposite of loading down a bill with enough unattractive amendments to kill it. There also are amendments that political scientists call saving and killer or poison-pill amendments. A saving amendment is essentially a compromise amendment that, if adopted, enhances prospects for the measure's enactment. A killer or poison-pill amendment deliberately strengthens a bill too much and turns a majority against the legislation.[43] Adoption of an amendment to include primaries in a congressional public financing bill, for example, is almost certain to kill the legislation because many House incumbents, particularly those from safe and one-party districts, oppose any measure that aids party challengers.

Importance of the Amending Process

Attempts are almost always made to amend controversial bills when they are considered in the Committee of the Whole. The amending process is a critical—and complex—stage for any bill. To summarize, some of the main features of the process are:

- Amendments in the Committee of the Whole are usually offered section by section under the five-minute rule.
- All amendments must be offered from the floor in written form.
- Amendments may not be repetitious. When an amendment is rejected, a member may not offer exactly the same proposal later.
- Any amendment may be challenged on a point of order before debate on the amendment has begun.
- Committee amendments are considered before those introduced by other legislators.
- Pro forma amendments ("Mr. Chairman, I move to strike the last word.") enable members to discuss the bill under consideration for five minutes, even though no change is intended.
- Amendments must be germane to the subject under consideration. Occasionally, nongermane amendments may slip by, either because members generally are agreed on their intent or because the Rules Committee has barred points of order against them.

VOTING

The House has a variety of methods of voting, with many votes occurring in the Committee of the Whole (see Box 5-2). A significant change in voting occurred on January 23, 1973, when electronic voting began. With electronic voting, which was authorized by the Legislative Reorganization Act of 1970, members insert a personalized card about the size of a credit card into one of the more than forty voting stations located on the House floor, and press one of three buttons: Yea, Nay, or Present. Each member's vote is displayed behind the Speaker's desk and on the wall panels over the press gallery. The system also is used to establish quorums. If electronic voting malfunctions, traditional methods are used. GOP House leader Bob Michel was not a fan of electronic voting because it quickened the pace of the House.

> It eliminates the time for informal chats with other members. C-SPAN is even more of a problem. Members now follow the affairs of the House from their offices, rushing to the floor to vote only at the last minute. Again, valuable face-to-face contact is gone.[44]

These technological changes have placed additional pressures on the floor managers. Electronic voting cut balloting time in half, from about thirty minutes under the traditional roll-call method, to no less than fifteen minutes. Further, recent changes in the rules have permitted the Speaker to postpone votes and schedule votes in clusters on matters such as passing bills or agreeing to suspension of the rules motions. The Speaker may reduce the time allowed for each vote in this procedure to five minutes.

Managers today have less time to coordinate floor activities during a vote. Members can enter the chamber through numerous doors, insert their cards and vote, then leave before the leadership has a chance to talk to them. As a result, both parties station monitors at all the doors to advise their colleagues when they enter and urge them to support the position of the floor manager or the party leadership.

From the floor managers' standpoint, the modern system has advantages and disadvantages. Managers have computer display terminals that show a continuous and changing record of the progress of a vote. However, they have less time to evaluate opposition to proposals and line up votes. Thus, floor managers today must work harder to build support before bills reach the floor. Meanwhile, problems such as the absence of one member or the unexpected vote switch of another can be spotted quickly on the computer consoles. Absent members can be summoned to the floor, and vote-switchers can be approached by persuasive members of the party.

On January 14, 1975, the House amended its rules to permit pairs in the Committee of the Whole. Pairing previously was limited to the House. Pairing is a voluntary arrangement between any two representatives on opposite sides of an issue. Wrote a noted House parliamentarian:

BOX 5-2   Methods of Voting in the House

The House regularly uses three types of votes: voice, division, and votes recorded by the name of the member (yeas and nays or recorded vote). Often, the House takes several votes on the same proposition, using the most simple method first and then increasingly more complex voting methods, before a decision is reached. A voice vote is the quickest method of voting and the type nearly always used when a proposition is first put to the membership. The presiding officer calls for the "ayes" and then the "noes," members shout in chorus on one side or the other, and the chair decides the result.

If the result of a voice vote is in doubt or a single member requests a further test, a division, or standing vote, may be demanded. In this case those in favor of the proposal and then those against it stand up while the chair takes a head count. Only vote totals are announced; there is no record of how individual members voted. Few issues are decided by division vote. After a voice vote, members will usually skip it and ask for a vote in which members are recorded by name. This kind of vote, which is nearly always taken using the electronic voting system, draws many more members to the chamber. It is called the yeas and nays or a recorded vote depending on the circumstances in which it is taken, but the result is identical.

The yeas and nays, provided for by the Constitution, is used only when the House itself is sitting, and never in the Committee of the Whole. This method of voting may be ordered by one-fifth of those present regardless of how few members are on the floor. House rules also provide that it may occur automatically whenever a quorum is not present on the floor when the question is put and any member objects to the vote on those grounds. The resulting vote both establishes a quorum and settles the question at issue.

A pair is essentially a "gentlemen's agreement," and the construction and interpretation of the terms, provisions, and conditions of a pair rests exclusively with the contracting Members. The rules do not specifically authorize them and the House does not interpret or construe them or consider questions or complaints arising out of their violation. Such questions must be determined by the interested Members themselves individually.[45]

Pairs are not counted in tabulating the final results of recorded votes. Pairs used to take three forms: (1) A general pair meant that two members were listed without any indication as to how either might have voted. (2) A specific pair indicated how the two absent legislators would have voted, one for and the other against. (3) A live pair matched two members, one present and one absent.

In a live pair, the member in attendance casts a vote, but then withdraws it and votes "present," announcing that he or she has a live pair with a colleague and identifying how each would have voted on the issue. A live pair subtracts one vote, "yea" or "nay," from the final tally and can influence the outcome of closely contested issues. Both parties have pair clerks to help

A recorded vote, provided for by House rules, may be demanded both in the House and in the Committee of the Whole, but it works differently in each case. In the House, it may be ordered upon demand of one-fifth of a quorum of 218, which is forty-four. In the Committee of the Whole a recorded vote is always ordered by twenty-five members.

In the Committee of the Whole, unlike the House, no means exists to force a vote automatically by claiming that a quorum (one hundred) is not present. In such cases, a member usually will demand a recorded vote and, pending that, make the point of order that a quorum is not present. By doing so the member gains time to ensure the presence of at least twenty-five supporters when the chair announces whether sufficient support exists for a recorded vote. If a quorum is not present, the chairman will order a quorum call to establish one before determining whether twenty-five members will support the demand for a recorded vote. The chairman has two choices: to order a regular quorum call, which summons all 435 members, whose names are recorded in the *Congressional Record* after the vote, or a notice quorum call, in which the chair stops the proceedings after one hundred members have responded and no permanent record of those responding is kept.

In many cases, to save time, enough members will rise informally to indicate their support for a recorded vote while the chair is still counting for a quorum; the point of order of no quorum will then be withdrawn and a recorded vote will occur. If both the quorum call and then the recorded vote are used the quorum call will be fifteen minutes long, followed, if ordered, by a recorded vote, which the chairman may reduce to five minutes.

SOURCE: Adapted from *Congressional Quarterly's Guide to Congress,* 5th ed. (Washington, D.C.: CQ Press, 2000), 496–497.

---

arrange these informal agreements. At the start of the 106th Congress (1999–2001), all pair voting except live pairs was eliminated. However, members may indicate in writing whether they would have voted for or against, and these statements appear in the *Congressional Record* immediately after the vote.

Factors in Voting

On any given day, legislators may be required to vote on measures ranging from foreign aid to abortion, from maritime subsidies to tax reform. It is nearly impossible for a member to be fully informed on every issue before the House. As one lawmaker said: "The sheer volume of votes is so great that there's no way you can weigh each and every issue."[46] Many lawmakers, as a result, follow the rational ignorance principle. They rely on cue-givers for guidance on matters beyond their special competence. These may be committee or party leaders, members of the state congressional delegation, trusted colleagues, staff aides, or floor managers.[47] "You want to know how Members are voting on an issue," a representative said, "you want to know how

Members from your delegation vote, and you want to know how Members who always vote the opposite of you are voting."[48] Party loyalty, constituency interests, and individual conscience are primary factors in determining a member's vote on any issue, but they are not the only factors. Members sometimes vote for proposals they oppose to prevent enactment of something worse or in the expectation that somewhere along the line the proposal will go down to defeat. Members, too, might vote one way on an authorization bill and another on the corresponding appropriations measure.

To mobilize winning coalitions is no easy task on divisive issues. The art of vote counting can be crucial to policy outcomes. For example, Speaker Foley extended the official voting period on a Clinton administration initiative to give him more time to persuade lawmakers to support the proposal. "At the end of the standard 15-minute roll-call period, opponents had a narrow majority, but the [Speaker] held the machines open for nearly 28 minutes while switching enough votes to prevail."[49] (The reverse charge—closing a vote with lawmakers still wanting to cast their ballot—reverberated through the House on June 21 and 22, 1995, during consideration of a closely contested amendment dealing with the elimination of the congressional Office of Technology Assessment.) Members use their votes, too, as trading material. In exchange for voting "yea" or "nay" on an issue, they may receive some project or favor that benefits their district.

Finally, the voting records of members can become a campaign issue. Representatives who miss numerous votes may have to explain their spotty congressional attendance record. Many interest groups contribute campaign funds to legislators whose votes are in accord with the groups' views. "If I cast a vote, I might have to answer for it," said a House member. "It may be an issue in the next campaign. Over and over I have to have a response to the question: Why did you do that?"[50] Liberal Democrat Mike Synar, who represented a conservative Oklahoma district for sixteen years until his 1994 electoral defeat and who cast many votes that antagonized his constituency, put it this way: "If you don't like fighting fires, don't be a fireman . . . and if you don't like voting, don't be a congressman."[51]

When voting on all amendments has been concluded, the Committee of the Whole rises (dissolves) and reports the bill back to the full House. (Rules from the Rules Committee typically provide that the Committee of the Whole rises automatically at the end of the amending process.) Then the chairman hands the gavel back to the Speaker, who resumes his place at the podium. The mace is returned to its pedestal on the table next to the podium, and a quorum becomes 218 members (a majority of the House). As prescribed in the rule, there is a standard sequence of events that takes place prior to the vote on final passage of a bill.

FINAL PROCEDURAL STEPS

After taking the chair, the Speaker announces that "under the rule [from the Rules Committee], the previous question is ordered." This means that no further debate is permitted on the measure or on amendments, no amendments other than those reported by the Committee of the Whole may be considered, and previously adopted amendments are not subject to further amendment. Then members, sitting as the House, consider the decisions taken in the Committee of the Whole.

The Speaker asks all the members to identify amendments on which they want separate recorded votes. The remaining amendments are decided en bloc by voice vote, after which the contested amendments are voted on individually. Except for motions to send a measure back to the reporting committee with instructions, only first-degree amendments adopted in the Committee of the Whole can now be considered. Separate recorded votes are not usually requested on amendments previously adopted in the Committee of the Whole unless the earlier votes were very close and the amendments highly controversial. On occasion, the House rejects amendments adopted in the Committee of the Whole.[52]

After all floor amendments are disposed of, there are two more steps before the final vote on passage. The first is engrossment and third reading. "The question is on engrossment and third reading of the bill," the Speaker declares. This is a pro forma question, which is approved quickly by voice vote. House rules provide that the bill be read by its title. (Before 1965 any legislator could demand that the bill be read in full, but the rules were changed to prevent this dilatory tactic.) Engrossment is the preparation of a final and accurate version of the bill by an enrolling clerk, for transmission to the Senate. This can be a complicated process, particularly if numerous amendments were adopted.

The second step is the recommittal motion, provided for in the rule from the Rules Committee. This is a privileged motion, protected and guaranteed by the rules of the House, that is the prerogative of the minority party. It gives opponents one last chance to obtain a recorded vote on their own proposals. Recommittal is a motion to return the bill to the committee that reported it; it is always made by a member opposed to the bill. Recommittal is in order only in the House, not in the Committee of the Whole.

There are two forms of the motion: a simple, or straight, motion to recommit and a motion that contains instructions to the reporting committee. A simple motion to recommit the bill to committee ("I move to recommit the bill to Committee A"), if adopted, in effect kills the bill, although technically it may be returned to the House floor later in the session. No debate is permitted on a simple motion to recommit.

Instructions in recommittal motions may embody amendments that were defeated in the Committee of the Whole. This is the only way amendments rejected earlier in the debate can be brought before the full House. Until 1970

BOX 5-3   Rules Changes Open the Process . . .

The rules package approved by the House on January 4, 1995, represented the most significant revision of House rules since enactment of the Legislative Reorganization Act of 1946.

Committees

- Three committees were abolished: District of Columbia, Merchant Marine and Fisheries, and Post Office and Civil Service. Several other committees were renamed.
- The jurisdiction of the Post Office and Civil Service Committee and the District of Columbia Committee was transferred to the Government Reform and Oversight Committee. Matters handled by the Merchant Marine and Fisheries Committee were split among three other committees. Several issues formerly handled by the Energy and Commerce Committee were parceled out to other committees.
- The total number of committee staff was cut by one-third.
- With three exceptions, no committee would be allowed more than five subcommittees.
- Staff hiring will be controlled by committee chairmen.
- Members may serve on no more than two standing committees and four subcommittees, except for chairmen and ranking members, who can serve ex officio on all subcommittees.
- A chairman or other designee may not cast an absent member's vote by proxy in committee.
- Committees must publish the members voting for or against all bills and amendments.
- Committees and subcommittees are barred from closing their meetings to the public (with certain exceptions).
- Committees must allow radio and television broadcasts, as well as still photography, of all open meetings.
- Bills that increase spending on existing programs must contain a cost estimate that shows the current cost of the programs.
- The Speaker may not send a bill to more than one committee simultaneously for consideration. The Speaker may refer a bill sequentially to other committees or parts of a bill to separate committees.

---

no debate was permitted on a recommittal motion. The Legislative Reorganization Act of that year authorized ten minutes of debate on recommittal motions with instructions. On occasion, a rule from the Rules Committee will authorize longer debate on recommittal motions with instructions.

Although House rules prohibit the Rules Committee from excluding a motion to recommit from a special rule, partisan conflict over the motion to recommit with instructions escalated when Democrats controlled the House. The Democratic-controlled committee issued rules with greater frequency that either eliminated or restricted the recommittal motion with instructions.

... But Strengthen the Reins of Power

Term Limits

- Speaker: no more than four consecutive two-year terms.
- Chairmen of committees and subcommittees: no more than three consecutive terms. The limits began with the 104th Congress.

Floor Procedures

- A three-fifths majority of members voting would be required to pass any bill, amendment, or conference report containing an increase in income tax rates.
- No retroactive tax increases that take effect prior to the date of enactment of the bill are allowed.
- Delegates and resident commissioners may no longer vote in or preside over the Committee of the Whole.
- Members may no longer delete or change remarks made on the floor in the *Congressional Record*—except for technical or grammatical corrections.
- Automatic roll-call votes are required on bills and conference reports that make appropriations and raise taxes.
- Members are guaranteed the right to offer so-called limitation amendments, which specify that no funds may be spent for a particular purpose, without having to defeat a motion to end amendments—unless the majority leader offers that motion.
- The minority leader or his designee is guaranteed the right to offer a motion to recommit with instructions on a bill under consideration in the House.
- Commemorative legislation may not be introduced or considered.

Administration

- The Office of the Doorkeeper was abolished.
- The House inspector general was instructed to complete an audit of the financial records of the House while it was under the control of the Democrats.
- Funding was abolished for more than twenty-five caucuses that received office space and budgets to operate in the House.

SOURCE: Adapted from *Congressional Quarterly Weekly Report,* January 7, 1995, 14–15.

The GOP staff director of the Rules Committee, Donald R. Wolfensberger, even wrote a report in 1990 entitled: "The Motion to Recommit in the House: The Rape of a Minority Right."

The GOP raged against special rules that prohibited Republicans from offering any floor amendments to legislation. The combination of restrictive rules and no recommittal motion with instructions meant that Republican policy alternatives never had an opportunity to be considered and voted upon. For their part, Democratic Speakers cited a 1934 precedent to overrule any GOP points of order against special rules that did not contain the recommittal motion with instructions. The precedent stated that under House rules the minority was guaranteed the right to offer a simple, or straight, motion to recommit, but it was not guaranteed the recommittal motion with instructions. When the 104th Congress began, the new GOP majority amended House rules to guarantee the minority's right to offer a motion to recommit with instructions if offered by the minority leader or a designee.[53] (This rule change originally had been proposed in 1993 by the bipartisan Joint Committee on the Organization of Congress.)

Recommittal motions with instructions commonly provide that the committee report "forthwith." If the recommittal motion is adopted, the committee chairman immediately reports back to the House in conformity with the instructions, and the bill, as modified by the instructions, is automatically before the House again. The committee chairman states: "Mr. Speaker, pursuant to the instructions of the House on the motion to recommit, I report the bill, H.R. 1234, back to the House with an amendment." The House votes separately on this amendment and, if adopted, then again on the pro forma engrossment and third reading questions, and finally on passage of the bill.

On a few occasions, the minority will offer a motion to recommit with instructions that the committee (or committees) report back to the House "promptly." This word is sometimes used instead of "forthwith" for at least two reasons. First, motions to recommit that contain the word "promptly" may outline a general statement of minority party policy—not detailed legislative language—which makes it easier for minority members to vote for it. Second, if the House adopted this kind of motion to recommit, it would kill the bill, and this may be the objective of the sponsor. For example, Minority Whip David E. Bonior, D-Mich., the leading House opponent of granting permanent normal trade relations with China, in 2000 offered a motion to recommit with instructions that the Committees on Ways and Means and International Relations report "promptly" back to the House with an amendment stating that if China attacked Taiwan, its permanent normal trade status with the United States would be automatically revoked.[54] Bonior's goal was to win a bipartisan majority and kill the bill, but his motion failed to be adopted.

Recommittal motions seldom are successful, but much depends on the size of the minority party in the House and political circumstances. Probably the most dramatic recommittal motion in recent Congresses occurred on September 25, 1984 (only a few weeks before national elections), when the Comprehensive Crime Control Act was enacted via the recommittal route. Rep. Dan Lungren, R-Calif., offered the recommittal motion with instructions containing the recodification of the criminal code, debated it for five minutes, and urged members to pass a crime package that "has been languishing here in the House since March of this year."[55] A Democratic opponent of the recommittal motion then took the floor and urged rejection of the motion in his five minutes.

To the surprise of nearly everyone, the recommittal motion was agreed to by a 243–166 vote. Then the continuing resolution to which the crime bill was attached was agreed to by the House. Democratic leaders were chagrined that the crime package had passed in this manner. "I think it was the wrong way" to pass major crime legislation after only ten minutes of debate, declared Speaker O'Neill.[56] When the next Congress convened, the House changed its rules to permit the majority floor manager—but not the minority floor manager—to request up to an hour of debate, equally divided, on a motion to recommit with instructions. This is a good example of the majority rule principle that undergirds House operations. (Another is the series of major rules changes made by Republicans when they took control of the 104th Congress (see Box 5-3 on pp. 174 and 175). Two Congresses later, under direction of Rules Chairman David Dreier, R-Calif., the House agreed to a comprehensive recodification of its rules, something that had not occurred since the 1880s.)

If the recommittal motion is rejected, the Speaker moves to the third step, the final vote on the whole bill. "The question is on the passage of the bill," he says. Normally, final passage is by a recorded vote. If the outcome is obvious, and the members are eager to be done with it, the measure may be passed by voice vote. When the results of the final vote have been announced, a pro forma motion to reconsider is made and laid on the table (postponed indefinitely) to prevent the bill from being reconsidered later. House rules state that a final vote is conclusive only if an opportunity was provided to reconsider it on the same day or the succeeding day.

NOTES

1. Traditionally, the majority party members sit to the Speaker's right, the minority to the left. In 1995, however, when Republicans took control of the 104th Congress after four decades of continuous minority status, they decided to remain seated where they were. Hence, when House Speaker J. Dennis Hastert, R-Ill., looks from the dais to his left, he sees his GOP colleagues; to his right are the Democrats.

2. During the 95th Congress (1977–1979), the House developed a regular system of scheduling floor sessions. This was done in response to the desires of members, committees, and party leaders. Members complained about problems in arranging their personal schedules and their inability to make firm commitments for meetings in their districts; committees wanted more time early in the session to work on legislation without being interrupted by floor meetings; and party leaders wished to better synchronize committee and floor action and use the time in session more effectively. As a result, the House by standing order varies its starting time: noon on Mondays and Tuesdays, 3 p.m. on Wednesdays, 11 a.m. on Thursdays and the balance of the week until May 15, when the convening time for Wednesdays through the balance of the week, including Saturdays if the House is in session, is advanced to 10 a.m. for the remainder of the session.

3. For guidelines on morning hour debate, see *Congressional Record,* May 12, 1995, H4901.

4. Jeffrey H. Birnbaum and Alan S. Murray, *Showdown at Gucci Gulch* (New York: Random House, 1987), 163.

5. Phil Kuntz, "Democrats' Defeat Raises Specter of Gridlock," *Congressional Quarterly Weekly Report,* August 13, 1994, 2311.

6. See Holly Idelson, "Clinton, Democrats Scramble to Save Anti-Crime Bill," *Congressional Quarterly Weekly Report,* August 13, 1994, 2340–2343; Holly Idelson and Richard Sammon, "Marathon Talks Produce New Anti-Crime Bill," *Congressional Quarterly Weekly Report,* August 20, 1994, 2449–2454; and David Masci, "$30 Billion Anti-Crime Bill Heads to Clinton's Desk," *Congressional Quarterly Weekly Report,* August 27, 1994, 2488–2493.

7. Juliana Gruenwald, "Parties Join to Oppose Treasury Bill," *Congressional Quarterly Weekly Report,* June 27, 1998, 1765.

8. Donald R. Wolfensberger, "Committees of the Whole: Their Evolution and Functions," *Congressional Record,* January 5, 1993, H31.

9. De Alva Stanwood Alexander, *History and Procedure of the House of Representatives* (New York: Burt Franklin, 1916), 257.

10. In the House sitting as the House, an hour is permitted for debate on amendments. "No member," the rule states, "shall occupy more than one hour in debate on any question in the House." Technically, then, all matters could be debated for 440 hours—1 hour each for the 435 representatives, 4 delegates (from the District of Columbia, the Virgin Islands, American Samoa, and Guam), and 1 resident commissioner (from Puerto Rico). In practice, measures are debated for only one hour in total and then are voted on.

11. For a description of the seventeenth-century English origins of the Committee of the Whole, see Alexander, *History and Procedure of the House of Representatives,* 257–258.

12. Technically, the first order of business in the Committee of the Whole is the reading of the bill. This usually is dispensed with either by unanimous consent or by the terms of the rule, which is the ordinary practice today.

13. Lizete Alvarez, "Taking a Job That Others Would Not," *New York Times,* December 19, 1998, B2.

14. *U.S. News & World Report,* August 20, 1984, 30.

15. *Washington Post,* October 22, 1983, A19.

16. *Congressional Record,* September 12, 1989, E3001.

17. *Congressional Record,* March 29, 1995, H3905. See E. Michael Myers, "Anatomy of a Speech: How Hyde Turned Tide," *The Hill,* April 5, 1995, 1.

18. *Congressional Record,* June 7, 1995, H5672–H5673; and *New York Times,* June 8, 1995, A11.

19. *Congressional Record,* May 24, 1983, H3257.

20. *Congressional Record,* January 12, 1991, H441. See Joseph M. Bessette, *The Mild Voice of Reason: Deliberative Democracy and American National Government* (Chicago, Ill.: University of Chicago Press, 1994).

21. *Congressional Record,* June 11, 1979, 14213–14215.

22. See *Congressional Record,* October 30, October 31, and November 2, 1987.

23. Nancy Roman, "Disaster Measure Doubles in Its Cost," *Washington Times,* June 5, 1997, A3.

24. *Congressional Record,* October 31, 1997, H9834.

25. *Congressional Record,* November 6, 1997, H10112.

26. *Constitution, Jefferson's Manual, and Rules of the House of Representatives,* 102d Cong., 2d sess., H. Doc. 102-405, 665.

27. Julie Rovner, "House Passes Labor-HHS Appropriations Bill," *Congressional Quarterly Weekly Report,* August 8, 1987, 1790.
28. *Congressional Record,* March 22, 1995, H3498–H3500.
29. "Amendment Procedure in the Committee of the Whole: A Brief Synopis," Parliamentary Outreach Program, Committee on Rules, June 3, 1997.
30. The Legislative Reorganization Act of 1970 provided that amendments published in the *Congressional Record* at least one day prior to their consideration in the Committee of the Whole are guaranteed ten minutes of debate time, regardless of any committee agreements to end debate on the bill. The objective is to prevent arbitrary closing of debate when important amendments are pending. The Rules Committee can waive this requirement.
31. *Congressional Record,* May 25, 1982, H2824. The amendment was not adopted.
32. *Procedure in the U.S. House of Representatives,* 97th Cong., 4th ed. (Washington, D.C.: Government Printing Office, 1982), 526.
33. Michael J. Malbin, "House Democrats Are Playing with a Strong Leadership Lineup," *National Journal,* June 18, 1977, 946. See also John F. Bibby, ed., *Congress off the Record* (Washington, D.C.: American Enterprise Institute for Public Policy Research, 1983), 23–24.
34. Richard F. Fenno Jr., *The Power of the Purse* (Boston: Little, Brown, 1966), 74.
35. Martin Gold, Michael Hugo, Hyde Murray, Peter Robinson, and A. L. "Pete" Singleton, *The Book on Congress* (Washington, D.C.: Big Eagle Publishing Co., 1992), 226.
36. See *Congressional Record,* May 7, 1996, H4482–H4484.
37. *Constitution, Jefferson's Manual, and Rules of the House of Representatives,* 226–227.
38. When amendments in the nature of substitutes are offered first, as many as eight amendments can be pending simultaneously on the House floor. Seldom does this situation occur because confusion is all too often the result.
39. Pat Towell, "After 42 Hours of Debate: Nuclear Freeze Resolution Finally Wins House Approval," *Congressional Quarterly Weekly Report,* May 7, 1983, 869.
40. Barry R. Weingast, "Fighting Fire with Fire: Amending Activity and Institutional Change in the Postreform Congress," in *The Postreform Congress,* ed. Roger H. Davidson (New York: St. Martin's Press, 1992), 165.
41. Customarily, the motion to strike also is used by members to obtain five more minutes of debate time.
42. *Congressional Record,* March 16, 1995, H3282.
43. See James M. Enelow and David H. Koehler, "The Amendment in Legislative Strategy: Sophisticated Voting in the U.S. Congress," *Journal of Politics* (May 1980): 396–413; and James M. Enelow, "Saving Amendments, Killer Amendments, and an Expected Utility Theory of Sophisticated Voting," *Journal of Politics* (November 1981): 1062–1089.
44. Donnie Radcliffe, "Many Hits, One Era," *Washington Post,* March 9, 1994, C4.
45. *Cannon's Procedure in the House of Representatives,* H. Doc. 86-122, 233. Clarence Cannon further notes (p. 231): "It is obviously impossible for all Members to be present at every roll call, and in cases of unavoidable absence the privilege of pairing is invaluable in preserving the rights of Members and the representation of constituencies."

46. *New York Times,* June 29, 1983, A14.
47. On factors influencing votes, see, for example, John W. Kingdon, *Congressmen's Voting Decisions* (New York: Harper & Row, 1973); and Donald P. Matthews and James A. Stimson, *Yeas and Nays* (New York: John Wiley & Sons, 1975).
48. *Congressional Record,* July 16, 1986, H4558.
49. David Rogers, "Plan to Create Line-Item Veto Survives a Vote," *Wall Street Journal,* April 29, 1993, A16.
50. *New York Times,* May 13, 1986, A24.
51. Jack Anderson and Michael Binstein, "Synar Stands His Ground," *Washington Post,* August 22, 1993, C7.
52. See, for example, Martha Bridegam and Pat Towell, "'Goodwill Games' Spark Sharp Exchange," *Congressional Quarterly Weekly Report,* June 27, 1987, 1386.
53. Some controversy surrounded Minority Leader Richard A. Gephardt's motion to recommit with instructions to a tax bill. See *Congressional Record,* April 5, 1995, H4331–H4332; and *Congressional Record,* April 6, 1995, H4340–H4341.
54. *Congressional Record,* May 24, 2000, H3744.
55. *Congressional Record,* September 25, 1984, H10129.
56. See Charles R. Wise, *The Dynamics of Legislation* (San Francisco, Calif.: Jossey-Bass Publishers, 1991).

CHAPTER 6

Scheduling Legislation in the Senate

R EPRESENTATIVES and senators work long days, not only on the floor and in committee but also in meetings with executive branch officials, constituents, pressure groups, and the media. They also must stay in contact with the diplomatic community, party leaders, and state and local officials. In addition, they make periodic trips home to attend important political functions, meet with constituents, or be present at campaign fund-raising events.

Of legislators in the two houses of Congress, senators lead the more harried existence. The legislative and committee workload is as heavy in the Senate as in the House, but it must be carried out by fewer lawmakers (100 senators compared with 435 House members), and in most cases senators represent a larger number of constituents. Senators are more often in the public eye and are called upon more frequently to comment on national and international policy. Senators not uncommonly are expected to be in two or more places at the same time (see Box 6-1). In such a situation, a senator must select the top priority event to attend in person and delegate staff members to cover the rest or, as a last resort, rely on a fellow senator to fill him in on what took place.

Given the role senators must play and the time restraints on them, the Senate's legislative scheduling system is much more flexible than the House's (see Table 6-1). The Senate has formal rules dictating floor procedure, but they are routinely set aside. Instead, the chamber relies on unanimous consent agreements (UCAs). The Senate's smaller size, as compared with the House, has infused informality into its deliberative processes. Senators also have significant parliamentary prerogatives, especially with respect to their ability to stymie floor action, and senators are not reluctant to wield these prerogatives to achieve individual or partisan objectives. As a result, floor decision making can be an uncertain or unruly affair. And, unlike the House, where the majority party led by the Speaker is in charge of scheduling, the majority and minority leaders in the Senate together largely shape the institution's program and agenda.

FLEXIBLE SCHEDULING SYSTEM

In response to the manifold pressures on members, the Senate has evolved a highly flexible legislative scheduling system that responds to the individual member's, as well as to institutional, needs. The system bears little resemblance to what the formal rules specify and rests largely on usage and informal practice. Senators' frustration with delays and uncertainty in scheduling

---

BOX 6-1 Schedule of Sen. Mike DeWine, R-Ohio
Thursday, May 25, 2000

8:30 AM **The National Center for Missing and Exploited Children and Fifth Annual Law Enforcement Awards Congressional Breakfast**

Location: Cannon Caucus Room (rm 345)
Notes: You will be presenting awards to two members of the Lancaster, Ohio, Police Dept. Karla and Amy R. to staff this event.

9:30 AM **Meeting with Sen. Voinovich, Dr. David Michaels with the DoE and Cong. Ted Strickland**

Location: SH-317
Notes: Dr. Michaels will give a briefing on the Portsmouth Oversight Investigation. Joy and Robert to staff.

10:00 AM **Testify before the International Security, Proliferation, and Federal Services Subcommittee**

Location: SD-226
Notes: Helen to staff.

11:00 AM **Photo op and brief stop-by with 22 students from Bluffton College in Ohio**

Location: Conference room
Notes: Urban poverty issues. Amanda and Karla to staff.

11:15 AM **Meeting with Robert and Stan [DeWine staff aides]**

Notes: DoE Appropriations bill

12:00 PM **Senators' Bible Study**

Location: S-214

12:00 PM **FYI—Luncheon sponsored by Ralph Regula to introduce the incoming chairman of the National Association of Manufacturers, W. R. Tim Timken Jr.**

---

sometimes prompts changes that may be observed at different times, depending on legislative workload and political circumstances, such as when the Senate is scurrying to move a backlog of business. To make progress in passing the thirteen general appropriations bills and a few other key legislative priorities given an abbreviated 2000 election-year schedule, Majority Leader Trent Lott, R-Miss., planned a five-day work week with votes on Mondays and Fridays.[1] The Senate has also tried a scheduling system of three weeks in session each month followed by one week off. This "gives Senators some predictability, to schedule their trips back home to their constituencies, or to catch up on committee work here or other work here," said Robert C. Byrd, W.Va., the Senate Democratic leader who instituted the change.[2] This

Location: H-219, Capitol
Notes: Tim Timken will assume the chairmanship in
September.

12:30 PM   **Group Lunch**
Location: Agriculture Comm. Rm. SR-328A
Notes: Menu: chicken piccata.

2:00 PM   **Brief stop-by meeting with former Vatican Ambassador and current RNC Catholic Task Force Chairman Tom Melady and Rob Bauer, Field Coordinator, and Todd Calongne, Director of the Chairman's staff**

Location: Laurel's office
Notes: Laurel will begin this meeting at 2:00 PM. She will
discuss the effort of the Task Force to organize in Ohio.
Laurel to staff.

2:00 PM   **FYI—Full Judiciary Committee Hearing**
Location: SD-226
Notes: Judicial nominations. Pete and Steve to staff.

2:30 PM   **Meeting with Robert and Helen** [DeWine staff aides]
Notes: Animal testing bill.

3:00 PM   **Meeting with Senator Bob Kerrey**
Location: Hart 141

4:00 PM   **Meeting with Pete, Anthony, Ann, and Robert** [DeWine staff aides]
Location: RMD's office
Notes: Project Exile Speech.

5:00 PM   **Meeting with Stephen M. Wolf, Chairman of U.S. Airways, James E. Goodwin, CEO of United, and Gary Slaiman**
Location: RMD's office
Notes: Merger. Pete and Laurel to staff.

scheduling change was agreed to informally by the unanimous consent of the senators, which reflects the chamber's basic operating principle.

Ostensibly, the three-week, one-week plan served individual and institutional objectives. Senators could conduct their constituency-related business and other work during the Senate's week off without fear of missing votes. This feature was especially attractive to members who must campaign for reelection and to those from the western United States. The Senate was expected to work five days a week during the three-week segment, including votes on Mondays and Fridays.

However, the three-week, one-week system was not regularly adhered to. As George J. Mitchell, D-Maine, who served as majority leader from 1989 to

TABLE 6-1 House and Senate Scheduling Compared

House	Senate
Important role for the Rules Committee	No equivalent body; instead, unanimous consent agreements govern floor action on measures
Majority party leaders, especially the Speaker, are the predominant force in scheduling	Majority party leaders control the flow of legislation to the floor in close consultation with minority party leaders
More formal process	Less formal process
Only key members are consulted in scheduling measures	Every reasonable effort is made to accommodate the scheduling requests of all senators
Elaborate system of formal calendars and special days for calling up measures	Heavy reliance on informal practice and personal accommodation in scheduling (Senate has only two calendars)
Party leaders can plan a rather firm schedule of daily and weekly business	Party leaders regularly juggle several measures to suit events and senators

1995, noted: "Because of its rules, the Senate schedule is inherently uncertain and not fully predictable."[3] One study found that the Senate infrequently followed the scheduling innovation, reverting instead to the "three-day workweek of the past—plus that new week off every month."[4] Figure 6-1 depicts the concentration of Senate work in the Tuesday-Thursday period during the 102d Congress (1991–1993) and contrasts the Senate pattern with the House's. (This pattern is typical of senatorial activity today.)

Senators still complain about scheduling conflicts and chaos ("[Senate] life is miserable," lamented Bob Kerrey, D-Neb.). Although scheduling improvements constitute a perennial reform topic, majority leaders (who are ultimately responsible for setting the Senate's schedule) usually strive to ensure certainty, predictability, and family-friendliness in the chamber's day-to-day work. "I tried my very best to make sure the Senate in fact is a family friendly workplace," remarked Majority Leader Lott. "[W]e have tried not to work into the wee hours of the night."[5] Leaders also make efforts to accommodate each senator's scheduling needs. "I had an inquiry this afternoon on when the votes will occur on Monday," said a GOP leader. "One of our colleagues on this side is attending a Little League baseball tournament where his son is involved and he cannot be back until 3 p.m., so he will be accommodated."[6]

The best-laid scheduling plans can always go awry in the Senate because individual senators have the capacity through various parliamentary devices to frustrate plans for moving the legislative agenda in a predictable fashion. Given the individualistic and increasingly partisan character of today's Senate, Republicans and Democrats commonly battle over agenda control.

Understandably, Majority Leader Lott wants the Senate to focus on the GOP's agenda; Democrats want, by contrast, the opportunity to advance their priorities by offering nonrelevant amendments to whatever vehicle (bill) lends itself to that objective. "It's got to be a Republican agenda, not a Ted Kennedy [Sen. Edward M. Kennedy, D-Mass.,] agenda," is how one GOP senator put it. Added another Republican, Lott must "show he's running the calendar, not a member of the minority."[7]

Senate leaders require flexibility in determining the Senate's business; they understand that scheduling is a significant strategic and political resource. If the Senate is gridlocked on a measure because of various stalling tactics, the majority leader might threaten to make members work long days, through the weekend, and even through a planned recess until the impasse is resolved. Majority Leader Lott "warned that a Saturday session could be necessary if there are unanticipated delays" in voting on legislation.[8] (During the entire

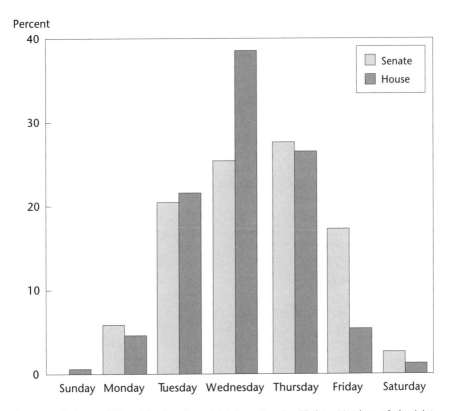

SOURCE: *Background Materials: Supplemental Information Provided to Members of the Joint Committee on the Organization of Congress,* 103d Cong., 1st sess. (1993), 1092.

FIGURE 6-1 Distribution of Senate and House Votes, 102d Congress, by Day of Week

1990s, the Senate met on a Saturday only twenty-two times out of more than sixteen hundred days in session. There were six Sunday sessions during the decade of the 1990s.) Alternatively, if senators agree on a date for a final vote on controversial legislation, the majority leader might extend a scheduled Senate recess for another week.

Strategic scheduling is part of deadline or end-game politics. Legislation may be scheduled during the closing weeks of a Congress to maximize political pressure for action. Lawmakers, too, are often willing to wait until the end of a Congress, "believing that he, she, or they will have maximum leverage at the end of the tunnel."[9] Or real or contrived crises can be generated as certain deadlines (the start of the fiscal year or the traditional August recess, for example) approach. The sense of urgency can heighten the pressure and stakes so members will act before the clock or calendar runs out.

Unlike House members, all senators have an opportunity to participate in scheduling legislation for floor action. Bob Dole, R-Kan., who was majority leader from 1985 to 1987 and 1995 to 1996, once reported: "The Senate leadership convened a special meeting this morning for all 100 Senators—81 Senators attended to discuss [the schedule for] wrapping up the year's business before adjournment."[10] This condition reflects both the comity that is usually prevalent in the Senate and the power that every member has under senatorial rules. "One person can tie this place into a knot," said a senator. "And two can do it even more beautifully."[11] Minor or noncontroversial bills are expedited to save time for major and controversial measures. Insofar as possible, action on important bills is scheduled to suit the convenience of members and to minimize conflicts with legislative activity taking place off the Senate floor. "The Senate operates largely on the basis of unanimous-consent agreements, comity, courtesy, and understanding," said veteran senator Byrd.[12]

The Senate's system for classifying measures for floor debate is simpler and more informal than the House system. In contrast to the House, with its five calendars, the Senate has only two: the Calendar of General Orders and the Executive Calendar. All legislation, major or minor, controversial or noncontroversial, is placed on the former; treaties and nominations under the Senate's advice and consent authority are placed on the latter.[13] Within the course of a single day, the Senate may consider measures on both the General Orders and Executive calendars. It may go from executive session to legislative session before finishing pending items on the Executive Calendar. (Filibustering a motion to enter or exit an executive session is not in order; however, the nomination or treaty to be taken up can be filibustered.)

Treaties are referred to the Foreign Relations Committee while presidential nominees are sent to the appropriate committee of jurisdiction. Unlike nominations or regular legislation, treaties do not die at the end of a Congress. For example, the Genocide Treaty was ratified in 1986, thirty-seven years after being submitted by President Harry S. Truman in 1949, by the required two-thirds vote of the Senate. By contrast, presidential nominations must be acted on in a session or they die, and as Senate Rule XXXI states, they must "again be made to the Senate by the President." Under the Constitution, presidents "shall have Power to fill up all Vacancies that may happen during the Recess of the Senate," a power that gives rise to periodic tension between the Senate and chief executive.

Relatively noncontroversial legislation in the House comes up under suspension of the rules procedure or by unanimous consent. Specific days of the month are designated for consideration of legislation on the Corrections Calendar or Private Calendar. The Senate has no comparable procedures. Formal Senate rules for calling up legislation—both major and minor—are cumbersome and consequently are generally ignored. One of these rules, for example, requires a daily calendar call, with measures brought up and debated in the order in which they appear on the calendar. (An example of a Senate calendar appears in Figure 6-2.) Were the Senate to follow that rule, it would lose virtually all flexibility in processing its workload.

At the start of each day, the majority leader often presents an overview of activities for the Senate, just as he announces the program for the next day or subsequent day at the conclusion of the daily session. Periodically, he indicates what the legislative agenda looks like for longer periods of time. Senators are kept informed of the legislative program through a variety of means, such as weekly whip notices (issued more frequently as needed by each party) listing the measures likely to be considered during the week (see Figure 6-3). The Senate's whip notices are less detailed than the House's, because Senate rules limit predictability in scheduling.

NONCONTROVERSIAL BILLS

Practically all noncontroversial measures are "called up by unanimous consent and enacted without debate," observed Senator Byrd. "In this regard, I have reference to private bills, most nominations on the Executive Calendar—which run into the thousands—and bills that are not of general interest." [14] He estimated that "easily 98 percent of the business of the Senate is called up by unanimous consent." [15] The leaders and staff aides in both parties check with senators to clear minor or noncontroversial legislation before such measures reach the floor. A single dissent will hold up floor action until the roadblock is cleared away. Once cleared, minor and noncontroversial bills generally take from several seconds to a few minutes to pass. "Locomotive velocity may develop at this point, as bills come up and pass through with no objection," Byrd noted.[16] These measures are considered typically at the end of daily Senate sessions, during the wrap-up period (see Box 6-2).

The Senate's small size, flexibility, and tradition of cooperation mean that the majority and minority leaders frequently can schedule noncontroversial legislation on a daily basis. Through informal floor discussions or colloquies, each examines the calendar to be sure the noncontroversial bills have been

SENATE OF THE UNITED STATES
ONE HUNDRED SIXTH CONGRESS

FIRST SESSION { CONVENED JANUARY 6, 1999
ADJOURNED NOVEMBER 19, 1999 } DAYS OF SESSION 162

SECOND SESSION { CONVENED JANUARY 24, 2000 } DAYS OF SESSION 48

CALENDAR OF BUSINESS

Monday, May 8, 2000

SENATE CONVENES AT 1:00 P.M.

PENDING BUSINESS

S. 2 (ORDER NO. 491)

A bill to extend programs and activities under the Elementary and Secondary Education Act of 1965. *(May 1, 2000.)*

UNFINISHED BUSINESS

H.R. 6 (ORDER NO. 437)

An act to amend the Internal Revenue Code of 1986 to reduce the marriage penalty by providing for adjustments to the standard deduction, 15-percent rate bracket, and earned income credit and to repeal the reduction of the refundable tax credits. *(Apr. 11, 2000.)*

(CONSENT AGREEMENTS ON P. 2)

PREPARED UNDER THE DIRECTION OF GARY SISCO,
SECRETARY OF THE SENATE

By DAVID J. TINSLEY, LEGISLATIVE CLERK

79-015

FIGURE 6-2 Senate *Calendar of Business*

cleared by interested senators on its side. The measures then are passed quickly by voice vote.

Minor and noncontroversial measures also may reach the Senate floor on a motion of any senator. However, the majority and minority leaders normally try to reach agreement in advance on the floor schedule and are likely to oppose action that will bring bills to the floor without prior clearance from them. The leaders' prerogative of receiving preferential recognition from the presiding officer—first the majority leader, followed by the minority leader—enables them to control the agenda of activities on the floor. As Senator Byrd explained: "A majority leader has enormous power when it comes to the schedule of the Senate, the scheduling of bills and resolutions and the programming of the Senate schedule. The majority leader has the first recognition power and that is a big arrow in his arsenal. . . . Nobody can get recognition before the majority leader."[17] A senator who attempts to bring a measure or matter to the floor without consulting the majority leader in advance may find the proposal subject to a tabling motion. (The motion to table kills the action to which it is directed.)

WHIP NOTICE

WEEK OF MAY 8

Monday, May 8

NO VOTES

The Senate will convene at 1:00 pm for a period of morning business.

At 3:00 pm, the Senate will begin consideration of the Lott/Gregg amendment re/ a teacher's bill of rights to S. 2, the Educational Opportunities Act.

Tuesday, May 9

VOTES EXPECTED THROUGHOUT THE DAY

By previous unanimous consent, the Senate will begin consideration of the Lieberman substitute amendment to S. 2.

At 12:30 pm, the Senate will recess until 2:15 pm for the weekly party lunches.

Further amendments to S. 2 are expected, therefore votes may occur throughout the day.

Wednesday, May 10 and Rest of the Week

The Senate will continue consideration of any pending business.

The House passed the conference report to H.R. 434, the African Growth and Opportunity Act, by a vote of 309-110 on Thursday, May 4. It is expected the Senate will begin consideration of the conference report this week.

If an agreement can be reached, the Senate could also begin consideration of S. 2045, the American Competitiveness in the Twenty-first Century Act of 2000 re/ H-1B Visas.

The Senate may consider any other legislation or nominations cleared for action.

FIGURE 6-3 Senate Whip Notice, Week of May 8, 2000

BOX 6-2 Wrapping Up the Senate's Day

Wrapup is when senators, by unanimous consent, at the end of the day agree to pass bill upon bill by voice vote and without a single word of debate. It occurs throughout the year, but in the waning days of a session, when floor time is scarce, many lawmakers find the time is right to get their bills passed.

Senators seek "to take advantage of the pressure of a recess deadline to pull people to the table, to resolve differences and break down barriers to compromise," said Bill Frist, R-Tenn. Because workdays often run well into the night during the end of sessions, "It's a lot easier to get things done in wrapup because people are home asleep and there are fewer people to object," Bob Kerrey, D-Neb., said. Furthermore, as Senate Parliamentarian Bob Dove explained, senators often use wrapup to pass mundane legislation and to finish up "on things they don't want to necessarily debate." Wrapup makes the upper chamber more efficient in passing legislation, Dove said.

Wrapup evolved from calendar Mondays, when the clerk would read titles of bills and resolutions, one right after the other, from the legislative calendar. If no senator stood to object, then the legislation would pass "just as fast as you could call up the bill," Dove said. Because calendar Mondays took up so much time, they were eliminated in favor of the "less stylized" wrapup, Dove said. Since Howard H. Baker Jr.'s reign as majority leader (1981–1985), Senate leaders have traded wish lists of bills, resolutions, and nominees. Initial negotiations are between the floor assistants and chiefs of staff, but Senate leaders Trent Lott, R-Miss., and Tom Daschle, D-S.D., often discuss the wish list on the floor during votes. The list is then hot-lined to all senators' offices via fax and e-mail to ferret out any objections.

Congressional scholars insist noncontroversial measures that could garner unanimous consent should not take up floor time. However, the Senate could use wrapup to evade the spotlight that naturally shines on debates and, in the process, pass major legislation. For example, the Senate in 1999 passed the $14.5 billion fiscal 2000 Interior appropriations conference report by unanimous consent without a word uttered on the numerous policy riders the White House opposed. For Democrats, supporting the Interior conference report in wrapup was part of their strategy. Because conference reports cannot be amended, Democrats decided not to grandstand on the Senate floor and instead fight that battle behind closed doors with budget negotiators.

The key to wrapup is bipartisan cooperation because the process relies on unanimous consent. When relations between the two leaders become raw, the effect is not only gridlock on the bill on the floor but also a near standstill of wrapup. Another primary consideration to successfully getting a bill through wrapup is to avoid drawing too much attention to it and thus inviting debate. Many senators do not want to reveal their wish lists. "The way to get this stuff done is not to announce we want to get it done," said Chris Madison, spokesman for Joseph R. Biden Jr., D-Del.

SOURCE: Adapted from Sumana Chatterjee, "Wrapup Turns Senate into Model of Efficiency," *CQ Daily Monitor,* November 16, 1999, 3.

MAJOR LEGISLATION

Once major Senate bills are reported from committee, the majority leader considers several questions. First, what measures should he call up? Here he receives input from numerous sources, such as committee chairmen, the minority leader, the White House, and the rank and file, and identifies both the must-pass and must-not-pass bills. Second, absent an emergency or deadline-driven situation, when should he take up legislation? In a workload-packed Senate, time is always a factor. "I want to see the votes," said Majority Leader Lott. "And I want to see an outline of what the parliamentary situation will be, because time is a consideration around here." [18] Finally, how can legislation be positioned so it can be taken up? On some bills, procedural or substantive controversy is absent from their consideration. On other measures, substance is at issue. On yet other legislation, controversy rages over procedure and substance, which is the most difficult scenario for getting a bill called up.

Once the majority leader determines which measure to call up from the legislative calendar, it can take one of two main routes to the floor: through unanimous consent or by motion ("I move to take up S. 1234."). Before these stages are reached, however, the legislation may be subject to the one-day rule, the two-day rule, or to "holds."

One-Day and Two-Day Rules

The one-day rule states that bills and reports must lie over on the calendar for one legislative day before they are eligible for floor consideration. This rule is seldom enforced and commonly is waived by unanimous consent. To speed up action, the majority leader states, "I ask unanimous consent that [these bills] be considered as having been on the calendar 1 legislative day for the purpose of the rules of the Senate." [19] There rarely is an objection to the request.

The two-day rule requires that printed committee reports accompanying legislation reported by a committee be available to members for at least two calendar days before those proposals are eligible for floor action. (The two-day rule was a three-day rule until the Senate changed it in February 1986.) This rule, too, may be waived by unanimous consent or by joint motion of the majority and minority leaders. However, the Senate usually observes the rule, sometimes to the chagrin of the majority leader, who has primary responsibility for scheduling the Senate's business.

When the Senate considered the controversial 1987 nomination of Robert H. Bork to the Supreme Court, Majority Leader Byrd wanted to facilitate floor action on the nominee. He repeatedly asked GOP leader Dole to join him in waiving the two-day rule. "Would the distinguished Republican leader indicate whether or not he is willing to join with me in waiving the 2-day rule?" asked Byrd. "I regret that I am not in a position now to waive the 2-day rule," answered Dole.[20] The discussion surrounding the two-day rule involved jockeying by both parties as they tried to expedite or stretch out debate on the proposed, and ultimately unsuccessful, Bork judgeship.

During the 104th Congress, when Dole was majority leader and Byrd was the Senate's senior Democrat (he had voluntarily relinquished his party leadership role at the start of the 101st Congress), Dole hoped to act quickly on legislation curbing unfunded federal mandates (when the costs of national programs are passed on to state and local governments). To hasten floor action on the unfunded mandates bill, Dole requested the two committees with jurisdiction (Budget and Governmental Affairs) not to submit committee reports with the measure. He did not want the bill delayed by the two-day rule or the Senate rule granting committee members three calendar days to file supplemental, additional, or minority views for inclusion in the report. (Unlike the House, the Senate has no formal rule requiring committee reports to accompany legislation. Senate committees, however, usually file committee reports.) Despite protests from each committee's Democratic members, neither panel issued a formal committee report. Instead, the two GOP committee chairmen filed substitute statements in the *Congressional Record*.[21]

Senator Byrd quickly made a floor issue of the speed with which the bill whizzed through committee. "The Senate is not up against a deadline," he said. "We're not up against an adjournment *sine die*." The measure, he argued, needed a thorough examination on the floor. He underscored the importance of formal committee reports, noting, for instance, their value "to any court in determining what the legislative intent is with regard to a particular bill."[22] For two weeks Senator Byrd led the Democratic effort to delay action on the GOP proposal. "We have what we know as 'Byrd-lock,' " quipped Majority Leader Dole.[23] After fifty-nine hours of debate on the bill and forty-four roll-call votes, the Senate finally enacted the legislation.[24] Majority Leader Lott has also experienced frustration with the two-day rule. "The Senators are exercising their right to object to waiving the 2-day rule. . . . But I hope that they will not do this for very long, because we have our work to do."[25]

Holds

Holds are an informal custom unique to the Senate. They permit any number of senators—individually or in clusters—to stop (sometimes permanently, sometimes temporarily) floor consideration of legislation or nominations simply by making requests of their party leaders not to take up such matters. Party leaders can move ahead anyway, but then they face the daunting prospect of overcoming a probable filibuster. Unlike filibusters, which are ostensibly educational and occur in full view of everyone, holds require no public utterance and occur in shrouded circumstances. Sometimes called the "silent filibuster," they are especially effective on limited or special purpose measures that attract little public or political attention. Must-pass legislation, such as continuing resolutions, cannot be killed by holds. Only senators place holds, but they may do so at the request of House members, lobbyists, or executive branch officials.

Relatively little is known about holds even among insiders in Washington. No public record is kept of who places holds, how they are done (often by letter to the party leader), how many holds are placed on any bill, or how long they will be honored by the leadership. Most holds, noted Senator Byrd, are used so senators "might be assured that they will be informed or contacted so they can be present when the matter is called up, or have an opportunity to offer an amendment."[26] The list of Democratic and Republican senators who have holds on various measures is kept by the respective leaders of each party, but this is restricted and closely held information.

Holds can forestall floor action because they are linked to the Senate's tradition of extended debate and unanimous consent agreements. Party leaders understand that to ignore holds can precipitate objections to unanimous consent requests or filibusters, which require sixty votes to break. Especially during the period when the Senate is rushing to adjourn, holds can be fatal. "At this stage in the year, you have a finite amount of time and an infinite amount of legislation. Either the hold goes away, changes are made to the legislation or the person with the hold wins," stated a Senate GOP leadership aide.[27] Holds are also used during the end-of-session rush by members who are searching for must-pass bills to which they can attach their favorite amendments. Sen. Phil Gramm, R-Texas, for example, in 1994 placed a hold on the Export Administration Act "so he [could] attempt to attach [his] home equity loan amendment."[28]

Holds are a more prominent feature of today's Senate because assertive senators recognize the political and policy potential inherent in this extraparliamentary practice. Holds "have come into a form of reverence which was never to be," exclaimed a senator.[29] Periodically, party leaders assert that senators cannot put indefinite or anonymous holds on matters, but the practice still flourishes because senators recognize the tactical benefits. On February 25, 1999, Majority Leader Lott and Minority Leader Tom Daschle, D-S.D., sent a Dear Colleague letter (published in the March 3, 1999, *Congressional Record*) to all senators announcing the end of secret holds. They wrote in part:

> [A]ll members wishing to place a hold on any legislation or executive calendar business shall notify the sponsor of the legislation and the committee of jurisdiction of their concerns. Further, written notification should be provided to the respective Leader stating their intentions regarding the bill or nomination.

However, no enforcement procedure is associated with this policy declaration, which means secret holds still exist. For example, for a while in 1999 no one knew who had secret holds on Richard Holbrooke, President Bill Clinton's nominee to be U.S. ambassador to the United Nations. Eventually it came out in press reports that Lott and several other senators had holds on the nominee.

Holds encourage bargaining not only among senators but also between the Senate and the executive branch. Sen. Jesse Helms, R-N.C., sometimes places holds on diplomatic and other nominations to extract concessions from the State Department and other federal agencies. Angry at President Clinton for allegedly breaking his June 1999 agreement that he would notify Republicans of any recess appointments to executive positions, Sen. James M. Inhofe, R-Okla., retaliated by placing holds in 2000 on all federal judicial appointments. Majority Leader Lott was sympathetic to Inhofe's holds. Yet he called up several judicial nominees anyway and succeeded in invoking cloture to end a filibuster. Holds have become so common on nominees that Minority Leader Daschle jokingly said that if senators do not have them, they ought to feel lonely. "You know, who's your holder? That seems to be the question of every nominee. It's almost a status symbol among senators. 'I have no holds. I'm going to have to pick out a nominee to get to know him or her a lot better.' It works that way. . . . 'Hello, I'm your holder. Come dance with me.'"[30]

UNANIMOUS CONSENT AGREEMENTS

If the Senate strictly observed every rule, it would become mired in a bog of parliamentary complications. Instead, the chamber expedites its business by unanimously agreeing to waive the rules. Any senator can object to a unanimous consent agreement. As Majority Leader Mitchell once said: "I regularly propound unanimous-consent requests on the floor, and I can assure [the senator] when Senators object we hear within seconds—within seconds. Frequently when I am in the middle of a sentence, the phone rings and staff comes running out to say, 'Senator so and so objects.'"[31] GOP and Democratic leaders "hot line" requests for unanimous consent agreements to all senators' offices via special telephone lines. Senators are provided a specific timeframe in which to object, otherwise the measure or matter will come to the floor. Unanimous consent agreements are often the product of intensive and extensive negotiations with drafts of agreements exchanged on and off the floor among concerned senators; once an accord is reached, each side will try to sell the UCA to its other colleagues.

By long-standing tradition, the business of the Senate is "largely transacted through unanimous-consent agreements," Massachusetts Republican Henry Cabot Lodge said in 1913. And, he continued, "not only the important unanimous-consent agreements which are reached often with much difficulty on large and generally contested measures, but constantly on all the small business of the Senate we depend on unanimous consent to enable us to transact the public business."[32] That statement holds true today. As one senator put it:

[T]he way the Senate conducts its business hour after hour, day after day, week after week, and year after year, is Senators voluntarily waive the rights which they possess under the rules. I would guess in the course of a typical week we probably enter into anywhere from 10 to 200 unanimous consent agreements, literally, where Senators by unanimous consent, with 100 Senators agreeing to yield some right that they may have—the right to debate, to offer amendments, the right to do this, that or the other thing—waive their rights so that the body may proceed in a way that seems expeditious.[33]

Once accepted, unanimous consent agreements are as binding on the Senate as any standing rule and may be set aside or modified only by unanimous consent. The Senate in October 1999 had agreed to a UCA that set a final date for a vote on the Comprehensive Nuclear Test Ban Treaty, a top priority of President Clinton's. However, the administration lacked the required two-thirds vote for approval and wanted to put off the vote. Intensive negotiations took place to determine a graceful way to avoid a showdown on the floor. However, as Sen. Joseph I. Lieberman, D-Conn., said, "the interesting procedural trick is that you need unanimous consent" to postpone the vote.[34] In the end, several conservative GOP senators refused to accept any change in the UCA, and the treaty went down to defeat. The vote "marked the first time an arms control agreement has been rejected by the Senate and only the sixth time in history that senators rejected any treaty."[35]

Overview

Two general types of unanimous consent permeate Senate operation: simple and complex. Both types set aside the rules, precedents, and orders of the Senate via the unanimous consent of all senators. A single objection ("I object") blocks a unanimous consent request. The two types share a general purpose: to do things on the floor that could not be done without unanimous consent. However, the complex form has large procedural and policy implications.

Simple UCAs. Simple unanimous consent requests are made from the floor by any senator; these almost always deal with routine business or noncontroversial actions. For example, senators regularly ask permission for staff members to be present on the floor during a debate. Simple unanimous consent requests also may rescind quorum calls, add senators as cosponsors of bills, insert material in the *Congressional Record,* or dispense with the reading of amendments.

From its beginning, the Senate provided a conducive environment for simple unanimous consent. Its small size, few rules, and informality encouraged the rise of this practice. Even several of the Senate's early rules incorporated unanimous consent provisions to speed the Senate's routine business. For example, a Senate rule adopted on April 16, 1789, stated: "Every bill shall receive three readings to its being passed; and the President [of the Senate] shall give notice at each, whether it be first, second, or third; which readings shall be on three different days, unless the Senate unanimously directs otherwise."

Complex UCAs. Complex unanimous consent agreements establish a tailor-made procedure for handling virtually anything considered on the Senate floor: bills, joint resolutions, simple resolutions, concurrent resolutions, amendments, nominations, conference reports, and treaties. Fundamentally, the Senate operates much differently with them than without them. As the Senate parliamentarians wrote: "Whereas the Senate Rules permit virtually unlimited debate, and very few restrictions on the right to offer amendments, these agreements usually limit time for debate and the right of Senators to offer amendments."[36] In effect, UCAs are a form of voluntary cloture (see Table 6-2). Senators generally accept the debate and amendments restrictions common to most UCAs largely for two overlapping reasons: They facilitate the processing of the Senate's workload and they serve the interests of individual senators, given that UCAs infuse predictability in floor scheduling.

UCAs are based on trust. Majority leaders will request and receive unanimous consent to modify UCAs if any senator believes he or she was misinformed or ill-informed with respect to its terms. As Majority Leader Mitchell said on one occasion:

> The agreement was reached in good faith, but I am now advised that due to a misunderstanding and an inadvertent error, a Senator's right to make a point of order was not protected and included in the agreement. That was an honest mistake. And since becoming majority leader, I have taken the position that whenever an agreement is reached that includes a provision placing a Senator at a disadvantage as a result of an inadvertent error or mistake, either by a Senator or staff, that the disadvantage should be removed and the agreement modified to reflect the circumstances which should have existed when the agreement was adopted.[37]

So many variations of complex agreements exist today that the term can neither comprehend nor distinguish them all adequately.

UCAs are proposed orally—usually by the majority leader—often after protracted negotiations among other party and committee leaders and key senators.[38] Once agreed to, they are formally recorded in the *Congressional Record,* the daily *Calendar of Business,* and in the *Senate Journal.* Such agreements may establish the sequential order in which measures will be taken up, pinpoint the time when measures are to reach the floor, and set rules for debate, including time limitations and, frequently, a requirement that all amendments be relevant to the bill under consideration. For example, a unanimous consent agreement could specify that the amendment offered by Senator A will have a time limit of twenty minutes equally divided between the two opposing sides or that the amendment cosponsored by Senators B and C will have a time limit of thirty minutes equally divided and controlled

TABLE 6-2 Purposes and Features of a Complex Unanimous Consent Agreement

Broad Purposes	General Features
Impose time limits on debate	A negotiated contract accepted by all senators
Expedite scheduling the Senate's workload	Changed only by another unanimous consent agreement
Establish predictability and permit flexibility	Comprehensive or partial in character
	Limits debate on measures and any motions related thereto
	Structures the amendment process
	Requires the germaneness or relevancy of amendments
	Waives points of order

in the usual form (that is, between the mover of the amendment and an opponent).

Commonly, party leaders are able to negotiate only partial, or incremental, unanimous consent agreements (covering parts but not the entire bill) before they call up the bill for floor action. Plenty of piecemeal unanimous consent agreements—limiting debate on specific amendments or deciding when to call up a measure—are hammered out on the floor. Party leaders and floor managers take what they can get when they can get it and work from there to more embracing unanimous consent agreements. It is "so hard to get these agreements," said one majority leader. "I find it is somewhat better to do them a little bit at a time." [39] Or as a congressional scholar wrote: "A dozen or more complex agreements are no longer uncommon for complicated contentious measures." [40]

The primary objective of unanimous consent agreements is to limit the time it takes to dispose of controversial issues in an institution noted for unlimited debate. These agreements, therefore, expedite action on legislation and structure floor deliberation. (Numerous precedents have evolved over time to govern UCAs.) Typically, agreements impose time limitations on every debatable—and thus delaying—motion, including amendments and final passage, points of order, or appeals from the rulings of the presiding officer. These agreements, however, may allow an unlimited number of amendments to be offered, thus permitting what Sen. Ted Stevens, R-Alaska, once dubbed a "time agreement filibuster."

A unanimous consent agreement could ban certain amendments or place time limits on them, preventing a time agreement filibuster. Thus, depending on what the circumstances warrant, party leaders can craft highly detailed, complex, and creative unanimous consent agreements to accommodate the diverse procedural contingencies that might arise on the floor. Their fundamental problem is winning consent from senators reluctant to waive any of their procedural prerogatives. As Senator Byrd once said: "The leader is the prisoner of Senators, and always has been. Any Senator can object to time agreements, they can make it difficult for every other Senator." [41]

Complex unanimous consent agreements usually specify the senators who are to control the time for debate on the bill and all amendments, and they provide that the time is to be controlled by senators on opposing sides of the issue. Common, too, is the requirement that amendments be relevant. Senate rules do permit nongermane floor amendments, but unanimous consent agreements often prohibit them to prevent extraneous issues from being taken up. Some agreements may also set the date and time for the vote on final passage of the measure. In an institution noted for procedural flexibility and sparseness (as compared with the House), unanimous consent agreements underscore the Senate's recognition that it needs to voluntarily impose additional rules on itself to dispatch its business.

Complex UCAs generally impose limitations on two of the most significant prerogatives associated with being a member of the Senate: the right of unlimited debate and the right to offer an unlimited number of floor amendments, even if they are nongermane. The irony of unanimous consent agreements is that, on the one hand, if they are accepted by everyone, the Senate can do almost anything it wants (an exception being, for example, that unanimous consent agreements cannot waive the constitutional requirement that veto overrides are to occur by recorded vote). On the other hand, if even one senator objects, then the Senate has difficulty accomplishing anything. In today's Senate, where individualism and partisanship are perhaps its paramount features, majority leaders have to work harder to negotiate unanimous consent agreements that accommodate the partisan and individual interests of senators.

Senate Leadership and UCAs

The majority leader generally has an important scheduling ally in the minority leader. In contrast to the House, where scheduling is the sole prerogative of the majority leadership, Senate scheduling traditionally involves the leaders of both parties. The Senate system derives not merely from equity but also from necessity, because Senate rules confer on each individual member formidable power to frustrate the legislative process, including the right to object to any unanimous consent request. The majority and minority leaders thus constantly consult with one another and with their top aides, other senators, executive officials, lobbyists, and key staff members on legislative scheduling.

Since the post-World War II period, all party leaders have relied extensively on unanimous consent agreements to process the Senate's workload.

During the majority leadership of Lyndon B. Johnson (1955–1961), they were often comprehensive in scope, identifying, for example, when a measure is to be taken up, when it is to be voted upon for final passage, and everything in between. Two subsequent majority leaders—Democrats Mike Mansfield of Montana, who held the post longer than any other senator (1961–1977), and Robert Byrd (1977–1981; 1987–1989)—are largely responsible for refining and extending the use of unanimous consent agreements. During their tenure UCAs became more complicated and governed floor action on a larger number of measures.

The personal styles of other majority leaders and the political context in which they served (the size of the majority party, for instance, or whether their party occupied the White House) also influenced how they employed unanimous consent agreements. For example, Howard H. Baker Jr., R-Tenn., majority leader from 1981 to 1985, brought measures to the floor without first obtaining comprehensive agreements. With the Senate and White House in GOP hands, the Democrats were reluctant to enter into broad agreements restricting their floor options because they had little idea of what amendments might surface. Thus, narrower agreements often were negotiated on the floor, typically regulating the consideration of a particular amendment or a series of amendments. Today, in a period of rampant individualism and partisanship, unanimous consent agreements tend to be piecemeal, such as establishing debate limits on specific amendments.

Reaching Agreement

The Senate's tradition of individual and minority rights means that strategic considerations often permeate the use and shape of unanimous consent agreements.

UCAs as Action-Forcing Devices. Two weeks prior to the scheduled mid-August 1986 recess of the Senate, Majority Leader Bob Dole circulated a unanimous consent agreement outlining how he planned to juggle floor action of four major measures: a Defense Department authorization bill, a debt ceiling extension measure, economic sanctions against South Africa, and aid to the contras (a paramilitary group) in Central America. The controversy between the parties involved the last two bills. Broad bipartisan support existed for economic sanctions against South Africa because of its policy of apartheid (racial separation), with Democrats urging a final vote by Friday, August 15. Aid to the contras, a priority of the Reagan administration, attracted only a bare majority of the Senate and almost all from GOP ranks.

After lengthy negotiations with Minority Leader Byrd and other senators, a unanimous consent agreement was reached that took Majority Leader Dole nearly an hour to read and that consumed three pages of the *Congressional Record*.[42] The agreement was "so complicated that senators admitted they could not understand it even after two or three readings."[43] Strategically, Dole's UCA forged an interdependent link between the two bills.

The UCA required the Senate to consider the contra aid package before South Africa sanctions. At Dole's insistence, a key clause had been added to the UCA. As Dole explained the provision, "unless cloture is invoked on both items, meaning South Africa and Contra aid, then this agreement is null and void, with the proviso . . . that as much of the August recess, as necessary, be null and void in order to complete action" on both proposals.[44] Not only did Dole threaten to delay the Senate's long-awaited August recess if these two issues were not resolved, but he also effectively choked off any Democratic incentive to filibuster the contra aid package. Furthermore, the agreement headed off dilatory action by senatorial opponents of South Africa sanctions.

On August 13, the Senate invoked cloture on both measures, thus assuring a final vote on each bill. Under the UCA, a cloture vote was to be taken first on contra aid. It failed on a 59–40 vote (sixty votes are needed). The UCA then required a cloture vote on sanctions against South Africa. Despite the Reagan administration's opposition to sanctions, cloture was overwhelmingly approved 89-11. Then another cloture attempt occurred on contra aid, because the UCA explicitly required cloture to be invoked on both measures. On the second attempt, cloture was invoked (62-37).

UCAs as Bargaining Chips. Party leaders understand that the business which comes before the Senate attracts differential interest and support among their colleagues. Some lawmakers are keenly interested in certain matters; others have little concern about these topics. This condition creates opportunities for bargaining when fashioning unanimous consent agreements.

Majority Leader George Mitchell in 1989 informed the Senate that he expected the Senate to complete action on a child care bill in a week's time. Minority Leader Dole pointed out GOP opposition to the measure but then raised the matter of the nomination of Chic Hecht, a former Republican senator from Nevada, to be ambassador to the Bahamas. Dole wanted expeditious Senate action on confirming Hecht, whose nomination was being delayed by Democrats. Dole said: "I hope that we could resolve [the Hecht] issue today because that may have an impact on how long it takes to get a unanimous-consent agreement on child care."[45]

Later that day, after extensive consultations with Senator Dole, Majority Leader Mitchell propounded a detailed UCA for the final disposition of the child care bill. No objection was made to Mitchell's request, because an understanding had been reached between Mitchell and Dole on the Hecht nomination. "The nomination of former Senator Hecht will be disposed of on Tuesday, July 11," stated Senator Mitchell. "And we hope it will be not later than 7 p.m. on that day."[46]

Partisan Overlay to UCAs. Both parties and individual senators assess the political and policy costs and benefits of going along with a unanimous consent agreement. Issues of position taking, electoral advantage, media coverage, and partisan advantage are among the many factors that influence

Senate acceptance of these compacts. A measure's controversialism may have little or no bearing on when or whether an accord is reached.

In the aftermath of President Clinton's impeachment trial and subsequent acquittal by the Senate, Majority Leader Lott wanted to accelerate action on popular issues and refocus public attention on legislative accomplishments. Lott called up a measure—waiving certain federal educational requirements and popularly referred to as "ed-flex"—that enjoyed broad bipartisan support among senators and the nation's governors. The bill easily passed the Senate on March 11, 1999, by a 98 to 1 vote. However, when the ed-flex measure had been called up two weeks earlier, it immediately bogged down in partisan and procedural wrangling over the ground rules for debating and amending the legislation.

"It's a bill we can get a [time limitation] agreement on and pass," declared Majority Leader Lott.[47] No unanimous consent agreement was forthcoming, however. Lott wanted the Senate to pass the modest educational measure quickly. Democrats, however, wanted to showcase the differences between the parties on education, especially with the 2000 elections as the backdrop, and offered a number of amendments advocated by President Clinton, such as reducing class size by hiring 100,000 more teachers. Minority Leader Daschle said to Lott: "Look. We will agree to these five or six amendments; we will agree to time limits and up-or-down votes of these five or six amendments; and then let's move on."[48] The last thing Lott wanted was to permit a high-profile debate of Democratic initiatives when Republicans hoped to claim education as one of their top priorities. "What they need to do is back off from all their amendments," declared Lott. "We set the agenda."[49]

Both sides were at a standoff. Republicans did not want to vote on the Democratic amendments. Yet they also realized Democrats had the votes to prevent final action on the popular bill. To determine if he could move the bill toward final passage, Lott employed a number of parliamentary maneuvers, such as filing cloture (hoping to invoke a germaneness requirement for amendments) and filling the amendment tree (preventing Democrats from offering their amendments). In the end, the two sides reached a unanimous consent agreement that served their respective purposes.

For Republicans, they achieved a final vote on the bill; moreover, they defeated the Democratic amendments on party-line votes. Politically, they also took credit for acting on an agenda issue that voters rate highly. Thus, passage of the legislation helped Republicans to recast their public image from the party that wanted to abolish the Department of Education to the party with a strong commitment to education. The immediate GOP cost before an agreement was reached was two weeks of gridlock and bitter partisanship.

Benefits rather than costs largely accrued to Democrats for rejecting attempts by Lott to reach an accord that limited their ability to offer amendments. They won media coverage of their educational proposals and gained the opportunity to offer and debate a series of prized amendments. Even though their proposals were rejected, Democrats knew they could always offer them again on another bill. A short-term cost for Democrats was an uptick of sharper partisanship between the two sides.

Scheduling involves numerous considerations. Party leaders must balance their interest in planning the Senate's business on a daily, weekly, and annual basis with (1) the needs of committees, which require concentrated periods of time, particularly early in the session, to process legislation assigned to them; (2) the needs of senators, who prefer some degree of predictability and certainty so they can schedule their time most efficiently; and (3) the needs of their party, which means considering an agenda that facilitates their continued majority status. These various imperatives mean that no matter how carefully Senate leaders plan the legislative agenda—the times and dates measures will be scheduled, and in what order they will be considered on the floor—they still must juggle bills to satisfy senators, take account of external events and political circumstances, and, where possible, influence policy outcomes in the interests of their own party. As Mitchell once said:

> The ability of any Senator to speak without limitations makes it impossible to establish total certainty with respect to scheduling. When there is added to that the different and very demanding schedules of 100 Senators, it is very difficult to organize business in a way that meets the convenience of everybody.[50]

THE TRACK SYSTEM

Another device sometimes used for scheduling purposes is the track system. The track system was instituted in the early 1970s by Majority Leader Mansfield with the concurrence of the minority leadership and other senators. It permits the Senate to have several pieces of legislation pending on the floor simultaneously by designating specific periods during the day when each proposal will be considered. The system is particularly beneficial when many important bills are awaiting floor action or when a protracted floor debate is taking place on a bill.

Before the initiation of the track system, legislative business halted during filibusters. The "two-track system enables the Senate to circumvent that barrier," said Majority Whip Alan Cranston, D-Calif. "[It] . . . can now continue to work on all other legislation on one 'track' while a filibuster against a particular piece of legislation is . . . in progress on the other 'track.'"[51] Use of the track system is implemented by the majority leader after obtaining the unanimous consent of the Senate. Or the different tracks can be put into place by agreement between the majority leader and the minority leader. On occasion, the Senate may operate on triple or quadruple tracks.

As the November 2000 elections drew nearer, Majority Leader Lott announced plans for double tracking the business of the Senate. "One track will be for appropriations bills and the other will be for legislation. When there is a lull in the appropriations process, then the Senate will be able to shift gears quickly and focus its attention on whatever legislation is pending on the legislative track." [52]

The use of unanimous consent agreements and the track system imposes a measure of discipline on the Senate. Formerly, senators could arrive in the midst of a debate on a banking bill, for example, obtain recognition from the chair, and launch into a lengthy discussion of the wheat harvest prospects. Today, complex agreements and the track system prevent that from happening. Now, senators generally know what measure will be considered on a specific day and at what time, when they are scheduled to speak on that bill, and how long they will have the floor.

SCHEDULING PROCEDURES COMPARED

The Senate has nothing that compares with the scheduling function of the House Rules Committee.[53] That panel regulates the flow of major bills to the floor, specifies the time for general debate, stipulates whether amendments can be offered, and decides if points of order are to be waived. The legislative route in the House is clearly marked by firm rules and precedents, but that is not so in the Senate. "Rules are never observed in this body," a president pro tempore observed, "they are only made to be broken. We are a law unto ourselves, and it is entirely immaterial in my judgment whether we have a code of rules or not." [54]

Nonetheless, unanimous consent agreements and the special rules drafted by the Rules Committee are similar in several respects (see Table 6-3). Each waives the rules of the respective chamber to permit timely consideration of important measures and amendments. Each must be approved by the members—in the Senate by unanimous consent of all senators and in the House by majority vote of the representatives. Each effectively sets the conditions for debate on the legislation in question and on all proposed amendments. And rules and unanimous consent agreements are formulated with the involvement of party leaders, although such participation in the House is generally limited to the majority party. The House leadership usually plays a significant part only for rules on crucial or controversial measures.

Among the more important differences between rules and unanimous consent agreements are that rules are drafted in public session by a standing committee, while unanimous consent agreements are often negotiated privately by senators and staff aides. Measures given a rule in the House commonly are taken up almost immediately, but unanimous consent agreements generally involve prospective action on bills.

The amendment process in each house also makes for important differences. Rules from the Rules Committee may limit the number of permissible amendments or prohibit them altogether. Senate unanimous consent agreements, except those prohibiting nongermane amendments, do not usually limit or forbid floor amendments. Senate practices regard an amendment as germane—even when it is not germane—if it is specifically enumerated in the

TABLE 6-3 Comparison of House Special Rule and Senate Unanimous Consent Agreement

House Special Rule	Senate Unanimous Consent Agreement
Specifies time for general debate	May specify time for debating the bill and amendments offered to the bill
Permits or prohibits amendments	Often restricts the offering of nonrelevant amendments
Formulated by Rules Committee in public session	Formulated by party leaders informally in private sessions; also on the Senate floor
Approved by majority vote of the House	Agreed to by unanimous consent of senators
Adoption generally results in immediate floor action on the bill	Adoption often aimed toward prospective floor action
Covers many aspects of floor procedure	Geared primarily to debate restrictions on amendments and final passage
Does not specify date and exact time for vote on final passage	May set date and exact time for vote on final passage
Effect is to waive House rules	Effect is to waive Senate rules

unanimous consent agreement. All senators must be willing to waive the germaneness requirement when the agreement is drawn up.

Finally, a special House rule specifies almost every significant floor procedure that will affect consideration of the bill. Complex agreements in the Senate focus on two points in particular: (1) setting limits on the debate time to be allowed for amendments, motions, points of order, and appeals from the rulings of the chair; and (2) structuring the amendment process. In general, procedural experimentation is easier to accomplish in the smaller Senate than in the 435-member House.

NOTES

1. Mark Preston, "Lott Wants Five-Day Workweek," *Roll Call*, May 11, 2000, 1.
2. *Congressional Record*, December 9, 1987, S17474.
3. *Congressional Record*, June 23, 1994, S7553.
4. Ilona Nickels, "Senate's 'Three Weeks On; One Week Off' Schedule," in *Background Materials: Supplemental Information Provided to Members of the Joint Committee on the Organization of Congress*, 103d Cong., 1st sess. (1993), 1050–1051; and Karen Foerstel, "Three-On, One-Off Senate Schedule: Where Did It Go?" *Roll Call*, July 1, 1991, 1.

5. *Congressional Record,* June 4, 1997, S5277.
6. *Congressional Record,* July 26, 1989, S8870.
7. Helen Dewar, "Senate Battle on Child Health Care Symbolizes Kennedy-Lott Power Struggle," *Washington Post,* May 23, 1997, A9.
8. *CQ Daily Monitor,* June 26, 1997, 2.
9. Norman Ornstein, "Let the End Games Begin," *Roll Call,* September 12, 1994, A23.
10. *Congressional Record,* November 17, 1989, S15948.
11. *New York Times,* May 21, 1987, B10.
12. *Congressional Record,* March 21, 1980, S2789. Sen. Robert C. Byrd, D-W.Va., wrote a multivolume Senate history and is widely regarded as the premier authority on the chamber's rules and precedents.
13. Each calendar is printed separately. There also are separate executive and legislative *Journals.* The General Orders calendar is found in the Senate *Calendar of Business,* which is printed each day the Senate is in session. Measures on the calendar are assigned a calendar order number. The Senate *Executive Calendar* appears whenever there is executive business.
14. *Congressional Record,* January 26, 1973, 2301. According to Senate rules, "Any rule may be suspended without advance notice by unanimous consent of the Senate."
15. *Congressional Record,* August 5, 1987, S11293.
16. *Congressional Record,* April 8, 1981, S3618.
17. *Congressional Record,* January 4, 1995, S39.
18. *CQ Daily Monitor,* June 10, 1996, 5.
19. *Congressional Record,* December 10, 1982, S14345.
20. *Congressional Record,* October 14, 1987, S14197.
21. *Congressional Record,* January 9, 1995, S646; and *Congressional Record,* January 11, 1995, S783.
22. *Congressional Record,* January 12, 1995, S858–S859.
23. Edwin Chen and Melissa Healy, "Byrd Dogs Republicans with Stall on GOP Proposals," *Los Angeles Times,* January 18, 1995, A5.
24. David Hosansky, "Chipping Away at Opposition, Senate Passes Mandates Bill," *Congressional Quarterly Weekly Report,* January 28, 1995, 276.
25. *Congressional Record,* June 19, 1997, S5903.
26. *Congressional Record,* February 24, 1986, S1512.
27. *CQ's Daily Monitor,* October 4, 1994, 5. For an informative study of holds, see Toby McIntosh, "Senate 'Holds' System Developing as Sophisticated Tactic for Leverage, Delay," *Daily Report for Executives* (No. 165), Bureau of National Affairs, August 26, 1991, C1–C5.
28. *National Journal's Congress Daily/AM,* October 5, 1994, 5.
29. *Congressional Record,* December 5, 1985, S16916.
30. Lawrence Goodrich, "Congressional Journal," *Christian Science Monitor,* November 28, 1997, 4.
31. *Congressional Record,* August 6, 1992, S11692.
32. *Congressional Record,* January 11, 1913, 1388.
33. *Congressional Record,* September 25, 1990, S13803.
34. *CQ Daily Monitor,* October 13, 1999, 2.
35. *CQ Daily Monitor,* October 14, 1999, 5.

36. Floyd Riddick and Alan Frumin, *Senate Procedure: Precedents and Practices* (Washington, D.C.: U.S. Government Printing Office, 1983), 1311.

37. *Congressional Record,* February 4, 1992, S872.

38. Unlike simple requests, which are formulated orally, complex unanimous consent agreements are formalized in writing and reported to senators by means of the *Congressional Record,* the front page of the daily *Calendar of Business,* and in party whip notices.

39. *Congressional Record,* September 13, 1994, S12793.

40. Steven S. Smith, *Call to Order* (Washington, D.C.: Brookings Institution, 1989), 115.

41. *Congressional Record,* June 1, 1989, S5939.

42. *Congressional Record,* August 9, 1986, S10952–S10955.

43. John Felton, "Senate's Climate of Partisanship Yields an Agreement of Unusual Complexity," *Congressional Quarterly Weekly Report,* August 16, 1986, 1878.

44. *Congressional Record,* August 9, 1986, S10952.

45. *Congressional Record,* June 21, 1989, S7026.

46. *Congressional Record,* June 21, 1989, S7067.

47. *CQ Daily Monitor,* March 8, 1999, 5.

48. *Congressional Record,* March 5, 1999, S2359.

49. Sue Kirchhoff and Sumana Chatterjee, "Flood of Democratic Amendments Stalls Senate's Efforts to Pass Bill on Flexibility in Education Aid," *Congressional Quarterly Weekly Report,* March 6, 1999, 550.

50. *Congressional Record,* July 20, 1990, S10183.

51. *Congressional Record,* January 21, 1975, 928.

52. Preston, "Lott Wants Five-Day Workweek," 38.

53. The Senate Rules and Administration Committee has jurisdiction over internal Senate matters but is not involved in scheduling bills for floor debate.

54. *Congressional Record,* December 18, 1876, 266.

CHAPTER 7

Senate Floor Procedure

A VISITOR who moves from the House gallery to the Senate gallery is struck immediately by the contrast in atmosphere. The Senate chamber is more sedate, it is quieter, and business is conducted at a more relaxed pace. The chamber is smaller and more intimate. Given their higher visibility and fewer number, senators are more easily recognizable than their House counterparts. Typically, only a handful of senators are present on the floor. The remainder are busy in committee meetings or occupied with constituent or other legislative business. All senators, however, generally arrive on the floor quickly in response to buzzers announcing roll-call votes or quorum calls.

The Senate chamber is ringed by an upper level of galleries for the press, visitors, and dignitaries. Four semicircular tiers of desks are arranged on the Senate floor (see Figure 7-1). Each of the one hundred senators has an assigned desk, complete with snuffbox and open inkwell. A broad aisle separates the Republicans, sitting on the right (facing the podium), from the Democrats, on the left. Depending on the makeup of the Senate, more seats may be on one side than the other. The Senate has no electronic voting machines; each senator responds aloud as his or her name is reached during a roll call. Both the Senate and the House employ microphones on the floor, but, unlike representatives, each senator has a microphone.

On the raised platform, the constitutional president of the Senate—the vice president of the United States—presides on expected close votes crucial to administration policy and may vote himself only to break a tie. The vice president usually is not present, however.[1] The Constitution provides for a Senate president pro tempore, elected by that body, to preside in the vice president's absence. The president pro tem usually is the most senior senator of the majority party. (Sometimes the Senate has also established the post of deputy president pro tempore.) In practice, each day's session is chaired by several temporary presiding officers—majority-party senators chosen by the president pro tem to serve on a rotating basis for about an hour.

Neither the president pro tem nor the presiding officer is analogous to the Speaker of the House, in part because neither possesses the political resources to exert such wide-ranging influence in the Senate. (One consequence is that rulings of the Senate presiding officer are often appealed and overturned by the Senate; the Speaker's parliamentary rulings in the House are seldom appealed and virtually never overturned.) The president pro tempore "has never been able to establish his authority as a party leader to the extent of the Majority Leader," said Sen. Robert C. Byrd, D-W.Va. (Byrd served as president

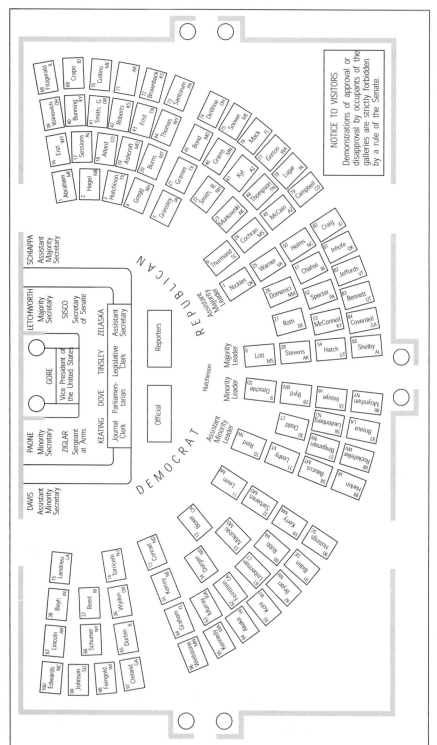

FIGURE 7-1 Senate Floor Plan and Seating Chart, as of February 2, 1999

pro tem from 1989 to 1995 and as majority leader from 1977 to 1981 and from 1987 to 1989.) "This is partly the result of the President pro tempore's irregular appointments and uncertain tenure over the years while serving in the absence of the Vice President."[2]

The principal elective leaders of the Senate are to be found at the two front desks on the center aisle, those assigned to the majority and minority leaders. To the left of the majority leader and to the right of the minority leader sit the party whips, second in command in the Senate party hierarchy. These party leaders, or their designees, remain on the floor at all times to protect their party's interests.

The leadership and individual senators are in frequent contact. To a much greater extent than in the House, each member has the power to influence the course of the legislative process on a daily basis. Any senator can disrupt the Senate's consideration of a bill more easily and with more telling effect than any one representative in the House. That this does not occur on a regular basis is a tribute to the operation of the Senate's system of unanimous consent, the skill of party leaders, and the long tradition of trust, accommodation, and reciprocal courtesy among members, which has survived periodic lapses into hard-line partisanship and confrontation.

LEGISLATIVE AND CALENDAR DAYS

The Senate, unlike the House, regularly distinguishes between a calendar day and a legislative day.[3] The former is the commonly understood notion of what constitutes a day—the twenty-four-hour period of time. The latter refers not to a day when the Senate is in session but to the period between a recess and an adjournment of the Senate. Recesses and adjournments determine the sequence of legislative days and calendar days. If the Senate adjourns at the end of a daily session, the legislative day ends with that calendar day. If, however, it chooses to recess, the legislative day is carried over to the next calendar day. For example, if the Senate recesses on May 3 and continues that practice for several calendar days, the legislative day remains May 3 even if the calendar day is May 21. However, once the Senate adjourns after a series of recesses, the legislative day and calendar day become the same.

The distinction between the types of days is important because many of the Senate's rules are tied to the legislative day. For instance, the "word 'day,' as used in the rules, unless it is specified as a calendar day, is construed to mean a legislative day," according to Senate precedents.[4] The decision to adjourn or recess is made either by unanimous consent or by majority vote on a motion made by the majority leader. If a quorum cannot be obtained, the Senate must adjourn. Adjournment favors senators trying to delay business because it may trigger series of time-consuming tactics when the Senate next convenes. The majority leader's decision to ask for a recess or an adjournment, therefore, can have some influence on controversial legislation before the Senate. Although party leaders make this determination, they often prefer recesses to adjournments. Recesses grant the leadership greater flexibility in shaping the Senate's daily business. Senate rules prescribe a daily order of business, but it is followed only when the Senate begins a new legislative day.

DAILY ORDER OF BUSINESS

Under resolutions adopted at the start of each Congress, the Senate generally convenes each day at noon. The leadership, by a unanimous consent request or motion, may modify the time on a day-to-day basis to stay abreast of the Senate's workload.

The regular order of business in the Senate, as in the House, begins with a prayer followed by the Pledge of Allegiance. Next is leader's time (usually ten minutes each to the majority leader and the minority leader). The majority leader, for example, might state what the Senate is expected to accomplish during that day or make a statement about a substantive matter. If neither leader wants any time, then the Senate typically either permits members who have requested time to make five-minute statements or resumes consideration of business under the terms of an earlier unanimous consent agreement.

The Senate, too, must keep and approve a *Journal* of the previous day's activities. The *Journal* usually is "deemed approved to date" by unanimous consent when the Senate adjourns or recesses at the end of each day. Any senator could object to the *Journal*'s approval and propose amendments to it, but this is an exceedingly rare occurrence. (In 1986 the Senate amended its rules to permit a nondebatable motion for the *Journal*'s approval. Previously, reading the *Journal* was sometimes used as a filibustering device.)

At the start of a new legislative day, the first two hours of Senate activity is called the morning hour—even if this period occurs in the afternoon. (The Senate can order that the morning hour be dispensed with. Recent Senates have not observed the morning hour.) Morning business is conducted during morning hour, including the receipt of messages, reports, and communications from the president, the House, and heads of executive branch departments. Bills and resolutions are introduced and referred to committee, committee reports filed, statements inserted in the *Congressional Record,* and brief speeches delivered. As Senator Byrd summarized:

> "Morning business" and the "morning hour" do not mean the same. The morning hour is the first two hours after the Senate convenes following an adjournment. Morning business is that period within the morning hour during which senators may introduce resolutions, bills, petitions, or memorials; committees may report matters, and certain matters come over from the previous day.[5]

Senators may speak during morning business only by unanimous consent, which is why the party leaders usually ask unanimous consent that a period be set aside for the transaction of routine morning business and that senators be allowed to speak therein, usually for up to five minutes. "[O]ne of the great opportunities that comes with having been elected a Member of the U.S. Senate is to participate . . . in what we call here morning business," said Sen. Joseph I. Lieberman, D-Conn., "which I have always seen as the people's forum, an opportunity to speak on the events of the day, both public and, in some senses, those that are more personal." [6]

The leadership may restrict or change morning business by unanimous consent. (Sometimes a single calendar day has several morning business periods or an entire day could be consumed by morning business.) Both parties increasingly use morning business to highlight their partisan agenda and goals. A nondebatable motion to proceed to any item on the calendar also is in order during the morning hour. Rarely is such a motion made during this period.

Following these preliminaries, the Senate then proceeds to unfinished business—legislation pending from a previous day. If there is no unfinished business, the majority leader or his designee offers a motion to take up a new measure that the leadership, after consultation with the minority leader and other interested senators, has scheduled for floor action. This is a critical juncture in the proceedings, for opponents of the bill could begin delaying tactics, such as a filibuster, to prevent it from being considered.

DEBATE IN THE MODERN SENATE

In the early Congresses, the Senate was characterized by protracted debates and great orators: Daniel Webster, John C. Calhoun, and Stephen A. Douglas on slavery, and later by Henry Cabot Lodge and others on the League of Nations. Today, senators are so busy, and the legislative agenda so crowded, that extended give-and-take among numerous senators is the exception rather than the rule. "In this United States Senate it is rare indeed to have one-third of the members present to hear debate," observed a senator. "There is dialogue and debate, but most of it does not take place on the floor under public scrutiny." [7]

Debate still serves to publicize issues, address constituencies, identify areas of consensus, and influence Senate votes. After one spirited floor session, a senator declared, "I was really undecided on the pending amendment, but [the] Senator so ably presented his case that I will join him" in opposing the amendment. [8] As another example, the first female African American senator, Carol Moseley-Braun, D-Ill. (1993–1999), gave a stirring address when the Senate took up a proposal to extend a patent for a Confederate flag insignia wanted by the United Daughters of the Confederacy. The "subject of her address was nothing less than a discourse on race in America" and it turned the tide against the measure. [9] However, not all speeches are so persuasive. As another senator said, "There almost never is a mind changed by debate on the floor of the Senate because, for the most part, no one is ever listening." Or senators have already committed themselves before debate begins.

Great debates can capture national attention and mobilize national sentiment on critical issues such as civil rights, health care, or Social Security. Debate, too, is used to reshape a party's public image with respect to issues ostensibly owned by the other party or to inoculate a party against campaign attacks. For example, in the lead-up to the November 2000 elections, and with opinion polls showing education to be a top-ranked issue for voters, the Senate debated a major education bill up for reauthorization. To distinguish their approach from Democrats, Senate Republicans argued for providing education block grants to the states and allowing governors the discretion to spend federal school aid dollars on their educational priorities. Democrats wanted to ensure sufficient funding for disadvantaged students, a traditional focus of the bill, and to refine the measure to make it more effective. "We've had the same debate for 35 years. This year, we have a different kind of debate," declared Sen. Slade Gorton, R-Wash. Both parties, too, were "rehearsing political attack lines in the event" the education bill fails to pass.[10]

But debate in the modern Senate often consists of prepared speeches perfunctorily read (or inserted in the *Congressional Record* without having been formally delivered before a largely empty chamber).[11] When intensive debate does occur, it is often among only a handful of senators with special interest in the legislation. To minimize personality clashes, the Senate (like the House) forbids first-person references during debate. "One of the reasons for the rule that a Senator must address another Senator through the Chair and not in the first person," stated Senator Byrd, "is to avoid casting aspersions, and causing acridness in debate and hurt feelings." [12]

Although the Senate is known for its principle of unlimited debate, debate can be restricted on four occasions. First, unanimous consent agreements typically limit debate on, for instance, bills, amendments, and various motions. Second, when the Senate invokes cloture (or Rule XXII), debate is limited to a specific number of hours. Third, the motion to table is nondebatable and is often used by floor managers to simultaneously stop debate on and to kill floor amendments. Rarely is a motion to table made on the bill itself, because if the motion were agreed to, it would kill the measure. Fourth, various statutes have debate-limiting features built into them. The Congressional Budget and Impoundment Control Act of 1974, for example, is replete with restrictions on debate, such as a two-hour limit on any amendment to the concurrent budget resolution and a ten-hour limit on the budget conference report.

Unlike the House, where the Speaker's recognition power is discretionary ("For what purpose does the gentlelady rise?"), the Senate presiding officer (addressed as either "Mr. President" or "Madam President") must recognize the first person seeking to speak unless the majority leader, minority leader, or one of the two floor managers is seeking recognition at the same time. Then Senate precedents stipulate that one of the four in the order mentioned has priority. Once a lawmaker is recognized, however, Senate precedents state that that senator may hold the floor for as long as he or she chooses. When senators yield the floor, others may be recognized to speak. The presiding officer may not put the pending measure or matter to a vote if senators are still seeking recognition to speak.

As in the House—even though only a scattering of members are on the floor—a quorum technically is present until a member suggests otherwise. Any senator may suggest the absence of a quorum. When this occurs the presiding officer is obligated to direct the clerk to call the roll of members. In contrast to House practice, the presiding officer may not first count the senators present to determine whether a quorum exists, except during postcloture proceedings. The calling of the roll is mandatory unless it is dispensed with by unanimous consent.

Quorum calls are commonly employed to give senators time to work out procedural arrangements (positive delay, as opposed to negative delay), such as a unanimous consent agreement, or to give a member scheduled to speak time to reach the floor. "What I would like to do is suggest the absence of a quorum," said a senator, "so that the parties involved here might sit down in the quiet of some room to see exactly how we can get this particular [amendment] to a point where we can vote up or down." [13] Once this is done, further calling of the roll to establish a quorum is dispensed with by unanimous consent. When Lyndon B. Johnson was majority leader (1955–1961), he "would ask for a quorum call and wait, sometimes for close to an hour, while the reading clerk droned slowly through the names. Then, when Johnson was ready for the Senate to resume, he would suspend the calling of the roll." [14] Cumulatively, the Senate spends considerable time on quorum calls—about six weeks of its work year, according to one calculation. [15]

Quorum calls to delay proceedings temporarily are to be distinguished from live quorums. Here a senator insists that at least a majority of the members come to the chamber and answer to their names. This can be a time-consuming process. Recalling that Sen. Strom Thurmond, R-S.C., once demanded a live quorum, a Senate colleague observed, "It took almost one hour to round up fifty-one Senators to respond to their names." [16] The two types of quorum calls are distinguished by the different number of bells that ring in members' offices and Senate committee rooms.

If the Senate officially discovers that it lacks a quorum, it has two options: (1) it must adjourn (recess if there is a previous order to that effect) or (2) it may vote to instruct the sergeant at arms to request (compel) the attendance of senators—"Mr. President, I move to instruct the Sergeant at Arms to request the attendance of absent Senators."

Television and Debate

In 1986, after years of consideration, the Senate authorized gavel-to-gavel coverage of its floor proceedings, which are carried over the Cable-Satellite Public Affairs Network (C-SPAN). Television has brought about some change in floor debate and activity. Speeches are more numerous, but they are better organized and livelier than before. Senators "are making better speeches," said Senator Byrd. "They are using more gestures and rhetorical flourishes, and it seems to me that overall, the debate has improved from a substantive point of view." [17]

Staff in senatorial offices regularly monitor floor debate to alert their bosses if issues are being discussed that require their attendance. Senators also watch floor proceedings from their offices, and what they observe may prompt them to go to the floor. "I came here to talk about this amendment," said Sen. Harry Reid, D-Nev., because "I watched with interest from my office." He continued, "I was especially impressed with, and was able to watch, the remarks of my colleague." [18] Senators, too, are using more props, graphs, and charts to illustrate their points. Some senators, to attract local media coverage, wait to offer floor amendments until it is prime time back home.

Television heightens public awareness of issues, of members, and of the Senate as an institution. Millions of C-SPAN viewers watch floor proceedings regularly, listen to the arguments for or against legislation, and then communicate (by letter, telephone, faxes, e-mail, or in other ways) their concerns to senators. Senatorial staff alert local television networks about their bosses' floor speeches (so segments might be broadcast back home), and party leaders monitor floor actions to ensure that arguably partisan statements are answered by someone with another viewpoint.

Party leaders may engage in image politics, as Republicans did in a 1995 debate on the constitutional balanced budget proposal. They pitted a youthful junior senator against an elderly senior senator, selecting thirty-seven-year-old freshman Rick Santorum, Pa., to challenge the arguments of seventy-eight-year-old Robert Byrd. "One GOP member said that was an 'image decision' by the leadership, designed to maximize the contrast for C-SPAN viewers between the old order and the new." [19] Senators, too, seek to attract national attention by coming up with catchy sound bites or dramatic statements that will get them on the nightly news shows. "This game is especially tempting for senators facing reelection campaigns," wrote a journalist, "since appearing on national television makes them look important and their opponents cannot get equal time." [20]

Floor Managers' Role

Floor managers have the major responsibility for guiding legislation to final passage. "I lean on the manager of the bill and the ranking [committee] members to carry the load" on the floor, Senator Byrd once observed.[21] Usually, two floor managers (one from each party from the reporting committee) are assigned per measure. In the case of multiply referred legislation, several majority and minority floor managers may be designated.

Senate floor managers, like their House counterparts, have varied responsibilities. For instance, they identify favorable times to schedule their legislation; they negotiate time-limitation agreements on amendments, work to efficiently dispose of them, or develop a manager's package encompassing scores of discrete amendments that can be agreed to by unanimous consent;

they may offer amendments to strengthen their bills as well as to counter proposed weakening amendments; they have to respond to any points of order raised against language in the legislation; and they must alert proponents when their support is needed on the floor. When Appropriations Chairman Ted Stevens, R-Alaska, manages legislation, he often wears either his Tasmanian Devil or Incredible Hulk tie to signal his clear intent to shepherd his committee-reported bill to enactment in an expeditious fashion.

Strategic calculations are a manager's stock in trade. For example, Sen. John C. Culver, D-Iowa (1975–1981), as a floor manager, was able to persuade Sen. William L. Scott, R-Va. (1973–1979), to offer a troublesome amendment at the most advantageous time from Culver's standpoint.

> The theory behind having Scott bring up the amendment now is that it is better to have such a proposal come up in the morning—a time when many senators are in committee meetings or in their offices and are more distracted than usual from the business that is taking place on the floor. Also, Culver figures that most of his colleagues will assume that at this point, especially after a long day of taking up amendments—and major ones—yesterday, only routine "housekeeping" amendments are being considered, and that they will pay less attention to the issue, be less eager to join the fray, than they might be later on.[22]

By Senate precedent, floor managers are accorded priority of recognition by the presiding officer. Explained Senator Byrd: "The manager of a bill also is entitled to preferential recognition—not ahead of the [majority leader and minority leader], but following in line, and is accorded that recognition generally by the Chair."[23]

Staff aides often assist floor managers. Senators rely more heavily on staff assistance during floor debate than do House members. Aides draft amendments and arguments and negotiate with aides of other senators to marshal support for legislation being considered.

BILLS CONSIDERED BY UNANIMOUS CONSENT

Unanimous consent agreements are crucial to the efficient operation of the legislative process in the Senate. A typical example of a unanimous consent agreement specifies the bill's number and its position on the General Orders Calendar (see Box 7-1).

Bipartisan trust is essential to the use of unanimous consent agreements. Occasionally, however, hard feelings can be generated over expectations or interpretations associated with unanimous consent agreements. For example, many senators expected to vote February 28, 1995, on final passage of a constitutional amendment to balance the budget (H. J. Res. 1). To the chagrin of opponents, Majority Leader Bob Dole, R- Kan., recessed the Senate because he was one vote short of the sixty-seven (or two-thirds) needed to pass a constitutional amendment. "I thought a deal was a deal," complained Minority Leader Tom Daschle, D-S.D.[24]

BOX 7-1　A Unanimous Consent Agreement

S. 744 (ORDER NO. 131)

4.—*Ordered,* That the Majority Leader, after consultation with the Democratic Leader, may proceed to the consideration of S. 744, a bill to provide for the continuation of higher education through the conveyance of certain public lands in the State of Alaska to the University of Alaska, and for other purposes; that immediately after the bill is reported, the committee amendment be agreed to as original text for the purpose of further amendment; that there be 4 hours for debate on the bill, equally divided and controlled between the Chairman and Ranking Member; that the only amendments in order be the following:

> Bingaman—2 relevant
> Murkowski—1 relevant

Ordered further, That no second degree amendments, or other first degree amendments, be in order; that debate time on the amendments be limited to 60 minutes each, equally divided and controlled in the usual form; that upon disposition of all amendments and the use or yielding back all time, the bill be read a third time and the Senate proceed to vote on passage of the bill. *(Nov. 19, 1999)*

SOURCE: Senate of the United States, *Calendar of Business,* 106th Cong., 2d sess., March 28, 2000, 2.

The stalling move . . . was technically allowed under the unanimous consent agreement that governed the last several days of the debate. The agreement only promised a final roll call "following the stacked votes" on proposed changes to the amendment on Feb. 28. It did not specify precisely when thereafter the final vote would occur, giving Dole the loophole he needed to claim extra time to search for the 67th vote needed to approve H. J. Res. 1. In addition, a majority leader is traditionally recognized when he calls for the Senate to go into recess.[25]

Dole was unable to find another vote, and the Senate defeated the centerpiece of the GOP's Contract with America. (When the outcome was plain, Senator Dole switched his vote from "yea" to "nay" and entered a motion to reconsider to comply with Senate rules requiring members to be on the prevailing side to be eligible to offer that motion, thus giving the Senate another chance to review and revote on the issue at some time in the future. Dole suggested he would call for another vote if he could round up one more supporter, but he never did.) Although relations between the parties remained tense for some time, the two party leaders of necessity continued to cooperate in crafting unanimous consent agreements.

The complex agreement in Box 7-1, like many others controlling floor action on legislation, reflects several general procedures common to many of these accords. First, the bill is to be called up at a time and date determined by the majority leader, after he consults with the minority leader. Second, a limited number of amendments (only three in this example) are in order and those must be relevant to the subject matter of the bill. Third, restrictions are placed on the length of debate on the bill (four hours) and the number of amendments, including a prohibition on second-degree amendments. Fourth, debate on amendments is limited to an hour for each with the time "divided and controlled in the usual form"—which means between the proponent of the amendment and an opponent. Finally, once the amendment process is concluded, provision is made for the Senate to "proceed to vote on passage of the bill."

Measures governed by unanimous consent agreements are commonly called up by the majority leader or the majority floor manager. Customarily, the presiding officer briefly summarizes the terms of the agreement, then recognizes the bill's floor manager, usually the chairman of the committee or subcommittee that handled the bill, for a short description of the legislation and its intent. The floor manager is followed by the ranking minority committee or subcommittee member, who presents similarly brief opening remarks. The Senate then is ready to debate and consider amendments to the bill.

THE AMENDING PROCESS

The Senate's amending process provides lawmakers an opportunity to make changes in the text of a measure or a pending amendment during floor consideration. Although the amending process can be complex, it is subject to certain conditions and principles. These conditions or principles, however, can be waived by unanimous consent of the membership.

Like the House, the Senate distinguishes among types (perfecting or substitute), degrees (first degree and second degree), and forms (motions to strike, to insert, or to strike and insert) of amendments. Further, certain factors affect any senator's eligibility to offer floor amendments. One factor is spatial. Are there any limbs (or places) left on the amendment tree? The Senate's volume of precedents, *Senate Procedure: Precedents and Practices*, presents four charts that depict the various number of amendments that may be pending at the same time. (The House effectively functions with only one amendment chart.) Which chart is in use on the Senate floor depends on whether the first amendment is a motion to insert (Chart 1); an amendment to strike (Chart 2); an amendment to strike and insert (Chart 3); or a complete substitute—an amendment that replaces the entire text of the pending bill (Chart 4). The simplest tree (Chart 1) permits a maximum of three amendments; the most complex tree (Chart 4) allows for as many as eleven amendments to be pending simultaneously (a rare occurrence).

Another factor that influences the amending stage is time. Is the amending process regulated by a time-limitation agreement that may specify when or in what order amendments are to be offered and which limits debate on each one? Still another factor is contextual. For instance, are there formal (the imposition of cloture, for example) or informal (the floor managers want to limit amendments to their bill) circumstances that impinge on the amending process?

Unlike the House, the Senate has neither a Committee of the Whole nor a five-minute rule for debating amendments. The Senate has no closed rules. Any measure is open to virtually an unlimited number of amendments unless a unanimous consent agreement specifies otherwise. On occasion, a floor manager may ask that a measure pass without amendments. Opponents still are likely to offer amendments, but if the floor manager has sufficient support they are likely to be voted down or tabled (killed). For example, the Agriculture Committee chairman and the ranking minority member put out the word on a farm relief bill they were managing that only technical amendments or amendments that did not add to the cost of the measure would receive their joint support. Otherwise, senators would have to debate their amendments in great detail, they said, and to answer pointed questions. The strategy worked—the only amendment offered to the bill was rejected. "We really stared them down," said Sen. Richard G. Lugar, R-Ind.[26]

Senators, unlike House members in the Committee of the Whole, can modify their own amendments without the need for unanimous consent or the majority approval of the chamber. A senator, for example, might propose an amendment that the floor manager will support if the language is discretionary, not mandatory. The senator can make the change on his or her own authority and facilitate the amendment's chances of being adopted by the Senate. These modifications are permissible until the Senate takes some action on the amendment, such as agreeing to take a vote on it or arranging a unanimous consent agreement limiting debate time. Senators sometimes quickly ask for action on their amendments because, even though they lose the right to modify them, they gain the right to offer amendments to their own amendments, should the need arise.

Senators must be recognized by the presiding officer before they can offer amendments. Officially reported committee amendments automatically take precedence over those offered by other members from the floor. Committee amendments are subject to further amendment from the floor.

Senators can propose amendments at any time to any section of a bill. This approach differs from the more orderly routine followed by the House, where the rules specify that each part of a measure be considered in sequential order, usually section by section. Senate custom gives individual senators greater leeway in offering and amending legislation. This flexibility means that a senator can eventually force virtually any issue to the floor through amendments and displace the best-laid agenda of any majority leader. To avoid having senators offer their favorite bill as an amendment to other measures or amendments, a majority leader may promise the lawmaker a specific time when the Senate will consider and vote on the legislation. Amendments

TABLE 7-1 Selected Bicameral Differences in the Amendment Process

House	Senate
Measures read for amendment section by section or title by title	Measures open to amendment at any point, unless a unanimous consent agreement states otherwise
Strict germaneness rule	No general germaneness rule
Amendment rights of members are commonly limited by the Rules Committee	Unlimited freedom for senators to offer amendments, unless unanimous consent agreement stipulates otherwise
Third-degree amendments are prohibited	Third-degree amendments are prohibited, but they can still be offered by unanimous consent
Five-minute rule for discussing amendments	No debate limit for amendments unless imposed by a unanimous consent agreement
Points of order against amendments must be raised after an amendment is read but before debate on it has begun	Points of order against amendments can be raised at any time
Representatives have no right, in the Committee of the Whole, to modify or withdraw amendments on their own authority	Senators have the right to modify or withdraw their amendments unless action (such as a call for a vote on the amendment) has been taken on it by the Senate

must be read by the Senate clerk, but this usually is dispensed with by unanimous consent unless an attempt is being made to delay the bill. Opposed to a bill, a senator said he planned to offer continuous and very long second-degree amendments to the bill and require that each be read in full. "It was a good old-fashioned filibuster," remarked a Senate aide.[27] (For several House-Senate differences in the amending process, see Table 7-1.)

Principle of Precedence

An important concept that shapes the Senate's amending process is precedence. While both the House and Senate have a rule specifying that only amendments in the first and second degree are permitted, basic differences exist in how each chamber interprets first- and second-degree amendments. This, in turn, affects the number of amendments that can be pending to a bill at the same time. In the Senate, even third-degree amendments occasionally are made in order by unanimous consent.

The principle of precedence determines which type of amendment (perfecting or substitute) may be offered when others are pending and the order in which those amendments are voted on. A perfecting amendment is one that alters language, either to the bill or to a pending amendment, but does not seek to substitute new text for the pending proposal. Perfecting amendments (which are always motions to strike, to insert, or to strike and insert) have precedence—or priority—over substitutes (always a motion to strike and insert). Thus, if Senator A offers a perfecting amendment to a bill (a first-degree amendment to insert) and Senator B then proposes a second-degree perfecting amendment to it, no other amendments are in order until the second-degree proposal is disposed of. And if the latter is adopted, other second-degree amendments—perfecting or substitute—may be offered until there are no unamended parts to alter.

Alternatively, Senator B may offer a second-degree substitute for Senator A's amendment to add something to the bill. Then Senator C, under the Senate's principle of precedence, can introduce a second-degree perfecting amendment to Senator A's amendment, which would be voted upon before the substitute. Figure 7-2 illustrates the amendment tree for this example. The order of offering amendments is the inverse of the order of voting. The basic principle is the "last offered amendment is the first to be voted on." Thus, lawmakers often calculate where they would like to be on the amendment tree depending in part on whether they want the first or last vote. Knowing that the first amendment is likely to be the target of many amendments, a senator may draft his amendment as second-degree perfecting so it will be voted on first. If a senator believes he has the votes to fend off any attempts at change, he might opt to offer his idea as a first-degree amendment. Predicting the optimal place on the amendment tree can be difficult, because much will depend on broader political dynamics and the kinds of ongoing substantive changes that amendments typically undergo on the floor.

The concept of filling the amendment tree has two basic meanings. First, as illustrated by the actions of Senator C, every available branch of the tree is filled according to the chart in play. Senators, as a result, cannot offer further amendments until a limb comes open. Second, as illustrated by the actions of Senators A and B, even though a branch of the tree is open, the principles of precedence prevent senators from offering any further amendment. That is, a motion of lower precedence—the second-degree substitute—cannot be proposed to a motion of higher precedence (the second-degree perfecting).

Strategic Uses of Amendments

Timing, strategy, lobbying, patience, and skillful drafting are important parts of the amending process. Prospects for amendments are influenced by these and other considerations, as filling the amendment tree, the second-degree strategy, the poison-pill approach, make-a-point amendments, and November amendments show.

Filling the Amendment Tree. With a Republican majority in the Senate, 1999 was the year of the amendment tree. When Democrats were in the

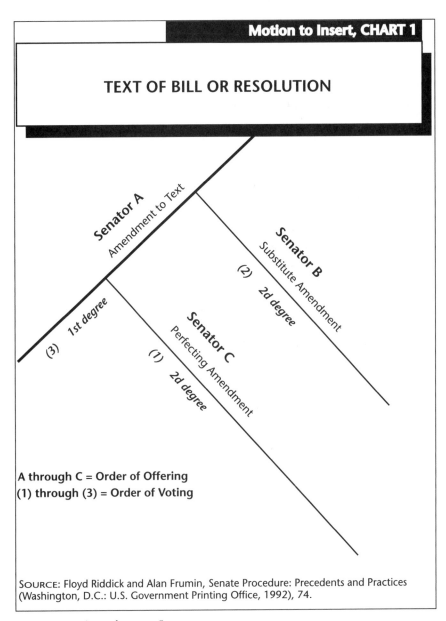

Motion to Insert, CHART 1

TEXT OF BILL OR RESOLUTION

Senator A
Amendment to Text
(3) 1st degree

Senator B
Substitute Amendment
(2) 2d degree

Senator C
Perfecting Amendment
(1) 2d degree

A through C = Order of Offering
(1) through (3) = Order of Voting

SOURCE: Floyd Riddick and Alan Frumin, Senate Procedure: Precedents and Practices (Washington, D.C.: U.S. Government Printing Office, 1992), 74.

FIGURE 7-2 Amendment to Insert

majority, they also did the same thing—but less frequently, they said. (No systematic studies identify the extent of tree building in recent years.) In the minority, Senate Democrats are on the lookout for openings to offer their policy priorities via floor amendments. "Keep in mind," said Minority Leader

Daschle, "we have so few opportunities to talk about our agenda if we can't talk about them in the form of amendments to bills." [28] Majority Leader Trent Lott, R-Miss., has different goals in managing the Senate. He wants to move the Senate's business without having to contend with nonrelevant Democratic amendments, and he needs to protect GOP senators from having to cast politically troublesome votes.

Although any senator can fill the amendment tree, the majority leader has special advantages if he chooses to use this parliamentary tactic. Lott is able to fill the tree easily because Senate precedents grant him preferential recognition. Thus, despite other precedents stating that senators lose the floor when they propose an amendment, Lott is able to offer amendment after amendment until the tree is filled. (The ultimate tree is achieved when Lott also fills a separate tree on the motion to recommit a bill with instructions. In the House, this is a preferential motion for the minority party. In the Senate, however, the motion is higher on the precedential ladder than motions to amend. Thus, Lott may concurrently fill the tree on a bill and then on the motion to recommit the measure to close off every possibility for Democratic amendments.)

Filling the tree is a controversial tactic that arouses the anger and frustration of senators, especially those in the minority party. Hence, it is not an everyday occurrence but is used to achieve different purposes. Its primary purpose is to prevent the minority party from offering controversial nonrelevant amendments that can attract public attention away from the majority's priorities. Democrats claim that Lott has attempted to make the Senate operate like the House, with its tighter rules for debating and amending legislation. "There is nothing deliberative about the Senate today," declared the minority leader. "We haven't been able to pass anything where the majority leader has filled the tree until he has torn the tree down." [29] Particularly galling to Democrats is when Lott asks to see proposed Democratic amendments in advance to determine if they should be offered to a specific measure. "But what our Republican colleagues continue to insist upon is that they act as an ad hoc rules committee," exclaimed Daschle. "They want to approve our amendments first. And only then will they allow our amendments to be considered once they have given their approval." Lott has answers to Daschle's complaints: Republicans set the agenda, and "we're not saying we have to see all their amendments. The [informal] rule around here is you give notice of amendments." [30] After he has filled the tree, Lott sometimes announces that he is willing to withdraw an amendment so senators can offer their proposals. However, he further stipulates that any amendment must be relevant to the subject matter of the bill. Democrats regularly turn down this deal.

Trees also sprout to force votes on issues. In mid-October 1999, for example, Minority Leader Daschle and Minority Whip Reid constructed a preemptive tree on campaign finance reform. Their objective was to force a Senate vote on the stronger House-passed bill compared with a narrowly tailored measure sponsored by Sens. John McCain, R-Ariz., and Russell Feingold,

D-Wis. The Democratic leaders filed cloture on their amendments to "set up a head-to-head matchup" between the House bill (offered as an amendment by Daschle) and the McCain-Feingold bill (introduced as an amendment by Reid to Daschle's amendment.) In the end, the Senate failed to enact any campaign finance reform measure. Finally, trees sometimes grow to protect a bill from divisive amendments that might fracture support for the legislation.

Second-Degree Strategy. In 1994 Majority Leader George J. Mitchell, D-Maine, employed second-degree amendments (using his priority of recognition) to block GOP attempts to broaden the scope of investigative hearings regarding President Bill Clinton's involvement with the Whitewater Development Corporation when he was governor of Arkansas. Democrats charged that Republicans were trying to embarrass the president; Republicans accused Democrats of unnecessarily limiting the scope of the inquiry. In a bitter partisan struggle, GOP senators began offering amendment after amendment to an airport improvements bill to widen the Whitewater hearings beyond what Democrats wanted. Every time a GOP senator offered a first-degree amendment to expand the Banking Committee's Whitewater inquiry, the majority leader (or his designee) used his right of first recognition by the presiding officer to offer a second-degree amendment that prevented an up or down vote on the GOP proposal. (Second-degree amendments are voted on before first-degree amendments, and if adopted, they replace or wipe out the first degree proposition.) As Sen. Don Nickles, R-Okla., stated:

> The majority leader . . . has offered the same amendment three or four times as a second-degree amendment to whatever first-degree amendment [that has been offered] from this side of the aisle. . . . [T]he majority leader has offered amendments that strike whatever amendment is offered on this side and inserted new language, and that new language is [the Mitchell plan for Whitewater hearings].[31]

Senate Republicans ended their opposition to Mitchell's plan in part because the public lacked interest in their efforts. (In a variation of the second-degree strategy of fending off unwanted amendments, Majority Leader Lott managed to eliminate objectionable items in a marriage penalty tax bill by offering a final amendment "striking the text of the bill and replacing it with the version originally reported by the Finance Committee."[32] The Senate then passed the bill in the form that Lott wanted.)

Poison-Pill Approach. One strategy of a bill's opponents is to load down the legislation with controversial amendments, possibly sparking a filibuster and jeopardizing Senate passage. "Overweight the plan, sabotage it with an unrealistic amendment," and that will ensure defeat of the legislation, noted Sen. Ernest F. Hollings, D-S.C.[33] Or as another senator said about a bill he opposed, "If this amendment worsens it a little more, then I'm for it."[34] Floor managers are on the alert for killer, or poison pill, amendments that can torpedo their legislation.

Make-a-Point Amendments. Senators sometimes offer amendments to make a point or to obtain something they want. For example, Sen. Jesse Helms, R-N.C., offered an amendment to "provide that the Endangered Species Act of 1973 shall not apply with respect to Fort Bragg, N.C." Senator Helms went on to explain that the army was having a problem in protecting several endangered species found on the Fort Bragg grounds, including the red-cockaded woodpecker. The Department of the Army, he said, had been required to set aside twelve thousand acres of land and to spend $5 million to protect the woodpecker.

"The last time I checked," said Helms, "the function of the Army is to defend the national security interests of the United States and not birds in trees."[35] Right after Senator Helms offered the amendment, the chairman of the Environment and Public Works Committee (which has jurisdiction over the Endangered Species Act) went to the floor and persuaded Helms to withdraw his amendment. The chairman noted that his committee would undertake a major review of the act and promised Helms a hearing on Fort Bragg's endangered species situation. The "proposition is fair," stated Senator Helms.[36]

November Amendments. Senators turn up the political heat on colleagues as the November elections get closer. A comment by Sen. Frank H. Murkowski, R-Alaska, underscores this use of the amending process. Amendments are being offered to a measure, Murkowski said, "with only one and only one purpose in mind. Let us be realistic. [This] is an opportunity for Senators on either side of the aisle, whether it be Democrats or Republicans, to develop ammunition to be used in some 30-second spot ad in the next political campaign. These votes are not about substance. They are strictly about politics, positioning, window dressing, and so forth."[37] The reverse approach is to work to avoid troublesome votes. Minority Leader Daschle has complained that Majority Leader Lott is trying to protect Republicans who have close November 2000 election contests from having to cast votes on gun control, the patients' bill of rights, or education. "They don't want to have votes on anything but naming airports," declared Daschle. Lott's spokesman replied: "The Democrats are just frustrated because we aren't voting on the things they want to vote on. Welcome to the minority."[38]

Voting on Amendments

The Senate has three types of voting: voice, division (standing), and roll call. Voice and division voting are similar to House procedures, but the Senate has nothing comparable to the electronic voting procedures of the House. The system of buzzers that summons senators to the floor is much like that of the

House. During a roll call, members respond yea or nay as their names are called alphabetically.

The Senate establishes the length of time for roll-call votes at the start of each Congress. When the 106th Congress convened in January 1999, the Senate agreed by unanimous consent:

> That for the duration of the 106th Congress, there be a limitation of 15 minutes each upon any roll call vote, with [a] warning signal to be sounded at the midway point, beginning at the last 7-1/2 minutes, and when roll call votes are of 10 minutes duration, the warning signal [is to] be sounded at the beginning of the last 7-1/2 minutes.

When votes are grouped back to back, referred to as stacking, the second and succeeding votes often occur, by unanimous consent, at ten-minute intervals. Prior to each vote in a stacked sequence, each side customarily is allowed at least one-minute to explain what the issue is about.[39]

Party leaders and floor managers make every effort to ensure that their supporters are on the floor when needed for a vote. "My experience convinces me," commented Senator Byrd, that voting "is the most critical step in the legislative process. . . . [The leaders and the floor managers must] have the right members at the right place and at the right time."[40]

Party leaders give advance notice of impending votes in whip notices and announcements from the floor. Occasionally, complex unanimous consent agreements specify the exact date and time for votes on final passage of a bill. The times for votes on amendments sometimes are agreed to by unanimous consent without elaborate negotiations during the debate on the bill. (Senators often get the yeas and nays ordered on their amendments, but this does not mean that a vote will occur anytime soon. All it means is that the vote will be a recorded vote.)

Recorded votes in the Senate usually can be obtained easily; only a sufficient second—one-fifth of the senators present—is needed, with a minimum of eleven required by the Constitution. If the minimum number is not on the floor at the time the request is made, a senator can summon other colleagues through a quorum call, try to get their support, and then renew the request for a roll-call vote. As Byrd explained: "If any Senator wants a roll call vote around here, he will ultimately get it. If he does not get it at first, he will put in a quorum and he will not let us call off the quorum. So we have to have a live quorum or give him the yeas and nays."[41] Most roll calls occur on amendments.

Cue-Givers. Senators, like representatives, rely on numerous cue-givers for guidance on voting because of the range and complexity of legislation. "When it comes to voting," a senator wrote, "an individual senator will rely heavily not only on the judgment of staff, his own and his committee's, but also on a select number of senators whose knowledge he has come to respect and whose general perspectives he shares."[42] The position of the reporting committee is an important factor to many senators. "A lot of members of the Senate," said another senator, "will arrive on the floor, and there's an amendment up that they really haven't had a chance to look at, and they'll just come up and ask, 'What's the committee position?' "[43]

Casting Procedural Votes. On controversial amendments, members often maneuver for procedural, instead of substantive, votes. A vote to table (kill) amendments or other motions is a classic ploy to avoid being recorded directly on politically sensitive policy issues. Senator Byrd has explained the difference:

> A motion to table is a procedural motion. It obfuscates the issue, and it makes possible an explanation by a Senator to his constituents, if he wishes to do so, that his vote was not on the merits of the issue. He can claim that he might have voted this way or he might have voted that way, if the Senate had voted up or down on the issue itself. But on a procedural motion, he can state he voted to table the amendment, and he can assign any number of reasons therefore, one of which would be that he did so in order that the Senate would get on with its work or about its business.[44]

Therefore, if a procedural vote can be arranged to kill or delay a bill, it is more likely to win the support of senators, who may prefer to duck the substantive issue. Moreover, senators generally support the party leadership on procedural votes. "[B]ecause this is a procedural vote . . . [members] traditionally stick with the leadership on such votes," declared a senator.[45]

Part of members' consideration in casting procedural or substantive votes involves their role in political campaigns. Votes are not simply used to make decisions or as trading material; they are used by interest group organizations, who select issues of concern to them, to characterize legislators as heroes or zeroes, depending on how members voted on the groups' chosen topics.

Like the House, the Senate permits vote pairing, either live or dead pairs. In a live pair, one senator is present on the floor during the vote. The practice is for the senator to cast his vote, "yea" or "nay," then withdraw it and announce, "I have a pair with the senator from [naming the state]. If he were present and voting, he would vote ["yea" or "nay"]. If I were at liberty to vote, I would vote ["yea" or "nay"]." In a dead pair, both senators are absent from the floor. Their positions are published after each roll call in the *Congressional Record.* Live and dead pairs are not tabulated on roll-call votes, but a live pair can affect the outcome of a vote. Explained Senator Byrd:

> The arranging of pairs has been decisive from time to time on very close votes, because it is possible to pair off enough present Senators to affect the outcome of the vote and perhaps make a difference of 1 or 2 votes which, had the Senators present not been paired, would have decided the issue opposite to the outcome that resulted.

Senators generally will not agree to give a live pair except on the condition that the outcome is not changed by virtue of the pair given.[46] In 1986 a live pair influenced the outcome of a controversial judicial nomination.[47]

Final Action on a Bill

"When no Senator seeks recognition," Senator Byrd explained, "the Chair automatically puts the question of adoption of amendments and passage of bills."[48] Thus, once the amending process is completed the Senate proceeds to a vote on final passage, unless a unanimous consent agreement has been made setting a later date and time for the final vote. The floor manager announces that no further amendments are pending. He then requests a third, and final, reading of the bill. The presiding officer orders the bill engrossed—put in the precise form in which it emerged from the Senate's amending process—and read a third time (the title of the bill only), a procedure that takes only a few seconds. Then the question is put on final passage of the measure.

The final vote is not over until the chair announces the outcome. Senate rules prohibit "any Senator from voting after the Chair has announced the decision," Senator Byrd pointed out. Senate rules provide "that the Chair cannot even entertain a unanimous consent request to suspend this rule."[49] Senators, like House members, may change their vote during the regular fifteen-minute voting period, which in the Senate is a minimum and not the maximum time allowed. For example, during an unusually lengthy Senate roll call dozens of senators switched their votes and defeated a proposal offered by Sen. Dale Bumpers, D-Ark. "I just want to announce that Dr. Cary's in his office for everyone whose arm is out of socket," exclaimed Bumpers.[50] (Dr. Freeman Cary was the Senate physician.)

After the result of the final vote on the bill has been announced, one more parliamentary step is required before Senate action is complete. This step is available only to the side that prevailed on the final vote. If the bill has been passed, a senator who voted for the bill, or who did not vote, makes a motion to reconsider the vote. (On a voice or standing vote, any senator can offer the motion.) Immediately thereafter, another proponent of the bill moves to table the motion to reconsider. By this procedural device Senate rules protect the bill from further consideration. Rarely does the motion to table fail. This procedure also is used after votes on amendments. The House procedure is basically identical.

BILLS WITHOUT UNANIMOUS CONSENT

Sometimes party leaders are unable to achieve unanimous consent agreements. This may happen for a variety of reasons: intense opposition to the bill by certain senators, a general desire for unrestricted debate and amendment, commitments by some senators to protect the interests of absent colleagues, or personal pique of some senators against party leaders. Passage of legislation then becomes a much more difficult task. Debate will be extensive and amendments will be numerous. Operating under the Senate's rules, this can be extremely time-consuming. Moreover, if one or more senators are intensely opposed to a bill, the well-known device of the filibuster may be threatened (as in the case of holds, this is another version of the silent filibuster) or used.[51] Near scheduled recesses or at the end of legislative sessions, the threat or use of filibusters is especially effective.

Determining when extended debate becomes a filibuster can be difficult, as a senator does not make a motion to filibuster a bill. Extended debate may occur because the issue warrants lengthy discussion. Extended debate also may occur because senators intend to stall action on measures. How to determine senators' intent during debates is often not an easy task. Senator Byrd once said, "I will be able to perceive one, because I know one when I see it."[52]

The filibuster is often viewed as the last recourse, forcing an almost complete stoppage of normal floor business—a situation most senators try to avoid. Filibusters also send signals to the majority leadership that sixty votes (to invoke cloture) may be needed to pass legislation. The Senate, unlike the House, is a supermajoritarian institution, because sixty votes (three-fifths of the membership) are commonly required to enact major and controversial legislation. The political reality often is, as Majority Leader Bob Dole observed, that "Everything in this Senate needs 60 votes."[53] Or as GOP senator Frank Murkowski expressed it: "It isn't good enough to have the majority. You've got to have 60 votes."[54] The filibuster (real or threatened) is a source of bargaining leverage for any senator. "The power to block the other person's bill gives you the power to influence the content," noted Sen. Thad Cochran, R-Miss.[55]

The Filibuster

Generally characterized in the public mind as a nonstop speech, a filibuster in the fullest sense employs every parliamentary maneuver and dilatory motion to delay, modify, or defeat legislation. Asked for filibustering pointers by a colleague, one senator said: "If it takes unanimous consent, object. If not, you make a little speech, suggest the absence of a quorum, then . . . use parliamentary procedures[,] . . . motions to adjourn, motions to recess." He added: "You have to have the floor protected 100 percent of the time."[56] Senators may also use filibustering tactics to force votes. For example, two days after the Million Mom March on Mother's Day, May 14, 2000, which was the largest gun control rally ever, Minority Leader Daschle deliberately gridlocked the Senate for five hours through quorum calls and other stalling tactics to successfully compel Majority Leader Lott to schedule votes on gun control issues.[57]

More has been written about extended debate in the Senate than about any other congressional procedure. Hollywood even glamorized the filibuster in a 1939 movie, *Mr. Smith Goes to Washington,* starring Jimmy Stewart. The filibuster permeates virtually all senatorial decision making. Measures might not be reported from committee or scheduled for floor action because senators are threatening a filibuster. "In many instances, it's the threat of a filibuster that keeps a bill from coming up," observed Senator Byrd.[58]

The filibuster has long been part of the Senate, but unrestricted debate aroused little concern during much of the nineteenth century. The number of senators was small, the workload was limited, and lengthy deliberations could be accommodated more easily. Since Rule XXII (cloture) was adopted in 1917, the number of filibusters has varied over time. Scholars have identified three distinct filibuster periods.

> The first lasts from roughly 1917 to 1937, in which the number of filibusters per Congress averages about 4.1. That period is followed by a quiet period between 1937 and 1968, where the mean number of filibusters is 2.1. In the 1970s, however, filibustering reaches new levels, before mushrooming in the 1980s and 1990s. Indeed, over the past twelve [89th to 101st] congresses, the number of filibusters has averaged 17.6.[59]

Defenders of the filibuster say it is needed to prevent bad bills from becoming law, protect minority rights against majority steamrollers, ensure thorough analysis of legislation, and dramatize issues for the public. As Senator Byrd put it:

> One of the things that makes the United States Senate the unique upper body that it is is the ability to talk at great length. And there have come times when the protection of a minority is highly beneficial to a nation. Many of the great causes in the history of the world were at first only supported by a minority. And it's been shown time and again that the minority can be right. So this is one of the things that's so important to the liberties of the people. As long as a people have a forum in which members can speak at length, the people's liberties will be safe.[60]

Opponents argue that the filibuster thwarts majority rule, delays or kills legislation, brings the Senate into disrepute, and permits small minorities to extort unwarranted concessions in bills supported by Senate majorities. Exasperated by the blocking actions of a dozen filibustering senators, Majority Leader George Mitchell in 1992 declared in frustration, citing an earlier test vote: "Only in the United States Senate and only in the last few days of a session can 85 Senators vote one way: Yes, for this bill; 12 Senators vote another way: No, against the bill—and the no's prevail."[61] With the close of the session as their ally, the dozen senators were set to launch a series of filibusters against the legislation; Mitchell realized that the lack of time prevented the Senate from proceeding to the measure. He later exclaimed: "What was intended to be minority rights is now a means of minority rule."[62]

These pro and con arguments highlight a dilemma: how to strike a balance between the right to debate and the need to decide. There is no easy answer. What is apparent is that the filibuster is a powerful bargaining device. Even the possibility of its use can force compromises in committee or on the floor. Senators of widely diverse viewpoints have resorted to it from time to time or have threatened to use it in order to influence legislation.

Every measure faces at least two primary filibusters: the first on the motion to take up the legislation and the second on consideration of the bill itself. The 1964 civil rights bill filibuster consumed sixteen days on the motion to take up the measure and fifty-seven days on the legislation itself. Those filibusters were unique in that they marked the first time the Senate had ever voted to end an extended debate on a civil rights bill. (Strom Thurmond set the filibuster record when he was a Democrat by speaking for twenty-four hours and eighteen minutes against the 1957 civil rights bill.)

Wider Use of Filibusters. Before the 1970s, conservative senators—often southern Democrats who used extended debate to defeat or delay civil rights measures—were almost the only users of filibusters. Recent decades witnessed an increase in the overall number of filibusters, including those conducted by moderate and liberal senators in each party. The filibuster is a "parliamentary tool available to liberals and conservatives who wish to dramatize issues in the only forum of our national government that provides for thorough analysis and unhurried consideration of proposed public laws." [63]

Furthermore, filibusters (and threats of filibusters) are occurring on issues of great national importance and visibility as well as on a wide range of less momentous topics. Lamented Majority Leader Mitchell:

> Not long ago the filibuster or threat of a filibuster was rarely undertaken in the Senate, being reserved for matters of grave national importance. That is no longer the case. . . . The threat of a filibuster is now a regular event in the Senate, weekly at least, sometimes daily. It is invoked by minorities of as few as one or two Senators and for reasons as trivial as a Senator's travel schedule. [64]

Several factors account for the increase in filibusters. First, new senators (many of whom are former House members socialized by rough partisan politics) prefer to push their own agendas even if the Senate's institutional activities grind to a halt. On occasion, one senator noted, senators are "determined to follow [their] own perspective even to the perversion, the distortion, and the destruction of the [legislative] process." [65] Second, filibusters have enhanced potency in an institution that is workload-packed and deadline-driven. Insufficient time is available to accommodate the manifold claims on the Senate's agenda. Thus, senators who simply indicate their intention to filibuster can exercise significant leverage.

Third, the internal incentives (the get-along, go-along approach, for example) that fostered deference to seniority and party leaders are gone. Professor Richard F. Fenno Jr., a noted congressional scholar, discussed how the 1950s Senate evolved from a "communitarian" institution, where senators were expected to use extended debate sparingly and only for high-stakes national issues, to today's "individualistic" Senate. With "more openness, more media visibility, more candidate-centered elections," more interest groups, more political obligations, and more staff, Senate newcomers are independent entrepreneurs unwilling to submerge their personal and political objectives "to the norms of any collectivity." [66] Senators have increased incentives for obstructive behavior. When Lyndon Johnson was majority leader, he exercised tight control over floor proceedings, including use of the filibuster.

> While Johnson went to great lengths to avoid filibusters, once they had begun
> . . . he tended to regard filibusters as a personal challenge to his stewardship.
> Instead of making an end run around the combatants . . . he often preferred to
> break the filibuster by keeping the Senate in session for long hours, even around
> the clock, and forcing the minority ultimately to give up in exhaustion. [67]

By contrast, contemporary party leaders may accommodate filibustering senators who have meetings to attend back home. Fourth, partisanship has contributed to gridlock and stalemate in the Senate. According to two scholars, "As the two parties became internally more cohesive and the differences between them grew larger, holding together a party-backed filibuster became significantly easier." [68]

Ending a Filibuster.   Besides mistakes that cause filibustering senators to lose the floor, two interrelated and broad methods of ending a filibuster are by informal compromise or by the formal Senate procedure used to terminate debate called cloture. [69] Frequently, cloture cannot be obtained unless compromises are made. Party leaders sometimes try "shuttle diplomacy" between the two sides, noted Senator Stevens, to avoid full-scale filibusters. [70]

Informal Compromise. The threat of filibusters can encourage policy-making compromises. During a filibuster, senators may meet in the cloakroom—off the Senate floor—or in the offices of the party leaders to conduct negotiations, which can go on day and night. The process may take several days or even weeks, depending on how controversial the bill is. If compromise fails, the odds increase that opponents of the legislation will win the battle and thus sidetrack the bill indefinitely. Alternatively, proponents may invoke cloture.

Cloture. After decades of determined resistance by many senators, the Senate in 1917 adopted Rule XXII, which gave the Senate the formal means (cloture) to end extended debate. Until that time, debate could be terminated only by unanimous consent, an impossibility in the face of a filibuster, or exhaustion. In 1893 Sen. Orville Platt, R-Conn., stated:

> There are just two ways under our rules by which a vote can be obtained. One
> is by getting unanimous consent—the consent of each Senator—to take a vote
> at a certain time. Next comes what is sometimes known as the process of "sitting it out," that is for the friends of a bill to remain in continuous session until the opponents of it are so physically exhausted that they can not struggle any
> longer. [71]

Unanimous consent and exhaustion have been the hardy perennials of Senate procedure.

Box 7-2   A Cloture Motion

MR. GRASSLEY. Mr. President, pursuant to the consent agreement, I now send a cloture motion to the desk.

THE PRESIDING OFFICER. The cloture motion having been presented under rule XXII, the Chair directs the clerk to read the motion.

The legislative clerk read as follows:

CLOTURE MOTION

We the undersigned Senators, in accordance with the provisions of rule XXII of the Standing Rules of the Senate, do hereby move to bring to a close debate on the Conference Report to accompany H.R. 434, The African Growth and Opportunity Act:

Trent Lott, Jon Kyl, Pat Roberts, Craig Thomas, Bill Frist, Paul Coverdell, James Inhofe, Orrin Hatch, Don Nickles, Larry Craig, Slade Gorton, Mitch McConnell, Peter Fitzgerald, Chuck Grassley, Phil Gramm, and Mike Crapo.

SOURCE: *Congressional Record*, May 10, 2000, S3788.

What finally prompted the Senate to adopt Rule XXII was a filibuster that had killed a bill to arm U.S. merchant ships against attacks by German submarines. President Woodrow Wilson strongly criticized the filibuster and called a special session of the Senate, which adopted the cloture rule on March 8, 1917, five weeks before war was declared.

Under Rule XXII a cloture petition signed by sixteen senators first must be filed with the presiding officer (see Box 7-2 and Box 7-3). Two days later, and one hour after the Senate convenes, the presiding officer must ascertain (unless waived by unanimous consent) whether a quorum is present. That having been established, the presiding officer is obliged to ask, "Is it the sense of the Senate that the debate shall be brought to a close?" A vote immediately is held. If three-fifths of the entire Senate membership (sixty of one hundred members) vote in favor, cloture is invoked. Thereafter, there is an additional thirty hours of debate with senators permitted to speak for no more than one hour on a first come, first served basis. Rule XXII also stipulates that first-degree amendments must be filed by 1 p.m. on the day following the filing of the cloture petition; second-degree amendments also must be filed in a timely manner—until one hour prior to the cloture vote. Before 1975, when the current three-fifths rule was adopted, a two-thirds majority of those senators present and voting was required to invoke cloture. (The two-thirds requirement still applies to proposals to amend the Senate's rules.)

No limit has been placed on the number of times cloture can be sought on a single piece of legislation. The record for cloture votes is eight, which occurred during the 100th Congress on a bill to limit campaign expenditures for Senate general election races. Majority Leader Byrd had made the spending-limit measure a priority, but Senate action was stymied by a three-month GOP-led filibuster.

Today, cloture is often used for purposes unrelated to ending talkathons. (Thus, counting the number of cloture votes is not a good indicator of how many filibusters occur in any year.) It is not unusual for Majority Leader Lott to file a cloture motion on a measure (or the motion to proceed) as soon as he asks the Senate to consider a certain bill. He may then withdraw the cloture motion and bring other matters to the floor, leaving the clotured-bill in a state of parliamentary limbo (not subject to debate or amendment) until the Senate votes two days later on whether to invoke Rule XXII. Minority Leader Daschle rails against this practice. "There is a time and a place for cloture," he said on one occasion, "but that time and place is not as soon as the bill is laid down." [72] On another occasion, he lamented: "I am reminded, again, as we file cloture, that the motion to invoke cloture is a motion to end debate. I am always amused by that phrase, 'end debate.' How do you end debate that you haven't even started?" [73]

In a Senate grown more individualistic and partisan, Majority Leader Lott will employ cloture to stop filibusters or other dilatory actions. But he often has another objective in mind: to prevent Democrats from offering their priorities as nongermane amendments to the pending bill. If invoked, Rule XXII

Box 7-3   Ending a Senate Filibuster

Cloture

   Day 1 Petition signed by sixteen members.
   Day 2 First-degree amendments are to be filed by 1 p.m.
   Day 3 Second-degree amendments are to be filed until one hour before the cloture vote.

A constitutional three-fifths (or sixty) vote is required to invoke cloture in the one-hundred-member chamber. A two-thirds vote is required to invoke cloture on proposals to change Senate rules.

Postcloture

   - Thirty-hour debate limit with time counted for votes, quorum calls, and other matters.
   - Amendments must be germane.
   - One-hour debate per senator.
   - Presiding officer can rule out dilatory motions on his own initiative without waiting for a point of order.
   - The measure on which cloture has been invoked remains the unfinished business of the Senate to the exclusion of all other business.

requires all amendments to be germane to the bill. "For the information of all Senators," said Sen. John W. Warner, R-Va., at the instruction of the majority leader, "a cloture motion was just filed on the [Defense Department] authorization bill in an effort to keep the bill free from extraneous matters."[74] On issues that divide the two parties, Lott is unlikely to attract the required sixty votes, but this may set the stage for continued negotiations between the two sides on how to structure the floor amendment process. Cloture, too, is used to test sentiment for or against a measure, expedite action on legislation, force votes that can be used against senators in election campaigns, permit party position-taking on issues, or, if it is invoked, keep unwanted amendments off the floor.

Recent Congresses have witnessed a marked increase in the use of cloture, including on the motion to proceed ("I move to call up S. 1234") to legislation or nominations. In the six Congresses from the 86th (1959–1961) through the 91st (1969–1971), a total of twenty-seven cloture votes were taken. That figure nearly doubled to fifty-three in the 105th Congress (1997–1999) alone (see Table 7-2). Majority Leader Mitchell noted the growth in the number of cloture motions filed on motions to proceed: from two in the 95th Congress (1977–1979) to the record-setting thirty-five in the 102nd Congress (1991–1993). Cloture was filed fourteen times on the motion to proceed during the 105th Congress.

In testimony presented to a joint reorganization committee, Mitchell highlighted the obstacle course that legislation must complete if opposition to it is strong.

> When a filibuster occurs or is threatened, a cloture motion to terminate debate must be filed. The vote on that motion cannot occur until two days after it is filed. So if a cloture motion were filed today, Tuesday, the vote on it would occur on Thursday. If three-fifths or more vote to invoke cloture, there are still up to thirty hours of debate on the motion, postcloture, or effectively two more days. So right now under Senate rules, cloture could be required up to six separate times on a single bill: on the motion to proceed to the bill, on the committee substitute, on the bill itself, and then . . . three times to get to conference with the House—[on the motions (1) to insist on Senate amendments, or disagree to House amendments, (2) to request a conference with the House, or (3) to authorize the chair to appoint conferees].[75]

Periodically, frustration with dilatory tactics gives rise to attempts to change Rule XXII. For example, when the 104th Congress began, Democratic senators Tom Harkin, Iowa, and Joseph Lieberman sought to amend Rule XXII with a "decreasing-scale" recommendation: sixty votes on the first try with the vote needed to invoke cloture "reduced by three on each subsequent vote, so that debate would be shut off with 57 votes on the second try, 54 on the third, and 51—a simple majority—on the fourth."[76] Senator Byrd argued strongly against the change, and, in the end, the Senate voted 76 to 19 to kill the Harkin-Lieberman proposal.[77] With neither party interested in

TABLE 7-2 Attempted and Successful Cloture Votes, 1919–1999

Congress		First Session Attempted	First Session Successful	Second Session Attempted	Second Session Successful	Total Attempted	Total Successful
66th	(1919-1921)	1	1	0	0	1	1
67th	(1921-1923)	1	0	1	0	2	0
68th	(1923-1925)	0	0	0	0	0	0
69th	(1925-1927)	0	0	2	1	2	1
70th	(1927-1929)	5	2	0	0	5	2
71st	(1929-1931)	0	0	0	0	0	0
72d	(1931-1933)	0	0	0	0	0	0
73d	(1933-1935)	1	0	0	0	1	0
74th	(1935-1937)	0	0	0	0	0	0
75th	(1937-1939)	0	0	2	0	2	0
76th	(1939-1941)	0	0	0	0	0	0
77th	(1941-1943)	0	0	1	0	1	0
78th	(1943-1945)	0	0	1	0	1	0
79th	(1945-1947)	0	0	4	0	4	0
80th	(1947-1949)	0	0	0	0	0	0
81st	(1949-1951)	0	0	2	0	2	0
82d	(1951-1953)	0	0	0	0	0	0
83d	(1953-1955)	0	0	1	0	1	0
84th	(1955-1957)	0	0	0	0	0	0
85th	(1957-1959)	0	0	0	0	0	0
86th	(1959-1961)	0	0	1	0	1	0
87th	(1961-1963)	1	0	3	1	4	1
88th	(1963-1965)	1	0	2	1	3	1
89th	(1965-1967)	2	1	5	0	7	1
90th	(1967-1969)	1	0	5	1	6	1
91st	(1969-1971)	2	0	4	0	6	0
92d	(1971-1973)	10	2	10	2	20	4
93d	(1973-1975)	10	2	21	7	31	9
94th	(1975-1977)	23	13	4	4	27	17
95th	(1977-1979)	5	1	8	2	13	3
96th	(1979-1981)	4	1	17	9	21	10
97th	(1981-1983)	7	2	20	7	27	9
98th	(1983-1985)	7	2	12	9	19	11
99th	(1985-1987)	9	1	14	9	23	10
100th	(1987-1989)	24	6	20	6	44	12
101st	(1989-1991)	9	6	15	5	24	11
102d	(1991-1993)	20	9	28	14	48	23
103d	(1993-1995)	20	4	22	10	42	14
104th	(1995-1997)	21	4	29	5	50	9
105th	(1997-1999)	24	7	29	11	53	18

SOURCE: *Congressional Quarterly's Guide to Congress*, 5th ed. (Washington, D.C.: CQ Press, 2000), 1116.

changing cloture, the Senate is, more than ever, a unanimous consent institution.

Final Vote on a Bill

Once cloture is invoked, filibusters by amendment are broken, and other delaying tactics have ended, the Senate proceeds to a final vote on the bill under consideration. If obstructionist tactics cannot be stopped, the leadership may withdraw the bill and proceed to other business.

On legislation not regulated by complex agreements and not the target of deliberate obstructionist tactics, the floor managers and party leaders try to fashion ad hoc agreements under which amendments can be disposed of. But because of the strong commitment in the Senate to giving every member ample opportunity to be heard, this can be a lengthy process. For example, one tax measure, which was not filibustered, consumed twenty-five days of debate. Two hundred nine amendments and motions were offered on the bill and 129 roll-call votes were taken. The length of debate on this legislation reflected its importance to senators and the country as well as the complexity of its provisions. While frustrating floor action is relatively easy, Senate rules make difficult bottling up legislation in committees and preventing it from reaching the floor.

PROCEDURES TO CIRCUMVENT COMMITTEES

Bypassing committees, while not an everyday occurrence in the Senate, is easier to accomplish than in the House. The House has a number of procedures for bringing to the floor bills that are blocked in committee, including the discharge petition, the power of extraction by the Rules Committee, and the suspension of the rules procedure. Except for suspension, which generally is used for relatively noncontroversial bills, these procedures are seldom employed and rarely successful.

In the Senate, at least four techniques are available: (1) use of nongermane amendments, also known as riders; (2) placing House-passed and Senate-introduced bills immediately on the Calendar of General Orders; (3) suspending Senate rules; and (4) implementing the discharge procedure. The first two are the most effective. The latter two are rarely used.

Nongermane Amendments

Unlike the House, the Senate has never had a rule requiring that amendments be germane to pending legislation. This feature probably ranks just below the filibuster as one of the Senate's most distinctive characteristics. "Amendments may be made," wrote Thomas Jefferson, "so as totally to alter the nature of the proposition." [78] A classic case occurred in 1965 when Sen. Everett McKinley Dirksen, R-Ill. (1951–1969), tried to add a proposal for a constitutional amendment on legislative reapportionment to a joint resolution designating August 6 to September 6 as National American Legion Baseball

Month. Dirksen's amendment had been blocked by the Judiciary Committee. An opponent of the proposal called the senator's attempt a "foul ball."

Periodically, the Senate has considered rules changes that would permit it to impose a germaneness requirement on floor amendments. Proponents argue that such a requirement would improve efficiency, expedite the workload, enhance relations with the House (which has a strict germaneness requirement), strengthen committees as centers of policy making, and promote predictability in scheduling. Opponents contend that the right of senators to offer nongermane amendments serves as a safeguard against capricious committee actions, permits any senator to raise important issues, and enables the Senate to respond quickly to new developments. "What is at stake [in the ability of senators to offer nongermane amendments] is the right of a minority—even a tiny minority, even one Senator—to raise an issue," declared one senator.[79]

In mid-May 2000, a bitter debate between Majority Leader Lott and Minority Leader Daschle occurred involving Daschle's effort to offer a nonbinding and nongermane sense-of-the-Senate amendment on gun control to a military construction appropriations bill. Two key procedural points set the context for their debate: Under Senate rules, amendments to general appropriations bills must be germane, but sense-of-the-Senate amendments have, by precedent, been considered germane. To prevent what he considered to be an abuse of the process—offering these nongermane and nonbinding amendments, often with campaign objectives in mind—Lott employed an unusual parliamentary maneuver. He offered his own sense-of-the-Senate amendment (urging enforcement of existing gun laws) to Daschle's (praising the Million Mom March for gun safety and urging Congress to enact gun control legislation), but then he raised a point of order against his own proposal. As Lott said: "Mr. President, I make a point of order that the pending Lott amendment violates rule XVI; that it is sense-of-the-Senate language on an appropriations bill, and that the Chair should rule on the germaneness question." Upholding long-standing Senate practice, the presiding officer ruled that "the point of order is not well taken."[80] The majority leader appealed the ruling of the presiding officer, and the Senate sided with Lott by overturning the ruling of the chair. (In 2000 the Senate also agreed that sixty votes are needed to add sense-of-the-Senate amendments to budget resolutions.)

Whether the Senate established a new precedent by its action in overturning the chair was not immediately clear because of uncertainty regarding both the intent of the Senate's action and how this ostensibly new precedent might be interpreted in subsequent similar cases. What is clear is sharp minority party dissatisfaction with the outcome. "What the majority leader is doing with this point of order is to basically close down debate on the floor of the Senate," declared Sen. Richard J. Durbin, D-Ill.[81] Lott disagreed. "What it is really about is getting the work of the Senate done, dealing with real bills and real issues, not playing games and saying: OK, we voted last year [on this hot topic]; we have not voted this year. OK, we voted last month; we have not voted this month." [82]

Germaneness sometimes has been a vexing issue for the Senate. On the one hand, the lack of a general prohibition on riders permits senators to raise and debate popular and unpopular issues and lessens the opportunity for arbitrary committee action. On the other hand, some senators complain that the practice wastes the Senate's time by permitting contentious debate on matters unrelated to the fundamental purpose of a pending bill.

Senate Prohibitions. Although the Senate does not have a general germaneness rule, the chamber requires germane amendments to pending legislation in four situations:

1. Unanimous consent agreements may contain a requirement that amendments are to be germane; today, the term "relevant" is employed because it is less restrictive.
2. Amendments to general appropriations bills.
3. When cloture has been invoked.
4. During consideration of concurrent budget resolutions and reconciliation bills.

When the Senate operates under a germaneness requirement, its tests for determining whether amendments are germane are stricter than those in the House. A Senate report noted that "a legislative amendment is germane if, and only if, it proposes to strike out or to change a number or date, or if its effect would be to restrict the scope of the measure or the powers it grants." [83] A presiding officer once noted, if an "amendment expands the effect of the bill or introduces new subject matter it is not germane." [84] Thus, if a farm bill dealt with five items—barley, wheat, rice, cotton, and soybeans—and a senator sought to amend the measure by adding a sixth item to the list, a germaneness point of order could be made against the amendment. Sense-of-the-Senate (or sense-of-Congress) amendments, which are nonbinding and generally symbolic in intent, and amendments to strike language are considered germane in most circumstances.

The Senate so narrowed its meaning of what constituted a germane amendment that when the germaneness requirement was in effect it prevented consideration of "policy alternatives that are highly pertinent but nonetheless nongermane because they expand the coverage of the bill or the powers it conveys." [85] The Senate needed a broader term to permit subject-related amendments to be offered to pending measures when they were governed by the germaneness stricture. Starting from the mid to late 1980s, the term that began to be employed is "relevancy." Hence, unanimous consent agreements today almost always use this term in describing what kinds of amendments are in order. Occasions have arisen when cloture has been invoked—which triggers the stricter germaneness standard—and a unanimous consent agreement has permitted selective relevant amendments to be offered postcloture. As Majority Leader Lott noted after cloture had been invoked,

"Under an additional consent, relevant trade amendments are in order in addition to the germaneness requirement under rule XXII." [86]

Placing Measures on the Calendar

When bills or joint resolutions are introduced in the Senate or passed by the House and sent to the Senate, they customarily are referred to a committee. According to Senate rules, all measures, including House-passed bills, must be read twice on different legislative days before they can be referred to committee; the procedure is seldom followed. If an objection is raised after the first reading, the second reading cannot occur until the next legislative day. After the second reading, the bill or joint resolution is sent to the appropriate committee. However, if an objection is raised at the second reading to further consideration of the bill, the measure is placed directly on the legislative calendar (see Box 7-4). Placing a bill on the calendar gives the leadership the option of calling up the House-passed measure or, if one exists, the Senate committee-reported version.

Rule XIV was increasingly used during the 1990s, especially the Lott years. [87] Although not used for the vast majority of measures, Rule XIV is often invoked on party issues of high priority. The majority leader may employ it to bypass committees because no time is available for lengthy committee review, concern has been raised that a bill might get stuck in committee, he wants an issue ready to be called up at his discretion, or the Senate wants to vote quickly on a measure. For instance, Lott used Rule XIV to place a major energy policy bill on the calendar in spring 2000. The procedural move "prevents the legislation from being split apart and shipped to three Senate committees" claiming jurisdiction. Lott "would be dooming the bill if he sent it to three committees" with only a limited amount of time left for Congress to complete its work. [88]

House-passed measures usually are held at the clerk's desk by unanimous consent. They are also held at the desk when similar Senate bills are pending on the calendar or are expected shortly to be reported out of committee.

Suspension of the Rules

Senate rules can be suspended, provided there is one day's written notice and the terms of the suspension motion are published in the *Record*. The rules are silent on the number of votes needed to suspend Senate rules. Precedents have required two-thirds of those present and voting to approve suspensions. The procedure is rarely used because it represents a challenge to the committee system and is open to dilatory tactics. In effect, three filibusters are possible on suspension motions: first, on the motion to suspend the rules; second, on the motion to take up the bill; and third, on the bill itself.

Suspension motions occasionally are made by senators who want to offer policy amendments to general appropriations measures. Policy amendments (legislative language) to appropriations measures are forbidden by Senate rules but can be made in order in various ways, including the suspension route.

BOX 7-4   Placing a Measure on the Calendar

May 10, 2000

MEASURE READ THE FIRST TIME—H.R. 4386

MR. BROWNBACK. Mr. President, I understand that H.R. 4386, which has just been received from the House, is at the desk. I ask for its first reading.

THE PRESIDING OFFICER. The clerk will report the bill by title.

A bill (H.R. 4386) to amend title XIX of the Social Security Act to provide medical assistance for certain women screened and found to have breast or cervical cancer under a federally funded screening program, to amend the Public Health Service Act and the Federal Food, Drug, and Cosmetic Act with respect to surveillance and information concerning the relationship between cervical cancer and the human papillomavirus (HPV), and for other purposes.

MR. BROWNBACK. Mr. President, I ask for its second reading and object to my own request.

THE PRESIDING OFFICER. Objection is heard. Under the rule, the bill will be read the second time the following day.

May 11, 2000

MEASURE PLACED ON CALENDAR—H.R. 4386

MR. BROWNBACK. Mr. President, I understand there is a bill at the desk due its second reading.

THE ACTING PRESIDENT pro tempore. The clerk will read the bill by title for the second time.

The senior assistant bill clerk read as follows:

A bill (H.R. 4386) to amend title XIX of the Social Security Act to provide medical assistance for certain women screened and found to have breast or cervical cancer under a federally funded screening program, to amend the Public Health Service Act and the Federal Food, Drug, and Cosmetic Act with respect to surveillance and information concerning the relationship between cervical cancer and the human papillomavirus (HPV), and for other purposes.

Mr. GRASSLEY. Mr. President, I object to further proceedings on this matter at this time.

THE ACTING PRESIDENT pro tempore. The bill will be placed on the calendar.

SOURCE: *Congressional Record*, May 10, 2000, S3852–S3853; and *Congressional Record*, May 11, 2000, S3858.

Discharge Petition

The formal process to discharge a bill from a committee under Rule XVII has taken place only fourteen times in the history of the Senate. It was last employed successfully in 1964. The prevailing sentiment is that the procedure undercuts the committee system and also that the rules governing its use are cumbersome. The discharge motion can be made by any senator only during the morning hour and must remain at the clerk's desk for one legislative day. Party leaders can forestall discharge motions for days or weeks by recessing, thus keeping the Senate in the same legislative day. If debate on the motion is not concluded within the morning hour, the motion is placed on the calendar where it faces the threat of a series of filibusters. A vote to discharge a committee of a bill requires a simple majority vote unless cloture must be invoked to stop a filibuster.

There is technically yet another way to bypass a Senate committee: by unanimous consent. The Senate can do almost anything it wants by unanimous consent. However, unanimous consent will not be obtained if a single member—presumably a member of the committee that would be bypassed—objects. (It is common practice for the Senate to discharge measures from committees by unanimous consent—meaning with the committee's permission.)

NOTES

1. During his service as vice president, John Adams (1789–1797) "cast 29 tie-breaking votes, more than any of his [forty-five] successors in that position." *Congressional Record,* April 21, 1987, S5204.
2. *Congressional Record,* May 21, 1980, S5674.
3. On November 17, 1982, for the first time since 1793, the House had two legislative days in the same calendar day. It adjourned at 1:19 p.m. (the first legislative day) and then reconvened at 4:00 p.m. (the second legislative day). Sharp partisanship stimulated the Democratic leadership to employ this rare scheduling device. On October 29, 1987, the House again adjourned and reconvened.
4. *Senate Procedure: Precedents and Practices,* 97th Cong., 1st sess., S. Doc. 97-2, 565.
5. *Congressional Record,* March 26, 1987, S3927.
6. *Congressional Record,* February 27, 1998, S1175.
7. *Congressional Record,* April 16, 1985, S4256.
8. *Congressional Record,* June 9, 1977, 18179.
9. *National Journal's CongressDaily/PM,* August 20, 1993, 4. See Mary McGrory, "Freshman Turns Senate Scarlet," *Washington Post,* July 27, 1993, A2.
10. Kenneth Cooper, "Battle May Be Brewing on Hill Over Renewal of Education Act," *Washington Post,* May 14, 2000, A10.

11. A Senate rule requires three hours of germane discussion at the beginning of each day's debate on a measure. Called the Pastore Rule after its sponsor, Sen. John O. Pastore, D-R.I. (1950–1976), its purpose is to confine debate to pending business.
12. *Congressional Record,* January 21, 1986, S8.
13. *Congressional Record,* May 21, 1987, S6979.
14. Rowland Evans and Robert Novak, *Lyndon B. Johnson: The Exercise of Power* (New York: New American Library, 1966), 115.
15. *Congressional Record,* October 31, 1985, 29990.
16. Joseph S. Clark, *Congress: The Sapless Branch* (New York: Harper & Row, 1964), 247–248.
17. *New York Times,* June 8, 1986, E5.
18. *Congressional Record,* September 27, 1993, S12550.
19. *CQ Daily Monitor,* February 24, 1995, 4.
20. Elizabeth Shogren, "Level of Debate in Senate Hits Comic Low," *Los Angeles Times,* August 25, 1994, A6.
21. *Congressional Record,* October 28, 1977, 5857.
22. Elizabeth Drew, *Senator* (New York: Simon & Schuster, 1979), 173–174.
23. *Congressional Record,* April 18, 1980, S3923. See also Stanley Bach, "Parliamentary Strategy and the Amendment Process: Rules and Case Studies of Congressional Action," *Polity* (Summer 1983): 573–592.
24. *Wall Street Journal,* March 2, 1995, A16.
25. *CQ Daily Monitor,* March 2, 1995, 5.
26. *New York Times,* May 6, 1987, B10.
27. John Bresnahan, "Democrats Angered by Senate Maneuvering on FEC," *Roll Call,* August 3, 1998, 3.
28. *CQ Daily Monitor,* February 24, 2000, 2.
29. *Congressional Record,* October 28, 1999, S1336.
30. John Bresnahan, "Daschle, Lott Argue about Notification on Amendments," *Roll Call,* June 21, 1999, 28.
31. *Congressional Record,* June 15, 1994, S6905.
32. Victoria Allred and Sumana Chatterjee, "Lott Pulls a New Trick Out of the Past," *Congressional Quarterly Weekly Report,* July 29, 2000, 1856.
33. *Congressional Record,* November 5, 1985, 30522.
34. *Washington Post,* July 24, 1991, A1.
35. *Congressional Record,* March 7, 1995, S3597.
36. *Congressional Record,* March 7, 1995, S3599.
37. *Congressional Record,* May 20, 1996, S5339.
38. *National Journal's Congress Daily/AM,* May 11, 2000, 5.
39. *Congressional Record,* April 1, 1998, S2896.
40. *Congressional Record,* January 26, 1973, 2301.
41. *Congressional Record,* December 9, 1987, S17476.
42. James L. Buckley, *If Men Were Angels* (New York: G. P. Putnam's Sons, 1975), 129.
43. Bernard Asbell, *The Senate Nobody Knows* (Garden City, N.Y.: Doubleday, 1978), 267.
44. *Congressional Record,* September 23, 1975, 29814.
45. *Congressional Record,* June 23, 1987, S8442.
46. *Congressional Record,* April 8, 1981, S3618.

47. Nadine Cohodas, "Decision on Manion Put Off after 'Roll of Dice' in Senate," *Congressional Quarterly Weekly Report,* June 28, 1986, 1508–1509.

48. *Congressional Record,* July 22, 1983, S10701.

49. *Congressional Record,* October 10, 1985, S13114.

50. *New York Times,* December 21, 1982, D29.

51. The word *filibuster* derives from the Dutch word *Vrijbuiter,* meaning freebooter. Passing into Spanish as *filibustero,* it was used to describe military adventurers from the United States who in the mid-1800s fomented insurrections against various Latin American governments. For an account of William Walker, filibusterer of the 1850s, see *Smithsonian,* June 1981, 117–128. The first legislative use of the word is said to have occurred in the House in 1853, when a representative accused his opponents of "filibustering against the United States." By 1863 the word *filibuster* had come to mean delaying action on the floor, but the term did not gain wide currency until the 1880s.

52. *Congressional Record,* July 18, 1983, S10216.

53. *Congressional Record,* July 20, 1995, 19662.

54. Doug Obey, "Alaska," *The Hill,* July 10, 1996, 27.

55. *Washington Post,* February 20, 1994, A13.

56. *New York Times,* December 12, 1982, 4E.

57. Nick Anderson, "Democrats Maneuver to Force Gun Vote," *Los Angeles Times,* May 17, 2000, A1.

58. *Washington Times,* November 17, 1987, A6.

59. Sarah Binder, Eric Lawrence, and Steven Smith, "Explaining Senate Change: The Rise in Filibustering, 1917–1996," paper presented at the annual meeting of the Midwest Political Science Association, April 10-12, 1997, 3.

60. *National Journal's CongressDaily/AM,* November 10, 1993, 1, 7.

61. *Congressional Record,* October 5, 1992, S16577.

62. *National Journal's CongressDaily/AM,* March 23, 1994, 8.

63. *Congressional Record,* February 26, 1979, 3232.

64. *Operations of Congress: Testimony of House and Senate Leaders,* hearing before the 1993 Joint Committee on the Organization of Congress, January 26, 1993, 50.

65. *Congressional Record,* September 27, 1984, S12137.

66. Richard F. Fenno Jr., "The Senate through the Looking Glass: The Debate over Television," *Legislative Studies Quarterly* (August 1989): 316.

67. *Congressional Record,* March 3, 1986, S1915.

68. Sarah Binder and Steven Smith, *Politics or Principle? Filibustering in the United States Senate* (Washington, D.C.: Brookings Institution, 1997), 15.

69. An example of a mistake that filibustering senators can make that cause them to lose the floor is violation of the two-speech rule, which forbids members from making a third speech on the same question in the same legislative day. For a contentious debate on the two-speech rule, see *Congressional Record,* September 25, 1986, S13687–S13710; and *Washington Post,* October 1, 1986, A17.

70. *Washington Post,* June 11, 1982, A11.

71. *Congressional Record,* September 21, 1893, 1636.

72. *Congressional Record,* July 7, 1998, S7565.

73. *Congressional Record,* March 28, 2000, S1832.

74. *Congressional Record,* June 19, 1998, S6666.

75. *Operations of Congress,* 116.
76. Mary Jacoby, "Harkin, Lieberman Take Up a Lonely Fight to Ban Filibuster—But How to Force Vote?" *Roll Call,* November 28, 1994, 24.
77. *Congressional Record,* January 5, 1995, S438.
78. *Constitution, Jefferson's Manual, and Rules of the House of Representatives,* 102d Cong., 2d sess., H. Doc. 102-405, 233.
79. *Congressional Record,* February 26, 1986, S1663.
80. *Congressional Record,* May 17, 2000, S4063.
81. *Congressional Record,* May 17, 2000, S4065.
82. *Congressional Record,* May 17, 2000, S4067.
83. *Report on Senate Operations, 1988,* Senate Committee on Rules and Administration, S Print 100-129, September 20, 1988, 55.
84. *Congressional Record,* February 9, 1982, S599.
85. *Congressional Record,* February 9, 1982, S599.
86. *Congressional Record,* November 2, 1999, S13632.
87. C. Lawrence Evans and Walter J. Oleszek, "Message Politics and Senate Procedure," paper presented at Florida International University for the conference "The Myth of Cool Judgment? Partisanship and Ideology in the Contemporary Senate," January 21-22, 2000.
88. *National Journal's CongressDaily/AM,* May 16, 2000, 10.

CHAPTER 8

Resolving House-Senate Differences

BEFORE LEGISLATION can be sent to the president for his consideration, it must be passed by both houses in identical form. House- and Senate-passed versions of the same bill frequently differ, sometimes only slightly but often on critical points. The two versions must be reconciled by mutual agreement. Whenever possible, this is done informally. However, a fair percentage of all bills passed by both chambers require action by a House-Senate conference committee—an ad hoc joint committee composed of members selected by each chamber to resolve differences on a particular bill in disagreement.[1] Of the 465 public laws enacted by the 103d Congress, 13 percent (or 62) went through conference.[2] Major and controversial legislation usually requires conference committee action.

Conference committees are called the third house of Congress. Here the final version of a bill is written, often by a small number of lawmakers. Decisions to add or drop provisions made during House or Senate consideration can be reversed at this lawmaking stage. Sen. Paul Wellstone, D-Minn., said:

> I used to teach political science classes. . . . You know, I feel guilty. I need to refund tuition to students for those 2 weeks I taught classes on the Congress. I was so off in terms of a lot of the decisionmaking.
>
> I should have focused on the conferences committees as the third House of Congress, because these folks can do any number of different things. And the thing that drives me crazy is you can have a situation where the Senate did not have a provision in the bill, and the conference committee just puts it in the bill. Then it comes back for an up-or-down vote. No opportunity to amend.
>
> Or you can have a situation where the Senate and the House pass bills with provisions in them and the conference takes it out. It is, I think, the least accountable part of decision making in Congress.[3]

OBSCURITY OF THE PROCESS

The conference committee process is older than Congress itself. State legislatures used conference committees before 1789 to reconcile differences between the chambers of their bicameral legislatures. The conference committee system was taken for granted when the first Congress convened, and it has been in use ever since.[4] Nevertheless, for many citizens the conference committee is little known or understood, compared with the other aspects of the legislative process.

Until the mid-1970s conference committees almost always met in secret sessions with no published record of their proceedings. The conference committees produced a conference committee report that showed the results of the secret negotiations, but the bargaining and deliberations that led to these results were not formally disclosed.

In one of the most significant reforms of congressional procedure, both chambers in 1975 adopted rules requiring open conference committee meetings unless a majority of the conference members (called conferees or managers) from either chamber voted in public to hold secret sessions. In 1977 the House went a step further, adopting a rule requiring the full House to vote to close a conference. This occurs usually on legislation dealing with national security. For instance, the head of the House conference delegation will offer the nondebatable motion to close the conference committee "to the public at such times as classified national security information is under consideration."[5]

Conferees still conduct much of their important business in secret, however. As thirty-eight-year-veteran senator Russell B. Long, D-La. (who voluntarily retired at the end of the 99th Congress), once noted in a statement that holds true today:

> The Senator knows when we started the openness thing we found it more and more difficult to get something agreed to in the conferences, it seemed to take forever. So what did we do? The Senator knows what we did. We would break up into smaller groups and then we would ask our chairman . . . to see if he could not find his opposite number on the House side and discuss this matter and come back and tell us what the chances would be of working out various and sundry possibilities.[6]

Relatively few complaints have been raised about closed sessions. Political commentators and others recognize the value of candid exchanges (away from the glare of special interest groups) in closed meetings. Further, reporters are usually kept well informed of the results of closed conferences. In today's open and video politics era, "secret" does not mean what it used to on Capitol Hill. On a few occasions, conference negotiating sessions have been televised over the Cable-Satellite Public Affairs Network (C-SPAN).

The conference committee is one of the most critical points in the legislative process. For several reasons, however, members of Congress may try to avoid this stage and resolve House-Senate differences on legislation without recourse to the conference committee process. First, pressure exists to approve the legislation quickly. Second, one house may be concerned that conferees of the other chamber will try to weaken (or filibuster) the legislation. For instance, on a nuclear waste storage bill, the House leadership "decided to go with the Senate version in an attempt to avoid a filibuster threatened by Nevada's [the site for storing nuclear waste] senators on any conference report to the legislation."[7] Third, a conference committee could become deadlocked—particularly in the weeks and days before the final adjournment of

Congress. Failure of the conferees to reach agreement before the end of a Congress means that the bill dies.

AGREEMENT WITHOUT A CONFERENCE

There are two principal ways of achieving bicameral agreement—each chamber approves the same bill—without a conference. First, one chamber can adopt verbatim the version of a bill produced by the other. This is a common occurrence and may involve informal consultation before or after passage of the bill by one chamber. Second, the two houses may send measures back and forth several times, amending each other's amendments, before they agree to identical language on all provisions of the legislation. The "ping-pong" approach may also be employed in combination with conference committee negotiations. Table 8-1 presents data on how often different procedures for reaching bicameral agreement were used in the 99th, 103d, and 105th Congresses.

House and Senate committee staff communicate regularly on legislation of mutual interest. Drafts of measures are exchanged for comment and consistency, companion bills are studied, and strategies are devised to facilitate passage in each chamber. Executive branch officials and pressure groups often participate in these informal strategy sessions. This kind of prior consultation frequently helps clear away obstacles to passage—allowing legislation to be approved by both houses in identical form, thus avoiding the need for a conference.

Consultation also may take place after a bill has passed one or both chambers. For example, on the first day of the 104th Congress, the House overwhelmingly passed the Congressional Accountability Act (H.R. 1), applying federal workplace safety and antidiscrimination laws to the legislative branch. When the legislation went to the Senate, members there wanted to make some changes. After consultations with the House sponsors of the legislation, the Senate passed S. 2, its version of the accountability act, and sent that measure to the House. To avoid the need for a conference committee, House Republican leaders decided to take up S. 2 under suspension of the rules, and it was passed by more than the two-thirds vote (390 to 0) required under that procedure. The House action cleared the legislation for submission to President Bill Clinton, who signed the measure into law.

Limits to Nonconference Tactics

Two points are worth noting about the ping-pong approach. First, a technical limit exists to the number of times measures may be shuffled between the chambers. The third-degree amendment prohibition applies to amendments between the House and Senate. Each chamber gets two shots at amending the amendments of the other body. "In short, after each chamber has passed the same bill for the first time (for example, the House passes a House bill and the Senate passes the House bill with Senate amendments), each chamber

TABLE 8-1 Bicameral Reconciliation of Legislation, 99th (1985–1987), 103d (1993–1995), and 105th (1997–1999) Congresses

Method of Reconciliation	99th Congress		103d Congress		105th Congress	
	Number	Percent	Number	Percent	Number	Percent
Simple adoption by one chamber of the version sent to it by the other	477	(72)	291	(63)	277	(70.5)
Amendments between the houses	133	(20)	112	(24)	77	(19.6)
Conference reports	39	(6)	46	(10)	39	(9.9)
Both conference reports and amendments between the houses	14	(2)	16	(30)	0	(0.0)
Public laws (total)	663		465		393	

SOURCE: 99th and 103d Congresses: Ilona Nickels, congressional specialist, Government Division, Congressional Research Service, Library of Congress; 105th Congress: Denise S. Feriozzi, Monroe Scholar, College of William and Mary.

may have one opportunity to amend the amendments of the other chamber." [8] Like many legislative procedures, the two-shot principle can be waived, ignored, or overturned. The Consolidated Omnibus Reconciliation Act of 1985, for example, bounced between the chambers a record-setting nine times.

Second, the back-and-forth alternative procedure is employed intentionally to avoid conferences and is feasible only when circumstances warrant its use. For instance, a House chairman may ask the chamber to concur in the Senate amendment to the House amendment to the Senate-passed bill. House approval is "appropriate parliamentary procedure, which allows us to avoid the trouble of a conference when faced with such small [bicameral] differences." [9] The House in this case agreed to the Senate amendment, which cleared the bill for the president. Lack of time also can prevent formation of conference committees and necessitate use of the back-and-forth approach.

PRECONFERENCE CONSIDERATIONS

It is often clear from the outset that controversial measures will end up in conference. Members plan their floor strategy accordingly. They make floor statements that emphasize their unyielding commitment to their own chamber's positions. In advance of a "House-Senate conference," noted one senator, "it is not unusual for the respective [chambers] to stake out positions for themselves and even to utter statements about their absolute intransigence, that sometimes does not always prevail when the conference convenes." [10]

Members frequently add expendable amendments to use as bargaining chips in conference. Such amendments can be traded away for other provisions considered more important. Use of such tactics has been refined to an art form by some senators. When Senator Long was Finance chairman (1965–1981), he usually came "to conference with a bill loaded up with amendments added on the Senate floor. . . . Long has plenty of things he is willing to jettison to save the goodies." [11] Members who sponsor floor amendments are mindful of the bargaining-chip ploy. As one senator remarked:

> I have been in this body long enough to beware of the chairman of a committee who says in an enticing voice, "Let me take the amendment to conference," because I think that is frequently the parliamentary equivalent of saying, "Let me take the child into the tower and I will strangle him to death." [12]

On another occasion, a colleague asked Sen. Bob Dole, R-Kan., if certain floor amendments would be dropped in conference. Dole responded, "I have indicated to the Senator from Ohio that we will certainly consider these carefully in conference before they are disposed of." [13]

With conference committees open, or at least subject to public review, conferees sometimes must put up a fight for such amendments before dropping them. Conferees understand, too, that some bargaining chips are more influential than others. Before these amendments are dropped, conferees will consider the implications of offending powerful members.

Another preconference tactic is for one chamber to deliberately keep out of its bill something it knows the other chamber wants. During a conference, the House conferees, for instance, may give in to the Senate, but only in return for Senate acceptance of something favored by the House. For these reasons, counting the number of times one house appeared to give in to the other is not a good indication of the winners and losers in conference.[14]

House and Senate floor managers also consider whether they want recorded votes on certain amendments when they are debated in their chamber. For example, one senator's strategy on an amendment he opposed was to seek a recorded vote on it "to beat the amendment, and beat it good, burying the issue in the Senate once and for all, and also putting him in a position to tell a Senate-House conference on the bill that the proposal was resoundingly defeated in the Senate." [15] Alternatively, floor managers sometimes prefer not to draw attention to amendments they oppose (or favor)—and thus hope to avoid taking roll-call votes—on the assumption that it then will be easier to drop (or advocate) them in conference.

Finally, members are sensitive to the overall contours of their bill and the margin of support for its passage on the floor. For example, many senators, including Republicans, were not strong supporters of the Contract with America, which was pushed by House Speaker Newt Gingrich, R-Ga. As a result, one GOP representative said that the "tactics are to [include nailing down] the firmest position [on a particular contract bill] because we still have to deal with the Senate and the White House." [16] Thus, if the Senate rewrites the House's position, "House leaders vow to fight for the House position in conferences with the Senate." [17]

CONFERENCE COMMITTEE PROCESS

The five major steps in the conference committee process are (1) requesting a conference, (2) selecting conferees, (3) bargaining in conference, such as negotiating objectives and procedural issues, (4) filing the conference committee report, and (5) taking final House and Senate action on the conference committee version of the bill.

Requesting a Conference

When the House passes a bill, which is then amended by the Senate and returned, the House has several options. It may refuse to take further action, in which case the measure dies; approve an entirely new version of the bill and send it to the Senate; agree to the Senate's amendments, negating the need for a conference; amend the Senate's amendments and return the measure once again to the Senate; or request a conference.

Occasionally, the Speaker may refer the Senate amendments, especially if they are nongermane to the House-passed measure, to the standing committee having jurisdiction over the subject matter of the amendments. More commonly, though, on major legislation, a member will ask and receive unanimous consent for the House to disagree to the Senate's amendments and request a conference with the Senate. The Speaker usually recognizes an appropriate committee member to make the unanimous consent request to go to conference on the bill. ("Mr. Speaker, I ask unanimous consent to take from the Speaker's table the bill H.R. 1234 with the Senate amendments thereto, disagree to the amendments of the Senate and ask for a conference with the Senate.")

If any representative objects to this request, the legislation can get to conference in three other ways. First, the House can suspend its rules (an action that requires a two-thirds vote) by adopting, for example, the following motion: "Mr. Speaker, I move to suspend the rules and take from the Speaker's table the bill H.R. 1234 with the Senate amendments thereto, disagree to the amendments of the Senate and ask for a conference with the Senate." If the legislation is controversial, this procedure is unlikely to be employed because of its supermajority requirements.

Second, the Rules Committee can report a rule sending a measure to conference. On occasion, the Rules Committee will report a rule that not only specifies how a House measure will be debated and amended but also provides for an automatic Senate hookup following completion of floor action on the bill. A hookup provision permits a companion Senate-passed measure to be immediately called up and the House-passed version inserted after the

Senate's bill number. Technically, the House and Senate have passed the same numbered measure (a requirement if a measure is sent to conference). The practical effect is that conference committee negotiations will involve two versions (the House's and Senate's) of the same bill.

Third, representatives can invoke House Rule XXII to get a measure to conference. This rule permits legislation to reach conference by majority vote of the House if a member of the committee of jurisdiction, typically the chairman, is authorized by his panel to offer the motion to go to conference. A chairman often will come to the floor armed with such authorization and alert the Speaker of this fact. Then, if a member objects to a unanimous consent request for a conference, the chairman will be immediately recognized by the Speaker to offer the Rule XXII motion. (Bills that are multiply referred to several committees require all committees with a primary or initial claim on the legislation, and that have reported the bill, to agree to the Rule XXII procedure.)

When the situation is reversed, and a Senate-passed bill is amended by the House and returned to the Senate, it is "held at the desk and almost always subsequently laid before the Senate by the Presiding Officer upon request or motion of a Senator [usually the manager of the bill.]" [18]

The House amendment or amendments may be dealt with in four ways by the Senate: (1) by adopting a motion to refer the amendment(s) to the appropriate standing committee, (2) by further amending the House amendments, (3) by agreeing to the House amendments (thus clearing the bill), or (4) by disagreeing to the House amendments, in which case a conference is requested by motion or unanimous consent.

Typically, the Senate gets to conference with the House by adopting this standard motion: "Mr. President, I move that the Senate insist on its amendments, request a conference with the House on the disagreeing votes thereon, and that the Chair be authorized to appoint conferees." This triple motion rolled into one—to insist (an alternative form is to "disagree to the House amendments" to the Senate-passed bill), to request, and to appoint—is rarely divided into discrete parts and voted upon separately, filibustered, or defeated. The normal routine for the Senate is to agree to the three-part motion by unanimous consent.

However, in a precedent-making move, GOP senators opposed to sending a campaign finance bill to conference during the waning days of the 103d Congress (1993–1995) launched filibusters against each part of the triple motion. "In the 210 years in the history of the United States Senate, never—until last week—has there been a series of filibusters on taking a bill to conference," stated Majority Leader George J. Mitchell, D-Maine.[19] With GOP expectations high for recapturing control of the Senate following the November 1994 elections, Republicans wanted to block action on this largely Democratic initiative. They were successful on both counts.

In another example of the difficulty the Senate encountered in proceeding to a conference with the House in the past decade, House and Senate leaders negotiated for months in 2000 on how to break a political and procedural stalemate and send a consumer bankruptcy bill to a conference committee. When the House passed the bankruptcy reform bill and sent it to the Senate, it was approved overwhelmingly (83 to 14); however, the bill also attracted amendments increasing the minimum wage and providing tax breaks to small businesses.[20] Because the Constitution requires tax legislation to originate in the House, any attempt to send the bankruptcy bill to conference would open it to a "blue-slip" rejection—a notification on blue paper to the Senate that it has contravened the constitutional prerogatives of the House. The bipartisan Senate leadership wanted "to split off the wage and tax provisions, sending them to one conference committee [the House had already approved a minimum wage and tax break bill] and the bankruptcy bill to another."[21] However, to accomplish this goal required unanimous consent, and two senators who opposed the bankruptcy bill objected.

For months things remained at a parliamentary standstill as top House and Senate leaders negotiated privately on how to resolve the impasse and get action on overhauling the bankruptcy laws. In the end, both chambers named unofficial conferees to participate in a "shadow" conference on bankruptcy reform that conducted its negotiations in secret and with little participation by House Democrats or key Senate Democrats. Subsequently, and in a good example of the procedural adhocracy that sometimes characterizes lawmaking on today's priority issues, GOP leaders worked to add the bankruptcy overhaul as a rider to a conference report on another bill.

Both chambers vote themselves into a state of disagreement before going to conference. Technically, each chamber goes to conference on one bill. One house will often take the other's bill, strike everything after the enacting clause, and then insert its own alternative. The conference meets to resolve differences on one bill, but there are House and Senate versions of the measure. On the patients' bill of rights bill, for example, the Senate in 2000 took up the House-passed measure, amended it with its own version, passed the legislation, and then requested a conference with the House.

Selecting Conferees

The selection of conferees is governed in both chambers by rules and precedent. For each occasion on which a bill is sent to conference, the House Speaker and the presiding officer of the Senate formally appoint the respective conferees. In practice, both chambers usually rely on the chairman and ranking minority member of the committee that originally considered and reported the bill to recommend the selections. Sometimes chairmen will delay in naming conferees to signal displeasure with the other body and to apply "leverage on the other body [and encourage it to] cave in on . . . key issues" even before a conference is formally convened.[22] Other factors, too, may slow the appointment of conferees. For instance, as a form of hostage politics, a senator may block the appointment of conferees on a bill he opposes until after they have been named on a measure he supports. Senators, too, may place holds on the conferee appointment process.

The Speaker and the presiding officer typically appoint conferees from the list given them in advance by the committee leaders, who select members of their own committees. (The Speaker, after the original appointment, also has the authority to remove managers or name additional conferees.) A member of another committee may be appointed when he or she has special knowledge of the subject matter or if the bill is of particular interest to the member's state or district. (Or members may be invited to attend the bicameral meetings without formally being named conferees, because of their specialized knowledge.) When a bill has been referred to several committees (multiple referral), it is common to have conferees from all the committees that handled it. With the new system of primary referrals that began with the 104th Congress, most House conferees are selected from the lead committee with other conferees named from the committees of secondary referral. (Party ratios on conference committees generally reflect the party membership in the House and Senate.)

House and Senate party leaders may get actively involved in naming conferees on issues of fundamental importance. For example, in a virtually unprecedented decision, Speaker Newt Gingrich in 1995 named a Democratic member, Gary A. Condit of California, as a conferee on unfunded mandates legislation. Condit, who ranked tenth in seniority on the committee of jurisdiction (Government Reform), supported GOP efforts to inhibit congressional passage of bills that impose financial costs on state governments. However, he could not persuade either the ranking Democrat on the Government Reform panel or Minority Leader Richard A. Gephardt, Mo., to appoint him as a conferee. (Under party rules, the "Democratic Leader shall make recommendations to the Speaker of all Democratic Members who shall serve as conferees.") Speaker Gingrich was amenable to the idea and appointed Condit to one of the designated GOP conferee slots. As a result, the House conference delegation was bipartisan: four Republicans and four Democrats. (Condit belonged to a conservative Democratic group called The Coalition, whose support Gingrich sought to help pass GOP legislation.)[23]

Speaker J. Dennis Hastert, R-Ill., exercised his authority to name conferees on the patients' bill of rights measure by stacking the conferees with House opponents of the legislation. To the chagrin of Hastert and other GOP leaders, the House enacted over their strong opposition a managed care proposal whose principal authors were Reps. Charlie Norwood, R-Ga., Greg Ganske, R-Iowa, and John D. Dingell, D-Mich. Their bipartisan proposal allowed patients to sue health maintenance organizations (HMOs), an idea that Hastert opposed. Hastert named thirteen GOP conferees, only one of whom supported the Norwood-Ganske-Dingell plan. In addition, the Speaker refused to name either Norwood or Ganske as conferees. "Is that stacking the deck, is that trying to subvert the will of the House, or what?" exclaimed Ganske.[24] Dingell offered to give Norwood, the prime author of the health plan, one of the Democrats' seven conferee slots but Norwood declined saying "that would kill any opportunity he might have to influence fellow Republicans."[25] President Clinton wrote to Hastert and asked him "to use your authority under the House rules to expand the conference committee to include members who accurately reflect the will of the House."[26]

House rules state that the Speaker shall "appoint no less than a majority [of conferees] who generally supported the House position as determined by the Speaker" as well as those "who are primarily responsible for the legislation." Parliamentarily, Hastert was able to skirt these guidelines because the Norwood-Ganske-Dingell bill was incorporated into a health access measure, and it was this legislation that was sent to conference with the other body. All thirteen GOP conferees, including freshman and physician Ernie Fletcher, Ky., voted for the access bill. (Seniority used to be a dominant criterion in the appointment of conferees, but junior members are now often selected.) On the Senate side, Majority Leader Trent Lott, R-Miss., broke with custom and designated Majority Whip Don Nickles, R-Okla., to head the Senate conference delegation instead of the chairman of the Senate panel that reported the managed care legislation—a sign that Lott wanted the GOP leadership to direct conference negotiations.

The trend in recent years has been to increase the size of conference delegations. In 1971 the average number of House conferees was eight; about twenty years later, twenty-five. In the same period, the average number of Senate conferees went from eight to a dozen.[27] Multiple committee consideration of megabills that cross-cut the jurisdiction of several panels is the driving force behind big conferences. One chamber cannot outvote the other by appointing more conferees, because each house votes as a unit, with a majority vote deciding each issue. Each house, in effect, has one vote ("yea" or "nay") to cast. However, large conference delegations affect the mechanics of conference decision making. They often divide into smaller groups called subconferences.

The largest conference in congressional history involved the 1981 omnibus budget reconciliation bill. "Over 250 Senators and Congressmen met in 58 [subconferences] to consider nearly 300 issues" in disagreement, noted Senate Majority Leader Howard H. Baker Jr., R- Tenn.[28] The use of subconferences enables bicameral negotiators to proceed on several fronts simultaneously and to expedite what is inherently (because of numbers) a more complex process.

The nature of the issues in disagreement may account most for the length of conferences on megabills. Large conference delegations invariably require more time to iron out bicameral differences. The diversity of views that need to be harmonized affects the pace of deliberations. The issues in disagreement are likely to be contentious. Having numerous conferees also facilitates access to the negotiations by lawmakers who are not conferees, interest groups, and executive officials. (Many conferences involve multilateral instead of bilateral negotiations, because scores of outside actors and interests can influence conference outcomes.) If large conferences become unwieldy even if they divide into subconferences, they often break down into smaller and smaller groups. This process was followed during a huge savings and loan conference, which embraced nearly one-quarter of the House, including every member of the House Banking Committee. As one House conferee put it:

> One hundred and two conferees were appointed and no progress was made until the four principals [the House and Senate Banking chairmen and ranking minority members] went behind closed doors. And I'm not complaining. If [the House Banking chairman] had not reduced the conference from 102 members to four, we would still be there arguing over this bill. He should get an Oscar for his starring role in, "Honey, I shrunk the conference."[29]

The rules, precedents, and customs of each chamber obligate conferees to try and uphold the position of their chamber. In addition, after either chamber has agreed to go to conference but before the conferees have officially been named, the House or Senate may adopt motions instructing their conferees, for instance, to sustain the majority position of the chamber on a particular amendment or provision (see Box 8-1). A member of the minority party is granted priority in the House to offer the motion to instruct and only one can be made at this stage. On the managed care health measure of the 106th Congress (1999–2001), the House voted to instruct the still-to-be named conferees to uphold a patient's right to sue his HMO. Instructions place additional political and moral pressure on the conferees and may strengthen their position in conference committee bargaining. "We need to give the House conferees some backbone to stand up to the Senate on this issue," declared a House member in support of a motion to instruct conferees.[30] However, instructions adopted by either chamber are not binding. (The practice is more common in the House than the Senate, in part because it appears unseemly to instruct senators.) Conferees may disregard the instructions, particularly when they feel the need for room to maneuver or compromise. The full House and Senate still have an opportunity to accept or reject the conference committee report on the bill, and a new conference may be requested if either house feels that its conferees have grossly violated their instructions.

During the early 1990s, when Democrats controlled the House, Republicans began to use the instruction motion to bring their issues before the chamber. In 1993 it was used eleven times; the following year, more than double that number. Only one motion to instruct can be offered prior to the appointment of conferees, and this motion is reserved to the minority. If a conference cannot reach agreement within twenty calendar days, however, House rules permit lawmakers to offer (with one day's notice) an unlimited number of instruction motions. During a more-than-twenty-day crime conference in 1994, for example, Republicans offered "nine motions to instruct conferees on, among other things, provisions regarding 'racial justice,' prison construction, and the death penalty."[31] In the minority, Democrats regularly

---

Box 8-1 **Instruction of Conferees**

APPOINTMENT OF CONFEREES ON H.R. 4103,
DEPARTMENT OF DEFENSE APPROPRIATIONS ACT, 1999

MR. YOUNG of Florida. Mr. Speaker, I ask unanimous consent to take from the Speaker's table the bill (H.R. 4103) making appropriations for the Department of Defense for the fiscal year ending September 30, 1999, and for other purposes, with Senate amendments thereto, disagree to the Senate amendments, and agree to the conference asked by the Senate.

THE SPEAKER pro tempore. Is there objection to the request of the gentleman from Florida?

MOTION TO INSTRUCT CONFEREES OFFERED BY MR. OBEY

MR. OBEY. Mr. Speaker, I offer a motion to instruct.

The Clerk read as follows:

MR. OBEY moves that the managers on the part of the House at the conference on the disagreeing votes of the two Houses on the bill, H.R. 4103, be instructed to reduce, within the scope of conference, the maximum amount possible from appropriations for low priority congressionally-directed projects not requested in the FY 1999 Defense Department budget request and apply those funds to alleviate high priority military readiness needs for spare parts, quality of life programs, training exercises, retention bonuses, and recruitment incentives.

SOURCE: *Congressional Record*, September 15, 1998, H7708.

---

offered instruction motions to force votes urging action by a stalled gun control conference that had made little progress more than a year after the Columbine High School shooting.

Party and committee leaders often devote considerable time to who gets named a conferee or who is passed over. Regularly, lawmakers lobby committee or party leaders to be chosen as conferees, because they are then strategically positioned to advance their substantive and political goals. On bills of great partisan and substantive importance, the top leaders of the House (by custom, the Speaker is not a conferee) or the Senate, including the majority leader, often are named conferees.

Bargaining in Conference

Before the conferees officially convene, informal preconference negotiations usually are held that commonly involve only key House and Senate staff aides but may also include committee members, party leaders, and others. And private preconference deal making goes on between the chambers and often only among majority party members without either the formal appointment of conferees or the participation of minority party members. "I have been appointed to conference committees in the Senate in name only," said Sen. Richard J. Durbin, D-Ill., "where my name will be read by the [presiding officer] and only the conference committee of Republicans goes off and meets, adopts a conference report, signs it, and sends it back to the floor without even inviting me to attend a session."[32]

No formal rules, such as quorum or proxy voting requirements, govern internal conference committee bargaining. The only stipulation is that the conferences must meet formally at least once in open session (unless they have taken appropriate steps to meet in private). The lack of rules is deliberate to foster an informal give-and-take environment conducive to reaching bicameral compromises, especially when the chambers have passed starkly different measures. Resolving the two chambers' versions of the patients' rights health legislation, for instance, was expected to be difficult. "It's akin to mating a chihuahua with a Great Dane," said Rep. Bill Thomas, Calif.[33]

A conference chairman is selected in ad hoc fashion, as no congressional rules dictate the procedure. On recurring measures that go to conference annually, such as appropriations and revenue bills, the chairmanship rotates between the two houses. On occasion, disputes arise as to which chamber's turn it is to chair. For example, the House chaired the surface transportation conference in 1991. As a result, the chairman of the Senate committee that reported the 1998 surface transportation bill believed it was the Senate's turn to head the overall conference. But the House Transportation chairman pointed out that the Senate had chaired the conference on a national highway bill in 1996 and argued that he should chair the conference. The Speaker and Senate majority leader subsequently agreed that it was the House's turn to chair the 1998 conference. As committee aides noted: "Can you spell 'ego'? It's about recognition more than anything."[34] However, the chairman plays an influential role in the conference process, arranging the time and place of meetings, the agenda of each session, and the order in which the disagreements are negotiated. The chairman sets the pace of conference bargaining, proposes compromises, and recommends tentative agreements.

Staff members, too, play an important role in conference deliberations. They draft compromise amendments, negotiate agreements, provide advice to members, and prepare the conference reports. Aides played a particularly important role during a complex conference on an omnibus budget reconciliation bill. According to the executive director of the House Budget Committee:

> The role of the staff has been not only to explore where there may be areas of agreement, but also to make the deal. How else are you going to get hundreds of issues resolved in a couple of weeks unless you give the staff some kind of license?[35]

Conference committee bargaining, like bargaining throughout the legislative process, is subject to outside pressure. Even before the mid-1970s sunshine rules that required open conference meetings, conferees were lobbied heavily by special interest groups, executive agency officials, and sometimes the president. On important measures, the president or presidential aides "write letters to conferees; . . . administration personnel show up at conference meetings; and the president freely threatens to use his veto unless conferees compromise."[36] During the conference on the patients' bill of rights, President Clinton in May 2000 invited House and Senate conferees to the White House to give them a pep talk on resolving their differences more expeditiously. The party leaders of Congress also get directly involved—brokering compromises or urging on bicameral negotiations to meet a certain timetable. Occasions also arise when the real negotiators are not the conferees but the top congressional leaders and administration officials who may convene in a summit to resolve the issues in disagreement. Their decisions are then implemented by the conferees.

Bargaining Objectives and Tactics.   Three key, and conflicting, objectives underlie the bargaining and informal give-and-take at conference sessions: (1) conferees usually want to sustain the position of their respective chambers on the bill; (2) they want to achieve a result acceptable to a majority of each chamber's conferees; and (3) they want to craft a compromise product that is acceptable to a majority of the membership of both chambers and one that the president will sign. These objectives cannot be upheld consistently. "We caved so quickly to the House side, it was like watching water go over a waterfall," exclaimed Sen. Joseph R. Biden Jr., D-Del., about a conference on an antiterrorism measure.[37]

The conferees may be able to reach compromises quickly on their differences. For example, splitting the difference on bills appropriating funds for federal programs is relatively painless. As one senator said, if the Senate bill contains a number, "say it is 200, and the House number is 100, if we cannot get together, we would say 'Let's make it 150. Let's split the difference.'"[38] Or logrolling may occur, for instance with House conferees agreeing to certain Senate-passed provisions to gain leverage to win acceptance of House-passed provisions elsewhere in the bill that are strongly supported by members of their own chamber. Offers and counteroffers are part of the often-exhausting conference process.

Conferees employ other techniques and tactics during the bargaining process. For example, if conferees chair subcommittees, they may convene hearings while the conference is under way to generate outside pressures on conference decision making. Senators may say that they cannot accept a House compromise offer because it would generate a filibuster in the Senate. Similarly, House conferees may say that a Senate offer is unacceptable because it violates House rules. To move stalled conference negotiations, lawmakers may try to force the House or Senate to vote again on the legislation in bicameral disagreement. One side may fight hard for a position on which it plans to yield, so the conferees can tell their parent chamber that they put up a good battle but the other side would not relent.

The bargaining skills of individual conferees can produce favorable results for their chamber's positions. One House staff aide reflected upon the skill of certain conferees during marathon bargaining sessions: "You're talking about a poker game," he said. "There are people with an enormous degree of patience who will just wait and wait and wait until the other side either slips or collapses or falls asleep." [39]

One tactic sometimes used to break a deadlock is for the conferees of one chamber to threaten to break off negotiations and return to their chamber for instructions—thereby reinforcing their position when negotiations resume. A House member once described this ploy as follows:

> Last year there was a difference of about $400 million between the House and Senate versions of the foreign aid appropriations [bill]. The chairman of the House delegation in the conference took a very firm position that we had to end up with slightly less than 50 percent of the difference as a matter of prestige. It was the day we [Congress] were to adjourn. We were in conference until about 10:30 p.m., and the Senate [conferees] wouldn't give in. I think the difference between conferees was only five or ten million dollars. The Senate was fighting for its prestige, and our chairman for his. At 10:30 he started to close his book [staff papers prepared for the conference] and he got up saying he would get instructions from the House. All the rest of our [House] conferees did the same. That prospect was too much for the senators. They capitulated. [40]

This example illustrates a number of factors in conference bargaining: the importance of timing and leadership; the influence of certain members on the negotiations; the impact of threats to convene another series of protracted meetings after one side receives instructions; the role that fatigue can play in resolving hotly contested issues; and the political and professional investment that senators and representatives have in upholding the prestige of their respective chamber and committees.

Another Approach for Appropriations Conferences. Most measures sent to conference are not spending measures, and they reach the conference stage in a manner that gives the conferees maximum bargaining flexibility and discretion. One of the chambers takes a bill from the other, strikes out everything after the enacting clause, and inserts a completely new version of the bill. This, as noted previously, is called an amendment in the nature of a substitute. In effect, the House and Senate are dealing with only one amendment in disagreement. In such cases, the conference committee can consider the versions of both houses (in effect, two entirely separate bills) and draft a third version of the legislation, provided that it is a reasonable (that is, germane) modification of either the House or Senate version.

Until the mid-1990s, the appropriations conferences always considered a number of discrete amendments in disagreement. By custom, the House initiates appropriations bills and the Senate would then adopt separate amendments to the various provisions in appropriations legislation. As a result, appropriations conferees enjoyed less latitude in arriving at compromises because relating the House provisions to the corresponding Senate amendment (which was numbered for the convenience of everyone) was not difficult. Also, the House-passed bill and Senate amendments dealt with specific amounts of money that are easy to compare.

An advantage enjoyed by the appropriators was that their conferences, unlike those dealing with one amendment in disagreement, could submit a partial conference report to their respective chambers. Everything they agreed upon was included in the partial conference report. Amendments on which they stilled disagreed, either in a technical (they have violated a rule, for example) or true (conflicts over policy) sense, were then submitted separately in each chamber without jeopardizing adoption of the partial report. Until recently, appropriations conferences reflected the combination approach to resolving bicameral differences on bills: a partial conference report was agreed to first and then the House and Senate sent amendments back and forth until they reached agreement.

When Republicans won control of Congress in the mid-1990s, their leadership decided to expedite action on these measures. No longer does the Senate adopt discrete, numbered amendments to appropriations bills; instead, it follows the practice of the other committees by striking the entire text of the House-passed bill and replacing it with a complete substitute amendment. The Senate can return at any time to its former way of handling appropriations bills sent to conference, and some sentiment may exist for that course (see Box 8-2).

Procedural Limits on Bargaining.   Theory and practice often diverge on whether the formal rules of either chamber inhibit the bargaining discretion of the conferees. Scope and germaneness are two procedural constraints—points of order can be raised against the conference report if they are violated. "Scope" is a complex technical term embedded in the respective rulebook of each chamber. It essentially means the conferees are not to add new matter, reopen provisions that both chambers agreed to, or exceed the range of the matters in disagreement committed to them; that is, conferees are not to write new law not previously considered and adopted by either body. For instance, Senate Rule XXVIII states that conferees "shall not insert in their report matter not committed to them by either House, nor shall they strike from the bill matter agreed to by both Houses." If, for example, the House authorizes $5 million for a program and the Senate authorizes $10 million, precedents state that the agreement must be sought within these high and low figures, which represent the scope of the bicameral disagreement. (Splitting the difference, $7.5 million in this case, is a common compromise device.) However, when words, not numbers, are in disagreement, judging whether a policy provision reworded by the conferees meets scope requirements is usually harder.

Today, violations of scope have become almost routine. In the House, special rules regularly waive all points of order against the conference report and its consideration in the House. In the Senate, a 1996 precedent has completely undermined Rule XXVIII. On October 3, 1996, when a point of or-

BOX 8-2 Senate Procedure Change on
Appropriations Bills

A little noticed change in the way the Senate writes its annual spending bills complicated life for appropriators as they approached the fiscal 1999 endgame. It robbed them of the ability to send a message through floor votes on specific issues when the House and Senate were at loggerheads.

Conferees were hung up over a House provision, in an agriculture spending measure (H.R. 4101), to block Food and Drug Administration approval of the RU-486 abortion pill or any similar drug. The Senate strongly opposed that provision.

Under the old way of doing business, conferees could sign off on an entire bill except for the item in dispute, then call a floor vote on the issue as an amendment in true disagreement. That would be a way of demonstrating the Senate's resolve to the House. Typically, such a provision would then be dropped from the bill.

After implementing the procedural change, the Senate could no longer stage such votes because of the way it drafts the bills. Instead of having a Senate bill consisting of one hundred or so individual amendments to the House bill, the Senate replaces the entire House text with its own language. That makes the whole bill the amendment in true disagreement; nothing is agreed to until everything is agreed to.

What prompted Senate appropriators to violate that old adage, "If it ain't broke, don't fix it"? In part, the change was designed to force conferees to make the hard decisions themselves instead of running back to the floor for reinforcements. It also aimed to block individual senators from using votes on items in true disagreement as a way to open up the rest of the conference report, given that such amendments could themselves be amended. So, for example, under old procedures, Democrats could have used a vote on RU-486 to force a vote on additional relief for distressed farmers.

SOURCE: Adapted from Andrew Taylor, "It's All or Nothing Now for Spending Bill Conferences: Change in Senate's Handling of Appropriations Process Ends Old Practice of Test Floor Votes," *CQ Daily Monitor*, October 1, 1998, 1, 5.

der was made that a conference report violated scope by adding new matter, the Senate presiding officer ruled: "[I]t is the opinion of the Chair that the conference report exceeds the scope, and the point of order is sustained."[41] The majority leader appealed the ruling of the chair, and the Senate voted to reject the chair's decision. This precedent now trumps Rule XXVIII and renders it a nullity. New lawmaking by Senate conferees is now the order of the day, subject only to the willingness of the House to adopt a special waiver rule for the conference report. The Senate could either reject the conference report or, on a future point of order, return to the status quo ante by overturning the presiding officer's ruling.

"Conferences are marvelous," exclaimed Sen. Alan K. Simpson, R-Wyo. "They're mystical. They're alchemy. It's absolutely dazzling what you can do."[42] For example, in fall 1999 conferees added a huge Labor-Health and Human Services (HHS) appropriations bill to a District of Columbia appropriations conference report. Congress was a month late in getting the appropriations bills enacted by the start of the fiscal year, and the majority leaders of each chamber were under pressure to get the spending measures passed to avoid any shutdown of governmental services. Hence, the $313.6 billion Labor-HHS bill and the $429 million D.C. appropriations measure were married. "Out of that marriage of elephant and ant," said Sen. Bob Graham, D-Fla., "we now have before the Senate the conference report on the District of Columbia with the enormous addition of a $313 billion Labor-HHS 'rider'."[43] Both houses agreed to the conference report.

The Senate is able to add amendments that are considered nongermane under House rules. For years, House conferees were faced with a take-it-or-leave-it proposition—accept the nongermane Senate amendments or lose the bill in its entirety, including the House-passed provisions, given that conference reports are not open to amendment. Members of the House expressed frustration over this recurring dilemma. The House finally acted against the Senate practice by adopting a 1972 rule change permitting separate votes on the nongermane portions of conference reports. The rule was designed to accommodate the Senate's right to offer nongermane amendments while protecting the procedural prerogatives of the House.

Any House member may make a point of order against a conference report when it is called up for final approval on the ground that it contains nongermane material. The member simply says, "Mr. Speaker, I make a point of order under House Rule XXII that the last section of the conference report contains nongermane material." Typically, special rules are obtained from the Rules Committee to protect the conference report against such points of order. Assuming there is no rule, the Speaker sustains the point of order; the representative who raised the objection on the floor then moves to reject the nongermane conference matter. Forty minutes of debate, equally divided between those who support and those who oppose the motion, are permitted under this procedure, after which the House votes on the motion to reject. If it is adopted, the nongermane material is deleted, and the question before the House is disposition of the remaining conference material minus the nongermane portion. Defeat of the motion permits the House to keep the nongermane matter in the conference report.

Filing the Conference Report

When a majority of the conferees from each chamber have reached agreement, they instruct committee staff aides to prepare a report explaining their conference decisions (see Figure 8-1 for an example of a conference report). In addition, conference reports must be accompanied by a joint explanatory

106TH CONGRESS 2d Session	HOUSE OF REPRESENTATIVES	REPORT 106-577

CONCURRENT RESOLUTION ON THE BUDGET FOR FISCAL YEAR 2001

APRIL 12, 2000.—Ordered to be printed

Mr. KASICH, from the committee of conference, submitted the following

CONFERENCE REPORT

[To accompany H. Con. Res. 290]

The committee of conference on the disagreeing votes of the two Houses on the amendment of the Senate to the concurrent resolution (H. Con. Res. 290), establishing the congressional budget for the United States Government for fiscal year 2001, revising the congressional budget for the United States Government for fiscal year 2000, and setting forth appropriate budgetary levels for each of fiscal years 2002 through 2005, having met, after full and free conference, have agreed to recommend and do recommend to their respective Houses as follows:

That the House recede from its disagreement to the amendment of the Senate and agree to the same with an amendment as follows:

In lieu of the matter proposed to be inserted by the Senate amendment, insert the following:

SECTION 1. CONCURRENT RESOLUTION ON THE BUDGET FOR FISCAL YEAR 2001.

(a) DECLARATION.—Congress declares that the concurrent resolution on the budget for fiscal year 2000 is hereby revised and replaced and that this is the concurrent resolution on the budget for fiscal year 2001 and that the appropriate budgetary levels for fiscal years 2002 through 2005 are hereby set forth.

(b) TABLE OF CONTENTS.—

Sec. 1. Concurrent resolution on the budget for fiscal year 2001.

TITLE I—LEVELS AND AMOUNTS

Sec. 101. Recommended levels and amounts.
Sec. 102. Major functional categories.
Sec. 103. Reconciliation in the House of Representatives.
Sec. 104. Reconciliation of revenue reductions in the Senate.

63–745

FIGURE 8-1 Conference Report

statement. This statement is prepared by the conferees (and appropriate staff) of both houses so that the explanation of what was decided upon will not be different in the two houses and thus subject to differing interpretations.

A majority of the conferees from each house—sometimes they are only from the majority party—must sign the report for it to be sent back to the House and Senate. When conferences end, the conferees sometimes scatter quickly, forcing staff members clutching official signature pages to track down managers for both Houses in their offices or in elevators, hallways, or restaurants. The parliamentarians will not accept photocopied signatures or other facsimiles.[44] After the necessary signatures are obtained, the conference committee has concluded its work. (Unlike reports of standing committees of each chamber, conference reports are prohibited by precedent from containing minority or additional viewpoints.)

Conference reports must be published in the *Congressional Record* before they are brought before the House or Senate for final action. House rules require a three-day layover for conference reports, which must be available to all members for reading at least two hours prior to floor consideration. Senate rules state that conference reports must be available on each senator's desk before they can be taken up on the floor. In each chamber, these rules can be set aside, usually by a rule from the House Rules Committee and by unanimous consent in the Senate.

Final Floor Action on Conference Reports

Once the conference report is agreed to and filed with the House and Senate, it must be acted upon by both chambers before it is cleared for the president. Customarily, the chamber that requests a conference acts last on the conference report, but only if the papers are in its possession. The papers are the official documents, such as the bill as originally passed by one chamber and the amendments added to it by the other chamber. Normally, the papers are held by the chamber that agreed to go to conference; that house then would be the first to consider the conference report. However, the papers may be transferred to the other chamber by agreement of the conference committee or one house may simply walk out with them.

Policy outcomes sometimes are influenced by which chamber acts first or last on the conference report. For example, the chairman of the committee that reported legislation creating the Department of Education got the House in 1979 to ask for a conference with the Senate. He wanted the House to act last on the conference report so that the parliamentary options available to the bill's opponents—who were more numerous in the House—would be limited.

The first chamber to act on a conference report has three options: adopt, reject, or recommit (return it to the conferees for further deliberation). When the first chamber to act adopts the conference report, however, this automatically dissolves the conference committee, and the other chamber is faced with a "yes" or "no" vote on the report. The chairman's strategy worked in the case of the Department of Education bill. After intense lobbying by the White House and various education groups, the House agreed to the conference report establishing the new department.

Sometimes motions are made in the first-acting chamber to recommit the conference report with instructions to the conferees that they take a specific action, such as adding or deleting matter. Sen. Phil Gramm, R-Texas, for example, offered a motion to recommit an agricultural conference report to the House-Senate conference committee with instructions that it reconsider the issue of food stamps for new immigrants. The Senate rejected Gramm's motion.[45] (The motion to instruct is a flexible procedure that can be made before, during, or after the conference. For an example of how a major program was terminated via the motion to instruct, see Box 8-3.)

Conference reports are privileged and may be brought up at almost any time the House and Senate are in session, subject to each chamber's requirement for the availability of conference reports, and typically with the prior approval of the leadership. The senior majority and minority conferees from each house's delegation normally act as the floor managers of the conference version. Both chambers require conference reports to be accepted or rejected in their entirety; they are not open to amendment.

In the Senate, conference reports are usually brought up by unanimous consent at a time agreed to by the party leaders and floor managers (see Box 8-4). Because conference reports are privileged, if any senator objects to the unanimous consent request the majority leader can offer a nondebatable motion to take up the conference report: "Mr. President, I move to proceed to the conference report to accompany S. 1234." The conference report itself, however, can be filibustered. (Commonly, conference reports are debated under a time-limitation agreement.) Furthermore, before the vote occurs on the leader's motion to proceed, any senator can request that the entire conference report be read. The reading of reports is typically waived but any senator has the right to force that it be done. Sen. Jesse Helms, R-N.C., for instance, required the clerk to read a 231-page conference report on an education measure because he was unhappy that conferees had removed a school prayer provision. "For more than five hours," noted one report, "clerks took turns reading the dreary rhetoric."[46]

In the House, there are three main routes to the floor for conference reports, which because of their privileged character can be called up at almost any time. Most conference reports are considered under the one-hour rule, with the time divided equally between the majority and minority floor managers. In 1985 the House changed its rules to permit one-third of the time to be assigned to a member who opposes the conference report if both the GOP and Democratic floor managers support it. Suspension of the rules is sometimes used to bring conference reports to the floor, but this is not a preferred procedure because it involves a severe requirement: a two-thirds instead of majority vote for adoption. Finally, a rule can be obtained from the Rules Committee (see Box 8-5). Conference managers often do this when they want to seek a waiver of the three-day layover requirement (either to meet deadlines or exploit favorable political circumstances) or to prevent points of order against the conference report for violations of scope or germaneness.

Conference reports are seldom rejected. As one congressional attorney explained:

BOX 8-3   Picking Procedural Locks

In their final bid to kill the superconducting super collider, Reps. Jim Slattery, D-Kan., and Sherwood Boehlert, R-N.Y., in 1993 had a mammoth task: to convince lawmakers that a complex parliamentary maneuver amounted to a vote to kill the $11 billion Texas-based atom smasher.

When the House first voted to end the big science project, the question was simple: "Do you want to kill the super collider?" The House responded with a resounding "yes," voting 280-150 to terminate the project. But after the Senate voted to restore the project and a House-Senate conference committee agreed, Slattery and Boehlert were shut out from getting another stand-alone vote on the issue.

Their only option was to try to ship the final spending bill back to negotiators with instructions to strip out the project. Lawmakers thus were presented with a more complicated question: "Do you want to vote 'nay' to the previous question on a motion to recommit the entire conference report, and then vote 'yea' on the next vote to amend the motion with instructions to kill the super collider?"

Before members vote on a final adoption of a conference report, House rules allow the minority to offer one motion—and only one motion—to recommit the conference report to committee for further deliberation. However, Slattery and Boehlert were not allowed to offer that motion. House rules and customs gave the nod to John T. Myers, R-Ind., the ranking minority leader of the subcommittee that wrote the bill and a supporter of the super collider. Myers's motion to recommit had no instructions, and had it prevailed, the final version of the energy and water spending bill would have immediately bounced back to the House with super collider funding intact.

The only way for Slattery and Boehlert to pick the procedural lock was to call for the previous question—a step that asks the House to shut off debate on the motion and to send the conference report back to committee. In this case, Slattery and Boehlert wanted House members to vote "nay" so they could alter Myers's motion. To walk lawmakers through this maze, Slattery and Boehlert handed out pink slips naming those who voted against the super collider and urged them to vote "no" on the previous question. The previous question subsequently was defeated, 159-264. Slattery then was able to amend Myers's motion to instruct conference negotiators to remove super collider funding from the bill. The House then voted on the motion to recommit as amended by Slattery to kill the super collider. Super collider opponents pulled out green leaflets that told the same lawmakers to vote "yea." They prevailed again, by a vote of 282-143.

SOURCE: Adapted from Mike Mills, "Picking Procedural Locks," *Congressional Quarterly Weekly Report,* October 23, 1993, 2867.

[The] chief reason conference reports pass is the basic rule that such reports must be adopted or rejected as a whole. No matter how distasteful any particular provision is, or how desirable some amendment would be, generally there is no way to amend a conference report; it can only be accepted or rejected as a whole. Thus, the question for Members is not how they feel about any particular provision, but how they feel about the bill as a whole, and they can always justify a vote for a conference report on the ground that they accepted the distasteful parts only to save the good ones.[47]

Outright rejection of a conference report kills the bill and may require a repetition of the entire legislative process. This becomes particularly significant in the weeks immediately before the final adjournment of a Congress, when members face the choice of accepting the bill as is; recommitting it to a conference committee, in all probability jeopardizing final approval; or killing the bill, knowing no time is left to move a revised bill through Congress.

Once both houses approve the conference report, the papers are delivered to the house that originated the measure. A copy of the bill as finally agreed to by Congress is prepared by an enrolling clerk. The enrolled bill is signed by the Speaker and presiding officer of the Senate, or by other authorized officers, and sent to the president. In a first-time-ever enrollment ceremony, Speaker Hastert and Senate President Pro Tempore Strom Thurmond, R-S.C., electronically signed a year 2000 (Y2K) liability bill and sent it via e-mail to the president. "For the first time in history Congress is sending an electronically signed bill to the president," declared Senate Majority Leader

---

Box 8-4   **Calling Up A Conference Report: Unanimous Consent Agreement**

UNANIMOUS CONSENT AGREEMENT—
CONFERENCE REPORT TO ACCOMPANY H.R. 2559

MR. ROBERTS. Mr. President, I ask unanimous consent that following the allotted times for morning business, the Senate then proceed to the conference report to accompany H.R. 2559, the crop insurance bill, and it be considered as having been read, and under the following time restraints: 1 hour under the control of Senator LUGAR; 1 hour under the control of Senator HARKIN; and 1 hour under the control of Senator WELLSTONE.

I further ask unanimous consent that following the use or yielding back of time, the Senate proceed to vote on the conference report, without any intervening action or debate.

THE PRESIDING OFFICER. Is there objection?

Without objection, it is so ordered.

Source: *Congressional Record*, May 25, 2000, S4412–S4413.

Box 8-5   Calling Up A Conference Report: House Rule

CONFERENCE REPORT ON H.R. 2559,
AGRICULTURAL RISK PROTECTION ACT OF 2000

MR. REYNOLDS. Mr. Speaker, by direction of the Committee on Rules, I call up House Resolution 512 and ask for its immediate consideration.

The Clerk read the resolution, as follows:
H. RES. 512
Resolved, That upon adoption of this resolution it shall be in order to consider the conference report to accompany the bill (H.R. 2559) to amend the Federal Crop Insurance Act to strengthen the safety net for agricultural producers by providing greater access to more affordable risk management tools and improved protection from production and income loss, to improve the efficiency and integrity of the Federal crop insurance program, and for other purposes. All points of order against the conference report and against its consideration are waived. The conference report shall be considered as read.

SOURCE: *Congressional Record,* May 25, 2000, H3816.

Lott.[48] Congress also transmitted a signed paper version of the measure to the White House.

Although most enrolled bills are sent quickly to the White House, sometimes there are delays of a few days or weeks in getting them there. A measure's length and complexity might slow its processing by the enrolling clerks or the delay might be intentional. For example, to eliminate a bill as a campaign issue and to free the president from electoral pressures, its transmittal can be timed so the chief executive has until after election day to decide whether to sign or veto (or pocket veto, if Congress has adjourned) the measure.[49]

PRESIDENTIAL APPROVAL OR VETO

Under the Constitution (Article I, Section 7), the president has a qualified veto power. The president's options are four. First, the president can sign measures into law. Second, the president can disapprove of legislative acts, subject to the ability of Congress during its two-year life to override the vetoes by a two-thirds vote of the members present and voting in each house. Once an enrolled bill is sent to the White House, the president has ten days, excluding Sundays, to sign or veto it. Third, if no action is taken within the ten-day period and Congress is in session, the bill automatically becomes law without the president's signature. Fourth, if the final adjournment (called *sine die*) of a Congress takes place before the ten-day period ends preventing the return of a bill and the president does not sign the measure, the legislation dies as a "pocket veto." Unlike a regular veto, Congress has no opportunity to override a pocket veto. Periodically, controversies erupt between Congress and the White House when presidents try to pocket veto measures when Congress is in recess.

Woodrow Wilson wrote that the president, in using the veto power, "acts not as the executive but as a third branch of the legislature." [50] The president can use the veto, or the threat of a veto, to advance legislative and political goals. Often, the threat of a veto is itself enough to persuade Congress to change its legislative course, because attracting the two-thirds vote required in each house to override presidential vetoes is difficult. Periodically, the administration will submit Statements of Administration Policy to Congress highlighting, for instance, the president's problems with certain legislation. One senator vividly described the president's power when he told the Senate why a conference committee agreed to a specific compromise: "There is another fundamental reason we did it—that is because we faced the veto, that great, big monster of a veto." [51]

Presidents use their veto power because they consider a measure to be unconstitutional, believe it encroaches on the chief executive's powers and duties, or hold that it represents ill-advised policies. When President Richard M. Nixon vetoed the 1973 War Powers Resolution (which Congress subsequently enacted by overriding his veto), he cited all three factors as the basis of his action. Vetoing bills because they cost too much is another favorite rationale of presidents.

The president receives recommendations from many quarters during the ten-day period allowed under the Constitution to decide whether to sign or veto legislation. He receives advice from the Office of Management and Budget (OMB), appropriate cabinet officers, White House aides, members of Congress, and scores of groups and officials. The OMB, for instance, once prepared a "menu" that contained an "A list" and a "B list." On the A list were provisions that merited a veto; on the B list were items that in some combination could trigger a veto. [52]

Presidents contemplate how vetoes can be employed to advance their electoral and policy agenda, especially when their party does not control Congress. As national elections approach, for example, presidents will use the veto against an opposition Congress to show how their policies differ from the other party's and thus highlight their fundamental beliefs to the electorate. Conversely, an opposition Congress will send measures to the White House that it expects the president to veto. "We are writing bills that Republicans will vote for, not necessarily what the [Democratic] president will sign," said a House GOP leadership aide. [53] This strategy can be called the politics of differentiation or contrast politics. Presidents Richard Nixon and Ronald Reagan vetoed bills on national television as a way to muster public support for their policies and to prevent an override by Congress. Meanwhile, presidents can be foiled by adroit congressional maneuvering.

PUBLIC LAW 106-177—MAR. 10, 2000   114 STAT. 35

Public Law 106–177
106th Congress

An Act

To reduce the incidence of child abuse and neglect, and for other purposes.

Mar. 10, 2000
[H.R. 764]

Be it enacted by the Senate and House of Representatives of the United States of America in Congress assembled,

TITLE I—THE CHILD ABUSE PREVENTION AND ENFORCEMENT ACT

Child Abuse
Prevention and
Enforcement Act.
Inter-
governmental
relations.
42 USC 3711
note.

SEC. 101. SHORT TITLE.

This title may be cited as the "Child Abuse Prevention and Enforcement Act".

SEC. 102. GRANT PROGRAM.

Section 102(b) of the Crime Identification Technology Act of 1998 (42 U.S.C. 14601(b)) is amended by striking "and" at the end of paragraph (15), by striking the period at the end of paragraph (16) and inserting "; and", and by adding after paragraph (16) the following:

"(17) the capability of the criminal justice system to deliver timely, accurate, and complete criminal history record information to child welfare agencies, organizations, and programs that are engaged in the assessment of risk and other activities related to the protection of children, including protection against child sexual abuse, and placement of children in foster care.".

SEC. 103. USE OF FUNDS UNDER BYRNE GRANT PROGRAM FOR CHILD PROTECTION.

Section 501(b) of title I of the Omnibus Crime Control and Safe Streets Act of 1968 (42 U.S.C. 3751) is amended—

(1) by striking "and" at the end of paragraph (25);
(2) by striking the period at the end of paragraph (26) and inserting a semicolon; and
(3) by adding at the end the following:

"(27) enforcing child abuse and neglect laws, including laws protecting against child sexual abuse, and promoting programs designed to prevent child abuse and neglect; and

"(28) establishing or supporting cooperative programs between law enforcement and media organizations, to collect, record, retain, and disseminate information useful in the identification and apprehension of suspected criminal offenders."

FIGURE 8-2 Public Law

Congress can attempt to force the president to approve unwanted measures by attaching them as riders to legislation the president regards as essential. Or the House or Senate might proceed slowly on measures of importance to the administration and on which it wants fast action until the president signs bills favored by the legislative branch.

When the president vetoes a measure, the Constitution provides that "he shall return it with his Objections to that House in which it shall have originated" and that chamber shall "proceed to reconsider it." This means that some action must be taken, but not necessarily a veto override vote. Neither chamber is under any obligation to schedule an override attempt. Party leaders may realize they have no chance to override and may not even attempt it. Because of popular support for the president's action, or for other reasons, the political environment may not be conducive to a successful override. Thus, a motion will be made to refer the message to committee rather than risk a loss on override.

If an override attempt fails in one chamber, the process ends and the bill dies. If it succeeds, the measure is sent to the other chamber, where a second successful override vote makes it law. The Constitution requires roll-call votes on override attempts.

Whether signed by the president, allowed to become law without his signature, or passed over a veto, the bill becomes a public law and is sent to the National Archives and Records Administration for deposit and publication in *Statutes at Large,* an annual volume that compiles all bills that have become law. (Figure 8-2 shows an example of a public law.)

NOTES

1. Ada G. McCown, *The Congressional Conference Committee* (New York: Columbia University Press, 1927), 12. See also Gilbert Steiner, *The Congressional Conference Committee, Seventieth to Eightieth Congresses* (Urbana, Ill.: University of Illinois Press, 1951); David J. Vogler, *The Third House: Conference Committees in the United States Congress* (Evanston, Ill.: Northwestern University Press, 1971); and Lawrence Longley and Walter J. Oleszek, *Bicameral Politics: Conference Committees in Congress* (New Haven, Conn.: Yale University Press, 1989).
2. Information compiled by Ilona Nickels, congressional specialist, Government Division, Congressional Research Service, Library of Congress.
3. *Congressional Record,* July 8, 1998, S7650.
4. Roy Swanstrom, *The United States Senate, 1787–1801,* 99th Cong., 1st sess., S. Doc. 99-19, 232.
5. *Congressional Record,* September 13, 1999, H8129.
6. *Congressional Record,* February 20, 1986, S1463.
7. *CQ Daily Monitor,* March 20, 2000, 3.
8. *Congressional Handbook,* U.S. Senate edition, 1994. Prepared by the Senate Committee on Rules and Administration. (Washington, D.C.: U.S. Government Printing Office, 1994), III-30.
9. *Congressional Record,* March 21, 1974, 7589. See also *Congressional Record,* April 10, 1974, 10569.
10. *Congressional Record,* December 20, 1982, S15757.
11. *National Journal,* May 22, 1976, 694.
12. Richard F. Fenno Jr., *The Power of the Purse* (Boston: Little, Brown, 1966), 610.
13. *Congressional Record,* May 17, 1984, S5969.

14. John Ferejohn, "Who Wins in Conference Committee?" *Journal of Politics* (November 1975): 1033–1046; and Walter J. Oleszek, "House-Senate Relationships: Comity and Conflict," *The Annals* (January 1974): 80–81.

15. Elizabeth Drew, *Senator* (New York: Simon & Schuster, 1979), 174.

16. *National Journal's CongressDaily/PM*, March 24, 1995, 4.

17. Andrew Taylor, "House's Magnum Opus Now Subject to Senate's Tender Mercies," *Congressional Quarterly Weekly Report*, April 1, 1995, 914.

18. *Enactment of a Law*, 97th Cong., 2d sess., S. Doc. 97-20, 24.

19. Ceci Connolly, "Legislation Goes Overboard as Legislators Eye the Exits," *Congressional Quarterly Weekly Report*, October 1, 1994, 2755.

20. Helen Dewar and Kathleen Day, "Senate Approves Bankruptcy Bill," *Washington Post*, February 3, 2000, A1.

21. *CQ Daily Monitor*, March 28, 2000, 5.

22. *Congressional Record*, July 18, 1985, H5937.

23. *Washington Times*, February 14, 1995, A11.

24. Mary Agnes Carey, "Hastert's Choice of Conferees Diminishes Prospects for Survival of House's Managed Care Bill," *Congressional Quarterly Weekly Report*, November 6, 1999, 2657.

25. William Welch, "Hastert Packs Panel with Opponents of HMO Bill," *USA Today*, November 4, 1999, 12A.

26. *National Journal's CongressDaily/AM*, November 5, 1999, 10.

27. Robert Alan Henning, "Between the Margins: Party Politics and Committee Power in Conference Committees of the U.S. House of Representatives," Ph.D. dissertation, University of California, Berkeley, 1997, 131.

28. *Congressional Record*, July 29, 1981, S8711.

29. *Congressional Record*, August 3, 1989, H5003.

30. *Congressional Record*, June 23, 1983, H4435.

31. *CQ's Daily Monitor*, August 8, 1994, 3.

32. *Congressional Record*, May 16, 2000, S3991.

33. Robert Pear, "Negotiators Stall on Patients' Rights Bill," *New York Times*, May 26, 2000, A15.

34. *National Journal's CongressDaily/PM*, April 17, 1998, 1.

35. *New York Times*, July 23, 1981, A19. See also Michael J. Malbin, *Unelected Representatives: Congressional Staff and the Future of Representative Government* (New York: Basic Books, 1980), chapter 5.

36. Ted Siff and Alan Weil, *Ruling Congress* (New York: Grossman, 1975), 184.

37. Laurie Kellman, "Senators Lament Cutting Anti-Terror Bill Features," *Washington Times*, April 17, 1996, A6.

38. *Congressional Record*, August 1, 1984, S9605.

39. *CQ's Congressional Insight*, October 19, 1990, 1.

40. Quoted in Charles L. Clapp, *The Congressman* (Washington, D.C.: Brookings Institution, 1962), 249.

41. *Congressional Record*, October 3, 1996, S12231.

42. Marc Lacey, "Senate Panel Opts to Split Bill on Immigration," *Los Angeles Times*, March 15, 1996, A8.

43. *Congressional Record*, November 1, 1999, S13597–S13598.

44. Martin Gold, Michael Hugo, Hyde Murray, Peter Robinson, and A. L. "Pete" Singleton, *The Book on Congress* (Washington, D.C.: Big Eagle Publishing Co., 1992), 343.

45. *Congressional Record,* May 12, 1998, S4665.

46. *Washington Post,* March 24, 1994, A18.

47. Charles Tiefer, *Congressional Practice and Procedure* (New York: Greenwood Press, 1989), 818.

48. Matthew Rarey, "Congress Breaks Into Cyberspace with Electronically Signed Bill," *Washington Times,* July 16, 1999, A3.

49. See, for example, John H. Cushman Jr., "Congress Lets President Delay His Tax Bill Veto," *New York Times,* October 23, 1992, A14.

50. Woodrow Wilson, *Congressional Government* (Boston: Houghton Mifflin, 1885), 52. Wilson wrote (p. 260) that the "president is no greater than his prerogative of veto makes him; he is, in other words, powerful rather as a branch of the legislature than as the titular head of the Executive."

51. *Congressional Record,* December 20, 1982, S15678.

52. *Washington Post,* October 15, 1986, A7.

53. Sam Dealey, "Veto Politics Stalls Congress: GOP Goes It Alone," *The Hill,* October 27, 1999, 1.

CHAPTER 9

Legislative Oversight

WHEN HARDWORKING Americans send their tax dollars to Washington . . . they expect their money to be spent wisely," stated House Speaker J. Dennis Hastert, R-Ill.[1] On the other side of the Capitol, Senate Majority Leader Trent Lott, R-Miss., declared: "I frankly think we haven't done enough in the area of investigations and oversight. I think Congress should spend more time in that area and less time churning out laws."[2] Lott added that fully a third of the Senate's time should be spent on oversight and investigations. The perspectives of the GOP leaders correspond to the general Republican view that government is too big in certain areas (the domestic social sector, for instance) and oversight is one way to shrink its role and reach. Many Democrats, by contrast, place more emphasis on making government work better and smarter than in reducing its size or scope.

Congressional oversight is the continuing review by the House and Senate, especially through its committee structure, of how effectively the executive branch is carrying out congressional mandates. Many laws passed by Congress are often general guidelines and sometimes their wording is deliberately vague or convoluted. The implementation of these laws commonly involves the drafting of administrative regulations by the executive agencies and day-to-day program management by agency officials. A key goal of legislative oversight is to hold executive officials accountable for their implementation of delegated authority. As one senator put it:

> I believe that oversight is one of the Congress's most important constitutional responsibilities. We must do more than write laws and decide policies. It is also our responsibility to perform the oversight necessary to insure that the administration enforces those laws as Congress intended.[3]

Congressional oversight looms large as a legislative activity during this era of reinventing, deinventing, reengineering, or rethinking the federal government's roles, because many Republicans and Democrats are trying to sort out which responsibilities are appropriate to the national government instead of to the states and localities or to the private sector. The Tenth Amendment to the Constitution ("The powers not delegated to the United States by the Constitution, nor prohibited by it to the states, are reserved to the states respectively, or to the people.") is being used by lawmakers to shift power back to the states. With respect to the private sector, Congress in 1998 passed the Federal Activities Inventory Reform Act, which requires agencies to inventory each federal job and determine whether it is inherently governmental or commercial and thus subject to being contracted out to the private sector.[4]

Congress employs oversight both to take stock of national governmental responsibilities and to ensure, as the Constitution states, that "the laws are faithfully executed" by federal administrators.

Constitutionally, oversight has been part of the principal functions of the legislative branch from the nation's beginning. Congress's power of the purse, its authority to pass laws that create programs and agencies, its power of impeachment and confirmation, and its right to investigate executive branch activities are among the explicit and implicit oversight functions rooted in the Constitution. The framers, according to historian Arthur M. Schlesinger Jr., believed the review function did not require specific mention in the Constitution. "[I]t was not considered necessary to make an explicit grant of such authority," wrote Schlesinger. "The power to make laws implied the power to see whether they were faithfully executed."[5] Or as Woodrow Wilson put it: "Quite as important as lawmaking is vigilant oversight of administration."[6]

Congress formalized its legislative oversight function in the Legislative Reorganization Act of 1946. That act required congressional committees to exercise "continuous watchfulness" of the agencies under their jurisdictions and implicitly divided oversight functions into three areas:

1. Authorizing committees (such as Agriculture, Banking, and Commerce) were required to review federal programs and agencies under their jurisdictions and to propose legislation to remedy deficiencies they uncovered.
2. Fiscal oversight was assigned to the Appropriations committees of each chamber, which were to scrutinize agency spending.
3. Wide-ranging investigative responsibility was assigned to the House Government Reform Committee and the Senate Governmental Affairs Committee to probe for inefficiency, waste, and corruption in the federal government. To some degree, all committees perform each type of oversight.

Each of the three overlapping types of oversight—legislative, fiscal, and investigative—aims to fulfill the basic goals or purposes of oversight, such as clarifying statutory intent; evaluating program administration and performance; eliminating waste, fraud, abuse, and red tape; reviewing whether programs have outlived their usefulness; ensuring that programs and agencies are administered in a cost-effective and economical manner; and correcting executive abuses of authority.

Congress has also enacted a number of other laws that indirectly strengthen its oversight capacities. These laws establish mechanisms, procedures, or entities within the executive branch that provide Congress with oversight-related information and assessments of administrative activities. They include statutes that address, for instance, paperwork reduction, the preparation of regular financial statements by individual departments and agencies, and the purchase of the most cost-effective information technology.

The Government Performance and Results Act of 1993 (GPRA or the Results Act) aims to promote more cost-effective federal spending by requiring agencies to set strategic goals (for instance, a statement of their basic missions and the resources required to achieve those objectives) and to prepare annual performance plans and annual performance reports, which are submitted to Congress and the president. A fundamental purpose of GPRA is to hold agencies accountable for the implementation of their performance goals. It will assist Congress in determining which programs are effective and which are ineffective by providing credible information on agency performance or nonperformance. GPRA may also help to reduce unnecessary duplication and overlap among federal agencies that implement similar policy areas. As House Majority Leader Dick Armey, R-Texas, noted as he held up a pizza box: "If this were a cheese pizza, it would be inspected by the [Food and Drug Administration]. If it were a pepperoni pizza, it would be inspected by the [U.S. Department of Agriculture]. . . . We definitely have a great deal of duplication here."[7]

How well the law will work in practice is still unclear, in part because the two parties view GPRA differently. "The Democrats see the Results Act as a way to deliver the same level of service, but do it better and more efficiently. They are not in this to cut a lot of programs out," said a GOP chairman of the House Government Reform Committee. "By contrast, Republican leaders see this as a way to justify devolution of functions to the states and thus eliminate a lot of things at the federal level."[8]

The Congressional Review Act of 1996 enables Congress to review and disapprove major agency rules and regulations. The act provided for expedited procedures if a lawmaker introduced a joint resolution of disapproval. Under the act, Congress has sixty legislative days to exercise a regulatory veto power; otherwise, the rules will go into effect. However, the law has been little used by Congress to block agency rules. For instance, Sen. Craig Thomas, R-Wyo., noted that between 1996 and 1999, "12,269 non-major rules and 186 major rules [those with a $100 million or more annual impact] were submitted to Congress by federal agencies. Only seven joint resolutions of disapproval were introduced, pertaining to five rules. None passed either House. In fact, none have even been debated on the floor of either House."[9] Various structural and interpretive flaws, such as "whether a disapproval resolution may be directed at part of a rule," account for its limited use.[10] Members also acknowledge that the law contains a fatal flaw: The president can veto the joint resolution of disapproval, which Congress is unlikely to override. However, the law does provide Congress with an information database on agency rulemaking.

Formalizing Oversight

The House and Senate have always had authority to investigate programs and agencies of the executive branch. The first congressional investigation in American history, in 1792, delved into the conduct of the government in the wars against the Indians. One of the broadest investigations was an 1861 inquiry into the conduct of the Civil War. Other notable probes have included investigations into the Crédit Mobilier in 1872–1873, the Money Trust in 1912, the Teapot Dome scandal in 1923, stock exchange operations in 1932–1934, and defense spending during World War II. A House and Senate select committee jointly investigated during the mid-1980s, with nationally televised hearings, the Iran-contra affair, which involved covert and deceptive operations by the National Security Council and others. Recently, House and Senate panels have conducted inquiries into the deficiencies and excesses of the Internal Revenue Service (IRS).

The 1946 reorganization act stated Congress's intention to exercise its investigative authority primarily through standing committees rather than by means of specially created investigating committees. (In 1995 the House amended its rules to grant explicit authority to the Speaker to appoint "special ad hoc oversight committees for the purpose of reviewing specific matters within the jurisdiction of two or more standing committees.") The 1946 act provided for continuous review of programs instead of sporadic hearings whenever errors, malfeasance, or injustices surfaced. The continuous watchfulness precept of the act implied that Congress henceforth would participate actively in administrative decision making, in line with the observation that "administration of a statute is, properly speaking, an extension of the legislative process." [11]

During the 1970s, both houses amended their rules to grant additional oversight authority to the standing committees. The Legislative Reorganization Act of 1970 rephrased in more explicit language the oversight duties of the committees and required most House and Senate panels to issue biennial reports on their oversight activities. The House Committee Reform Amendments of 1974 assigned special oversight responsibilities to several standing committees; the Senate adopted the same approach, called comprehensive policy oversight, when it adopted the Committee System Reorganization Amendments of 1977. Both special oversight and comprehensive policy oversight are akin to the broad review authority granted the House Government Reform Committee and the Senate Governmental Affairs Committee.

Explained Sen. Adlai E. Stevenson III, D-Ill. (1970–1981), floor manager during Senate debate on the 1977 change:

> Standing committees are directed and permitted to undertake investigations and make recommendations in broad policy areas—for example, nutrition, aging, environmental protection, or consumer affairs—even though they lack legislative jurisdiction over some aspects of the subject. Such oversight authority involves subjects that generally cut across the jurisdictions of several committees. Presently, no single committee has a comprehensive overview of these policy areas. [This rule change] corrects that. It assigns certain committees the right to undertake comprehensive review of broad policy issues. [12]

Rules Governing Oversight

Other notable changes were made in House and Senate rules regarding oversight:

- The House directed its committees to create oversight subcommittees, undertake future research and forecasting, and review the impact of tax expenditures (credits, incentives, and the like) on matters that fall within their respective jurisdictions.[13]

- The Senate required each standing committee to include regulatory impact statements in committee reports accompanying the legislation it sends to the floor. One of these statements, for instance, might evaluate the amount of additional paperwork that would result from enactment of a proposed bill.
- Passage of the 1974 Congressional Budget and Impoundment Control Act strengthened Congress's review capabilities by directing the General Accounting Office (GAO)—a legislative support agency of Congress—to assist House and Senate committees in program evaluation and in the development of "methods for assessing and reporting actual program performance."

In 1995 the House adopted a new rule requiring all standing committees to prepare by February 15 of the first session of each Congress a comprehensive oversight plan. The objective was "to ensure that committees make a more concerted, coordinated and conscientious effort to develop meaningful oversight plans at the beginning of each Congress and to follow through on their implementation, with a view to examining the full range of laws under their jurisdiction over a period of five Congresses."[14] Four years later, in a move designed to encourage more monitoring of administrative performance, the House amended its rules to permit committees to have a sixth subcommittee (under House rules, most standing committees are limited to five subcommittees) if it is an oversight subcommittee.

Congress requires these additional oversight devices because it faces an executive establishment of massive size and diffuse direction. As a scholar wrote: "[W]e should not deceive ourselves into thinking that the Federal Government of the future will be a shrinking violet, retreating to the modest proportions it had in George Washington's or Grover Cleveland's time."[15] Although the call for less government is especially strong today and many elective officials declare that "the era of big government is over," the federal government will continue to exercise a large role in defense, international policy making, law enforcement, national economic management, environmental protection, health, and numerous other areas.

Congress needs a variety of oversight techniques to hold agencies accountable so that if one technique proves to be ineffective, committees and members can employ others singly or in combination.

TECHNIQUES OF OVERSIGHT

The objectives of oversight vary from committee to committee. The focus may be on promoting administrative efficiency and economy in government; protecting and supporting favored policies and programs; airing an administration's failures and wrongdoing or its achievements; publicizing a particular member's or a committee's goals; reasserting congressional authority vis-à-vis the executive branch; or assuaging the interests of pressure groups.

Hearings and Investigations

The traditional method of exercising congressional oversight is through committee hearings and investigations into executive branch operations. Legislators need to know how effectively federal programs are working and how well agency officials are responding to committee directives. And they want to know the scope and intensity of public support for government programs to assess the need for legislative changes.

For more than two hundred years, Congress has conducted investigations of varying types with varying results. There have been abuses and excesses, successes and accomplishments. Although no explicit provision in the Constitution authorizes Congress to conduct investigations, the Supreme Court has decided in several cases that the investigative function is essential to the legislative function. In *Watkins v. United States* (1957), for example, the Court declared that the "power of the Congress to conduct investigations is inherent in the legislative process. That power is broad. It encompasses inquiries concerning the administration of existing laws as well as proposed or possibly needed statutes." The Supreme Court has also made clear that the investigative power is not unlimited, and Congress has no authority, for instance, "to expose for the sake of exposure." Congress, too, has established procedures (for example, the right of witnesses before investigative hearings to be accompanied by their own counsel) to ensure that individuals are treated fairly when they testify before committees.

The success or failure of investigating panels hinges on the skill of their committee leaders, the degree of bipartisan cooperation among members, and good preparatory work by competent staff. Surprise and luck are also factors. As Sen. Daniel K. Inouye, D-Hawaii, the only veteran of both the Watergate and Iran-contra investigating committees, noted:

> I happened to be [at a hearing on Watergate] . . . and the question was asked by one of the Republican staffers [Fred Thompson, minority counsel and now a GOP senator from Tennessee] to one of the lesser witnesses [former Nixon White House aide Alexander P. Butterfield]. Thompson asked, "Mr. Butterfield, are you aware of any listening devices in the Oval Office of the President?" Butterfield responded, "I was aware of listening devices, yes sir."[16]

The rest, said Senator Inouye, was history.

Although excessive use of hearings and investigations can bog down governmental processes, judicious use of such tools helps to maintain a more responsive bureaucracy while supplying Congress with information needed to formulate new legislation and to inform the public.[17] Committee members and committee staffs may conduct oversight hearings around the country (field hearings) to watch public programs in operation and to take testimony from citizens and local officials.

Legislative Veto

In 1932 Congress began to include provisions in statutes that, while delegating authority to the executive branch, reserved to Congress the right to approve or disapprove executive actions based on that authority within a specified time period. This procedure, known as the legislative veto, allows one or both chambers, by majority vote, to veto certain executive branch initiatives, decisions, and regulations. (Sometimes Congress authorizes committees—the committee veto—to approve, or disapprove, executive actions [see Box 9-1].)

The legislative veto was an attractive oversight technique because, even though Congress seldom exercised its veto prerogative to overturn agency decisions, committees and members felt the practice kept federal administrators sensitive and responsive to congressional interests. It was employed in legislation dealing with both domestic and international issues. The legislative veto also served executive branch purposes by permitting agencies to make binding decisions without going through the lengthy lawmaking process.

On June 23, 1983, however, the Supreme Court declared in a historic decision, *Immigration and Naturalization Service v. Chadha,* that the legislative veto was unconstitutional. In a 7-2 vote, the Court majority said the device violated the separation of powers, the principle of bicameralism, and the presentation clause of the Constitution (legislation passed by both chambers must be presented to the president for his signature or veto). The decision, wrote Justice Byron R. White in a dissent, "strikes down in one fell swoop provisions in more laws enacted by Congress than the court has cumulatively invalidated in its entire history."

Despite the *Chadha* ruling, Congress still employs legislative and committee vetoes. As scholar Louis Fisher pointed out:

> In response to the Court's ruling, Congress repealed some legislative vetoes and replaced them with joint resolutions, which satisfy the [Supreme Court's] ruling because joint resolutions must pass both Houses and be presented to the President. However, Congress has also continued to enact legislative vetoes to handle certain situations. From June 23, 1983 to the end of the [105th Congress, more than four hundred legislative vetoes] (generally the committee-veto variety) have been enacted into law.[18]

Congress and the executive branch adapted to the post-*Chadha* era largely through informal accommodations and statutory adjustments. On the one hand, executive agencies want discretion and flexibility in running their programs; on the other hand, Congress is generally unwilling to grant open-ended authority to executive entities. The legislative and committee vetoes remain important review devices, because both branches recognize their value.

Authorizing Process as Oversight

Congress not only has the authority to create or abolish executive agencies and transfer functions between or among them, but it also can enact "statutes authorizing the activities of the departments, prescribing their internal

> **Box 9-1   A Committee Veto**
>
> For the appropriation account "Transportation Administrative Service Center," no assessments may be levied against any program, budget activity, subactivity or project funded by this statute "unless notice of such assessments and the basis therefore are presented to the House and Senate Committees on Appropriations and are approved by such Committees." Department of Transportation and Related Agencies Appropriations Act 1998, 111 Stat. 1426 (1997).
>
> SOURCE: Cited in *Congressional Oversight Manual* (Congressional Research Service, June 25, 1999), 91.

organization and regulating their procedures and work methods." [19] The authorization process is an important oversight tool. As a House member observed during debate on a bill to require annual congressional authorization of the Federal Communications Commission (FCC):

> Our subcommittee hearings disclosed that the FCC needs direction, needs guidance, needs legislation, and needs leadership from us in helping to establish program priorities. Regular oversight through the reauthorization process, as all of us know in Congress, is necessary, and nothing brings everybody's attention to spending more forthrightly than when we go through the reauthorization process.[20]

Significant issues are often raised during the authorization process. In a political environment where reining in government is a popular refrain, lawmakers may ask such questions as: Can an agency be made smaller? If a program or agency did not exist, would it be created today? Should agencies and cabinet departments be merged or consolidated? What fundamental changes need to be made in how various agencies operate? In an era of downsizing, what and whose federal jobs should be cut?

The authorizing process, however, is often not exercised effectively as an oversight tool. Many programs and agencies fail to be reauthorized for years, yet they still continue to operate because appropriators provide funding for them. Congress, for instance, has "failed to reauthorize the Justice Department since 1980." [21] While lawmakers give many reasons for failing to reauthorize federal programs or entities (conflict between the chambers and branches or too little time, for example), the consequence is "increasingly poor congressional oversight over federal programs." [22]

Appropriations Process as Oversight

Congress probably exercises its most effective oversight of agencies and programs through the appropriations process. By cutting off or reducing funds, Congress can abolish agencies or curtail programs. By increasing funds, it can build up neglected program areas. In either case, it has formidable power to shape ongoing public policies. The power is exercised mainly by the House and Senate Appropriations committees, particularly through their powerful subcommittees, whose broad budgetary recommendations are only infrequently changed by the full committee or by the House and Senate.

The Appropriations committees define the precise purpose for which money may be spent, they adjust funding levels, and they often attach provisos prohibiting expenditures for certain purposes. The appropriations process as an oversight technique, notes congressional budget expert Allen Schick, is comparable to a Janus-like weapon: "The stick of spending reductions in case agencies cannot satisfactorily defend their budget requests and past performance, and the carrot of more money if agencies produce convincing success stories or the promise of future results." [23]

In a period of fundamental concern about the size and role of the national government, the appropriations process can be a potent tool for advancing party objectives and requiring federal officials to justify the continued existence of their programs and agencies. Appropriators are well positioned to take the lead in making spending cuts. For example, in a February 2000 report to Speaker Dennis Hastert, House Appropriations Chairman C. W. Bill Young, R-Fla., stated that since the GOP takeover of Congress in 1995, the Appropriations panel "has terminated 285 programs for a savings of $3.6 billion to taxpayers." [24]

Members may also add riders to appropriations measures (or the bills may include spending limitations when reported from committee) that restrict or prohibit agencies from carrying out certain functions. (Riders are policy provisos; limitations are restrictions on spending, but the distinction between the two is sometimes difficult to delineate because prohibitions on spending affect policy.) The GOP-controlled House, for instance, passed legislation in June 2000 that barred the federal Occupational Safety and Health Administration (OSHA) from using federal funds to promulgate new ergonomics regulations designed to prevent repetitive-motion injuries by workers. OSHA "wants to complete its rulemaking before President [Bill] Clinton leaves office, and the [ergonomics provision] would push that decision into 2001, when Republicans hope to control the White House." [25] Supporters argue that the ergonomics "regulations would impose needless, costly burdens on employers who are already seeking to improve workplace safety." [26]

Mindful that the president often has the whip hand when Congress fails to enact its appropriations bills by the start of the fiscal year (October 1), House Republican leaders in 2000 urged their partisan colleagues not to add divisive riders to appropriations measures. "GOP leaders argued that if Republicans hoped to wrap up their work well before the election and deny the Democrats the opportunity to keep them pinned down in Washington, they will have to show some restraint." [27] Nonetheless, several GOP lawmakers continued to offer controversial riders or spending limitations.

Inspectors General

Congress, too, has created statutory offices of inspectors general (IGs) in nearly sixty major federal agencies and departments. IGs are located in every cabinet department and major agency, including the Central Intelligence Agency (CIA). Granted wide latitude and independence by the Inspectors General Act of 1978, as amended in 1988, these officials conduct investigations and audits of their agencies to improve efficiency, end waste and fraud, and discourage mismanagement. IGs keep Congress fully and currently informed about federal activities, problems, and program performance through the issuance of periodic reports. As the IG of the Department of Health and Human Services said about her job: "I believe that a successful IG must . . . be willing to go beyond just the traditional after-the-fact investigations and audits. Instead, the IG should . . . not just detect, but also prevent fraud and abuse." [28]

Lawmakers like the idea of having an independent office of inspector general located within an agency performing a watchdog role for Congress. The House, in the wake of internal bank and Post Office scandals, created its own Office of Inspector General in 1992; the position was filled the next year. One function of the House's IG is to conduct periodic audits of the chamber's financial activities. (The House contracted in 1995 with a major accounting firm—Price Waterhouse—to conduct a comprehensive auditing review of its spending practices.)

Nonstatutory, Informal Controls

Congress has various informal ways to influence federal administrators. Executive officials, conscious of Congress's power over the purse strings, are attuned to the nuances of congressional language in hearings, floor debate, committee reports, and conference reports. For example, in committee reports the verbs *expects, urges, recommends, desires,* and *feels* display in roughly descending order how obligatory a committee comment or viewpoint is intended to be. [29] If federal administrators believe congressional directives to be unwise, they are more likely to ask for informal consultation with members and committee staff than to seek new laws or resolutions. Executive officials are in frequent contact with committee members and staff. Analyzing the House Appropriations Committee's relationship with the federal bureaucracy, one scholar wrote:

> [There] is a continuing and sometimes almost daily pattern of contacts between the Committee on Appropriations and the executive branch. When Congress is not in session, communication continues by telephone or even, on occasion, by visits to the homes of members of the committee. If the full story were ever known, the record probably would disclose a complex network of relationships between members of the Committee on Appropriations and its staff and officials, particularly budget officers, in the executive branch. [30]

Such informal contacts enable committees to exercise policy influence in areas where statutory methods might be inappropriate or ineffective. Informed methods of program review are probably the most prevalent techniques of oversight.

Members sometimes urge their colleagues, administrative agencies, and the courts to exercise caution in interpreting committee reports, floor debate, and other nonstatutory devices as expressions of the intent of Congress. Abner J. Mikva, one of the few public officials to have served in all three national branches of government (he was a House member, federal judge, and President Clinton's White House counsel), recounted a story about the pitfalls of interpreting a bill's legislative history:

> I remember when [Rep. Morris K.] Mo Udall [(D-Ariz., 1961–1991)] was managing the strip-mining bill, and there had been all sorts of problems getting it through. They'd put together a very delicate coalition of support. One problem was whether the states or the feds would run the program. One member got up and asked, "Isn't it a fact that under this bill the states will continue to exercise sovereignty over strip mining?" And Mo replied, "You're absolutely right." A little later someone else got up and asked, "Now is it clear that the Federal Government will have the final say on strip mining?" And Mo replied, "You're absolutely right." Later, in the cloakroom, I said, "Mo, they can't both be right." And Mo said, "You're absolutely right." [31]

Interpreting statutory intent is a hot issue on the Supreme Court because legal phraseology is often ambiguous. Justice Antonin Scalia advocates rejection of conflicting and unvoted-upon committee hearings, reports, or floor debate (congressional history) in clarifying statutory language. Instead, judges should focus on the exact legal language and the statutory text in which it is embedded (the plain meaning principle) rather than picking and choosing among reports (written by unelected staff aides) or floor debate to clarify statutory construction. Justice Stephen G. Breyer, by contrast, recommends use of congressional history in statutory interpretation so judges can better understand the goals and objectives of the legislation signed into law. [32]

General Accounting Office Audits

The General Accounting Office, created by the Budget and Accounting Act of 1921, is known as Congress's watchdog. Among its primary functions is to conduct audits and investigations of executive agencies and programs at the request of committees and members of Congress to make sure that public funds are properly spent. In addition, it conducts field investigations of administrative activities, prescribes accounting standards for the executive branch, prepares policy analyses, and provides legal opinions with respect to government actions and activities. With a staff of about thirty-three hundred, GAO submits hundreds of reports to Congress annually on ways to root out waste and fraud in government programs and to promote program performance. For example, a 2000 GAO report identified sixty-one federal programs that "could be eliminated or greatly scaled back to save billions of dollars annually." [33] GAO studies frequently lead to the introduction of legislation, congressional hearings, or cost-saving administrative changes. The head of the GAO, the comptroller general, is appointed for a single fifteen-year term by the president, subject to the advice and consent of the Senate. The GAO works only for Congress.

Reporting Requirements

Numerous laws require executive agencies to submit periodic reports to Congress and its committees. As one scholar explained:

> Reporting requirements are provisions in law requiring the executive branch to submit specified information to Congress or committees of Congress. Their basic purpose is to provide data and analysis Congress needs to oversee the implementation of legislation and foreign policy by the executive branch.[34]

Some reports are of minimal value because they are couched in broad language that reveals little about program implementation; others may be more specific. Some reports address large policy issues; others, the narrow interests of a small number of lawmakers. (One way to resolve problems in the legislative process, such as mobilizing support from lawmakers who are uncertain about the worth of a program or activity, is to ask an agency for a report.) Generally, however, the report requirement encourages self-evaluation by the executive branch and promotes agency accountability to Congress. For example, when Congress became exasperated with Pentagon delays in implementing a major reorganization of defense offices, it directed the secretary of the army "to report every 30 days to Congress on what he [was] doing to put the legislation into place." [35]

Periodically, Congress and the executive branch recommend the elimination of certain reports (more than four thousand reports currently are submitted to Congress). Sometimes the impulse to eliminate reports reflects legislative and executive concern about micromanagement of executive affairs by legislative committees. The ever-present tension (even distrust) that suffuses legislative-executive relations explains to a large degree why Congress gets involved in managerial details and demands reports from federal entities. "We wrote an extraordinary amount of detail into the Clean Air Act," said one House member, "because we didn't trust the Environmental Protection Agency . . . with too much discretion." [36] The concern about reporting requirements involves seeking an appropriate weighing of Congress's need for information to conduct evaluations of agencies and programs against the imposition of burdensome, costly, or irrelevant obligations on executive entities.

Ad Hoc Groups

Numerous informal groups and caucuses of Senate and House members focus on specific issues and programs and monitor executive branch activities. For example, the Congressional Automotive Caucus works with appropriate government agencies to resolve issues associated with the automobile industry.

Outside organizations also provide Congress with information on inadequacies in federal programs and other problems with the bureaucracy and exert pressure for more ambitious oversight. For instance, a private group called Citizens Against Government Waste annually identifies federal projects that, in their judgment, are a waste of taxpayers' dollars.[37] Many of these groups employ computers "to assist them in research on such subjects as the performance of Governmental agencies."[38] Think tanks such as the Brookings Institution and the Heritage Foundation periodically study public policy issues and advise members of Congress and others on how well federal agencies and programs are working. A joint project of Syracuse University's Maxwell School of Citizenship and Public Policy and the magazine *Government Executive* has rated agencies' performance and issued report cards on their management capacities. "We hope through continuous, comprehensive scrutiny to give citizens and lawmakers information they can use to better evaluate agency performance."[39]

Congress receives much free advice from various groups on how to cut back the size of government and, alternatively, how to make federal programs and departments work more effectively as well as which national activities might be candidates for expansion.

Senate Confirmation Process

High-ranking public officials are chosen by the president "by and with the Advice and Consent of the Senate," in accord with the Constitution. In general, the Senate gives presidents wide latitude in selecting cabinet members, but it closely scrutinizes judicial and diplomatic appointments as well as nominees to regulatory boards and commissions. Increasingly in recent years, Senate committees are probing the qualifications, independence, and policy predilections of presidential nominees, seeking information on everything from physical health to financial assets. Today, nominees often complain about lengthy delays that can turn the process into an ordeal. A survey of top-level appointees who served in the Reagan, Bush, and Clinton administrations found that more "than half of the appointees confirmed between 1984 and 1999 waited five months or more to enter office; just one-sixth of the appointees who were confirmed between 1964 and 1984 waited that long."[40] However, as Sen. Robert C. Byrd, D-W.Va., pointed out, if the Senate "rushes through a nomination without adequate investigation, it is accused of 'consent without advice' or 'half rubber, half stamp.' "[41]

Nomination hearings establish a public record of the policy views of nominees, on which appointed officials can be called to account at a later time. "We all ask questions at confirmation hearings, hoping to obtain answers that affect actions," observed Sen. Carl Levin, D-Mich.[42] Committees, too, may take nominees to task for the way their agencies have addressed management problems. For example, when the nominee for deputy director for management at the Office of Management and Budget (OMB) appeared before the Senate Governmental Affairs Committee, Chairman Fred Thompson, R-Tenn., criticized OMB's efforts to improve agency performance and pointed out that federal agencies "have not addressed half of the 'high-risk' programs identified by congressional auditors as vulnerable to waste, fraud, and abuse."[43] Committees may also extract pledges from nominees that they will testify at hearings when requested to do so, with the not-so-subtle threat that otherwise the appointee's name will not be sent to the full Senate for action.

Program Evaluation

Program evaluation is an approach to oversight that uses social science and management methodology, such as surveys, cost-benefit analyses, and efficiency studies, to assess the effectiveness of ongoing programs. It is a special type of oversight that has been specifically provided for in many agency appropriations bills since the late 1960s and in the 1974 Congressional Budget and Impoundment Control Act. The studies often are carried out by the GAO and by the executive agencies themselves.[44]

Despite the multiplicity of methods to evaluate programs, members sometimes disagree about how to measure performance. Several factors frequently account for their divergent perspectives. People may not agree on the objectives of certain programs. Public laws often are the products of conflicts and compromises, and when those compromises are translated into legislative language, ambiguity about program goals may be the result. Many policies have competing objectives or produce unintended results. In addition, no agreement may have been reached about criteria—quantitative or qualitative—for determining program success or failure. Finally, even if decision makers agree on objectives and criteria, they may interpret the assessments differently. Members and committees who support particular programs are unlikely to view with favor evaluations that recommend repeal or revision of those programs.

Casework

Each senator's and representative's office handles thousands of requests each year from constituents seeking help in dealing with executive agencies. The requests range from inquiries about lost Social Security checks or delayed pension payments to disaster relief assistance and complicated tax appeals to the Internal Revenue Service. "Constituents perceive casework in nonpolitical terms," wrote two scholars. "They *expect* their representatives to provide [this service]."[45] As a House member wrote:

> Last year, one of my constituents, a 63-year old man who requires kidney dialysis, discovered that he would no longer be receiving Medicare because the Social Security Administration thought he was dead. Like residents of Southern Indiana who have problems dealing with the federal bureaucracy, this man contacted my district office and asked for help. Without difficulty, he convinced my

staff that he was indeed alive, and we in turn convinced the Social Security Administration to resume sending him benefits.[46]

Most congressional offices employ specialists, called case workers, to process these types of petitions. Depending on the importance or complexity of a case, a member himself may contact federal officials, bring up the matter in committee, or discuss the case on the floor. Casework has the positive effect of bringing quirks in the administrative machinery to members' attention. And solutions to an individual constituent's problems can suggest legislative remedies on a broader scale.

To enlist the support of citizens in rooting out mismanagement by federal agencies, a chairman of the House Budget Committee "created a Web site that encourages everyone who logs on to report government waste and abuse in their local community (www.house.gov/budget)."[47]

Support-Agency Studies

Congress has two support agencies besides the GAO: the Congressional Research Service and the Congressional Budget Office. Each prepares (or contracts for) reports or studies to assist committees and members in reviewing federal agency activities, expenditures, and performance. Their analyses can spark legislation to correct administrative shortcomings.

Resolutions of Inquiry

On infrequent occasions, a House member will introduce a privileged simple resolution, called a resolution of inquiry, which requests the president or the head of an executive department to furnish specific factual information and documentation to the House about the administration of a particular federal program. (A resolution of inquiry enjoys its privileged status only if it asks for facts and not opinion from the executive branch.) When Leon E. Panetta, D-Calif., was a House member (he left in 1993 to become President Clinton's White House chief of staff), he explained some objectives of a resolution of inquiry: "It is a vehicle to provide information to Congress, to foster cooperation between the executive and legislative branches, and to encourage auditing of how taxpayers' dollars are spent."[48] House precedents state that the "effectiveness of such a resolution derives from comity between the branches of government rather than from any element of compulsion."[49]

In the mid-1990s the House considered a resolution of inquiry reported by the Banking Committee. It asked President Clinton, within fourteen legislative days, to provide the House with information on his use of the Exchange Stabilization Fund to shore up the value of Mexico's faltering currency. By a vote of 407 to 21, the House adopted the resolution of inquiry, which requested a large number of specific documents from the president, such as any document containing "a description of the activities of the central bank of Mexico."[50] A member of the president's own party introduced this resolution of inquiry, even though such resolutions "are usually introduced by partisan opponents of the president, who seek to embarrass him by asking for potentially damaging details about his actions."[51] The Clinton administration provided the Banking Committee with, among other items, "more than 3,200 pages of unclassified documents and 475 pages of classified documents."[52]

Oversight by Individual Members

Some members conduct their own personal reviews of agency activities and develop ways to publicize what they believe to be examples of governmental waste and inefficiency. Sen. William Proxmire, D-Wis. (1957–1989), periodically bestowed a Golden Fleece Award on agencies that, in his estimation, wastefully spend tax dollars.[53] Rep. Berkley W. Bedell, D-Iowa (1975–1987), utilized another technique:

> One of the practices I have is to make unannounced visits to the executive branch of the Government. I simply select an agency at random, open a door, walk in, and start asking questions of the people who work in that office.[54]

On occasion, individual members will conduct ad hoc field oversight hearings. These sessions usually permit constituents to testify about their problems with federal agencies. They usually garner favorable publicity for the legislator, too.

Impeachment

The ultimate check on the executive and judicial branch is the removal power, and it is vested exclusively in Congress. As Article II, Section 4 of the Constitution states: "The President, Vice President, and all Civil Officers of the United States, shall be removed from office on Impeachment for, and Conviction of, Treason, Bribery, or other high Crimes and misdemeanors." The House has the authority to impeach an official by majority vote. (Impeachment, in effect, is the formal lodging of charges against a person.) House trial managers then prosecute the case before the Senate, where a two-thirds vote is required for conviction. In the history of the United States, the House has impeached seventeen individuals—two presidents, one Supreme Court justice, one senator, one cabinet officer, and twelve federal judges. Of those, seven judges were tried, convicted, and removed from office.

OVERSIGHT TRENDS

While some legislators and scholars complain that congressional oversight is irregular and shallow, recent Congresses in the judgment of several scholars have seen a surge of legislative interest in the process.[55] As one specialist of the oversight process explained:

> There are no authoritative, comprehensive statistics on the amount of oversight or even the number of specialized investigations throughout the history of Congress. This absence is, in part, because scholars have disagreed as to what

constitutes oversight and, therefore, how it should be measured. Nonetheless, some statistics . . . are available. . . . [T]hese data tend to show that Congress has increased its oversight activity over history, particularly over the past three decades.[56]

Today, there is considerable interest in oversight because a fundamental topic of the national debate is the appropriate role of the national government. As Senator Thompson put it: "The two most important questions policymakers must ask themselves are, 'What should government be doing?' and 'At what level of government should it be done?' " People may react negatively to big government in the abstract, but voters want more rather than less government in many areas, such as health or environmental protection.

Among other factors that have contributed to heightened interest in oversight are:

- Public dissatisfaction with and concern about governmental waste, fraud, program performance, and escalating expenditures.
- Congressional assertiveness and distrust of the executive branch in the wake of such events as the Vietnam War, Watergate, the Iran-contra affair, and revelations of abuses by agencies such as the CIA, Federal Bureau of Investigation (FBI), and IRS.
- The influx of representatives and senators who are skeptical about the national government's ability to resolve public problems.
- The proliferation of federal programs and regulations that touch the lives of practically every citizen; citizens in turn inform their elected officials about problems they encounter with federal agencies.
- The proliferation of interest groups and trade associations that pressure Congress to examine governmental actions that affect their special interests.
- The availability of staff resources and procedural tools, which permits the new breed of aggressive legislators to scrutinize federal activities.
- Aggressive investigative reporting into executive activities by the print and broadcast media.

Perhaps surprisingly, the apparent switch from the politics of fiscal austerity to the politics of fiscal abundance still compels members and committees to scrutinize program activities and expenditures. For example, House and Senate GOP leaders have targeted government waste and federal fat as one way to find additional monies (or offsets) for programs they favor while still maintaining limits on spending. Making fraud, waste, and abuse a top GOP priority is electorally appealing to voters who favor a smaller government. Democrats contend that Republicans often cut the wrong programs and that they want to curb spending to make room in the budget for big tax cuts for the wealthy.

Divided government (one party in control of the White House; the other, Congress) provides another incentive for oversight. Opposition lawmakers, for example, monitor and supervise agency activities and, at the same time, they are on the lookout for ways to politically bash the administration. The Clinton White House complained about the oversight activities of House Republicans. "It seems a pattern has developed where [they] are requesting information not so they can evaluate the effectiveness of the government's performance," stated a White House spokesman, "but so that they can use [requests for information to] thwart those who might be carrying out the laws as they've been properly passed by Congress." In response, a House GOP spokesperson said: "For . . . years [federal executives have] gotten nothing from Democratic oversight chairman but postcards from Hawaii saying, 'Wish you were here.' "[57]

Because relations between the GOP-controlled Congress and the Clinton White House were marred by sharp conflict, a large number of investigatory probes of the administration were launched. Congressional Democrats, based on their own findings, charge that most have been politically motivated.[58] Some scholars of Congress share this general view. "There is such visceral hatred of the President among Republicans on the Hill that it oftentimes leads to quite destructive uses of oversight tools. In this intensely politicized environment, it's easy for the bureaucracy to become a whipping boy," said Thomas Mann of the Brookings Institution.[59] Speaker Hastert has urged committees to conduct more programmatic reviews of agencies rather than undertake unwarranted media-focused attacks on administration officials or programs. As former House member Lee H. Hamilton, D-Ind., said at a bipartisan congressional oversight forum sponsored by Speaker Hastert and House Rules Chairman David Dreier, R-Calif.: "[S]pending too much time on personal investigations weakens the oversight function of Congress. It consumes Executive Branch time and resources and, more importantly, diverts congressional time and resources away from the more constructive work of policy oversight."[60]

LACK OF CONSENSUS ON OVERSIGHT

Despite the heightened focus on legislative review activities and Congress's augmentation of its staff, budget, and authority for oversight, many members and commentators still fault congressional efforts in this area. As Senator Thomas of Wyoming said:

> Congressional oversight is something that, unfortunately, we probably don't do as much as we should. That is what committee meetings are for. That is what audits are for. When you pass a law and say here is where we want to go, then you have to say: How are we getting there? We don't do that well.[61]

Several factors help to account for this general perception, although those who are the targets of oversight—executive branch officials—no doubt prefer to be left alone.

First, no clear consensus has emerged on how to measure oversight, quantitatively or qualitatively. As a result, members' anxiety about Congress's ability to review the massive federal establishment remains high. Quantitatively, no one knows how much oversight Congress is doing. However, undercounting characterizes statistical analyses of oversight no matter what definition of that activity is employed. Part of the problem is that legislative review is a ubiquitous activity carried out by many entities: committees, members' offices, legislative support agencies, and committee and personal staff aides. Almost any committee hearing, for example, even ones ostensibly devoted to formulating new legislation, might pay considerable attention to reviewing past policy implementation. Qualitatively, little agreement exists among members on the criteria that can be used to evaluate effective oversight.

Second, some legislators hold oversight objectives that appear impossible to meet. They would like to see Congress conduct comprehensive reviews of the entire executive establishment. They find Congress's selective and unsystematic oversight approach generally unsatisfactory even when there is more of it. Oversight is too often a guerrilla foray rather than the continuous watchfulness contemplated by the 1946 Legislative Reorganization Act. Congress performs, two scholars noted, dual types of oversight: "fire-alarm" and "police-patrol." The former occurs when outside events or public interest trigger agency reviews; it is episodic and reactive in character. The latter is proactive and involves deliberate House and Senate decisions to oversee certain federal activities.[62]

Third, some committees and individual members believe they have minimal impact on the bureaucracy. Exclaimed Rep. Jim Wright, D-Texas, who served as Speaker from 1987 to 1989:

> Fighting the red tape and the overregulation of bureaucratic rulemaking and guideline writing are among the most frustrating things any of us have had to do in Congress—it is almost like trying to fight a pillow. You can hit it—knock it over in the corner—and it just lies there and regroups. You feel sometimes as though you are trying to wrestle an octopus. No sooner do you get a hammerlock on one of his tentacles than the other seven are strangling you.[63]

To many new members of Congress, the best way to handle this problem is to eliminate or downsize agencies or programs.

Fourth, oversight may produce more questions than answers. Congress finds it easier "to highlight what's going wrong and to blame it on someone," declared a senator, "than to try to determine what to do about it."[64] More oversight still can mean that agency problems remain uncorrected.

Fifth, Congress seeks to shape executive actions to its own objectives, not simply to conduct or commission neutral evaluation studies of departmental activities. Oversight is part of the legislative-executive tug-of-war that characterizes the U.S. separation of powers system. According to one commentator:

> The key issue for Congress is not administrative performance but its ability to influence agency actions. Congress is interested in performance, but it expresses this interest by seeking dominion over agencies. The distribution of political

power between the legislative and executive branches, not simply [or even mainly] the quality of programs, is at stake.[65]

A fragmented and assertive Congress is sometimes frustrated by its inability to control and coordinate a fragmented and sophisticated bureaucracy. Congress, for instance, confronts the issue of whom to hold accountable for program performance when a contractor work force carries out the bulk of a department's activities with federal employees charged with supervising this third party or shadow group of employees. The Energy Department has 20,000 federal employees but a contractor work force of 140,000 people.[66] Thousands of nonfederal employees—defense contractors, state and local officials, or university administrators—increasingly carry out activities once performed by civil servants. As a result, it is harder for Congress to hold accountable those who administer policies or deliver services.

Another development that has the potential to weaken congressional oversight is lockbox government. Federal officials are looking for ways to avoid the constraints of the congressional appropriations process by encouraging the passage of laws that give them a guaranteed funding stream for a specific activity. For instance, federal oil and gas royalties flow into the Land and Conservation Fund to be spent on congressionally designated environmental programs. A consequence of removing agencies and programs from the regular appropriations process is that it robs "legislators of an opportunity to hold agency officials accountable for policy decisions. If functions are spun off to private organizations, oversight could be weakened further."[67]

Despite Congress's general interest in oversight, other considerations limit effective performance. Legislators still have too little time to devote to their myriad tasks, including oversight. Huge investments of time, energy, and staff assistance are required to ferret out administrative inadequacies. Some members are reluctant to support massive investigations that may reveal only that a program is working fairly well, not a determination that attracts much constituent attention or media coverage. "Effective oversight is, of necessity, time-consuming and tedious," said a Republican senator. "To do it right, you have to hear an endless stream of witnesses, review numerous records, and at the end of it you may find an agency was doing everything right. It is much more fun to create a new program."[68]

Many members, however, accept that much of their effort in this area is unglamorous. The review process sometimes is inhibited by the alliances that develop between committees, agencies, and clientele groups. Examples of these subgovernments or iron triangles, as the alliances are called, are the axis of the House and Senate Veterans' Affairs committees, the Department of Veterans Affairs, and the veterans groups, and the combine of the congressional Agriculture committees, the Department of Agriculture, and the various farm groups. Each component of such an alliance usually is supportive of the other. In such cases, committees find it harder to review agency programs critically absent a countervailing view of them.

Finally, some members and scholars say that Congress lacks electoral, political, and institutional incentives for oversight. As a result, some legislators are "insufficiently dissatisfied with their oversight behavior to feel a strong enough stimulus to alter existing patterns."[69]

NOTES

1. Audrey Hudson, "House Republicans Say Cutting Waste Is Top Priority," *Washington Times,* April 5, 2000, A3.
2. Karen Foerstel, "Senate GOP Leaders Expand Agenda of Investigations Again, This Time to Bipartisan Annoyance," *Congressional Quarterly Weekly Report,* September 25, 1999, 2217.
3. *Congressional Record,* June 21, 1983, S8822. For several studies on oversight, see Morris S. Ogul, *Congress Oversees the Bureaucracy* (Pittsburgh, Pa.: University of Pittsburgh Press, 1976). Professor Ogul's book contains a lengthy bibliography on oversight. See also Frederick Kaiser, "Congressional Oversight of the Presidency," *The Annals* (September 1988): 75–89; Christopher Foreman, *Signals from the Hill: Congressional Oversight and Social Regulation* (New Haven, Conn.: Yale University Press, 1988); and Joel Aberbach, *Keeping a Watchful Eye: The Politics of Congressional Oversight* (Washington, D.C.: Brookings Institution, 1990).
4. See Nancy Ferris, "Targeting Jobs," *Government Executive,* December 1999, 20–27.
5. Arthur M. Schlesinger Jr. and Roger Burns, eds., *Congress Investigates: A Documented History, 1792–1974,* vol. 1 (New York: Chelsea House, 1975), xix.
6. Woodrow Wilson, *Congressional Government* (Boston: Houghton Mifflin, 1885), 297.
7. Jennifer Kabbany, "Armey Targets Waste in Federal Agencies," *Washington Times,* February 12, 1999, A6.
8. Dick Kirschten, "Overlooking Management," *Government Executive,* June 1999, 16.
9. *Congressional Record,* June 6, 2000, S4566.
10. Morton Rosenberg, "Whatever Happened to Congressional Review of Agency Rulemaking?: A Brief Overview, Assessment, and Proposal for Reform," *Administrative Law Review* (Fall 1999): 1060.
11. David B. Truman, *The Governmental Process* (New York: Alfred Knopf, 1953), 439. The continuous watchfulness provision was retitled legislative "review" in the Legislative Reorganization Act of 1970. That act also directed House and Senate committees to submit biennial reports on their oversight activities.
12. *Congressional Record,* February 1, 1977, 2897.
13. Michael J. Malbin, *Unelected Representatives* (New York: Basic Books, 1979). See chapter 6 for an analysis of a House oversight subcommittee in action.
14. *Congressional Record,* January 4, 1995, H35.
15. *Workshop on Congressional Oversight and Investigations,* H. Doc. 96-217, 96th Cong., 1st sess. (1979), 198.

16. *Washington Post,* March 17, 1994, A15.
17. Congressional requests for executive agency information may be blocked by executive privilege. See Bernard Schwartz, "Executive Privilege and Congressional Investigatory Power," *California Law Review* (March 1959): 3–50; Raoul Berger, *Executive Privilege: A Constitutional Myth* (Cambridge, Mass.: Harvard University Press, 1974); *U.S. v. Nixon,* 418 U.S. 683 (1974); and "Symposium: *United States v. Nixon,*" *UCLA Law Review* (October 1974): 1–40.
18. Information supplied by Louis Fisher, senior specialist on the separation of powers, Government Division, Congressional Research Service, Library of Congress. See Louis Fisher, "The Legislative Veto Invalidation: It Survives," *Law and Contemporary Problems* (Autumn 1993): 273–292.
19. Joseph P. Harris, *Congressional Control of Administration* (Washington, D.C.: Brookings Institution, 1964), 284.
20. Quoted in Louis Fisher, "Annual Authorizations: Durable Roadblocks to Biennial Budgeting," *Public Budgeting and Finance* (Spring 1983): 38.
21. David Baumann, "Undersupply of Oversight," *Government Executive,* June 2000, 50.
22. David Baumann, "Government on Autopilot," *National Journal,* March 13, 1999, 689.
23. *Workshop on Congressional Oversight and Investigations,* 199.
24. *National Journal's CongressDaily/PM,* February 11, 2000, 1.
25. David Rogers, "House Approves Delay in Ergonomics Standards," *Wall Street Journal,* June 9, 2000, A10.
26. Nick Anderson, "House Votes against Worker Injury Rules," *Los Angeles Times,* June 9, 2000, A1.
27. Eric Pianin, "From GOP Leaders, A Plea against Riders," *Washington Post,* May 22, 2000, A19.
28. *The Inspectors General Act: 20 Years Later,* Hearings before the Senate Committee on Governmental Affairs, S. Hrg. 105-737, 105 Cong., 2d sess. (September 9, 1998), 4.
29. Michael Kirst, *Government without Passing Laws* (Chapel Hill, N.C.: University of North Carolina Press, 1969), 37. See also William Rhode, *Committee Clearance of Administrative Decisions* (East Lansing, Mich.: Michigan State University Press, 1959).
30. Holbert N. Carroll, *The House of Representatives and Foreign Affairs,* rev. ed. (Boston: Little, Brown, 1966), 172. A good example of nonstatutory controls involves the reprogramming of funds within executive accounts. Reprogramming refers to the expenditure of funds for purposes not originally intended when Congress approved the department's budget. Agencies secure approval for reprogramming from the appropriate House and Senate committees.
31. *New York Times,* May 12, 1983, B8. See also *New York Times,* October 22, 1982, A16.
32. See, for example, Robert A. Katzmann, "Justice Breyer: A Rival for Scalia on the Hill's Intent," *Roll Call,* May 30, 1994, 5, 15. See also Cornell Clayton, "Separate Branches—Separate Politics: Judicial Enforcement of Congressional Intent," *Political Science Quarterly* (Winter 1994–1995): 843–872; *Interbranch Relations,* Hearings before the Joint Committee on the Organization of Congress, 103 Cong., 1 sess. (June 29, 1993); and Robert Pear, "With

Rights Act Comes Fight to Clarify Congress's Intent," *New York Times,* November 18, 1991, A1.

33. Eric Pianin, "GOP Targets 61 Programs for Cuts," *Washington Post,* February 2, 2000, A19.

34. Ellen C. Collier, "Foreign Policy by Reporting Requirement," *Washington Quarterly* (Winter 1988): 75.

35. *New York Times,* December 31, 1987, A20.

36. Phillip Davis, "After Losing Pollution Battle, White House Seizes Victory," May 23, 1992, 1440. See also Pamela Fessler, "Complaints Are Stacking Up as Hill Piles on Reports," *Congressional Quarterly Weekly Report,* September 7, 1991, 2562–2566.

37. *National Journal CongressDaily/AM,* February 16, 1995, 4.

38. *New York Times,* August 26, 1983, A14.

39. Anne Laurent, "Measuring Up," *Government Executive,* March 2000, 11.

40. See *The Merit and Reputation of an Administration: Presidential Appointees on the Appointments Process, A Report on a Survey Conducted by Princeton Survey Research Associates on Behalf of the Presidential Appointee Initiative* (Washington, D.C.: Brookings Institution and Heritage Foundation, April 28, 2000).

41. *Congressional Record,* July 29, 1987, S21504.

42. *New York Times,* April 14, 1983, B10.

43. Stephen Barr, "OMB Nominee Gets Earful at Confirmation Hearing," *Washington Post,* September 16, 1999, A11.

44. See, for example, Robert T. Nakamura and Frank Smallwood, *The Politics of Policy Implementation* (New York: St. Martin's Press, 1980); George C. Edwards III, *Implementing Public Policy* (Washington, D.C.: CQ Press, 1980); and *Program Evaluation: Improving the Flow of Information to the Congress,* General Accounting Office Report, GAO/PEMD-95-1, January 1995, 84.

45. John R. Johannes and John C. McAdams, "Entrepreneurs or Agent: Congressmen and the Distribution of Casework, 1977–1978," *Western Political Quarterly* (September 1987): 549.

46. Lee H. Hamilton, "Constituent Service and Representation," *The New Bureaucrat* (Summer 1992): 12.

47. Audrey Hudson, "Billions Wasted by Government, Study Shows," *Washington Times,* January 5, 2000, A8.

48. *Congressional Record,* July 14, 1988, E2397.

49. Richard S. Beth, *Resolutions of Inquiry in the House of Representatives: A Brief Description,* Congressional Research Service Report 87-365 (April 22, 1987), 2.

50. *Congressional Record,* March 1, 1995, H2444–H2458.

51. Benjamin Sheffner, "Rare Parliamentary Tactic Used to Hit Mexico Policy," *Roll Call,* March 2, 1995, 3.

52. Mike Mills, "Treasury Says Congress Given Papers on Mexico," *Washington Post,* April 7, 1995, F1.

53. See *Christian Science Monitor,* August 5, 1982, 1.

54. *Congressional Record,* June 8, 1983, H3737.

55. See especially, Aberbach, *Keeping a Watchful Eye.*

56. *History of the United States House of Representatives, 1789–1994,* H. Doc. 103-324 (Washington, D.C.: Government Printing Office, 1994), 262. Fred-

erick Kaiser, specialist, Congressional Research Service, Library of Congress, wrote this study's chapter on oversight.

57. Paul Bedard, "White House Fumes at Probes," *Washington Times,* April 7, 1995, A1.

58. *Congressional Record,* June 25, 1998, H5316–H5324.

59. Dick Kirschten, "Rating Elected Officials," *Government Executive,* December 1999, 16.

60. *Congressional Record,* July 19, 1999, E1586.

61. *Congressional Record,* June 12, 2000, S4945.

62. Matthew D. McCubbins and Thomas Schwartz, "Congressional Oversight Overlooked: Police Patrols versus Fire Alarms," *American Journal of Political Science* (February 1984): 165–179.

63. *Workshop on Congressional Oversight and Investigations,* 5.

64. *Workshop on Congressional Oversight and Investigations,* 144.

65. Allen Schick, "Politics through Law: Congressional Limitations on Executive Discretion," in *Both Ends of the Avenue,* ed. Anthony King (Washington, D.C.: American Enterprise Institute for Public Policy Research, 1983), 166.

66. Timothy Noah, "So What Do People at the Energy Department Do All Day Long?" *Wall Street Journal,* December 15, 1994, A8.

67. Alasdair Roberts, "Lockbox Government," *Government Executive,* May 2000, 28.

68. *Congress Speaks: A Survey of the 100th Congress* (Washington, D.C.: Center for Responsive Politics, 1988), 163.

69. Morris S. Ogul, "Congressional Oversight: Structures and Incentives," in *Congress Reconsidered,* 2d ed., ed. Lawrence C. Dodd and Bruce I. Oppenheimer (Washington, D.C.: CQ Press, 1981), 330.

CHAPTER 10

A Dynamic Process

ANYONE who views lawmaking in Congress as a precise, neat process of drafting, debating, and approving legislation overlooks the dynamic forces at work on Capitol Hill. It is not a static institution.

For better or worse, the interests, pressures, perceptions, and prejudices of members of Congress change quickly, a result, in part, of the election cycle, but also of other conditions and influences. The demands made by the presidency and the courts, international events, lobbying groups, and media disclosures are some of the ever-present forces that affect lawmaking. Congress is an institution in which procedures reflect and, in turn, perpetuate the messiness, openness, pragmatism, compromise, and deliberateness so characteristic of much American policy making. As a House chairman said: "Legislation is like a chess game more than anything else. It is a seemingly endless series of moves, until ultimately somebody prevails through exhaustion, or brilliance, or because of overwhelming public sentiment for their side." [1]

At every stage of the legislative process a new winning coalition must be formed to carry a policy recommendation up the next rung of the legislative ladder; otherwise, its progress is jeopardized. And that coalition changes, as the forces that mold it change. While coalitions are formed to advance legislation, others may form to tear it down. If opponents fail in one session of Congress, they always can come back in the next to try again. In the judgment of Sen. Alan K. Simpson, R-Wyo.:

> In politics there are no right answers, only a continuing flow of compromises between groups resulting in a changing, cloudy, and ambiguous series of public decisions where appetite and ambition compete openly with knowledge and wisdom. [2]

Despite its built-in—and frequently beneficial—inefficiencies, Congress's policy-making role is firmly grounded in the Constitution. The preeminent place envisioned for Congress by the authors of the Constitution has been modified by the growth of executive power in the twentieth century. But the constitutional separation of powers has preserved for Congress an independent role that distinguishes it from legislative bodies in most other democracies.

Moreover, the power balance between Congress and the president is constantly in flux. During the mid-1990s, unlike earlier periods when presidential initiatives dominated the airwaves, the nation's agenda was driven more from Congress than from the White House. This unusual circumstance occurred, according to Speaker Newt Gingrich, R-Ga., because the country wanted to debate the core proposals of the GOP's agenda (a smaller national government, tax cuts, overhaul of the welfare system, and so on) and the Clinton administration, "temporarily at least, lost its sense of authority with the country." [3] This power imbalance righted itself when House Republicans moved beyond the triumphal one-hundred-day stage to the government shutdowns of late 1995 and early 1996, which the public blamed them for and when their popular standing took a nosedive.

The mechanics of legislating influence the policy-making process. Procedural details and nuances have a crucial policy impact, and understanding why certain policies are adopted and others are not is impossible without an appreciation of the rules governing the process. Substance, in short, can be shaped through procedure. The Senate's tradition of lengthy debate is "a wonderful tool to . . . expose legislation to more careful consideration," said Senate Minority Leader Tom Daschle, D-S.D. "You hold many of these pieces of legislation up to the light of day and share the concerns you have with the American public, and that exposure is extremely powerful." [4]

Congress's informal procedures and practices are often as important as its formal rules. For instance, neither chamber needed rules changes to permit lawmaking through megabills, which derived in large measure from legislative-executive conflict and members' need for political cover. In the case of the GOP's Contract with America, lawmakers could say to lobbyists, "Gee, I'd like to be with you on that, but I've got to stick with the contract." [5]

Moreover, no rules changes mandated that legislators must play both the inside (maneuvering behind the scenes in Congress to pick up support for legislation) and the outside (generating public support) game to push controversial legislation through the House and Senate. "Being a good legislator means you have to do both," remarked House Democratic leader Richard A. Gephardt, D-Mo. "If you are going to pass important legislation, you have to both deal with Members and put together coalitions in the country." [6]

The rules of the game are as important in illuminating the outcomes of the legislative process as they are in comprehending who wins at any competition—the presidential nominating system, for example. The electoral strategy of a presidential candidate in the general campaign cannot be fully appreciated without understanding the electoral college or the techniques of raising campaign funds. Similarly, one cannot comprehend the behavior of members of Congress as participants in policy formation without knowledge of the formal and informal rules and procedures under which they operate.

Congressional rules and practices have an effect on policy outcomes. For example, the requirement for an extraordinary majority of the Senate to invoke cloture gives to a well-organized minority the ability to block passage of legislation desired by a majority. Civil rights legislation was repeatedly delayed in the 1950s and 1960s by the opponents' use of the filibuster.

However, the rules themselves may change in response to events or policy goals. Some rules are modified or ignored, while new ones come out of struggles over a particular problem. The mixed results and unanticipated consequences that attend some procedural revisions can even disgruntle members who originally supported rules changes. For instance, simplifying the complexities of the budget process is no easy task when 535 lawmakers want a say in how and what fiscal decisions are made.

An ostensibly procedural decision also can be used to mask a policy objective. When members vote to table a bill, procedurally it appears as if they are merely postponing consideration of it. Nevertheless, such a procedure usually sidetracks the legislation permanently, while allowing members to say they did not take a position on the measure.

Important, too, are the differences in the way the two chambers operate. Each chamber functions under rules and procedures that reflect its basic constitutional design. A close examination of the differences as well as the similarities between the two bodies is indispensable to an accurate understanding of how Congress functions. Unlike those of the House, said Sen. Robert C. Byrd, D-W.Va., the rules in the Senate favor the minority: "They were meant to favor the minority to prevent the majority from running over the minority. That is why there is a Senate. That is why this Senate ought to remain a Senate and not become a second House of Representatives."[7]

The most significant and enduring feature of the rules is that they usually require bills to pass through a labyrinth of decision points before they can become law. Generally, passing legislation is more difficult than defeating it. The multiple decision points make necessary a constant cycle of coalition building—by means of the various bargaining techniques—to move legislation past each potential roadblock. The shifting coalitions combine, dissolve, and recombine in response to the widely varying issues and needs of members. Unlike in the past, when a few barons dominated legislative policy making, today's Congress operates in an environment where scores of members have some—and often significant—bargaining power.

Coalition building is possible primarily for two reasons. First, members of Congress, who represent diverse constituencies, are not equally concerned about every item on the legislative agenda. Second, members pursue many objectives other than the enactment of legislation. They may seek reelection, election to higher office, appointment to prestigious committees, or personal conveniences such as additional staff or office space. These conditions create numerous opportunities for coalition building through the three types of bargaining—logrolling, compromise, and the distribution of nonlegislative favors (primarily by the congressional leadership).

Another factor determining whether a series of majority coalitions can be built is the extent to which members are in general agreement that a law is required or inevitable on a particular subject. Members may have widely divergent views on the solution to the problem, but they usually will work to compromise their differences when dealing with must-pass legislation.

Time influences the entire congressional process. As the two-year cycle of a Congress runs its course, every procedural device that can be employed has a policy consequence—either delaying or speeding up the processing of legislation. Frequently, as the countdown to final adjournment occurs, the bargaining process shifts into high gear. Bills that have been deadlocked for months are moved along swiftly as logrolling and compromises save bills in which members have a vested interest. Deadlines and threatened or actual procedural and policy crises frequently activate the lawmaking process. The end game is often played in the legislative process.

> [T]he sharpness of the ideological, political, and partisan divisions [in contemporary Congresses] means that most controversial areas come down to end games; every major player is willing to wait, believing that he, she, or they will have maximum leverage at the end of the tunnel.[8]

Stalled legislation dies if not enacted before Congress's final adjournment.

During the past decade, Congress has undergone significant transformations. Some of the changes resulted from the GOP takeover of Congress after Republicans had been the House minority for forty years; other changes have been under way for some time. Together, they have influenced the character of Congress's procedural and policy politics. Seven important developments highlight significant legislative trends:

Centralization of Authority in the Speakership. Recent Speakers of the House, such as Jim Wright, D-Texas (1987–1989) and Thomas S. Foley, D-Wash. (1989–1995), had an impressive array of formal and informal powers that strengthened their hand in the lawmaking process. None, however, compares with Speaker Newt Gingrich's exercise of authority in the House and in the larger political system. Strongly supported by party colleagues, especially junior Republicans, Gingrich took command of the House as few leaders before him. Not only did he set the nation's agenda when he assumed the Speakership, functioning as the House's chief executive officer and relying on Majority Leader Dick Armey of Texas to be the chief operating officer on the House floor, but he also bypassed the custom of seniority to handpick loyalists to chair committees crucial to the success of the Republican agenda. As one congressional journalist put it:

> The notion of a House that's balkanized into legislative fiefdoms . . . has become antiquated. Instead, the House is driven by a Speaker who wields extraordinary power and by rank-and-file Members who are intent on proving to a skeptical public that they can change how Washington works.[9]

In an unprecedented event and path-breaking expansion of the bully-pulpit role long associated with presidents, Speaker Gingrich requested and received free, prime-viewing television time to address the nation following House action on the Contract with America.[10] (Congressional history demonstrates that centralized authority is not a permanent condition in either chamber; instead, the forces of centralization versus decentralization are constantly in play, and they regularly adjust and reconfigure in response to new conditions and circumstances.)

Of the four most recent Speakers—Thomas P. "Tip" O'Neill Jr. (D-Mass.), Wright, Foley, and Gingrich—only O'Neill left office voluntarily. Wright resigned from the House for ethical infractions, Foley lost his House seat, and Gingrich left the House in large measure because he lost the support of many GOP colleagues. Speaker J. Dennis Hastert, R-Ill., operates much differently than Gingrich in his leadership post, stressing the regular order, more consultation with the rank and file, and greater reliance on the committee chairs. However, Hastert still exercises significant top-down command of the House and his party. Like Gingrich, if the situation warrants it, Hastert is not reluctant to bypass standing committees, utilize task forces, select party loyalists as conferees, threaten party sanctions against uncooperative partisan colleagues, instruct committee chairs to deal with certain bills, or construct majorities in the narrowly divided House exclusively from within GOP ranks. As one of Hastert's top lieutenants, Majority Whip Tom DeLay, R-Texas, said about moving the thirteen general appropriations bills: In 1999, "we told our appropriators that if they'd write the bills reflecting Republican values, we'd provide the votes, and we did. This year, we'll have to do it again. It's a little tougher because it's an election year, but we're doing it." [11]

The heightened partisanship in the House and Senate motivates leaders in both chambers—majority and minority—to encourage, and often get, party loyalty on various key votes. "Procedure is always a party vote," emphasized Majority Whip DeLay.[12] The top majority and minority leaders of the House and Senate rely heavily on consensus and consultation with their partisan colleagues. Their persuasive powers and the assistance they can provide promote support for leadership decisions. Probably more compelling is the argument made by majority leaders to their partisans that if they are to maintain control, they must stick together and do whatever it takes politically and procedurally to retain their status. Similarly, when the chambers are narrowly divided, minority leaders urge their members to follow the leadership's playbook because it will lead to majority control. "Without unity, we really can't make ourselves heard," noted Senate Minority Leader Daschle. "When you have multi-voices, you have no voice." [13]

Procedural-Policy Choreography. Both congressional parties in each chamber regularly employ a mix of political strategies to win outside support for their fundamental procedural and policy priorities. They have theme teams, message boards, and scores of party sessions to coordinate and transmit a clear and coherent message to the public. They also hire consultants to assist them in devising effective communications strategies and employing words as political weapons. For example, House Republicans were provided by Public Opinion Strategies, a Virginia-based firm, with "sample phrases to use in criticizing a Democratic drug benefit plan, including complaints that the proposal was 'too restrictive, too confusing' and would involve 'politicians and Washington bureaucrats setting drug prices.'" [14] A key objective of this effort is to frame the national debate in a way that mobilizes public support behind GOP or Democratic congressional objectives and that rebuts attacks by opponents. Both congressional parties employ field hearings, rallies, focus groups, polls and surveys, town meetings, news conferences, talk radio appearances, Internet outlets, newspaper articles, media events, bus tours, and more with the primary objective of winning public support for their causes and candidates.

Making major policy innovations today usually requires combining various external campaigning techniques with internal procedural coordination (for example, who should offer amendments, when, how, and should they be agreed to, modified, or killed). The hoped-for objective of these efforts is building extra political pressure to pass priority legislation. Another dimension to the inside-outside game is to hold or win power by trying to keep the other party on the defensive by portraying them, for example, as "tax-and-spend" Democrats or "extreme" Republicans. Thus, the distinction between campaigning and governing is blurred or sometimes obliterated in the House or Senate. Parties in both chambers regularly use the floor to spotlight their priorities and to activate outside supporters. Several lawmakers phrased it as follows: "Legislating [today] becomes campaigning by another name," said Sen. Joseph I. Lieberman, D-Conn.; "The Senate has become a campaign platform, " said Sen. Robert F. Bennett, R-Utah; and "More and more, the Congress is not passing real legislation, it is passing institutional press releases aimed far more at sending political messages than they are at solving problems," said Rep. David R. Obey, D-Wis.[15]

Congress and the Information Age.   Congress is fast becoming wired to a high-tech world that enables members, party leaders, and constituents to communicate politically to shape the legislative process. As Speaker Gingrich, a strong advocate for making Congress state of the art in communications technology, said:

> We will change the rules of the House to require that all documents and conference reports and all committee reports be filed electronically as well as in writing and that they cannot be filed until they are available to any citizen who wants to pull them up simultaneously so that information is available to every citizen in the country at the same moment that it is available to the highest paid Washington lobbyist.[16]

Technology has had and will have an impact on Congress. The agenda of Congress has been transformed because of developments in technology, telecommunications, and other aspects of the information age. Issues of electronic commerce, Internet security, privacy, copyright, censorship, and much more increasingly occupy the attention of lawmakers. Electronic advocacy has added a plebiscitary quality to congressional policy making. Today, many citizens and interest groups make their preferences known almost instantaneously to lawmakers. An important issue for Congress is how to achieve an effective balance between representative government (where policy usually proceeds slowly) and electronic democracy (where fast action is often the objective). E-campaigning and fund raising appear to be the wave of the future as technology is employed by candidates to devise more customized and targeted electoral contests. Although the House and Senate are both wired institutions, each prohibits the use of electronic devices, such as laptop computers, in the chamber. However, a new generation of lawmakers, for whom electronic devices are second nature, in time will win election to Congress. They may insist that the rules be changed to allow individual lawmakers to bring electronic devices into the chamber. The cyber-Congress may harness more effectively the use of computerized technology to review executive branch performance and to monitor the cost-effectiveness of various federal programs.

Ad Hoc Lawmaking. Today, ad hoc lawmaking is a growth industry on Capitol Hill. At least two different tracks are available for the consideration of legislation. On the first track are measures that follow traditional textbook lawmaking—introduction of a bill, referral to committee, hearings and markup, floor deliberation and conference action, and presidential consideration. On the second track are the priority measures of each party as well as so-called run-of-the-mill measures that get caught up in partisan battles and may become hostages to larger concerns. In these cases, ad hoc lawmaking is often the name of the game. Members find new uses for old rules, employ innovative devices, or bypass traditional procedures and processes altogether to achieve their political and policy objectives. In a hard-to-govern era because of factors such as sharper partisanship, razor-thin congressional majorities, and divided government, new and unexpected procedural twists to lawmaking are to be expected.

The politics of procedure is different today compared with earlier periods. Before, procedural issues were basically an insider's game driven largely by various tactical considerations (logrolls or compromises, for instance) associated with forging winning coalitions. Today, the process of building coalitions is inseparable from larger, outside political forces (the power of interest groups, the intensity of media coverage, and so on) that influence how Congress operates. The result is a lawmaking process that is more free-flowing and less predictable than in the past.

Resurgence of Sharp Partisanship. Parties have always been important in the modern Congress. Among other things, they organize the House and Senate and advocate substantive agendas. Partisanship is important and useful because it identifies the principles and ideals that orient each party. However, recent Congresses have witnessed heightened political rancor between the parties. Various scholars have highlighted the reasons for this development.[17] Although bitter partisanship in the 1990s was more evident in the House (in part because of GOP members' frustration with their long minority status, ended by the November 1994 elections) than the Senate, it surfaces more frequently in that chamber, too, even with its reputation for greater reciprocity among its smaller membership. "When I came to the Senate in 1959," said Senator Byrd, "there was partisanship. Everett Dirksen was a partisan. Mike Mansfield was a partisan. But they were not bitter partisans. We didn't have the negativism, the bitter partisanship that we have seen rule the Senate . . . and it is getting worse." [18] The breakdown of civility in an environment of partisan polarization compounds the ability of either chamber to produce legislation. When procedural rules are used solely for dilatory or message purposes, sometimes blocking legislation to affect election outcomes, it becomes that much harder for lawmakers to work together in a collegial manner.

Congress and the Challenge from the Supreme Court.   Since the mid-1990s, the Supreme Court has not been reluctant to constrict congressional power, especially when it affects the power of the states. The Supreme Court "has struck down parts or all of 22 federal laws since 1995, including the Gun-Free School Zones Act, the Religious Freedom Restoration Act, and several statutes that make states vulnerable to being sued—an unprecedented run that seems certain to open a new front in the political battle over the future direction of the Supreme Court." [19] In the opinion of Clinton administration solicitor general Seth Waxman, "[T]he extraordinary act of one branch of government declaring that the other two branches have violated the Constitution has become a commonplace." [20]

From the New Deal to at least the early 1990s, the Court has broadly interpreted the power of Congress to address social problems through its constitutional authority either to regulate interstate commerce or to enforce the due process and equal protection clauses of the Fourteenth Amendment. Through its recent decisions, the Court has indicated its willingness to overturn laws in those areas if they adversely affect state sovereignty or if they stray too far from Congress's enumerated powers. Whether the Court will continue in this direction is unclear, but the potential consequences for Congress are significant both in what and how it addresses various issues. As University of Virginia law professor A. E. Dick Howard stated: "There are enough cases now where I think Congress ought to think of it as a wake-up call. . . . Routine congressional drafting becomes freighted with constitutional consideration." [21]

A related development also bears watching for its impact on Congress: the use of lawsuits instead of laws to set social policy. "Over the last few years, the legal system has begun to overtake the legislative process as a vehicle to resolve contentious debates, particularly over unpopular products, when Congress is unwilling to act." [22] Litigation involving the firearms and tobacco industries are recent examples. The objective of these suits is to force these industries, upon threat of huge financial penalties, to make agreements (increasing the price of cigarettes or putting safety locks on guns) that normally are the purview of Congress. As an analyst pointed out: "The Founders created Congress to set national policy. They didn't intend for policy to be fashioned by lawsuits."[23]

The Surplus Era.   Budget surpluses in the non-Social Security part of the budget continue to grow. If these monies materialize, Congress will face a new lawmaking dynamic: what to do with the so-called surplus. The new era of surpluses promises to be just as controversial as the old one of deficit reduction. Both parties appear eager to reduce the national debt, but they differ on the size of any tax cuts; how much to invest in health, education, defense, or other areas; and what changes to make in Medicare (redesigning it) and Social Security (permitting private retirement accounts). Congress may need to rewrite its budget rules, drafted for deficit reduction, to reflect the new surplus reality. Equally significant is whether surpluses will permit lawmakers and presidents to shift from incremental to comprehensive policy initiatives.

And so the dynamic interplay between policy making and the rules continues. Precedents and practices are revised or abandoned and new ones established, often with great difficulty, in response to changing needs and pressures. "We always learn in this organization, even though we may think the rules are fixed and firm," stated a senator, "how the fertility of the minds of the Members manages to find ways to expand those rules."[24] Or as Senator Byrd pointed out, the "Senate doesn't operate under the rules it operated under when I came here and that existed up until a few years ago."[25]

Congress's dynamism is ensured by the regular infusion of new members, changing events and conditions, and the fluctuating expectations of citizens. If Congress reduces or increases its lawmaking activity, it usually is not by accident but as a reaction to members' perceptions of what their constituents and the country want. For its part, the nation expects Congress to use its considerable powers and policy-making procedures to help resolve, or at least allay, the pressing issues facing the country.

NOTES

1. *Washington Post,* June 26, 1983, A14.
2. *Congressional Record,* May 20, 1987, S6798.
3. David S. Cloud, "Speaker Wants His Platform to Rival the Presidency," *Congressional Quarterly Weekly Report,* February 4, 1995, 331.
4. *New York Times,* April 9, 1995, 18.
5. *Newsweek,* January 16, 1995, 18.
6. Richard Cohen, "Taking Advantage of Tax Reform Means Different Strokes for Different Folks," *National Journal,* June 22, 1985, 1459.
7. *Congressional Record,* February 23, 1988, S1124.
8. Norman Ornstein, "Let the End Games Begin," *Roll Call,* September 12, 1994, A-23.
9. Richard Cohen, "The Transformers," *National Journal,* March 4, 1995, 528–529.

10. *New York Times,* April 8, 1995, 1.
11. Daniel Parks, Karen Foerstel, and Andrew Taylor, "Politics of Parsimony Slows GOP Efforts to Move Spending Measures," *Congressional Quarterly Weekly Report,* June 10, 2000, 1381.
12. David Rogers and Jeannie Cummings, "Democrats Aim to Stir Public as Impeachment Nears," *Wall Street Journal,* December 14, 1998, A20.
13. Eliza Newlin Carney, "Running Interference," *National Journal,* November 22, 1997, 2362.
14. *CQ Daily Monitor,* June 13, 2000, 2.
15. The quote by Senator Lieberman is from Phil Keisling, "Trade-Offs in a Political Career," *Washington Monthly,* March 2000, 46; Senator Bennett, *CQ's Daily Monitor,* May 23, 2000, 3; and Representative Obey, *Congressional Record,* June 18, 1999, H4643.
16. Albert Eisele, "The New Electronic Populism," *The Hill,* January 4, 1995, 20.
17. See, for example, David W. Rohde, *Parties and Leaders in the Postreform House* (Chicago, Ill.: University of Chicago Press, 1991).
18. *Los Angeles Times,* January 30, 1995, A12.
19. Tony Mauro, "Split Branches," *Legal Times,* May 22, 2000, 8.
20. Quoted in Stuart Taylor Jr., "The Tipping Point," *National Journal,* June 10, 2000, 1816.
21. Dan Carney, "High Court Shows Inclination to Rein In Congress," *Congressional Quarterly Weekly Report,* January 25, 1997, 241.
22. Barry Meider, "Bringing Lawsuits to Do What Congress Won't," *New York Times,* March 26, 2000, E3.
23. Stuart Taylor Jr., "Guns and Tobacco: Government by Litigation," *National Journal,* March 25, 2000, 930.
24. *Congressional Record,* February 26, 1988, S1521.
25. *Congressional Record,* July 26, 2000, S7614.

Glossary of Congressional Terms

Act. The term for legislation once it has passed both houses of Congress and has been signed by the president or passed over his veto, thus becoming law. Also used in parliamentary terminology for a bill that has been passed by one house and engrossed. (See **Engrossed Bill, Law.**)

Adjournment *Sine Die*. Adjournment without definitely fixing a day for reconvening; literally "adjournment without a day." Usually used to connote the final adjournment of a session of Congress. A session can continue until noon, January 3, of the following year, when, under the Twentieth Amendment to the Constitution, it automatically terminates. Both houses must agree to a concurrent resolution for either house to adjourn for more than three days.

Adjournment to a Day Certain. Adjournment under a motion or resolution that fixes the next time of meeting. Under the Constitution, neither house can adjourn for more than three days without the concurrence of the other. A session of Congress is not ended by adjournment to a day certain.

Amendment. A proposal of a member of Congress to alter the language, provisions, or stipulations in a bill or in another amendment. An amendment usually is printed, debated, and voted upon in the same manner as a bill.

Amendment in the Nature of a Substitute. An amendment that seeks to replace the entire text of a bill. Passage of this type of amendment strikes out everything after the enacting clause and inserts a new version of the bill. A substitute amendment proposes to replace the entire text of a pending amendment.

Appeal. A member's challenge of a ruling or decision made by the presiding officer of the chamber. In the Senate, the senator appeals to members of the chamber to override the decision. If carried by a majority vote, the appeal nullifies the chair's ruling. In the House, the decision of the Speaker traditionally has been final; seldom are appeals made to the members to reverse the Speaker's stand. To appeal a ruling is considered an attack on the Speaker.

Appropriations Bill. A bill that gives legal authority to spend or obligate money from the Treasury. The Constitution disallows money to be drawn from the Treasury "but in Consequence of Appropriations made by Law."

An appropriations bill usually provides the monies approved by authorization bills, but not necessarily the full amount permissible under the authorization measures. By congressional custom, an appropriations bill originates in the House, and it is not supposed to be considered by the full House or Senate until the related authorization measure is enacted. In

309

addition to general appropriations bills, there are two specialized types. (See **Continuing Resolution, Supplemental Appropriations Bill.**)

Authorization Bill. Basic, substantive legislation that establishes or continues the legal operation of a federal program or agency, either indefinitely or for a specific period of time, or which sanctions a particular type of obligation or expenditure. An authorization normally is a prerequisite for an appropriation or other kind of budget authority. Under the rules of both the House and Senate, the appropriation for a program or agency may not be considered until its authorization has been considered. An authorization also may limit the amount of budget authority to be provided or may authorize the appropriation of "such sums as may be necessary."

Bills. Most legislative proposals before Congress are in the form of bills and are designated by H.R. in the House of Representatives or S. in the Senate, according to the house in which they originate, and by a number assigned in the order in which they are introduced during the two-year period of a congressional term. Public bills deal with general questions and become public laws if approved by Congress and signed by the president. Private bills deal with individual matters such as claims against the government, immigration and naturalization cases, and land titles, and they become private laws if approved and signed. (See also **Concurrent Resolution, Joint Resolution, Resolution.**)

Bills Introduced. In both the House and the Senate, any number of members may join in introducing a single bill or resolution. The first member listed is the sponsor of the bill, and all members' names following the sponsor's are the bill's cosponsors. Many bills are committee bills and are introduced under the name of the chairman of the committee or subcommittee. All appropriations bills fall into this category. A committee frequently holds hearings on a number of related bills and may agree to one of them or to an entirely new bill. When introduced, a bill is referred to the committee or committees that have jurisdiction over the subject with which the bill is concerned. Under the standing rules of the House and Senate, bills are referred by the Speaker in the House and by the presiding officer in the Senate. In practice, the House and Senate parliamentarians act for these officials and refer the vast majority of bills. (See also **Clean Bill, Report.**)

Budget Authority. Authority to enter into obligations that will result in immediate or future outlays involving federal funds. The basic forms of budget authority are appropriations, contract authority, and borrowing authority. Budget authority may be classified by (1) the period of availability (one-year, multiple-year, or without a time limitation), (2) the timing of congressional action (current or permanent), or (3) the manner of determining the amount available (definite or indefinite).

Calendar. An agenda or list of business awaiting possible action by each chamber. The House uses five legislative calendars. (See **Corrections, Discharge, House, Private, and Union Calendars.**)

In the Senate, all legislative matters reported from committee go on one calendar. They are listed in the order in which committees report them, or the Senate places them on the calendar, but they may be called up out of order by the majority leader, either by obtaining unanimous consent of the Senate or by a motion to call up a bill. The Senate uses one nonlegislative calendar; this is used for treaties and nominations. (See **Executive Calendar.**)

Calendar Wednesday. In the House, committees, on Wednesdays, may be called in the order in which they appear in Rule XV of the House, for the purpose of bringing up any bills from either the House or the Union Calendar, except bills that are privileged. General debate is limited to two hours. Bills called up from the Union Calendar are considered in Committee of the Whole. Calendar Wednesday is not observed during the last two weeks of a session and may be dispensed with at other times by a two-thirds vote. This procedure is rarely used and routinely is dispensed with by unanimous consent.

Clean Bill. Frequently after a committee has finished a major revision of a bill, one of the committee members, usually the chairman, will assemble the changes and what is left of the original bill into a new measure and introduce it as a clean bill. The revised measure, which is given a new number, is then referred back to the committee, which reports it to the floor for consideration. This often is a timesaver, as committee-recommended changes in a clean bill do not have to be considered and voted on by the chamber. Reporting a clean House bill also protects committee amendments that might be subject to points of order concerning germaneness.

Cloture. The formal procedure by which a filibuster can be ended in the Senate. A motion for cloture can apply to any measure before the Senate, including a proposal to change the chamber's rules. A cloture motion requires the signatures of sixteen senators to be introduced, and to end a filibuster the cloture motion must obtain the votes of three-fifths of the entire Senate membership (sixty if there are no vacancies). However, to end a filibuster against a proposal to amend the standing rules of the Senate, a two-thirds vote of senators present and voting is required. The cloture request is put to a roll-call vote one hour after the Senate meets on the second day following introduction of the motion. If approved, cloture limits each senator to one hour of debate. The bill or amendment in question comes to a final vote after thirty hours of consideration (including debate time and the time it takes to conduct roll calls, quorum calls, and other procedural motions). (See **Filibuster.**)

Committee. A division of the House or Senate that prepares legislation for action by the parent chamber or makes investigations as directed by the parent chamber. Most standing committees are divided into subcommittees, which study legislation, hold hearings, and report bills, with or without amendments, to the full committee. Only the full committee, not a subcommittee, can report legislation to the House or Senate.

Committee of the Whole. The working title of what is formally the Committee of the Whole House on the state of the Union. The membership is comprised of all House members sitting as a committee. Any one hundred members who are present on the floor of the chamber comprise a quorum of the committee. Usually, any legislation must have passed through the regular legislative committee or the Appropriations Committee and must have been placed on the calendar before it can be heard by the Committee of the Whole. Technically, the Committee of the Whole considers only bills directly or indirectly appropriating money, authorizing appropriations, or involving taxes or charges on the public. Because the Committee of the Whole need number only one hundred representatives, a quorum is more readily attained, and legislative business is expedited. Before 1971, members' positions were not individually recorded on votes taken in Committee of the Whole.

When the full House resolves itself into the Committee of the Whole, it supplants the Speaker with a chairman. A measure is debated and amendments may be proposed, with votes on amendments as needed. When the committee completes its work on the measure, it dissolves itself by rising. The Speaker returns, and the chairman of the Committee of the Whole reports to the House that the committee's work has been completed. At this time members may demand a roll-call vote on any first degree amendment adopted in the Committee of the Whole.

Concurrent Resolution. A concurrent resolution, designated H. Con. Res. or S. Con. Res., must be adopted by both houses, but it is not sent to the president for his signature and therefore does not have the force of law. A concurrent resolution, for example, is used to fix the time for adjournment of a Congress. It also is used as the vehicle for expressing the sense of Congress on various foreign policy and domestic issues, and it serves as the vehicle for coordinated decisions on the federal budget under the 1974 Congressional Budget and Impoundment Control Act. (See also **Bills, Joint Resolution, Resolution.**)

Conference. A meeting between representatives of the House and the Senate to reconcile differences when the chambers pass dissimilar versions of the same bill. Members of the conference committee are appointed formally by the Speaker and the presiding officer of the Senate and are called managers for their respective chambers.

A majority of the managers for each house must reach agreement on the provisions of the bill (usually a compromise between the versions of the two chambers) before it can be considered by either chamber in the form of a conference report. When the conference report goes to the floor, it cannot be amended, and, if it is not approved by both chambers, the bill may go back to conference or a new conference may be convened. Informal practices largely govern the conduct of conference committees.

Bills that are passed by both houses with only minor differences need not be sent to conference. Either chamber may concur in the other's amendments, completing action on the legislation. Sometimes leaders of the committees of jurisdiction work out an informal compromise instead of having a formal conference.

Continuing Resolution. A joint resolution drafted by Congress that continues appropriations for specific ongoing activities of a government department or departments when a fiscal year begins and Congress has not yet enacted all of the regular appropriations bills for that year. The continuing resolution usually specifies a maximum rate at which the agency may incur obligations. This usually is based on the rate for the previous year, the president's budget request, or an appropriation bill for that year passed by either or both houses of Congress, but not cleared.

Corrections Calendar. A House Calendar, established in 1995, to which relatively noncontroversial legislation is assigned. To be eligible for placement on the Corrections Calendar, measures must have been favorably reported from committees and assigned to either the House or Union calendars. The Corrections Calendar is in order, at the Speaker's discretion, on the second and fourth Tuesdays (Correction Days) of each month. Debate on bills correcting overly burdensome, arbitrary, or costly laws and regulations is limited to one hour. Further, no amendments are permitted (unless offered by the chairman of the primary committee of jurisdiction) and a three-fifths vote is required to pass correction bills.

Dilatory Motion. A motion made for the purpose of killing time and preventing action on a bill or amendment. House rules outlaw dilatory motions, but enforcement is largely within the discretion of the Speaker or chairman of the Committee of the Whole. The Senate does not have a rule banning dilatory motions, except under cloture.

Discharge a Committee. Occasionally, attempts are made to relieve a committee from jurisdiction over a measure before it. This is attempted more often in the House than in the Senate, and the procedure rarely is successful.

In the House, if a committee does not report a bill within thirty days after the measure is referred to it, any member may file a discharge motion. Once offered, the motion is treated as a petition needing the signatures of 218 members (a majority of the House). After the required signatures have been obtained, there is a delay of seven days. Thereafter, on the second and fourth Mondays of each month, except during the last six days of a session, any member who has signed the petition must be recognized, if he so desires, to move that the committee be discharged. Debate on the motion to discharge is limited to twenty minutes, and, if the motion is carried, consideration of the bill becomes a matter of high privilege.

If a resolution to consider a bill is held up in the Rules Committee for more than seven legislative days, any member may enter a motion to discharge the committee. The motion is handled like any other discharge petition in the House. (For Senate procedure, see **Discharge Resolution.**)

Discharge Calendar. The House calendar to which motions to discharge committees are referred when they have the required number of signatures (218) and are awaiting floor action.

Discharge Petition. (See **Discharge a Committee.**)

Discharge Resolution. In the Senate, a special motion that any senator may introduce to relieve a committee from consideration of a bill before it. The resolution can be called up for Senate approval or disapproval in the same manner as any other Senate business. (For House procedure, see **Discharge a Committee.**)

Division Vote. (See **Standing Vote.**)

Enacting Clause. Key phrase in bills beginning, "Be it enacted by the Senate and House of Representatives. . . ." A successful motion to strike it from legislation kills the measure.

Engrossed Bill. The final copy of a bill as passed by one chamber, with the text as amended by floor action and certified by the clerk of the House or the secretary of the Senate.

Enrolled Bill. The final copy of a bill that has been passed in identical form by both chambers. It is certified by an officer of the house of origin (clerk of the House or secretary of the Senate) and then sent on for the signatures of the House Speaker, the Senate president pro tempore, and the president of the United States. An enrolled bill is printed on parchment.

Executive Calendar. This is a nonlegislative calendar in the Senate on which treaties and nominations are listed.

Filibuster. A time-delaying tactic associated with the Senate and used by a minority in an effort to prevent a vote on a bill or amendment that probably would pass if voted upon directly. The most common method is to take advantage of the Senate's rules permitting unlimited debate, but other forms of parliamentary maneuvering may be used. The stricter rules used by the House make filibusters more difficult, but delaying tactics are employed occasionally through various procedural devices allowed by House rules. (See **Cloture.**)

Five-Minute Rule. A debate-limiting rule of the House that is invoked when the House sits as the Committee of the Whole. Under the rule, a member offering an amendment is allowed to speak five minutes in favor, and an opponent of the amendment is allowed to speak five minutes in opposition. Debate is then closed. In practice, amendments regularly are debated more than ten minutes, with members gaining the floor by offering pro forma amendments or obtaining unanimous consent to speak longer than five minutes. (See **Strike Out the Last Word.**)

Germane. Pertaining to the subject matter of the legislation at hand. House amendments must be germane to the bill being considered. The Senate requires that amendments be germane when they are proposed to general appropriation bills, bills being considered once cloture has been adopted, or, frequently, when proceeding under a unanimous consent agreement placing a time limit on consideration of a bill. The 1974 budget act also requires that amendments to concurrent budget resolutions be germane. In the House, floor debate must be germane, and the first three hours of debate each day in the Senate must be germane to the pending business.

House Calendar. A listing for action by the House of public bills that do not directly or indirectly appropriate money or raise revenue.

Joint Resolution. A joint resolution, designated H.J Res. or S.J. Res., requires the approval of both houses and the signature of the president, just as a bill does, and has the force of law if approved. No practical difference exists between a bill and a joint resolution.

A joint resolution generally is used to deal with a limited matter such as a single appropriation. Joint resolutions also are used to propose amendments to the Constitution. They must pass both chambers in identical form but do not require a presidential signature; they become a part of the Constitution when three-fourths of the states have ratified them.

Law. An act of Congress that has been signed by the president or passed over his veto by Congress. Public bills, when signed, become public laws and are cited by the letters P.L. and a hyphenated number. The two digits before the hyphen correspond to the Congress, and the one or more digits after the hyphen refer to the numerical sequence in which the bills were signed by the president during that Congress. Private bills, when signed, become private laws.

Legislative Day. The day extending from the time either house meets after an adjournment until the time it next adjourns. Because the House normally adjourns from day to day, legislative days and calendar days usually coincide. But in the Senate, a legislative day may, and frequently does, extend over several calendar days. (See **Recess.**)

Legislative Veto. A procedure permitting either the House or Senate, or both chambers, to review proposed executive branch regulations or actions and to block or modify those with which they disagree. The specifics of the procedure may vary, but Congress generally provides for a legislative veto by including in a bill a provision that administrative rules or action taken to implement the law are to go into effect at the end of a designated period of time unless blocked by either or both houses (even committees) of Congress. Another version of the veto provides for congressional reconsideration and rejection of regulations already in effect. The Supreme Court on June 23, 1983, restricted the form and use of the legislative veto, ruling that it is an unconstitutional violation of the lawmaking procedure provided in the Constitution.

Majority Leader. The majority leader is elected by members of the majority party. In the Senate, in consultation with the minority leader and other senators, the majority leader directs the legislative schedule and serves as party spokesperson and chief strategist. In the House, the majority leader is second to the Speaker in the majority party's leadership and serves as the party's "field general" on the floor.

Majority Whip. In effect, the assistant majority leader in either the House or Senate. The majority whip helps marshal majority forces in support of party strategy and legislation.

Marking Up a Bill. Going through the contents of a piece of legislation in committee or subcommittee, considering its provisions in large and small portions, acting on amendments to provisions and proposed revisions to the language, inserting new sections and phraseology, and so on. If the bill is extensively amended, the committee's version may be introduced as a separate bill, with a new number, before being considered by the full House or Senate. (See **Clean Bill.**)

Minority Leader. Floor leader for the minority party in each chamber.

Minority Whip. Performs duties of whip for the minority party.

Motion. In the House or Senate chamber, a request by a member to institute any one of a wide array of parliamentary actions. A member moves for a certain procedure, the consideration of a measure, and so on. The precedence of motions, and whether they are debatable, is set forth in the House and Senate manuals.

One-Minute Speeches. Addresses by House members at the beginning of a legislative day. The speeches may cover any subject but are limited to one minute's duration.

Override a Veto. If the president disapproves a bill and sends it back to Congress with his objections, Congress may try to override his veto and enact the bill into law. Neither house is required to attempt to override a veto. The override of a veto requires a recorded vote with a two-thirds majority in each chamber. The question put to each house is: "Shall the bill pass, the objections of the president to the contrary notwithstanding?" (See also **Pocket Veto, Veto.**)

Pair. A voluntary arrangement between two lawmakers, usually on opposite sides of an issue. If passage of the measure requires a two-thirds majority vote, a pair would require two members favoring the action to one opposed to it. The names of lawmakers pairing on a given vote and their stands, if known, are printed in the *Congressional Record*.

PAYGO (Pay-As-You-Go). A procedure established in the Budget Enforcement Act of 1990 requiring that mandatory spending or revenue legislation increasing the deficit must be offset to avoid a sequester of certain financial accounts. (See **Sequestration.**)

Pocket Veto. The act of the president in withholding approval of a bill after Congress has adjourned. When Congress is in session, a bill becomes law without the president's signature if the president does not act upon it within ten days, excluding Sundays, of receiving it. But if Congress adjourns *sine die* within that ten-day period, the bill will die even if the president does not formally veto it. (See also **Veto.**)

Point of Order. An objection raised by a member that the chamber is departing from rules governing its conduct of business. The objector cites the rule violated, and the chair sustains the objection if correctly made. Order is restored by the chair's suspending proceedings of the chamber until it conforms to the prescribed order of business.

President of the Senate. Under the Constitution, the vice president of the United States presides over the Senate. In the vice president's absence, the president pro tempore, or a senator designated by the president pro tempore, presides over the chamber.

President Pro Tempore. The chief officer of the Senate in the absence of the vice president; literally, but loosely, "president for a time." The president pro tempore is elected by the full membership of the Senate. The recent practice has been to choose the senator of the majority party with the longest period of continuous service.

Previous Question. A motion for the previous question, when carried, has the effect of cutting off all debate, preventing the offering of further amendments, and forcing a vote on the pending matter. In the House, the previous question is not permitted in the Committee of the Whole. The motion for the previous question is a debate-limiting device and is not in order in the Senate.

Private Calendar. In the House, private bills dealing with individual matters such as claims against the government, immigration, and land titles are put on this calendar. The private calendar must be called on the first Tuesday of each month; the Speaker may call it on the third Tuesday of each month as well.

Privilege. Privilege relates to the rights of members of Congress and to the relative priority of the motions and actions they may make in their respective chambers. The two are distinct. Privileged questions deal with legislative business. Questions of privilege concern members themselves.

Privileged Questions. The order in which bills, motions, and other legislative measures are considered by Congress is governed by strict priorities. A motion to table, for instance, is more privileged than a motion to recommit. Thus, a motion to recommit can be superseded by a motion to table, and a vote would be forced on the latter motion only. A motion to adjourn, however, takes precedence over a tabling motion and thus is considered of the highest privilege. (See also **Questions of Privilege.**)

Pro Forma Amendment. (See **Strike Out the Last Word.**)

Questions of Privilege. These are matters affecting members of Congress individually or collectively. Matters affecting the rights, safety, dignity, and integrity of proceedings of the House or Senate as a whole are questions of privilege in both chambers.

Questions involving individual members are called questions of personal privilege. A member rising to ask a question of personal privilege is given precedence over almost all other proceedings. An annotation in the House rules points out that the privilege is derived chiefly from the Constitution, which gives a member a conditional immunity from arrest and an unconditional freedom to speak in the House. (See also **Privileged Questions.**)

Quorum. The number of members whose presence is necessary for the transaction of business. In the Senate and House, it is a majority of the membership. A quorum is one hundred in the Committee of the Whole. If a point of order is made that a quorum is not present, the only business that is in order is either a motion to adjourn or a motion to direct the sergeant-at-arms to request the attendance of absentees.

Readings of Bills. Traditional parliamentary procedure requires bills to be read three times before they are passed. This custom is of little modern significance. Normally a bill is considered to have its first reading when it is introduced and printed, by title, in the *Congressional Record*. In the House, its second reading comes when floor consideration begins. (This is the most likely point at which a reading of the bill does take place, if there is any.) The second reading in the Senate is supposed to occur on the legislative day after the measure is introduced, but before it is referred to committee. The third reading (again, by title) takes place when floor action has been completed on amendments.

Recess. Distinguished from adjournment in that a recess does not end a legislative day and therefore does not interrupt unfinished business. The rules in each house set forth certain matters to be taken up and disposed of at the beginning of each legislative day. The House usually adjourns from day to day. The Senate often recesses, thus meeting on the same legislative day for several calendar days or even weeks at a time. (See **Adjournment.**)

Recognition. The power of recognition of a member is lodged in the Speaker of the House and the presiding officer of the Senate. The presiding officer names the member who will speak first when two or more members simultaneously request recognition.

Recommit to Committee. A motion, made on the floor after a bill has been debated, to return it to the committee that reported it. If approved, recommittal usually is considered a death blow to the bill. In the House, a motion to recommit can be made only by a member opposed to the bill, and, in recognizing a member to make the motion, the Speaker gives preference to members of the minority party over majority party members.

A motion to recommit may include instructions to the committee to report the bill again with specific amendments or by a certain date. Or, the instructions may direct that a particular study be made, with no definite deadline for further action. If the recommittal motion includes instructions to "report the bill back forthwith" and the motion is adopted, floor action on the bill continues; the committee does not reconsider the legislation.

Reconsider a Vote. A motion to reconsider the vote by which an action was taken has, until it is disposed of, the effect of putting the action in abeyance. In the Senate, the motion can be made only by a member who voted on the prevailing side of the original question or by a member who did not vote at all. In the House, it can be made only by a member on the prevailing side.

A common practice in the Senate after close votes on an issue is a motion to reconsider, followed by a motion to table the motion to reconsider. On this motion to table, senators usually vote as they voted on the original question, which allows the motion to table to prevail, assuming there are no switches. The matter then is finally closed and further motions to reconsider are not entertained. In the House, as a routine precaution, a motion to reconsider usually is made every time a measure is passed. Such a motion almost always is tabled immediately, thus eliminating the possibility of future reconsideration, except by unanimous consent. Motions to reconsider must be entered in the Senate within the next two days of session after the original vote has been taken. In the House they must be entered either on the same day or on the next succeeding day the House is in session.

Recorded Vote. A vote upon which each member's stand is individually made known. In the Senate, this is accomplished through a roll call of the entire membership, to which each senator on the floor must answer "yea," "nay," or, if he does not wish to vote, "present." Since January 1973, the House has used an electronic voting system for recorded votes, including yea-and-nay votes formerly taken by roll calls. When not required by the Constitution, a recorded vote can be obtained on questions in the House on the demand of one-fifth (forty-four members) of a quorum or one-fourth (twenty-five members) of a quorum in the Committee of the Whole. (See **Yeas and Nays.**)

Report. Both a verb and a noun as a congressional term. A committee that has been examining a bill referred to it by the parent chamber reports its findings and recommendations to the chamber when it completes consideration and returns the measure. This process is called reporting a bill.

A report is the document setting forth the committee's explanation of its action. Senate and House reports are numbered separately and are designated S. Rept. or H. Rept. When a committee report is not unanimous, the dissenting committee members may file a statement of their views, called minority views and referred to as a minority report. Members in disagreement with some provisions of a bill may file additional or supplementary views. Sometimes a bill is reported without a committee recommendation. Adverse reports occasionally are submitted by legislative committees. When a committee is opposed to a bill, it usually fails to report the measure at all. Some laws require that committee reports, favorable or adverse, be made.

Resolution. A simple resolution, designated H. Res. or S. Res., deals with matters entirely within the prerogatives of one house or the other. It requires neither passage by the other chamber nor approval by the president, and it does not have the force of law. Most resolutions deal with the rules or procedures of one house. They also are used to express the sentiments of a single house, such as condolences to the family of a deceased member, or to comment on foreign policy or executive business. A simple resolution is the vehicle for a rule from the House Rules Committee. (See also **Concurrent Resolution, Joint Resolution, Rules.**)

Rider. An amendment, usually not germane, which its sponsor hopes to get through more easily by including it in other legislation. Riders become law if the bills embodying them are enacted. Amendments providing legislative directives in appropriations bills are outstanding examples of riders, though technically legislation is banned from appropriations bills. The House, unlike the Senate, has a strict germaneness rule; thus, riders usually are Senate devices to get legislation enacted quickly or to bypass lengthy House consideration and, possibly, opposition.

Rules. The term has two specific congressional meanings. A rule may be a standing order governing the conduct of House or Senate business and listed among the permanent rules of either chamber. The rules deal with such matters as the duties of officers, the order of business, admission to the floor, parliamentary procedures on handling amendments and voting, and jurisdictions of committees.

In the House, a rule also may be a resolution reported by the Rules Committee to govern the handling of a particular bill on the floor. The committee may report a rule, also called a special order, in the form of a simple resolution. If the resolution is adopted by the House, the temporary rule becomes as valid as any standing rule and lapses only after action has been completed on the measure to which it pertains. A rule sets the time limit on general debate. It also may waive points of order against provisions of the bill in question, such as nongermane language, or against certain amendments intended to be proposed to the bill from the floor. It may even forbid all amendments or all amendments except those proposed by the legislative committee that handled the bill. In this instance, it is known as a closed or gag rule as opposed to an open rule, which puts no limitation on floor amendments, thus leaving the bill completely open to alteration by the adoption of germane amendments.

Senatorial Courtesy. Sometimes referred to as "the courtesy of the Senate," it is a general practice—with no written rule—applied to consideration of executive nominations. Generally, it means that nominees from a state are not to be confirmed unless they have been approved by the senators of the president's party of that state, with other senators following their colleagues' lead in the attitude they take toward consideration of such nominations.

Sequestration. The cancellation (or withholding) of budgetary resources. Once canceled, sequestered funds are no longer available for obligation or expenditure.

Speaker. The presiding officer of the House of Representatives and the overall leader of the majority party in the chamber. The Speaker is selected by the caucus of the majority party's members and formally elected by the full House at the beginning of each new Congress.

Standing Committee. (See **Committee.**)

Standing Vote. A nonrecorded vote used in both the House and the Senate. (A standing vote also is called a division vote.) Members in favor of a proposal stand and are counted by the presiding officer. Then members opposed stand and are counted. There is no record of how individual members voted.

Strike Out the Last Word. A motion whereby a House member is entitled to speak for five minutes on an amendment then being debated by the chamber. A member gains recognition from the chair by moving to strike out the last word of the amendment or section of the bill under consideration. The motion is pro forma, requires no vote, and does not change the amendment being debated.

Substitute. A discreet amendment or entire bill introduced in place of the pending legislative business. Passage of a substitute measure kills the original measure by supplanting it. The substitute also may be amended. (See also **Amendment in the Nature of a Substitute.**)

Supplemental Appropriations Bill. Legislation appropriating funds after the regular annual appropriations bill for a federal department or agency has been enacted. A supplemental appropriation provides additional budget authority beyond original estimates for programs or activities, including new programs authorized after the enactment of the regular appropriations act. (See also **Appropriations Bill.**)

Suspend the Rules. Often a time-saving procedure for passing bills in the House. The wording of the motion, which may be made by any member recognized by the Speaker, is: "I move to suspend the rules and pass the bill. . . ." A favorable vote by two-thirds of those present is required for passage. Debate is limited to forty minutes and no amendments from the floor are permitted. If a two-thirds favorable vote is not attained, the bill may be considered later under regular procedures. The suspension procedure is in order every Monday and Tuesday and is intended to be reserved for noncontroversial bills.

Table a Bill. A motion to lay on the table is not debatable in either house, and usually it is a method of making a final, adverse disposition of a matter. Tabling motions on amendments are effective debate-ending devices in the Senate.

Treaties. Executive proposals—in the form of resolutions of ratification—that must be submitted to the Senate for approval by two-thirds of the senators present. Treaties are normally sent to the Foreign Relations Committee for scrutiny before the Senate takes action. Foreign Relations has jurisdiction over virtually all treaties. Treaties are read three times and debated on the floor in much the same manner as legislative proposals. After approval by the Senate, treaties are formally ratified by the president. Unlike legislative documents, however, treaties do not die at the end of a Congress but remain live proposals until acted on by the Senate or withdrawn by the president.

Unanimous Consent. Proceedings of the House or Senate and action on legislation often take place upon the unanimous consent of the chamber, whether or not a rule of the chamber is being violated. Unanimous consent is used to expedite floor action and frequently is used in a routine fashion. For example, a senator may request the unanimous consent of the Senate to have specified members of his staff present on the floor during debate on an amendment.

Unanimous Consent Agreement. A device used in the Senate to expedite legislation. Much of the Senate's legislative business, dealing with both minor and controversial issues, is conducted through unanimous consent or unanimous consent agreements. On major legislation, such agreements usually are printed and transmitted to all senators in advance of floor debate. Once agreed to, they are binding on all members unless the Senate, by unanimous consent, agrees to modify them. An agreement may list the order in which various bills are to be considered, specify the length of time bills and amendments are to be debated and when they are to be voted upon, and, frequently, require that all amendments introduced be relevant to the bill under consideration. In this regard, unanimous consent agreements are similar to the rules issued by the House Rules Committee for bills pending in the House. (See **Rules.**)

Union Calendar. Bills that directly or indirectly appropriate money or raise revenue are placed on this calendar of the House according to the date they are reported from committee.

Veto. Disapproval by the president of a bill or joint resolution (other than one proposing an amendment to the Constitution). When Congress is in session, the president must veto a bill within ten days, excluding Sundays, of receiving it; otherwise, the bill becomes law without the president's signature. When the president vetoes a bill, it must be returned to the house of origin with a message stating the president's objections. (See also **Override a Veto, Pocket Veto.**)

Voice Vote. In either the House or Senate, members answer "aye" or "no" in chorus, and the presiding officer decides the result. The term also is used loosely to indicate action by unanimous consent or without objection.

Yeas and Nays. The Constitution requires that yea-and-nay votes be taken and recorded when requested by one-fifth of the members present. In the House, the Speaker determines whether one-fifth of the members present requested a vote. In the Senate, practice requires only eleven members. The Constitution requires the yeas and nays on a veto override attempt. (See **Recorded Vote.**)

Yielding. When a member has been recognized to speak, no other member may speak without permission from the member recognized. This permission is called yielding and usually is requested in the form, "Will the gentleman yield to me for a question?" While this activity occasionally is seen in the Senate, the Senate has no rule or practice to parcel out time, other than in unanimous consent agreements.

Selected Bibliography

Chapter 1. Congress and Lawmaking

Arnold, R. Douglas. *The Logic of Congressional Action*. New Haven, Conn.: Yale University Press, 1990.

Bacon, Donald C., Roger H. Davidson, and Morton Keller, eds. *The Encyclopedia of the United States Congress*. 4 vols. New York: Simon & Schuster, 1995.

Binder, Sarah A. *Minority Rights, Majority Rule: Partisanship and the Development of Congress*. New York: Cambridge University Press, 1997.

Davidson, Roger H., and Walter J. Oleszek. *Congress and Its Members*. 7th ed. Washington, D.C.: CQ Press, 2000.

Gross, Bertram M. *The Legislative Struggle*. New York: McGraw-Hill, 1953.

Koempel, Michael L., and Judy Schneider. *Congressional Deskbook 2000*. Alexandria, Va.: TheCapitol.Net Inc., 2000.

Lee, Frances E., and Bruce I. Oppenheimer. *Sizing Up the Senate: The Unequal Consequences of Equal Representation*. Chicago, Ill.: University of Chicago Press, 1999.

Luce, Robert. *Legislative Procedures*. Boston: Houghton Mifflin, 1922.

___. *Legislative Assemblies*. Boston: Houghton Mifflin, 1924.

___. *Legislative Principles*. Boston: Houghton Mifflin, 1930.

___. *Legislative Problems*. Boston: Houghton Mifflin, 1935.

Silbey, Joel H., ed. *Encyclopedia of the American Legislative System*. 3 vols. New York: Charles Scribner's Sons, 1994.

Tiefer, Charles. *Congressional Practice and Procedure: A Reference, Research, and Legislative Guide*. New York: Greenwood Press, 1989.

Chapter 2. The Congressional Budget Process

Fenno, Richard F., Jr. *The Power of the Purse*. Boston: Little, Brown, 1966.

Munson, Richard. *The Cardinals of Capitol Hill*. New York: Grove Press, 1993.

Palazzolo, Daniel J. *Done Deal? The Politics of the 1997 Budget Agreement*. Chatham, N.J.: Chatham House, 1999.

Schick, Allen. *Congress and Money*. Washington, D.C.: Urban Institute Press, 1980.

___. *The Capacity to Budget*. Washington, D.C.: Urban Institute Press, 1990.

___. *The Federal Budget: Politics, Policy, Process*. Revised edition. Washington, D.C.: Brookings Institution Press, 2000.

Strahan, Randall. *New Ways and Means: Reform and Change in a Congressional Committee*. Chapel Hill: University of North Carolina Press, 1990.

Wildavsky, Aaron. *The Politics of the Budgetary Process*. 4th ed. Boston: Little, Brown, 1984.

Wilmerding, Lucius. *The Spending Power*. New Haven, Conn.: Yale University Press, 1943.

Chapter 3. Preliminary Legislative Action

Cooper, Joseph. *The Origins of the Standing Committees and the Development of the Modern House.* Rice University Monograph in Political Science, vol. 56, no. 3, Summer 1970.

Davidson, Roger H., and Walter J. Oleszek. *Congress against Itself.* Bloomington: Indiana University Press, 1977.

Deering, Christopher J., and Steven S. Smith. *Committees in Congress.* 3d ed. Washington, D.C.: CQ Press, 1997.

Evans, C. Lawrence. *Leadership in Committee.* Ann Arbor: University of Michigan Press, 1991.

Fenno, Richard F., Jr. *Congressmen in Committees.* Boston: Little, Brown, 1973.

King, David C. *Turf Wars: How Congressional Committees Claim Jurisdiction.* Chicago, Ill.: University of Chicago Press, 1997.

Krehbiel, Keith. *Information and Legislative Organization.* Ann Arbor: University of Michigan Press, 1991.

Maltzman, Forrest. *Competing Principals: Committees, Parties, and the Organization of Congress.* Ann Arbor: University of Michigan Press, 1997.

Wilson, Woodrow. *Congressional Government.* Boston: Houghton Mifflin, 1885.

Chapter 4. Scheduling Legislation in the House

Cooper, Joseph, and David W. Brady. "Institutional Context and Leadership Style: The House from Cannon to Rayburn." *American Political Science Review,* June 1981, pp. 411–425.

Cox, Gary W., and Mathew D. McCubbins. *Legislative Leviathan: Party Government in the House.* Berkeley: University of California Press, 1993.

Hardeman, D. B., and Donald C. Bacon. *Rayburn.* Austin: Texas Monthly Press, 1987.

"A History of the Committee on Rules." Committee Print, 97th Cong., 2d sess. Washington, D.C.: Government Printing Office, 1983.

Peters, Ronald M., Jr. *The American Speakership.* 2d ed. Baltimore, Md.: Johns Hopkins University Press, 1997.

Rae, Nicol, and Colton C. Campbell. *New Majority or Old Minority? The Impact of Republicans on Congress.* Lanham, Md.: Rowan and Littlefield Publishers, 1999.

Rohde, David. *Parties and Leaders in the Postreform House.* Chicago, Ill.: University of Chicago Press, 1991.

Chapter 5. House Floor Procedure

Alexander, DeAlva Stanwood. *History and Procedure of the House of Representatives.* Boston: Houghton Mifflin, 1916.

Bach, Stanley, and Steven S. Smith. *Managing Uncertainty in the House of Representatives: Adaptation and Innovation in Special Rules.* Washington, D.C.: Brookings Institution, 1988.

Damon, Richard E. "The Standing Rules of the U.S. House of Representatives." Ph.D. dissertation, Columbia University, 1971.

Froman, Lewis A. *The Congressional Process: Strategies, Rules, and Procedures.* Boston: Little, Brown, 1967.

Harlow, Ralph V. *The History of Legislative Methods in the Period before 1825.* New Haven, Conn.: Yale University Press, 1917.

MacNeil, Neil. *Forge of Democracy: The House of Representatives.* New York: David McKay, 1963.

Polsby, Nelson W. "The Institutionalization of the House of Representatives." *American Political Science Review,* March 1968, pp. 144–168.

Sinclair, Barbara. *Legislators, Leaders, and Lawmaking: The U.S. House of Representatives in the Postreform Era.* Baltimore, Md.: Johns Hopkins University Press, 1995.

Smith, Steven S. *Call to Order: Floor Politics in the House and Senate.* Washington, D.C.: Brookings Institution, 1989.

Chapter 6. Scheduling Legislation in the Senate

Clark, Joseph S. *The Senate Establishment.* New York: Hill & Wang, 1963.

Ehrenhalt, Alan. "Special Report: The Individualist Senate." *Congressional Quarterly Weekly Report,* September 4, 1982, pp. 2175–2182.

Fenno, Richard F., Jr. *Learning to Legislate: The Senate Education of Arlen Specter.* Washington, D.C.: CQ Press, 1991.

Harris, Fred R. *Deadlock or Decision: The U.S. Senate and the Rise of National Politics.* New York: Oxford University Press, 1993.

Hibbing, John R., ed. *The Changing World of the U.S. Senate.* Berkeley, Calif.: IGS Press, 1990.

Rudman, Warren. *Combat: Twelve Years in the U.S. Senate.* New York: Random House, 1996.

Chapter 7. Senate Floor Procedure

Binder, Sarah A., and Steven S. Smith. *Politics or Principle? Filibustering in the United States Senate.* Washington, D.C.: Brookings Institution Press, 1997.

Burdette, Franklin L. *Filibustering in the Senate.* Princeton, N.J.: Princeton University Press, 1940.

Evans, Rowland, and Robert Novak. *Lyndon B. Johnson: The Exercise of Power.* New York: New American Library, 1966.

Harris, Joseph P. *The Advice and Consent of the Senate.* Berkeley: University of California Press, 1953.

Matthews, Donald. *U.S. Senators and Their World.* Chapel Hill: University of North Carolina Press, 1960.

Shuman, Howard E. "Senate Rules and the Civil Rights Bill: A Case Study." *American Political Science Review,* December 1957, pp. 955–975.

Sinclair, Barbara. *The Transformation of the U.S. Senate.* Baltimore, Md.: Johns Hopkins University Press, 1989.

Chapter 8. Resolving House-Senate Differences

Fenno, Richard F., Jr. *The United States Senate: A Bicameral Perspective.* Washington, D.C.: American Enterprise Institute for Public Policy Research, 1982.

Longley, Lawrence D., and Walter J. Oleszek. *Bicameral Politics: Conference Committees in Congress.* New Haven, Conn.: Yale University Press, 1989.

McCown, Ada C. *The Congressional Conference Committee.* New York: Columbia University Press, 1927.

Pressman, Jeffrey L. *House vs. Senate: Conflict in the Appropriations Process.* New Haven, Conn.: Yale University Press, 1966.

Steiner, Gilbert. *The Congressional Conference Committee, Seventieth to Eightieth Congresses.* Urbana: University of Illinois Press, 1951.

Vogler, David J. *The Third House: Conference Committees in the U.S. Congress.* Evanston, Ill.: Northwestern University Press, 1971.

Chapter 9. Legislative Oversight

Aberbach, Joel D. *Keeping a Watchful Eye: The Politics of Congressional Oversight.* Washington, D.C.: Brookings Institution, 1990.

Bond, Jon R., and Richard Fleisher, eds. *Polarized Politics: Congress and the President in a Partisan Era.* Washington, D.C.: CQ Press, 2000.

Fisher, Louis. *Constitutional Conflicts between Congress and the President.* 4th ed., revised. Lawrence: University of Kansas Press, 1997.

Foreman, Christopher H. *Signals from the Hill: Congressional Oversight and the Challenge of Social Regulation.* New Haven, Conn.: Yale University Press, 1988.

Gilmour, Robert S., and Alexis A. Halley, eds. *Who Makes Public Policy: The Struggle for Control between Congress and the Executive.* Chatham, N.J.: Chatham House, 1994.

Harris, Joseph P. *Congressional Control of Administration.* Washington, D.C.: Brookings Institution, 1964.

Light, Paul C. *Monitoring Government: Inspectors General and the Search for Accountability.* Washington, D.C.: Brookings Institution, 1993.

Ogul, Morris S. *Congress Oversees the Bureaucracy.* Pittsburgh, Pa.: University of Pittsburgh Press, 1976.

West, William F. *Controlling the Bureaucracy.* Armonk, N.Y.: M. E. Sharp, 1995.

Chapter 10. A Dynamic Process

Bailey, Stephen K. *Congress Makes a Law.* New York: Columbia University Press, 1950.

Birnbaum, Jeffrey H., and Alan S. Murray. *Showdown at Gucci Gulch.* New York: Random House, 1987.

Casey, Chris. *The Hill on the Net: Congress Enters the Information Age.* Chestnut Hill, Mass.: Academic Press Inc., 1996.

Davidson, Roger H., ed. *The Postreform Congress.* New York: St. Martin's Press, 1992.

Evans, C. Lawrence, and Walter J. Oleszek. *Congress under Fire: Reform Politics and the Republican Majority.* Boston: Houghton Mifflin, 1997.

Hibbing, John R., and Elizabeth Thiess-Morse. *Congress as Public Enemy.* New York: Cambridge University Press, 1995.

Jones, Charles O. "A Way of Life and Law." *American Political Science Review,* March 1995, pp. 1–9.

Krehbiel, Keith. *Pivotal Politics: A Theory of Lawmaking.* Chicago, Ill.: University of Chicago Press, 1998.

Redman, Eric. *The Dance of Legislation.* New York: Simon & Schuster, 1973.

Sinclair, Barbara. *Unorthodox Lawmaking.* 2d ed. Washington, D.C.: CQ Press, 2000.

Sundquist, James L. *The Decline and Resurgence of Congress.* Washington, D.C.: Brookings Institution, 1981.

Wolfensberger, Donald R. *Congress and the People: Deliberative Democracy on Trial.* Washington, D.C.: Woodrow Wilson Center Press, 2000.

SELECTED INTERNET SOURCES

Architect of the Capitol (http://www.aoc.gov)
C-SPAN (http://www.c-span.org)
CNN/Time (http://www.cnn.com/ALLPOLITICS)
Clerk of the House (http://www.clerkweb.house.gov)
Congressional Budget Office (http://www.cbo.gov)
Congressional Quarterly (http://www.cq.com)
General Accounting Office (http://www.gao.gov)
Government Printing Office (http://www.access.gpo.gov)
The Hill (http://www.hillnews.com)
House of Representatives (http://www.house.gov)
Library of Congress (http://www.thomas.loc.gov)
National Journal (http://www.nationaljournal.com)
Roll Call (http://www.rollcall.com)
Senate (http://www.senate.gov)
Washington Post (http://www.washingtonpost.com)
White House (http://www.whitehouse.gov)

Index

Aberbach, Joel, 294, 297
Abortion, 53–54, 123, 261*b*
Abscam scandal, 116–117
Adams, John Quincy, 49
AFDC. *See* Aid to Families with Dependent Children
Agencies, 275–276, 280, 282, 283, 284, 285. *See also* Government, federal; individual agencies by name
Agenda of the American People, 141. *See also* Contract with America
Aid to Families with Dependent Children (AFDC), 47
AIR-21. *See* Aviation Investment and Reform Act for the 21st Century
Alaska, 216*b*
Albert, Carl (D-Okla.), 140
Albert Gore Jr. Mud Dump Site, 80
Alexander, De Alva Stanwood (R-N.Y.), 152, 178
Allred, Victoria, 242
Alvarez, Lizete, 178
Amendments
  amendment tree, 220–223
  to appropriations bills, 53, 54–55, 151, 237, 239–240
  as bargaining chips, 249
  cloture and, 232
  cue-givers, 225–226
  degrees of, 219, 220, 223, 232, 247
  in the nature of a substitute, 259
  in true disagreement, 261*b*
  make-a-point, 224
  nongermane, 236–239
  November, 224
  perfecting, 220
  poison-pill, 223–224
  policy, 239–240
  reconciliation process, 249, 251, 260, 261*b*
  sense-of-the-Senate, 237, 238
  substitute, 220
  voting, 220, 223, 224–227
Anderson, Jack, 180
Anderson, Nick, 243, 295
Antiterrorism legislation, 258

Appointments. *See* Nominations and appointments
Appropriations. *See also* Budget process; Entitlement programs
  amendments to bills, 238
  appropriations process as oversight, 281–282
  budget reform and, 56
  conference committees, 259–260
  continuing resolutions, 53, 58
  definition, types and structure, 43, 45, 46–47
  discretionary spending, 47, 62, 69
  general appropriations bills, 45, 49
  germaneness, 54–56, 60
  highway and transit spending, 52
  legislation in appropriations bills, 53, 54–55, 151, 237, 239–240
  limitations, 282
  lockbox government and, 293
  mega or omnibus bills, 58, 62
  process of, 259–260
  Republican Party and, 302
  riders, 53–55, 103, 262, 282
  rules, 49–50, 53–56, 128
Appropriations—specific legislation
  Department of Agriculture, 261*b*
  Department of Health, Education, and Welfare, 53–54
  Department of Health and Human Services, 159, 262
  Department of Interior, 55
  Department of Labor, 53–54, 159, 262
  Department of Treasury and Postal Service, 151
  District of Columbia, 262
  foreign aid, 259
Archer, Bill (R-Texas), 160
Armey, Dick (R-Texas), 157, 276, 301
Asbell, Bernard, 242
Ashbrook, John (R-Ohio), 129
Audits, 283, 284–285, 288. *See also* Legislative oversight
Authorizations. *See also* Budget process
  authorizing process and oversight, 280–281

backdoor measures, 52
budget resolution, 58
definition and purposes, 43–44
permanent to temporary, 45
presidential rescission, 65
reauthorizations, 43
review of programs, 275
rules, 49–50, 53–56
Aviation Investment and Reform Act for the
21st Century (AIR-21), 52

Babington, Charles, 74
Babson, Jennifer, 146
Baby boomers, 68, 70–71, 72
Bach, Stanley, 242
Baker, Howard H., Jr. (R-Tenn.), 62, 73, 190,
199, 254
Balutis, Alan B., 39
Bankruptcy reform bill, 252
Bargaining, 229–230, 249, 257–262, 300,
301. See also Coalitions
Barr, Stephen, 296
Barry, John M., 37
Bauman, Robert (R-Md.), 129, 147
Baumann, David, 295
Bedard, Paul, 297
Bedell, Berkley W. (D-Iowa), 289
Benenson, Bob, 147
Bennett, Robert F. (R-Utah), 303
Berger, Raoul, 295
Bessette, Joseph M., 178
Beth, Richard S., 147, 296
Bibby, John F., 179
Biden, Joseph R. (D-Del.), 258
Bills. See also Committees; Filibusters; Legislation; Reconciliation process
amendments, 158–168, 173, 217–227
appropriations, 127
assignment to calendars, 110
blue-slip rejection, 252
clean-bill procedure, 102
consideration in committee, 86–103, 239
debate, 153–158
engrossment and final reading, 173, 227
enrollment, 267–268
fast-track procedures, 142, 144
final action, 227
"in order" days, 110, 112, 115, 116,
139
introduction of, 75
legislative drafting, 83–84
legislative history, 284
markup, 95–101
motion to table, 212

multiple and split referrals, 84–86, 162,
164, 251, 253
numbering system for, 79–80, 103
numbers introduced and passed, 76, 77
presidential action, 268–271
reading of, 159, 160, 173, 178n12, 239
referral procedures, 79–86, 162, 253
riders, 162–163, 238, 262
scheduling, 109–144, 187–204
Senate floor procedure, 207–241
suspension, 11
time limits, 85, 86
unanimous consent agreements and, 84,
106n5, 215–217, 227–236
voting, 169–172, 226, 236
Binder, Sarah, 243
Binstein, Michael, 180
Birnbaum, Jeffrey H., 178
Biskupic, Joan, 108
Bliley, Thomas (R-Va.), 15–16, 78–79, 87b,
91
Boehlert, Sherwood (R-N.Y.), 266
Bolling, Richard W. (D-Mo.), 131, 156,
167
Bonior, David (D-Mich.), 9, 176
Bork, Robert H., 95, 191–192
Boyer, Dave, 147
Bradley, Bill (D-N.J.), 28
Bresnahan, John, 242
Breyer, Stephen G., 103, 284
Bridegam, Martha, 180
Brooke, Edward W. (R-Mass.), 54
Brookings Institution, 286
Brown, Everett Somerville, 72
Brown, William Holmes, 6b
Buckley, James L., 242
Budget and Accounting Act of 1921, 42, 284
Budget Enforcement Acts of 1990, 1997
(BEA), 41, 68–69, 70
Budget issues
balanced budget amendment, 214, 215
deficits, 15, 37n23, 41, 56, 66–67, 68–69,
70
emergencies, 70
federal budget, 43
indexing, 42
national debt, 41, 71, 72
off- and on-budget, 51–52, 71
reconciliation process, 15, 63–64
reforms, 56
surplus era, 69–72, 293, 306
uncontrollable spending, 42–43
Budget process. See also Appropriations; Authorizations; Budget Enforcement Act;

Congressional Budget and Impoundment Control Act of 1974
authorization-appropriations process, 43–56
budget authority, 47–48
budget crosswalk, 61
changes in, 300
committees, 48
concurrent budget resolution, 58–61, 62, 70
conference report, 60–61, 65
continuing resolutions, 53, 58
differences between House and Senate, 50–51
evolution of, 66–69
firewalls, 69
main phases of, 43
outlays, 47
pay-as-you-go (PAYGO) procedures, 69, 70–71
reconciliation, 15, 59, 61–65
reprogramming of funds, 295n30
sequestration, 69
spending caps, 69–70
timetable, 58, 59b, 61
Bumpers, Dale (D-Ark.), 227
Bush, George W., 100
Butterfield, Alexander P., 279
Byrd, Robert C. (D-W.Va.)
    as authority on Senate rules and precedents, 205n12
    campaign reform, 232–233
    as chairman of Appropriations Committee, 53
    holds, 193
    nomination of Bork, Robert H., 191
    paired votes, 226
    references, 39
    roll call votes, 225
    Rule XXII changes, 234
    as Senate Majority Leader, 199
    as senior Democrat, 192
    view of committee reports, 192
    view of filibusters, 228, 229
    view of majority leader, 189, 198
    view of morning hour and morning business, 210
    view of nomination process, 286
    view of president pro tempore, 207, 209
    view of Senate partisanship, 305
    view of Senate proceedings, 6, 25, 182, 186, 187, 212, 213–214, 215, 225, 226, 227, 300, 306

Byrd Rule, 56, 64–65

Cable-Satellite Public Affairs Network (C-SPAN)
    coverage of conference negotiations, 246
    debates on, 155
    effects of, 26, 31, 169, 213–214
Calendar of Business, 196, 205n13
Calendars. See House of Representatives; Senate
Calendars of the United States House of Representatives and History of Legislation, 110, 111
Calhoun, John C., 211
Calmes, Jackie, 39, 108
Campaigns and campaigning, 134, 172, 183, 232, 303
Cannon, Clarence A. (D-Mo.), 6b, 9, 37, 180
Cannon, Joseph G. (R-Ill.), 118, 141
Cannon's Precedents of the House of Representatives, 6b
Carey, Mary Agnes, 272
Carney, Dan, 307
Carney, Eliza Newlin, 307
Carroll, Holbert N., 295
Carter (Jimmy) administration, 85
Cary, Freeman, 227
Catholic Charities, 89
Caucuses, 60, 140, 285–286
CBO. See Congressional Budget Office
Central Intelligence Agency (CIA), 283, 290
Chairmen. See Committees
Chamber of Commerce, U.S., 2
Chatterjee, Sumana, 206, 242
Chen, Edwin, 37, 205
Chen, Ping, 145, 146
Child care legislation, 200
CIA. See Central Intelligence Agency
Cigler, Allan J., 40
Citizens Against Government Waste, 286
Civil rights, 90, 299
Civil Rights Act of 1964, 15, 230
Civil War, 276
Clapp, Charles L., 39, 272
Clark, Joseph S., 242
Clayton, Cornell, 295
Clean Air Act, 96, 285
Clinton, Bill
    Congressional Accountability Act, 247
    Exchange Stabilization Fund, 288–289
    fiscal 2001 budget, 70
    impeachment, 95, 105b
    juvenile justice legislation, 2
    line-item veto, 65, 66

managed care legislation, 254
1994 crime bill, 151
North American Free Trade Agreement, 30
Omnibus Reconciliation Act of 1993, 69
patients' bill of rights legislation, 258
prescription drugs for elderly, 144
2000 Interior appropriations bill, 55
use of budget surplus, 71
Whitewater hearings, 223
Clinton (Bill) administration, 41, 291, 299
Clinton v. City of New York (1998), 66
Cloud, David S., 38, 306
Cloture, 228, 231–236, 238, 299
Clymer, Adam, 37
Coalition, The, 253
Coalitions, 21–22, 172, 298, 299, 300, 304.
    See also Bargaining
Cochran, Thad (R-Miss.), 228
Cogan, John F., 74
Cohen, Richard E., 38, 103, 108, 306
Cohodas, Nadine, 243
Cold war, 41
"College of Cardinals," 48, 61
Collender, Stanley E., 73
Collier, Ellen C., 296
Colmer, William M. (D-Miss.), 140
Columbine High School, 1, 256
Committees. *See also* House of Representa-
    tives—committees; Senate—committees
alliances, 18
amendment process, 98, 99
authorizing and appropriating, 48, 51–53,
    67, 72n7, 275
bill consideration, 86–88, 114
blocking legislation, 138–142
bypassing, 1, 15, 16, 103, 105–106
chairmen, 89–91, 95, 96, 97, 98, 99,
    107n26, 114, 128, 257
conference committees, 1, 60–61,
    245–247, 250–268
hearings, 88, 89, 91–95, 279, 292
jurisdiction and mandate, 8, 17–18, 75,
    77, 81–82, 83–86
legislative oversight, 277, 278–279
markup, 95–101
members, 89–90, 91
minority party issues, 89–90, 93b
negotiations in, 91
nomination process, 286–287
partisanship in, 103, 105–106
the report, 101–103, 192
rules, 92, 93b, 96, 97, 101, 174b
seniority issues, 90, 92
staff, 107n26, 108n29

terms of office, 27
use of technology, 92
votes, 98–99, 101–102
witnesses, 89, 94, 107n24
Committee System Reorganization Amend-
    ments of 1977, 277
Comprehensive Crime Control Act of 1984,
    176–177
Comprehensive Nuclear Test Ban Treaty,
    195
Comptroller general, 285
Condit, Gary A. (D-Calif.), 69, 253
Conference committees. *See* Committees;
    Reconciliation process
Congress. *See also* Committees; House of
    Representatives; Senate
adjournment, 268–269, 301
audits, 284–285
bicameralism, 29
budget process enforcement, 66
centralization, 301–302
changes in, 301–306
coalition building, 21–22
conflict in, 9–10
constituents, 34–35
constitutional authority, 142
controls, 283–284
culture of, 17
cycle of, 17, 22–23, 88
differences in chambers, 300
electronic devices in, 304
functions of rules and procedures, 5–10,
    12–13
introduction of bills, 78–79
lawmaking of, 13–16
leadership of, 18b, 62
legislative oversight, 274–294
legislative process, 298–306
media relationships, 31–34
minority party rights, 9, 10
parliamentarians, 12
policy and decision making, 2–5,
    10–22
power in, 10, 11, 17–20, 28
pressures on members, 30–36, 181, 186,
    190
public opinion strategies, 302–303
regulatory veto, 276
reports to, 285
resolution of disapproval, 276
task forces in, 15
term limits, 105b
veto overrides, 31, 268, 271
voting in, 10–11

Congress–80th, 116
Congress–82d, 116
Congress–91st, 129
Congres–92d, 129
Congress–93d, 129
Congress–94th, 86, 129
Congres–95th, 129
Congress–98th, 141
Congress–99th, 150, 247, 248*t*
Congress–100th, 137, 232
Congress–101st, 137
Congress–102d
  cloture, 234
  multiple referrals, 86
  Senate scheduling, 184, 185*f*
  session hours, 15
Congress–103d
  bicameral reconciliation of legislation,
    247, 248*t*
  bill numbering, 79
  District of Columbia, 115
  filibusters, 251
  legislation passed, 245
  private bills, 116
  session hours, 15
  use of rules, 131, 137
Congress–104th
  amendment of Rule XXII, 234
  bill numbering, 79
  corrections measures, 112
  District of Columbia, 115
  first 100 days, 15, 20, 21*t*
  multiple referrals, 86
  private bills, 116
  Republicans in, 26, 29, 122
  use of reconciliation, 62
  use of rules, 122, 131, 132–133, 137, 176
Congress–105th
  bicameral reconciliation of legislation,
    247, 248*t*
  campaign finance legislation, 135*b*
  cloture, 234
  corrections measures, 112
  private bills, 116
  use of rules, 131, 133, 137
Congress–106th
  bill numbering, 79
  discharge petitions, 139–140
  House rules, 24, 114, 136
  membership, 28
  pair voting, 170–171
  Rules Committee, 119
  time for roll call votes, 225
  use of task forces, 103

Congress–107th, 22, 90
Congressional Accountability Act of 1995, 8,
    79, 247
Congressional Automotive Caucus, 285–286
Congressional Black Caucus, 60
Congressional Budget and Impoundment
    Control Act of 1974 (PL 93-344)
  budget timetable, 58, 59*b*
  Byrd Rule, 64–65, 66
  concurrent budget resolution, 58–61
  conference report, 60–61, 65
  congressional review capabilities, 278
  debate on, 212
  enforcement of, 66
  floor manager for, 156
  impoundments, 65–66
  new entities created, 57–58
  points of order, 66
  program evaluation, 287
  reasons for, 56
  reconciliation, 61–64
  as rulemaking statutes, 7*b*
Congressional Budget Office (CBO), 57–58,
    288
Congressional Record
  amendments, 130, 134
  conference reports, 264
  legislative programs and agenda, 142
  prepared speeches, 212
  presentation of bills in, 78, 121, 159,
    161
  signers of discharge petitions, 138, 139
  as source for informal practices, 7*b*
  suspension of Senate rules, 239
  unanimous consent agreements, 196, 199
  votes and voting, 171, 226
Congressional Research Service, 288
Congressional Review Act of 1996, 276
Connolly, Ceci, 272
Conservative Action Team, 151
Consolidated Omnibus Reconciliation Act of
    1985, 248
Constituents and constituencies, 34–35
Constitution–amendments
  Balanced Budget, 214, 215
  Equal Rights, 114
  Fourteenth, 305
  line-item veto, 66
  reapportionment, 236
  Sixteenth, 42
  Tenth, 274
  term limits, 133
Constitution–articles
  Article I, 3, 42, 106*n*6, 268

Article II, 3, 289
Article III, 3
Constitution–clauses
due process, 305
elastic, 3
equal protection, 305
presentation, 280
supremacy, 4
Constitution–issues
budget issues, 41–42, 45, 48–49, 214, 215
checks and balances, 4–5
congressional role and authority, 2, 31,
142, 268, 271, 275, 298, 305
expulsion of members of Congress, 10
federalism, 4–5
impeachment, 289
legislative oversight, 275, 279
legislative veto, 280
limited government, 3
nominations and appointments, 286
origin of tax legislation, 252
president pro tempore, 106n6, 207
president's role, 31, 268
rules of procedure, 5, 6b
Senate voting, 225
separation of powers, 3–4, 5, 42, 280,
292, 298–299
unconstitutional legislation, 305
vetoes, 268–269, 271
vice president's role, 106n6, 207
Continuing resolutions, See Budget process
Contra aid legislation, 199–200
Contract with America (1994-1995)
bill numbering and, 79
bypassing committees, 103, 105
congressional procedures and, 15
congressional term limits, 105b
effects of, 29, 299
Gingrich, Newt and, 301
limitation of debate, 122–123
passage of, 20, 122, 215–216, 249–250
precursor to, 141
term limits, 133
use of rules, 133
Conyers, John, Jr., (D-Mich.), 163
Cook, Rhodes, 39
Cooper, Kenneth, 241
Cox, Christopher (R-Calif.), 83
"Crackup of Committees," (Cohen), 103
Craig, Larry E. (R-Idaho), 32
Cranston, Alan (D-Calif.), 202
Crédit Mobilier, 276
Crime bills (1994, 1996), 151, 163, 176, 255
Cronkite, Walter, 34

Culver, John C. (D-Iowa), 215
Cummings, Jeannie, 307
Cushman, John H., Jr., 273

Daschle, Tom (D-S.D.)
campaign finance reform, 222
gun control issues, 228, 237
as Senate Minority Leader, 201, 215, 302
Senate Technology and Communications
Committee, 32, 33
use of amendments, 221–222
use of holds, 193, 194
view of cloture, 233
view of Lott, Trent, 224
view of Senate debate, 299
Dauster, William G., 74
Davidson, Roger H., 38, 73, 179
Davis, Phillip, 296
Day, Kathleen, 272
Days, legislative and calendar, 209–210, 211,
241n3, 243n69
Dealey, Sam, 273
Debate. See House of Representatives
Decision making. See Policy and decision
making
DeLay, Tom (R-Texas), 36, 302
Democratic Caucus, 140
Democratic Party
amendment trees, 220–222
bankruptcy legislation, 251–252
budget surplus, 71
committee issues, 27, 90
conservatives, 253
educational issues, 201–202, 212
House rules, 129, 130, 132–133, 135, 174,
175–176
Interior appropriations, 190
motions to instruct, 255–256
obstructionist tactics, 157–158
103d Congress, 137
Senate agenda, 185
Southern Democrats, 90, 230
term limits, 134
view of government, 274
view of Government Performance and Results Act, 276
Whitewater hearings, 223
Department of Agriculture, 276
Department of the Army, 224, 285
Department of Defense, 234
Department of Education, 129, 156, 264
Department of Energy, 293
Department of Health, Education, and Wel-
fare (HEW), 53–54, 283

Department of the Interior, 55
Department of Justice, 281
Department of Labor, 53–54
Department of Veterans Affairs, 293–294
Deschler, Lewis, 6
Deschler-Brown Precedents of the United States House of Representatives, 6b, 24
Deschler's Precedents of the United States House of Representatives, 6b, 24
Destler, I.M., 147
Dewar, Helen, 205, 272
DeWine, Mike (R-Ohio), 182b
Dingell, John D. (D-Mich.), 2, 12, 253–254
Dirksen, Everett McKinley (R-Ill.), 236–237, 305
Discharge petition, 138–140, 241
District of Columbia, 110, 262
Dodd, Lawrence C., 38, 297
Doherty, Carroll, 107
Dole, Bob (R-Kan.)
    amendments, 249
    as Senate Majority Leader, 192, 215–216
    as Senate Minority Leader, 191
    Senate scheduling, 186
    unanimous consent agreements, 199–200, 215–216
    view of Senate voting, 228
Domenici, Pete V. (R-N.M.), 47, 100
Dornan, Robert K. (R-Calif.), 157–158
Douglas, Stephen A., 211
Dove, Bob, 190
Dreier, David (R-Calif.), 134, 135–136, 177
Drew, Elizabeth, 242, 272
Durbin, Richard J. (D-Ill.), 237, 257

E-Agenda, 144
Earmarking, 51, 52
Economic issues, 41, 72. *See also* Budget issues
E-Contract 2000, 144
Education legislation, 201, 212, 216b
Edwards, George C., 296
Ehrenhalt, Alan, 145, 146
Eilperin, Juliet, 37
Eisele, Albert, 307
Elections, 28–29. *See also* Campaigns and campaigning
Ellwood, John William, 72
Elving, Ronald, 108
Emerson, Bill (R-Mo.), 160
Endangered Species Act of 1973, 224
Enelow, James M., 179–180
Engler, John, 112

Entitlement programs
    as direct or mandatory spending, 47
    growth of, 52–53, 67–68
    legal basis, 45
    pay-as-you-go procedures, 69, 70
    reconciliation and, 61–62
Environmental issues, 55
Environmental Protection Agency (EPA), 285
Equal Rights Amendment (ERA), 114
Ergonomics, 282
Evans, C. Lawrence, 244
Evans, Rowland, 242
Exchange Stabilization Fund, 288–289
Executive branch. *See also* Presidents and the presidency
    budget issues, 47, 62
    executive privilege, 295n17
    expenditures by, 42
    legislative oversight of, 274, 291, 295n17
    legislative veto, 280
    presidential bills and proposals, 78
    pressures on Congress, 30–31, 298
    public distrust of, 290
    reporting requirements, 285

Fair Labor Standards Act of 1938, 139
Family planning, 81–82
FBI. *See* Federal Bureau of Investigation
FCC. *See* Federal Communications Commission
FDA. *See* Food and Drug Administration
Federal Activities Inventory Reform Act of 1998, 274
Federal Bureau of Investigation (FBI), 290
Federal Communications Commission (FCC), 281
Federal Pay Raise Act of 1960, 139
Federal Reserve, 41
Federalist, The, 41–42
Feingold, Russell (D-Wis.), 222–223
Felton, John, 206
Fenno, Richard F., Jr., 9, 38, 39, 179, 230, 243, 271
Ferejohn, John, 272
Ferris, Nancy, 294
Fessler, Pamela, 296
Filibusters
    as bargaining device, 229–230
    budget process, 60, 64
    campaign finance reform, 251
    civil rights legislation, 299
    in committees, 98
    conference reports, 265

criticism and defense of, 229
ending of, 231–236
extended debate and, 228
history of the word, 243n51
increased use of, 6–7, 15, 230–231
Johnson, Lyndon B. and, 231
losing the floor in, 243n69
in Senate executive session, 186
Senate Journal, 210
Senate track system, 202
shutdown rule, 132
silent filibusters, 192, 228
unanimous consent agreements and, 197,
    200, 227–228
votes to break, 25
Filson, Lawrence E., 107
Firearms, 305. *See also* Gun control legislation
Fisher, Louis, 73, 280, 295
Fletcher, Ernie (R-Ky.), 254
Foerstel, Karen, 74, 204, 294, 307
Foley, Thomas S. (D-Wash.), 29, 155, 162,
    172, 301, 302
Food and Drug Administration (FDA), 261b,
    276
Food stamps, 64–65
Ford, Paul L., 37
Foreman, Christopher, 294
Frank, Barney (D-Mass.), 101, 127
Franklin, Daniel P., 73
Frist, Bill (R-Tenn.), 190
Frumin, Alan, 206

Gallop polls, 26. *See also* Public opinion
Ganske, Greg (R-Iowa), 253–254
GAO. *See* General Accounting Office
Gates, Bill, 92
General Accounting Office (GAO), 42, 65,
    278, 284–285, 287
Genocide Treaty, 186
George III, 3
Gephardt, Richard A. (D-Mo.), 32, 119, 158,
    253, 299
Gibbons, Sam M. (D-Fla.), 160
Gingrich, Newt (R-Ga.)
    Calendar Wednesday, 141
    campaign finance legislation, 135b
    centralization of authority, 20
    committee issues, 90, 133
    Contract with America, 249–250
    "Corrections Day," 112
    as Speaker of the House, 26, 253, 301,
        302
    use of task forces, 15

view of congressional role, 298–299
view of C-SPAN, 26
view of electronic age, 303
view of rules of House, 10
view of sequence of amendments, 131
War Powers Resolution of 1973, 155
Godfrey, John, 147
Gold, Martin, 145, 179, 272
Golden Fleece Awards, 289
Goldwater, Barry (R-Ariz.), 54
Gonzalez, Elian, 116
Goodrich, Lawrence, 72, 205
Gore, Al, 1, 80, 91
Gorton, Slade (R-Wash.), 212
Goss, Porter J. (R-Fla.), 119
Government Executive, 286
Government, federal. *See also* Constitution,
    issues
    checks and balances, 4
    divided, 290–291, 304
    emergency spending, 70
    federalism and, 4–5
    iron triangles, 293–294
    legislative oversight of, 274, 275, 290,
        291–292
    limited, 3, 278, 290
    spending for key programs, 68f
    shutdowns, 62, 299
Government Performance and Results Act of
    1993 (GPRA), 275–276
Government, state, 4–5, 305
GPRA. *See* Government Performance and
    Results Act of 1993
Graham, Bob (D-Fla.), 60, 262
Gramm, Phil (R-Texas), 37n23, 78–79, 193,
    264–265
Green, Michael, 39
Gribbin, August, 39
Gruenwald, Juliana, 178
Gun control legislation, 1, 99, 105b, 228,
    237–238, 256
Gun-Free School Zones Act, 305
Guns, 305

Hager, George, 73
Hamilton, Alexander, 2
Hamilton, Lee H., 296
Harkin, Tom (D-Iowa), 234
Harris, Douglas, 39
Harris, Joseph P., 295
Hastert, J. Dennis (R-Ill.)
    committee issues, 133
    electronic bill signing, 267–268

as Speaker of the House, 16, 26, 78, 119, 253–254, 302
use of task forces, 103
view of tax dollars, 274
Hatch, Orrin (R-Utah), 1
Healey, Jon, 73
Healy, Melissa, 205
Health issues, 103
Health maintenance organizations (HMOs), 253
Heaphey, James J., 39
Hearings. *See* Committees
Hecht, Chic, 200
Heclo, Hugh, 38
Heinz, John P., 40
Helms, Jesse (R-N.C.), 194, 224, 265
Henning, Robert Alan, 272
Henry, Ed, 39
Heritage Foundation, 286
HEW. *See* Department of Health, Education, and Welfare
Hill, Jeffrey S., 145
Hinds, Asher C., 6*b*, 38
Hinds' Precedents of the House of Representatives, 6*b*
HMOs. *See* Health maintenance organizations
Holbrooke, Richard, 193–194
Hollings, Ernest F. (D-S.C.), 37*n*23, 81, 223
Hook, Janet, 38, 72, 146
Hosansky, David, 205
House of Representatives. *See also* Congress; Legislation; Speaker of the House
amendments, 158–168, 203, 217, 249, 251, 265
audits of, 283, 284–285
budget process, 50, 60
calendars, 110–112, 115–117, 120, 139, 141–142, 187
casework, 287–288
characteristics, 25–28
compared to Senate, 23–30, 50–51, 96–97, 101*t*, 181, 186, 187, 217–218, 219t, 227, 236, 238
"Corrections Day," 112
debate, 153–158, 167, 262
floor managers, 155–156, 159, 169, 177, 249
floor procedure, 148–177
House chamber, 148, 149
impeachment, 289
introduction of bills, 75

leadership, 18–19*b*, 55, 82, 109, 130, 138, 142, 151, 158, 203, 253, 256, 258, 302
legislative process, 80, 81, 109–144, 148–177, 227, 236, 245–271, 302
mace, 152–153, 172
minority rights in, 9
political culture of, 129
precedents, 6*b*, 24–25, 53, 85, 137, 138, 140, 141, 142, 162, 163, 176
question of privilege, 157–158
resolving House-Senate differences, 245–271
scheduling, 109–144, 150, 177*n*2, 203
speeches in, 26
view of Senate, 29
votes, 25, 113, 116, 120, 177
House of Representatives—committees. *See also* Committees
amendments, 162
authorizing, 48, 55
circumventing, 236
with direct access to the floor, 117
discharge petitions, 138–140
energy issues, 38*n*27
hearings, 92, 120
Internet, 83
number and size, 100, 107*n*7
reform of, 167
role of, 139
select, 118
staff, 257
standing committees, 82*b*, 118
Year 2000 Readiness and Responsibility Act, 87*b*
House of Representatives—committees by name
Agriculture, 81, 92, 293–294
Appropriations, 48, 49, 50, 61, 62, 81–82, 115, 117, 282, 283
Armed Services, 84
Banking, 99, 255, 288–289
Budget, 57, 58, 60, 61, 64, 117, 257
Commerce, 83, 84, 87*b*, 105*b*
Committee of the Whole, 55, 115, 129, 150, 151–153, 161, 168, 172, 173
Economic and Educational Opportunities, 140
Education and the Workforce, 81, 100
Government Reform, 115, 140, 253, 275, 277
House Administration, 117
International Relations, 81–82, 84
Judiciary, 83, 99, 103, 105*b*, 140

Rules, 1, 60, 64, 103, 109, 117, 118–137, 140–141, 150, 159, 161, 164, 174, 203, 250, 262
Standards of Official Conduct, 117, 118
Transportation and Infrastructure, 51, 84, 257
Veterans' Affairs, 81, 293–294
Ways and Means, 55, 81, 83, 84
House of Representatives—rules
adoption of the rule, 137–138, 150–151
amendments, 122, 123, 126, 129, 130, 131–133, 134, 135b, 137, 144, 152, 160–168, 173, 203–204, 219, 247, 265
budget process, 53, 55, 60, 64
changes in, 174–177
characteristics and purposes, 25, 120–121
committee issues, 72, 81, 88, 92, 93b, 97, 98, 101, 102, 128, 161–162
Committee of the Whole, 152, 173
compared to unanimous consent agreements, 203–204
conference committee and report, 246, 250–251, 252, 254, 255, 257, 260, 264, 265, 268b
Corrections Calendar, 112
creative rules, 128–137
debate, 112, 113, 115, 120, 121, 122, 123, 129, 130, 132, 134, 137, 139, 141, 142, 152, 153, 159, 173–174
discharge petitions, 138–139, 140–141
fast-track procedures, 142, 144
fiscal powers, 151–152
germaneness, 162, 163, 164b, 168, 237, 260, 262
highway and transit spending, 52
hookup provisions, 250–251
legislative oversight, 277–279
legislative process, 82, 84, 112, 118–137, 175b
motions, 55, 167, 173–176
pairing, 169–171, 180n45
points of order, 66, 118, 122, 126–128, 145n20, 162–163, 262
quorum in the House, 148, 152, 172
recommittal, 173–176
referral process, 85, 129, 162
role of the Rules Committee, 119–122, 262
scope, 260
strike the enacting clause, 167–168
structured and self-executing, 130–131
tax or tariff proposals, 55
time-structured, 134–135

votes and voting, 113–114, 120, 129, 131, 133, 135, 137, 152, 165, 169–172, 176, 177, 250, 265
House of Representatives—specific rules
bifurcated rules, 136–137
Calendar Wednesday, 141–142
Committee of the Whole, 152, 173
Corrections Calendar, 112
five-minute rule, 115, 159–161, 168
king- and queen-of-the-hill rules, 131–132, 133–134, 135b
multiple stage rules, 132
one-hour rule, 116, 120, 121, 137, 153, 178n10, 265
one-third rule, 265
open, closed, and modified rules, 122–126, 132–133, 135b, 136, 159
Rule X, 87b
Rule XVI, 165
Rule XXII, 251, 262
shutdown rule, 132
special rules, 118, 122–137, 145n20
structured and self-executing rules, 130–131
suspension of the rules, 112–115, 138, 162, 187, 250, 265
waiver and martial law rules, 126–128, 145n20
House Practice: A Guide to the Rules, Precedents, and Procedures of the House (1996), 7b
Howard, A.E. Dick, 305
Hudson, Audrey, 294, 296
Hugo, Michael, 145, 179, 272
Hutchison, Kay Bailey (R-Texas), 54–55
Hyde, Henry J. (R-Ill.), 54, 87b, 105b, 154–155

Idelson, Holly, 178
IGs. See Inspectors general
Immigration and Naturalization Service v. Chadha (1983), 280
Impeachment, 289
Impoundments, 56, 65–66
Incumbents, 29
Inhofe, James M. (R-Okla.), 26, 138, 194
Inouye, Daniel K. (D-Hawaii), 279
Inspectors general (IGs), 283
Inspectors General Act of 1978, 283
Interest groups, 11, 13, 100, 226, 290, 293–294
Internal Revenue Service (IRS), 94, 277, 290

Internet. *See* Technology
Iran-contra scandal, 95, 277, 279
Iron triangles. *See* Government, federal
IRS. *See* Internal Revenue Service

Jackson, Robert, 3
Jacoby, Mary, 146, 244
Jefferson, Thomas, 5, 37, 165, 236
Jefferson's Manual, 6, 7b
Johannes, John R., 296
Johnson, Donald Bruce, 38
Johnson, Lyndon B. (D-Texas), 22, 90, 199, 213, 231
Joint resolutions, 280
Jones, Charles O., 38, 145
Journal (House of Representatives), 157

Kabbany, Jennifer, 294
Kaiser, Frederick, 294, 297
Kalb, Deborah, 37
Katzmann, Robert A., 108, 295
Kearns, Doris, 38
Keisling, Phil, 307
Kellman, Laurie, 272
Kennedy, Edward, 75
Kennedy, John F., 20, 119
Kennedy-Kassebaum bill, 80
Kerry, Bob (D-Neb.), 184, 190
King, Anthony, 38, 297
King, David C., 106, 107
King, Martin Luther, Jr., 112
Kingdon, John W., 180
Kirchhoff, Sue, 206
Kirschten, Dick, 294, 297
Kirst, Michael, 295
Koby, Michael, 108
Koehler, David H., 179
Kosterlitz, Julie, 146
Koszczuk, Jackie, 40
Krishnakumar, Anita, 73
Kriz, Margaret, 37
Kronholz, June, 106
Kuntz, Phil, 178

Lacey, Marc, 272
Lambro, Donald, 74
Land and Conservation Fund, 293
Laumann, Edward O., 40
Laurent, Anne, 296
Lautenberg, Frank (D-N.J.), 29, 34
Lawmaking, 13–16. *See also* Bills; House of Representatives; Legislation; Senate
Lawrence, Eric, 243
Leach, Jim (R-Iowa), 78–79

Lee, Francis, 39
Legislation. *See also* Bills; Committees; House of Representatives; Senate; specific legislation by name
ad hoc lawmaking, 304
adjournment and, 301
amending, 98
blocked in committee, 138–142
campaign reform, 134, 135b
categories of, 77–79
"Christmas tree," 69
coalitions and, 300
congressional cycle and, 22–23, 300–301
congressional oversight, 275–276
House and Senate compared, 101t, 252
interpretation of, 102–103
naming and numbering, 75, 79–80, 103
national emergencies, 123
omnibus and megabills, 15, 58, 62, 68, 94, 129, 254, 299
oversight, 275–276
privileged, 117–118
procedures and process, 11, 14, 20–22, 155, 298–306
regulation and, 274
rescission bills, 65
riders, 103
scheduling, 109–144, 181–204
stalled, 301
title page, 270
Legislation—specific. *See also* Appropriations—specific legislation
airport improvements, 223
antiterrorism, 258
banking, 78–79
bankruptcy, 251–252
campaign reform, 134, 135b
child care, 200
Contra aid, 199–200
defense, 132
District of Columbia, 115–116
gun control, 1, 99, 105b, 228, 237–238, 256
juvenile justice, 1–2
managed care, 253, 254, 255
marriage tax, 223
Medicare reform, 15–16
minimum wage, 136, 252
national emergencies, 123
patients' bill of rights, 252, 253, 257, 258
prescription drug benefit, 302–303
savings and loan, 255
stripmining, 284
super collider, 266

tax, 236, 252
trade, 144
transportation, 257
veterans, 114
Legislative branch. *See* Congress
Legislative oversight, 274–294
Legislative process, 298–306. *See also* House of Representatives; Senate
Legislative Reorganization Acts of 1946, 1970 (PL 79-601, PL 91-510)
amendments and debate, 179*n*30
bill referrals, 84
committee witnesses, 107*n*24
electronic voting, 169
oversight functions, 275, 277, 294*n*11
as rulemaking statutes, 7*b*
rules changes, 174
Legislative veto, 276, 280
Levin, Carl (D-Mich.), 286
Lieberman, Joseph I. (D-Conn.), 41, 195, 211, 234, 303
Limitation riders. *See* Appropriations
Line-Item Veto Act of 1996, 65
Litigation, 305–306
Lobbies and lobbying, 35–36, 98, 99
Locke, John, 3
Lodge, Henry Cabot, 194, 211
Logrolling, 21, 22, 155, 258, 300, 301
Long, Russell B. (D-La.), 67, 246, 249
Longley, Lawrence, 39, 271
Loomis, Burdett A., 40
Lott, Trent (R-Miss.)
gas tax cut, 105
gun control issues, 228, 237
and Holbrooke, Richard, 193–194
as Senate Majority Leader, 78, 182, 184, 185, 191, 201, 202–203, 222, 237–238, 254
Senate Rule XVI, 55
tax reform bill, 150–151
use of cloture votes, 233, 238–239
use of holds, 193
use of Rule XIV, 239
use of sequential referral, 85
use of task forces, 16, 103
view of investigations and oversight, 274
view of two-day rule, 192
Love, Alice, 40
Luce, Robert, 72
Lugar, Richard G. (R-Ind.), 218
Lungren, Dan (R-Calif.), 176

McAdams, John C., 296
McCain, John (R-Ariz.), 222–223

McCloskey, Frank (D-Ind.), 158
McCormack, John W. (D-Mass.), 12
McCown, Ada G., 271
McCubbins, Matthew D., 297
McGrory, Mary, 241
McIntosh, Toby, 205
McIntyre, Richard D. (R-Ind.), 158
Mackaman, Frank H., 145
Madison, Chris, 190
Madison, James, 2, 3, 37, 41–42
Malbin, Michael J., 179, 272, 294
Maloney, Carolyn B. (D-N.Y.), 135*b*
Managed care legislation, 253, 255
Mansfield, Mike (D-Mont.), 15, 199, 202, 305
Markup. *See* Committees
Martinez, Gebe, 40
Masci, David, 178
Mason, Alpheus Thomas, 37
Matsunaga, Spark M., 145, 146
Matthews, Donald P., 180
Mauro, Tony, 307
Maxwell School of Citizenship and Public Policy, 286
Mayhew, David, 40
Media
coverage of conference committees, 246
coverage of House and Senate, 25–26, 27
Gingrich, Newt and, 301
investigative reporting, 290
pressures on Congress, 31–34, 98
television and debate, 213–214
Medicaid, 67
Medicare, 15–16, 67–68, 70–71
Meehan, Martin T. (D-Mass.), 134, 135*b*
Meider, Barry, 307
Merchant marine, 84
Mexico, 288–289
Meyers, Roy T., 72
Michel, Robert H. (R-Ill.), 11, 122, 145, 154, 169
Mikva, Abner J., 284
Miller, Matthew, 74
Million Mom March (2000), 228, 237
Mills, Mike, 107, 296
Mills, Wilbur D. (D-Ark.), 123
Minimum wage legislation, 136, 252
Mitchell, Alison, 74
Mitchell, George J. (D-Maine)
as Senate Majority Leader, 19, 194, 196, 200
view of cloture, 234
view of filibusters, 229, 230, 234, 251

view of Senate schedule, 183–184
Whitewater hearings, 223
Moakley, Joe (D-Mass.), 130, 132–133
Mollison, Andrew, 39
Mondale, Walter, 35, 40
Money Trust, 276–277
Montesquieu, Charles-Louis, 3
Morella, Constance A. (R-Md.), 20
Morning hour, 210
Morse, Wayne (D-Ore.), 23
Moseley-Braun, Carol (D-Ill.), 211
Motions, 55, 167
    to amend, 222, 266
    in conference committee, 250, 251, 255,
        265
    to discharge (*See also* Discharge petition;
        Rules), 140–141, 241
    to instruct, 255, 264–265
    to proceed (*See also* Cloture; Committees;
        Reconciliation process), 233, 234,
        265
    to recommit, 173–176, 222, 264–265, 266
    to reconsider, 227
    to reject nongermane matter, 262
    to rise, 55
    to suspend the rules, 239–240
    to table, 212, 226, 227, 300
Mr. Smith Goes to Washington (film), 228
Munson, Richard, 72, 73
Murkowski, Frank H. (R-Alaska), 224,
    228
Murray, Alan S., 178
Murray, Hyde, 145, 179, 272
Myers, E. Michael, 178
Myers, John T. (R-Ind.), 266

Nader, Ralph, 30, 94
NAFTA. *See* North American Free Trade
    Agreement
Nakamura, Robert T., 296
Natcher, William H. (D-Ky.), 159
National American Legion Baseball Month,
    236–237
National Rifle Association (NRA), 2, 99
National Sea Grant College Program Reau-
    thorization Act of 1998 (PL 105-16), 44
National security, 246
Nelson, Robert L., 40
Nevada, 246
New Frontier, 119
Nickles, Don (R-Okla.), 16, 82–83, 223, 254
Nickles, Ilona, 204, 271
Nixon, Richard M., 56, 269
Noah, Timothy, 297

Nominations and appointments, 186–187,
    193–194, 286–287
North American Free Trade Agreement
    (NAFTA), 30
Norton, Eleanor Holmes, 115
Norwood, Charlie (R-Ga.), 253–254
Novak, Robert, 242
NRA. *See* National Rifle Association
Nuclear freeze proposals, 154, 165–166
Nuclear waste storage bill, 246

Obey, David R. (D-Wis.), 50, 81, 167–168,
    303
Obey, Doug, 243
Occupational Safety and Health Administra-
    tion (OSHA), 282
Office of Inspector General, 283
Office of Legislative Counsel, 83
Office of Management and Budget (OMB),
    61, 71, 269, 286–287
Office of Technology Assessment (OTA), 172
Ogul, Morris S., 294, 297
Oleszek, Walter J., 38, 39, 244, 271, 272
OMB. *See* Office of Management and Bud-
    get
Omnibus bills. *See* Legislation
Omnibus Reconciliation Act of 1993, 69
O'Neill, Thomas P. "Tip," Jr. (D-Mass.)
    Equal Rights Amendment, 114
    as Speaker of the House, 302
    speech on Lebanon, 154
    tax reform bill, 151
    use of ad hoc committee, 85
    use of task forces, 15
    view of Comprehensive Crime Control
        Act, 177
    view of rules and the Rules Committee,
        121, 137
    view of Speaker of the House, 109
Operation Desert Storm, 70
Oppenheimer, Bruce I., 39, 107, 145, 297
Ornstein, Norman J., 39, 40, 205, 306
OSHA. *See* Occupational Safety and Health
    Administration
OTA. *See* Office of Technology Assessment

Pairing. *See* Voting
Palmer, Elizabeth, 108
Panetta, Leon E. (D-Calif.), 288
Parks, Daniel, 307
Parliament (England), 152
Parliamentarians and parliamentary principles
    amendments, 131–132
    bill referrals, 80, 83, 84, 85–86

committee issues, 97
role of, 106n6
unanimous consent agreements, 196
Partisanship. *See also* Political parties
amendments and, 131, 221–223, 224
budget issues, 43, 57–58, 70, 71
committee issues, 103, 105–106, 162
Contract with America, 20
ed-flex legislation, 201
effects of, 15, 129–130
filibusters and, 231
in the House of Representatives, 136–137, 148
increases in, 302, 304–305
obstructionism and, 157–158, 304
riders to appropriations bills, 55
Rules Committee, 119
in the Senate, 184, 190, 198, 209, 211, 304–305
unanimous consent agreements, 198, 199, 200–201
Whitewater hearings, 223
Pastore, John O. (D-R.I.), 242n11
Pastore Rule, 242n11
Patient's bill of rights legislation, 252, 253, 257, 258
Pay-as-you-go procedures (PAYGO). *See* Budget process
Peabody, Robert L., 39, 145
Pear, Robert, 272, 295
Pepper, Claude (D-Fla.), 140
Perot, Ross, 138
Persian Gulf War, 155
Peters, John G., 38
Pianin, Eric, 37, 74, 295, 296
Platt, Orville (R-Conn.), 231
Plumer, William (N.H.), 49
Plungis, Jeff, 73
Policy and decision making
amendment process, 165–166
committee role, 284
conference committee, 245–246, 254, 264
Congress and, 298, 300–301, 302–303
policy incubation, 25
process and procedure, 150–151, 299–301
role of committees in, 162, 277
role of Congress, 277
role of deliberation, 155
use of lawsuits, 305
Political issues
amendments, 220–224
authorization process, 281

budget process, 66–67
budget surplus, 71–72
conference committees, 251–253, 256, 259
fiscal austerity and abundance, 290
House rules, 134–136
lawmaking, 298, 302, 304
legislative versus executive branch, 292–293
message sending, 32
modification of mandatory spending levels, 47
motion to recommit, 176
public opinion strategies, 302–303
scheduling, 109, 144, 186
unanimous consent agreements, 199, 200–201
vetoes, 269, 271
voting, 220, 226
Political parties. *See also* Partisanship
educational issues, 212
floor managers, 153–154
leadership, 82–83, 214
public opinion strategies, 302–303
role in Congress, 18–19, 304
rules, 7b, 90
Rules Committee and, 121
use of amendments by, 163, 166–167
Polsby, Nelson W., 39, 145
Pomery, Earl (D-N.D.), 7–8, 37
Pool, Bob, 108
Pope, Charles, 73
Pork-barrel spending, 168
Power
congressional, 10, 11, 17–20, 28
constitutional separation of, 3–4, 5, 42, 280, 292, 298–299
House of Represeatives, 151–152
Speaker of the House, 18b, 109, 110, 114, 118, 207, 212, 277
Precedents
appropriations, 45
bill referrals, 83, 85
continuing resolutions, 53
effects of, 16–17
limitation riders, 53
sources of, 6b
Precedents—House of Representatives
amendments, 162
announcements by party leaders, 142
bringing legislation before the House, 141
compilations, 6b, 24
motions to recommit, 176
power of extraction, 140
proposal of substitute rules, 137

referrals, 85
signers of discharge petitions, 138
unauthorized programs in continuing resolutions, 53
Precedents—Senate
amendments, 217, 222
compilations, 6b, 24–25
precedents versus rules, 54–55
priority of floor recognition, 212, 222
unanimous consent agreements, 197
violations of scope, 260–261
Prescription drug benefit legislation, 302–303
President pro tempore, 80, 106n6, 207, 209
Presidents and the presidency. See also Executive branch
bully pulpit role, 30–31
electoral strategies, 299
fiscal authority, 42
impoundments, 65–66
line-item veto, 65–66
nominations and appointments, 187, 286–287
presidential bills and proposals, 78
pressures on Congress, 30–31, 269
role of, 31
veto or approval, 258, 268–271, 276
Presiding officer of the Senate. See President pro tempore; Vice president
Preston, Mark, 204, 206
Price, David E. (D-N.C.), 31–32, 39
Price Waterhouse, 283
Priest, Dana, 108
Procedure in the U.S. House of Representatives, 6b
Procedures. See also Bills; Legislation; House of Representatives; Rules; Senate
bypassing committee referral, 1, 15, 16
congressional cycle and, 22–23
evolution of, 6–7, 15
functions of, 5–10
policy making and, 11–13
regular order, 13, 20
suspension of the rules, 12
Program evaluation, 287
Proxmire, William (D-Wis.), 289
Public opinion, 26, 34, 56, 67, 302–303
Public Opinion Strategies, 302

Quorum
Committee of the Whole, 152
House of Representatives, 148, 152, 172
markups, 97

Senate, 209, 213, 225, 232
use of electronic voting, 169

Radcliffe, Donnie, 180
Rainmundo, Jeff, 38
Rarey, Matthew, 273
Rayburn, Sam (D-Texas), 90, 119
Reagan, Ronald, 62, 66–67. 150–151, 269
Reagan (Ronald) administration, 199, 200
Reconciliation process. See also Bargaining; Budget process
agreement without a conference, 247–248
amendments, 267
appropriations, 259–260, 261b
bargaining, 257–262, 300
conference committees, 1, 60–61, 245–248, 249, 250–268
general characteristics, 245
megabills, 254–255
obscurity of the process, 245–247, 249
preconference considerations, 248–250
report of the conference committee, 255, 260–265, 267
rules, 257, 267
Referrals. See Bills
Reid, Harry (D-Nev.), 214, 222
Reischauer, Robert D., 41, 71–72
Religious Freedom Restoration Act, 305
Reports
committee, 101–103, 192
conference, 60–61, 65, 255, 264, 265, 267
to Congress, 285
executive branch, 285
Republican Party. See also Contract with America
agenda, 298–299, 301
amendment process, 132–133, 221–222
bankruptcy legislation, 251–252
campaign reform, 134, 135b
committee issues, 27, 90, 257
Corrections Day, 112
District of Columbia, 115
educational issues, 201, 212
House rules, 122, 127, 129, 130, 132–133, 135–136, 175
juvenile justice bill, 1
minimum wage legislation, 136
obstructionist tactics, 157–158
seating in the House of Representatives, 177n1
speeches in Congress, 26
"Talking Points," 33
tax cuts and savings, 71, 282
tax reform bill, 150–151

term limits, 133–134
use of instruction motion, 255
view of government, 274
view of Government Performance and Results Act, 276
Whitewater hearings, 223
Resolutions of inquiry, 288–289
Results Act. *See* Government Performance and Results Act of 1993
Rhode, William, 295
Rich, Spencer, 108
Riddick, Floyd, 206
Rieselbach, Leroy N., 38
Riley, Richard W., 75
Ripley, Randall B., 107
Roberts, Alasdair, 297
Roberts, Pat (R-Kan.), 28
Robinson, James A., 145
Robinson, Peter, 145, 179, 272
Rockefeller, John D., IV (D-W.Va.), 32–33
Rogers, Chester W., 38
Rogers, David, 180, 295, 307
Rohde, David W., 38, 39, 307
Roman, Nancy, 179
Roosevelt, Theodore, 30
Rosenberg, Morton, 294
Rosenstiel, Thomas B., 39
Rostenkowski, Dan (D-Ill.), 55–56, 100–101
Roth, William V., Jr. (R-Del.), 99
Roukema, Marge (R-N.J.), 100
Rouselot, John (R-Calif.), 129
Rovner, Julie, 106, 179
Rudman, Warren B. (R-N.H.), 37*n*23
Rules. *See also* House of Representatives—rules; Precedents; Procedures; Senate—rules
amendments, 60
authorizations-appropriations, 49, 51*t*, 53–56
changes in, 299–300
committee issues, 92, 93*b*, 96, 97, 101, 123, 126
complexity of, 24–25
congressional policy making and, 10–17, 299
exceptions, 53
functions of, 5–10
germaneness, 54–56, 60, 102, 160
legislative process, 122–137
major sources of, 6*b*
party rules, 7*n*, 24*b*
points of order, 53, 54, 66, 97, 101, 102
regular orders, 13
sample rule, 124–125

special orders, 13
statutory rules, 7*b*
suspension of, 12
taxes and tariffs, 55–56, 123
understanding of, 12
voting in House and Senate, 10–11
Rules of the House of Representatives (House Manual), 6*b*

Salant, Jonathan, 145
Salisbury, Robert H., 40
Sammon, Richard, 178
Sanders, Bernard (I-Vt.), 151
Santorum, Rick (R-Pa.), 214
Savings and loan legislation, 255
Saxon, H. James (R-N.J.), 80
Scalia, Antonin, 102–103, 284
Schick, Allen, 72, 73, 74, 282, 297
Schlesinger, Arthur M., Jr., 275, 294
Schlesinger, Jacob, 74
Schneier, Edward V., 38
Schumer, Charles E. (D-N.Y.), 11, 17
Schwartz, Thomas, 297
Scott, William L. (R-Va.), 215
Senate. *See also* Congress; Filibusters; Legislation; President pro tempore; Unanimous consent agreements
amendments, 203, 212, 215, 217–227, 236, 249, 251, 260, 261*b*
budget process, 50–51, 60, 63*b*
calendars, 186, 187, 188, 190, 191, 205*n*13, 239, 240*b*, 241*n*3
casework, 287–288
characteristics of, 15, 25–28, 186, 187, 193, 195, 207, 209, 230–231
compared to House, 23–30, 50–51, 96–97, 101*t*, 181, 184*t*, 186, 187, 207, 217–218, 219*t*, 236, 238
confirmation process, 286–287
daily order of business, 210–211
debate, 187, 190, 197, 202, 211–215, 228, 232–233, 236, 299
decision making, 181
floor managers, 212, 214–215, 218, 223–224, 227, 236, 249
floor procedure, 207–241
holds, 192–194, 253
impeachment, 289
introduction of bills, 75, 211
legislative process, 80, 82, 84–85, 187–204, 207–241, 245–271
minority rights in, 9
motions, 189
partisanship in, 184

pay-as-you-go procedures, 69
precedents, 6*b*, 24–25, 54–55, 197, 212, 222
presiding officer, 18*b*
quorum and sufficient second, 213, 225, 232
resolving House-Senate differences, 245–271
scheduling, 181–204, 211
Senate chamber, 207, 208
staff, 181, 187, 215
supermajority votes, 60, 61, 64, 66, 82
track system, 202–203
view of House of Representatives, 29–30
voting, 25, 182, 186, 207, 213, 224–227, 232
whips and whip notices, 187, 189*f*, 209, 225
wrapup, 190
Senate—committees. *See also* Committees
amendments, 218
authorizing, 48, 50
energy, 85
conference committees, 251–252
numbers of, 107*n*7
procedures to circumvent, 236–241, 251
reports by, 192
standing committees, 106th Congress, 82*b*
Senate—committees by name
Agriculture, Nutrition, and Forestry, 64–65, 81, 218, 293–294
Appropriations, 48, 49, 50, 61, 62, 282
Banking, 223
Budget, 57, 58, 60, 61, 64, 100, 192
Commerce, 85
Energy and Natural Resources, 85, 92
Environment and Public Works, 96, 224
Finance, 81, 83, 85, 94, 223
Foreign Relations, 95, 96, 186
Governmental Affairs, 192, 275, 277
Health, Education, Labor, and Pensions (HELPS), 83
Judiciary, 92, 95
Natural Resources, 85
Rules and Administration, 206*n*53
Technology and Communications, 32–33
Veterans' Affairs, 81, 293–294
Senate—leadership. *See also* individuals by name
adjournments and recesses, 209–210
amendments, 222, 236
conference committees, 253, 256, 258
filibusters, 231
holds, 192, 193

power of, 207
referrals, 82–83, 239
scheduling, 184, 185–186, 187, 189, 191, 202
structure of, 18*b*, 19*b*
unanimous consent agreements, 197, 198–199, 217
voting, 225, 236
wrapup, 190
Senate—rules. *See also* Rules; Unanimous consent agreements
ad hoc committees, 85
adjournment and recesses, 209–210, 213
amendments, 60, 196, 198, 203–204, 217, 218, 219, 222, 233–234, 236–237, 247, 265
budget process, 53, 54, 60, 64
characteristics of, 25, 300
committee issues, 81, 92, 96, 97, 98, 101, 102
closed, 218
cloture, 212, 229, 231–236, 238–239
conference committee and report, 252, 260, 264, 265
days (legislative and calendar), 209–210
debate, 196, 198, 217, 242*n*11
discharge petitions, 241
germaneness and relevancy, 54, 60, 64, 198, 203–204, 233–234, 236–239, 242*n*11, 260, 262
leadership, 223
legislative oversight, 277–279
legislative process, 82, 187
points of order, 66, 237
principle of precedence, 219–220
quorum, 209, 213
scheduling and, 183–184, 203
scope, 260
suspension of, 239–240
term limits, 27
unanimous consent agreements, 181, 195, 196, 198
voting, 227, 237, 241, 265, 299
Senate—specific rules
Byrd Rule, 56, 64–65
one-day rule, 191
Rule XIV, 1, 106, 239
Rule XVI, 54–55, 237
Rule XVII, 241
Rule XXII, 212, 229, 231–236, 238–239
Rule XXVIII, 260–261
Rule XXXI, 187
three-fifths rule, 232
two-day rule, 191–192

two-speech rule, 243n69
two-thirds rule, 232
Senate Journal, 196, 205n13, 210
*Senate Manual Containing the Standing
   Rules, Orders, Laws, and Resolutions
   Affecting the Business of the United
   States Senate*, 6b
Senate Procedure: Precedents and Practices,
   6b, 217
Senate Republican Conference, 32
Serrano, Jose E. (D-N.Y.), 15
Shaw, Clay (R-Fla.), 106
Shays, Christopher (R-Conn.), 134, 135b
Sheffner, Benjamin, 296
Shepnick, Philippe, 106
Sherman Anti-Trust Act of 1890, 83
Shogren, Elizabeth, 72, 242
Shuster, Bud (R-Pa.), 51, 52
Siff, Ted, 272
Simon, Paul (D-Ill.), 100, 108
Simpson, Alan K. (R-Wyo.), 22, 262, 298
Simpson, Glenn, 40
Singleton, A.L. "Pete," 145, 179, 272
Slade, Michael, 108
Slattery, Jim (D-Kan.), 266
Smallwood, Frank, 296
Smith, Howard W. (D-Va.), 118–119
Smith, Steven S., 206, 243
Snowe, Olympia J. (R-Maine), 30
Sobel, Lindsay, 39
Social issues, 55
Social Security, 67–68, 71–72
Solomon, Gerald B.H. (R-N.Y.), 105n,
   122–123, 132–133
South Africa, 199–200
Speaker of the House. *See also* individuals
   by name
   bill referrals, 80, 85, 86
   centralization of authority in, 301–302
   Committee of the Whole, 152
   Journal (House of Representatives), 157
   reconciliation process, 250, 253
   role and power, 18b, 109, 110, 114, 118,
      207, 212, 277
   Rules Committee and, 119
   time limits, 85, 86
   votes and voting, 137, 152
   whip notices, 142
Specter, Arlen (R-Pa.), 94
Staff, congressional
   committee, 107n26, 108n29
   House of Representatives, 257
   role of, 27
   Senate, 181, 187, 215

Statutes at Large, 271
Steiner, Gilbert Y., 73, 271
Stenholm, Charles W. (D-Texas), 22, 32, 66,
   123
Stevens, Ted (R-Alaska), 54, 97–98, 197,
   215, 231
Stevenson, Adlai E., III (D-Ill.), 277
Stewart, Jimmy, 228
Stimson, James A., 180
Strip-mining legislation, 284
Sunshine rules, 257–258
Super collider legislation, 266
Supreme Court, 4, 95, 279, 284, 305–306
Surface transportation legislation, 257
Surplus. *See* Budget issues
Swanstrom, Roy, 271
Synar, Mike (D-Okla.), 172
Syracuse University, 286

Tax issues
   airline, 52
   gasoline, 52, 105
   increases, 105b
   interest groups, 100
   legislation, 236, 252
   marriage tax, 223
   pay-as-you-go procedures, 69, 70
   reductions, 62–63, 64, 72, 100, 136,
      144
   reform bill, 150–151
   rules, 55–56, 128b
   taxpayer abuses, 94
   use of closed rules, 123
Taylor, Andrew, 272, 307
Taylor, Elizabeth, 94
Taylor, Stuart, Jr., 307
TEA-21. *See* Transportation Equity Act of
   the 21st Century
Teapot Dome scandal, 276
Teamsters Union, 95
Technology
   Congress and the information age,
      303–304
   electronic signing, 267–268
   electronic voting, 169
   Internet, 83, 92, 98
   teleconferences, 92
   teledemocracy, 30, 31–32, 34–35
Tiefer, Charles, 273
Telecommunications Act of 1996, 83
Term limits, 27, 105b, 133–134, 175b
Thomas, Bill (R-Calif.), 257
Thomas, Clarence, 95
Thomas, Craig (R-Wyo.), 276, 291

Thompson, Fred (R-Tenn.), 279, 286–287, 290
Thurmond, Strom (R-S.C.), 213, 230, 267–268
Tobacco issues, 16, 36, 82–83, 85, 305
Toner, Robin, 39
Torricelli, Robert (D-N.J.), 28
Towell, Pat, 179, 180
Traffic Safety Act of 1966, 94
Transportation Equity Act of the 21st Century (TEA-21), 52
Treaties, 186
Truman, David B., 294
Truman, Harry S, 11, 186
Trust funds, 51, 52, 71

UCAs. *See* Unanimous consent agreements
Udall, Morris K. "Mo" (D-Ariz.), 284
Unanimous consent agreements (UCAs)
   amendment procedure, 160, 161, 217, 218, 219, 228, 238
   bills and, 84, 106n5, 110, 112, 215–217
   calling of the roll, 213
   comparison to House rules, 203–204
   conference committee and report, 250, 251, 265, 267b
   debate and, 212
   discharge petitions, 241
   examples of, 199–200, 201–202, 216b
   failure to achieve, 227–236
   germaneness and relevancy, 238–239
   in the House, 141, 187, 251
   in the Senate, 25, 181, 187, 190, 191, 194–202, 210, 211, 227–236, 238
   partial and incremental, 197, 199
   purposes and agreements, 199–202
   simple and complex, 195–198, 206n38
   veto overrides, 198
   voting, 225
Unfunded mandates, 121–122, 192, 253
United Daughters of the Confederacy, 211
Universities, 5, 7, 8, 9, 10
Unsafe at Any Speed (Nader), 94
Upton, Fred (R-Mich.), 144
U.S. Court of Claims, 117
U.S. Term Limits Inc. v. Thornton (1995), 134

VandeHei, Jim, 147
Veterans, 114
Veto
   Bush, George and, 79
   committee, 280, 281b
      House rules and, 136
      legislative, 280
      line-item veto, 65–66
      pocket veto, 269
      political reasons for, 269
      procedure, 271
      regulatory, 276
      use of riders, 163, 269–270
      votes to override, 31, 268
Vice president, 18b, 106n6, 207
Victor, Kirk, 108
Vietnam War, 45, 95
Vobejda, Barbara, 108
Vogler, David J., 107, 271
Voinovich, George V. (R-Ohio), 84
Voting
   for amendments, 220
   cloture, 228, 231–236, 238, 299
   in committees, 98–99, 101–102
   conference report, 266
   for constitutional amendments, 134
   cue-givers, 225–226
   electronic voting, 129, 169, 224
   in House of Representatives, 169–172, 250
   procedural issues, 226
   recorded votes, 129, 225
   roll call, 169, 225
   in Senate, 224–227, 228, 231
   stacking, 225
   vote pairing, 169–171, 180n45, 226–227

Waggonner, Joe D., Jr. (D-La.), 167
Walker, Jack L. 38
Wall Street Journal, 138
Wallison, Ethan, 146, 147
War Powers Resolution of 1973, 155, 269
Warner, John W. (R-Va.), 234
Washington, D.C. *See* District of Columbia
Watergate scandal, 45, 95, 279
Watkins v. United States (1957), 279
Waxman, Seth, 305
Web sites, 143, 146n26, 288
Webster, Daniel, 211
Weil, Alan, 272
Weingast, Barry R., 179
Welch, Susan, 38
Welch, William, 272
Welfare reform, 89, 90, 160
Wellstone, Paul (D-Minn.), 245
Whips and whip notices, 142, 143, 187, 189f, 209, 225
White, Byron R., 280
Whitewater Development Corporation, 223
Williams, Kenneth C., 145

Wilson, Woodrow, 23, 38, 232, 269, 273, 275, 294
Wise, Charles R., 180
Wolfensberger, Donald R., 146, 175, 178
World War II, 276
Wright, Gerald C., Jr., 38
Wright, Jim (D-Texas)
  resignation, 302
  as Speaker of the House, 157, 301
  view of amendment strategies, 161
  view of House and Senate rules, 25, 119
  view of overregulation, 292
  view of scheduling, 109

Yang, John, 37
Year 2000 Readiness and Responsibility Act, 87b, 151
Young, C.W. Bill (R-Fla.), 67, 282
Youngstown Co. v. Sawyer (343 U.S. 579, 635), 3